GENDER & NEOLIBERALISM

The All India Democratic Women's Association & Globalization Politics

Published in India in 2013 by
Tulika Books
35 A/1 Shahpur Jat, New Delhi 110 049
tulikabooks.wordpress.com

First edition (hardback) 2013

ISBN: 978-93-82381-23-5

For sale only in India and South Asia

Printed at Chaman Offset, Delhi 110 002

For

Vijay, Zalia and Rosa

Contents

Anderson, Karen Kukil, Maida Goodwin, and the archival legacy of Kate Weigand. Also, Francisca de Haan helped to winkle out important materials from the Aletta Institute for Women's History in Amsterdam. The Nehru Memorial Museum and Library Archives in New Delhi and the P.C. Joshi Archives in Jawaharlal Nehru University, New Delhi are staffed by resourceful people who guided my opening requests for materials with skill. Early in the process of research, discussions with Barbara Sicherman, Joan Hedrick, Laura Lovett and Rob Corber shaped my research decisions in important ways. A special thanks to Revan Schendler; she read through an early draft of the manuscript and gave sage advice about revisions. My editors at Tulika Books, Indu Chandrasekhar and Rakhi Sehgal provided their creative and careful thinking and firm belief in the project; while Vikas Rawal created maps just in time. Also, my editors at Routledge, Benjamin Holtzman and Max Novick backed the project early and didn't give up hope.

To my intrepid colleagues in the Study of Women and Gender Program, the Five College Women's Studies Research Center, the Environmental Science and Policy Program, and the concentrations in Community Engagement and Social Change, South Asia and Sustainable Food who push to make even administrative details creative and far-seeing. Especially, I would like to thank my co-conspirators for all the work we've done together: Payal Banerjee, Riché Barnes, Carrie Baker, Lucy Mule, Bosiljka Glumac, Lester Tomé, Ambreen Hai, Susannah Howe, Arlene Avakian, Daniel Rivers, Liz Pryor, Eeva Sointu, Hye-Kyung Kang, Paula Giddings, Margaret Hunt, Laura Lovett, Shisuka Hsieh, Al Mosley, Kim Kono, Kevin Quashie, Jayne Mercier, Marjorie Senechal, Rick Fantasia, Vicky Spelman, Elliot Fratkin, Crystal Jones, Alex Keller, Darcy Buerkle, Nadya Sbaiti, Abdelkader Berrahmoun, Lorna Peterson, Nancy Sternbach, Gary Lehring, Nancy Whittier, Susan Van Dyne, Marilyn Schuster, Joanne Corbin, Yoosun Park, Joanne Benkley, Greg White, Drew Guswa, Byron Zamboanga, Marsha Pruett, Phil Peake and David Smith.

The Five College Inter-Asian Political Cultures writing workshop as well as the Asian American writing workshop were valuable resources over all the years I have lived in the Pioneer Valley. Miliann Kang, Diana Yoon, Floyd Cheung, Richard Chu, Kavita Datla, Paula Chakravartty, Amrita Basu, Srirupa Roy, Svati Shah and Krupa Shandilya were among the many inspiring people who fuelled these vibrant working groups. Also, for Kasturi Ray and Gautam Premnath who formed the backbone of my first writing group very many years ago; they set the standard for generous and critical readings of numerous drafts of this project. Across time and space, close friends and comrades often made all the difference, especially Marilyn Filley, Arabella Holzbog, Erin Keesey, Sorayya Khan, Naeem Inayatullah, April Flowers, Durba Ghosh, Brian Steinberg, Libero della Piana, Edmund Campos, Zaira

Rivera Casellas, Polly Moran, Raza and Ali Mir, Alisa Gallo, Kehaulani Kauanui, Sunaina Maira, and Rupal Oza.

The infrastructure for long-term research is daily and reproductive: my family in its many, ever-widening circles gave me immeasurable support over the years. My aunts, Radha and Brinda, and my uncles, Prannoy and Prakash, with their sense of fun, commitment, willingness to start an adventure and foster a debate, spurred me to write this book. For new venues to write and think, my parents, Margaret and Peter, fully indulged the necessity of digging clams and dropping baited hooks into the ocean alongside writing. My mother-in-law Soni, who always sees the possibilities of the future, was generous with her encouragement throughout. For everyone in my family who asked about the project and listened actively to long answers, I can only marvel at your patience. I want to thank especially my sister and brother who are also my best friends, Kathy and Phil, and my closest cousins who I couldn't live without: Atiya, Tara, Shonali, Mimi, Riku, Arjun, Tinku, Karuna, Mandakini, Surojit, Lulu, Rohini, Emily, Nick, Tim, Melissa, Ahmed, Nasik, Yasin, Mike and Margie. To the next generation, who provide hope for the future, I send love to Sebastian, Simone, Vivan, Gautam, Gaurav, Ayesha, Saira, Ahilya, Jack, Margot, Sahil, Diya, Piya, Max, Finley, Sonita, Salig, Sameer. Also to my sisters and brothers-in-law, Leela, Meera, Jojo, Harish and Rani who opened their homes to me more times than I can count. For carrying alongside me an enduring vision for what should and can be, for imagining time as an ever-open vista, unyielding intellectual support as well as sustaining meals and clean floors, no one surpasses Vijay Prashad. His unwavering support made the book possible. Together with Zalia and Rosa Maya, daughters who make every day worth getting up at the break of dawn, I give my love and thanks to a family that never tires of turning our next corner together.

Born in the years I began my research of AIDWA, I will never forget my nephew Ishan Bose-Pyne. His laughter and unstinting love for this world are in every page of this book.

The cover of a Tamil Nadu Democratic Women's Association pamphlet from the late 1970s for a campaign against dowry practices. The title reads: *We Will Break the Shackles of Dowry!*

Introduction

In 1991, the Indian government publicly mandated a new agenda known as liberalization. The agenda was the domestic variant of neoliberalism, namely the giving over of large areas of the state and social life to the private business sector. In every aspect of their lives, people experienced the impact of liberalization. Survival in agricultural areas was damaged, cultural imaginations of people were foreshortened and the well-being of the most vulnerable people became more precarious. Liberalization produced a churning of Indian society, with grotesque social consequences. Religious and communal violence increased; in 1992, the anti-Muslim riots in India after tearing down the Babri Masjid in Ayodhya signalled future carnage. Caste conflict intensified. The Mandal Commission recommendations to reserve more seats for lower-caste students, among other policy suggestions, were enacted in 1989. The vociferous protests in response to these new reservation policies revealed the hardening of caste hierarchies across the country. Landlordism gained new weapons. The blatant theft of common lands and the loss of political will around land reform matched the private property dogma of the new world order. Conspicuous consumption spiralled upwards, putting pressure on gendered traditions of accruing capital. Dowry harassment became an epidemic, with the overt violence and even murder of daughters-in-law often linked to demands for ongoing payments and goods from the woman's natal family. The precarious social value of women eroded further in these patriarchal economic regimes. Old social, religious and class fissures took on incendiary new forms with liberalization, and social justice movements were caught in the crossfire.

The Indian women's movement, with its amalgamation of non-governmental organizations (NGOs), autonomous feminist groups and national mass women's organizations, were knocked sideways by the rapid changes in India's political terrain. Groups across the movement saw the weaknesses in their organizing strategies and reassessed their goals. While some retreated, others found ways to carve their own place in the upheaval of old certainties. This book follows the response of one national mass organization, the All India Democratic Women's Association (AIDWA), that chose to directly oppose liberalization and the combustible forces it fuelled. As a left-wing women's organization with the bulk of its membership among rural and urban poor working women, and bolstered by its ideological tenets that sought to combat feudal and capitalist forms of women's oppression and exploitation, AIDWA did not blink. For the first ten years of its existence, AIDWA had operated with a theory that working women could unite with middle-class women on common issues such as high commodity prices and anti-woman violence. After 1991, this theory was seen to be insufficient.

AIDWA formed in 1981 as a federal women's organization with state-based units located across India. Socialist women's mass organizations in states like Maharashtra, Tamil Nadu, Andhra Pradesh, Tripura, as well as Kerala and West Bengal, coalesced into a national federation with a founding membership of 590,000 women. By 2006, its membership grew to 10 million women. These membership numbers are striking for a few reasons. First, AIDWA became one of the largest women's organizations in the world. Second, poor rural women alongside poor urban working women formed the largest base of its membership. Even more salient, AIDWA accomplished this during the high point of neoliberalism, a doctrine composed of economic and social policies that typically work to render mass organizing ineffective if not almost impossible.

A central question of this book is how AIDWA managed to grow so rapidly across India, with its strength built from among the women most severely disenfranchised by neoliberal policies and governance. My contention is that during the 1990s, AIDWA pivoted away from its earlier understanding of primarily organizing women around common issues that crossed class and community locations, toward a new theory of inter-sectoralism that enabled its success. As it grew to become a large mass organization for women, activists at local levels developed methods that successfully organized people within *and* outside of their work places, inside their communities and beyond the norms of those community affiliations. In the process, inter-sectoral organizing created a stronger organizational fabric to resist the fragmentation of and competition between peoples and interests that are the hallmark of neoliberalism.

During the late 1980s, state and national leaders of AIDWA began to develop a sectoral theory of women's gendered lives. A sectoral theory of women's lives embeds an understanding of those social groupings in a systemic and historical class analysis. The term sectoral is not a new one: sectors or sections are words used interchangeably by members to describe the particular social groupings (such as those around religion, caste, class, location and work status) that structure a polity and define people's lives within that polity. Early on in their organizing, AIDWA members defined sectoral issues nominally more than analytically. That is, sectoral issues denoted the specific needs of a sub-category of particularly oppressed women that demanded greater knowledge and targeted political attention. After the anti-Sikh riots in Delhi in 1984, the visibility and political mobilization of anti-Muslim and other communal tensions rose. In the early 1990s, liberalization policies infiltrated into Indian governance itself. In this context, AIDWA members' identification and analysis of particularly vulnerable sectors of women facilitated the emergence of a more integrated inter-sectoral method of organizing in the mid-1990s.

Inter-sectoral organizing refers to how this sectoral analysis of women in neoliberal India produced specific strategies, tactics and even goals in AIDWA's political practices. I first heard the term 'inter-sectoral organizing' from Brinda Karat, the general secretary who led the organization from 1993 until 2004. Inter-sectoral organizing methods paid heed to the overlapping rather than discrete or bounded facets of women's lives. AIDWA members at the state and national levels combined their attention to specific women's issues, with inter-sectoral organizing between these often porous and inter-related issues. As an organizing method, inter-sectoral organizing sought to create bridges of solidarity between distinct and seemingly conflicting groups of women. I use the term inter-sectoralism to describe these connections between AIDWA's ongoing conceptualization of women's sectoral issues and its inter-sectoral organizing.

Inter-sectoralism took the lived conflicts around women's differences as the daily stuff of women's inequality. To know and then effectively challenge rural Dalit women's oppression, for example, demanded a class analysis of agricultural day-labourers, bonded workers and landholders with very small plots of land. It required an understanding of the sexual politics of power and the gendered untouchability practices in rural localities. In addition, it had to take into account the sites where overlapping structures of casteist and feudal hierarchies met class exploitation and time-honed patriarchal systems of gender oppression. Campaigns fought Dalit women's oppression through methods like public exposure and condemnation of atrocities. These campaigns sought to dismantle accepted caste norms through laws on the books alongside careful ideological work within the organization itself, so that anti-casteist activism became every AIDWA member's struggle, not just a Dalit women's issue.

The organization's sectoral analysis sought to understand the specificities of an increasingly competitive and fragmented social polity. Its inter-sectoral organizing efforts attempted to knit anew the solidarities between women that could reach across these exclusionary, if not violent divisions. Sectoral analyses and inter-sectoral organizing sought to foster movement leaders from precisely these oppressed and marginalized sectors of women. They also sought to build a stronger unity against divisions of caste, class and religious bigotry, but it was a unity reconceived. Karat described this method as 'inter-sectoral, inter-class and crossing', to explain their seemingly risky campaigns that linked women's political activism across class, religious and caste lines within the organization's membership and beyond (Brinda Karat interview, 24 December 2004). Sectoral analyses and inter-sectoral organizing methods lived and breathed along the grain of neoliberalism and communalism to better derail their logics of fragmentation and their momentum towards antagonistic competition.

Attention to AIDWA's activism during the 1990s and early 2000s reveals what might seem obvious. It shows that organizing large numbers of women is tremendously difficult. The daily tasks for local, unpaid activists are sometimes tedious, such as ongoing communication, the logistics of membership and the details of campaigns. At the core of this book are the stories of many women who worked at all levels of the organization, from local unit members to national leaders, who lived mainly in rural Haryana, rural and urban parts of Tamil Nadu, and New Delhi. These women took part in a highly visible and an often dangerous political refusal of neoliberalism. Their campaigns, many of which are still ongoing, share a long-term goal to replenish the uneven social fabric. Yet each campaign, whether for access to common lands, women's physical and sexual safety, or for caste-based autonomy and equality, had its own complexities marked by each locality's history. The campaigns described in this book open up another set of questions about how AIDWA functions as a leftist women's organization: in its membership, its decision-making, its leadership structures and its internal reproduction. If neoliberalism partly inspired sectoral analyses and inter-sectoral organizing methods, this book explores what allowed that counter-response to emerge from AIDWA.

AIDWA has deep ties with the Communist Party of India (Marxist) (CPI[M] or CPM). It is politically independent of the CPM, but is part of the Party's universe of mass organizations. AIDWA shares with the CPM a general orientation toward the Indian state and political economy. It also leverages its own power through the Party and its other mass organizations (labour union, and youth, agricultural worker, agricultural cultivator and student organizations). Many of its national and state-level leaders are also members of the CPM who regard bringing women into radical politics as integral to their Marxist commitment to fighting for socialism. AIDWA is an enduring and militant part of the women's movement in India, focused on mobilizing the largest numbers of women to determine their own lives and build a more just future.

Membership of AIDWA is open to any woman regardless of her political affiliation, as long as she upholds the central organizational tenets of equality, emancipation and the liberation of women. From its beginning, AIDWA has been an education for both the CPM and the larger women's movement. It pushed its left allies to give more prominence to women's issues like dowry violence, and sexual violence in the home and by the state. It also pioneered new ways for feminists to approach struggles against casteism and religious communalism through an attention to the gender and class specificities of these bigotries.

This book provides the first major study of AIDWA to look at its geographical reach (across the country) and its class depth (from middle-class women to landless women). It is also the first major study to look at AIDWA since its ground-breaking organizing strategy (inter-sectoral organizing) led to an expansion of its membership in the 1990s and 2000s. The earlier work (notably Amrita Basu 1992 and Raka Ray 1999) was published before this expansion. These previous studies are based on work in one or two states, and do not tackle the rural and urban parts of AIDWA. The sheer productive force of AIDWA's activism during the 1990s and into the 2000s, and the lack of attention given to it by scholars of the Indian women's movement beg further analysis.

AIDWA's differences from the autonomous women's movement in its organizing methods, its membership base and its ongoing adherence to socialist ideals do not fully explain why it merits so little academic attention. Many early books written about the Indian women's movement gave primary attention to autonomous groups and were written by women active in these groups (Kumar 1993; Gandhi and Shah 1991; Sunder Rajan, ed. 1999). Even the more recent work that provides a richly informative window on feminist NGOs, small women's collectives and governmental women's agencies has little to say about any of the national leftist women's organizations (to name just a few of these: Writers and Nagar 2006; Dave 2011; Govinda 2009). Collections of essays purporting to represent South Asian feminisms and gender politics in India also carry an impoverished view of the movement as a complex whole (Nivedita Menon, ed. 1999; Maitrayee Chaudhuri, ed. 2003; Ray and Katzenstein, eds. 2005; Ritu Menon, ed. 2011; Loomba and Lukose, eds. 2012).

Apart from Ray (1999) and Basu (1992), the academic literature on AIDWA is minimal. There are, however, two other kinds of writings on its analysis and activism. The first is AIDWA's own texts. There are the documents produced for its national conferences held every three years. AIDWA publishes magazines in many states, in a host of languages. Each campaign and major issue that AIDWA selects to analyse generates pamphlets and research documents. These are not kept in a central archive, but are to be found in the many offices of AIDWA across the country and in the homes of AIDWA activists. The second is the work of journalists who cover AIDWA's campaigns and turn to the organization for its opinion on the myriad issues germane to its activism. Most magazines and newspapers tend to avoid AIDWA, but a few dedicated journalists, such as Asha Krishnakumar and T.K. Rajalakshmi, have followed AIDWA's work over the years. None of these writings can afford to stand outside the time of their production – they are about events and struggles that are ongoing and decisive. This means that none of these texts take the longer view in order to assess AIDWA's transformation from 1981 to the present.

This research project began in the early 1990s. It took me from the byways of Haryana to the fisher communities of Tamil Nadu, from activists' homes in Mumbai to the streets of Kolkata, from the headquarters of AIDWA in Delhi to the legal clinic in the capital's working-class areas. I have interviewed members of AIDWA at the national level, state level, district level and unit level. I have interviewed its veteran members and its newest members. Most of my ethnographic research I gathered through multiple visits to particular campaigns' localities, sometimes over an eight-year span. I spoke with members at all levels of these campaigns. Longer oral history interviews with national, state and local leaders augmented my understanding, and shed light on how members saw their activism and their organization. As with most theories of political praxis, sectoral analysis has multiple locations for its articulation, none of them authoritative or unidimensional. I drew from archival historical research and ephemeral political materials like pamphlets, position papers and speeches to trace this emerging theory of activism and to map its past. These traces of written evidence alongside the memories of how campaigns unfolded reveal the contours of how local and state units developed its inter-sectoral praxis.

Globalization Politics and the Indian Women's Movement

The Gandhian–Nehruvian discourse of Prime Minister Indira Gandhi's governance in the 1970s, and less so of her son Rajiv Gandhi in the 1980s, around solving the plight of the rural poor had all but disappeared in the 1990s. With its strength in embattled agricultural locations, AIDWA grew in response to these difficult and distinctly neoliberal conditions. Notably, the continual growth of AIDWA over the 1990s and into the 2000s was among the very women who carried the heaviest burdens due to neoliberal policies of decreased access to affordable food, potable water, and avenues to own land and hold jobs to support themselves. During the period of the NGO-ization of the Indian women's movement and the dominance of neoliberalism, AIDWA saw substantial increases in the number of women who paid their one-rupee yearly due to join the organization. The individualization of survival, its membership suggests, was not the only response to a globalized market economy. AIDWA grew because of its ideology about women's activism and its socialist goals for their emancipation. AIDWA grew because it continued to embrace politics that sought to reach the greatest number of women.

Despite the fact that the women's movement in India recognized that neoliberalism was a women's issue, the facets of the movement responded to this insight differently. NGOs, autonomous women's groups and left-wing national organizations like AIDWA, each developed their own strategies in response to it. The autonomous women's groups suffered a crisis of nerve in this period. In 1994, the Centre for Women's Development Studies (CWDS) in Delhi hosted a regional workshop for women's movement groups in western India, predominantly from Gujarat and Maharashtra.[1] The publication of the proceedings documented the consensus that the autonomous women's movement had failed 'to establish links with mass[es] of women and find a language to build necessary rapport' (Sharma 2003: 4565). This failure, in part, led to the rise in women's communal and casteist political mobilization. As self-critical discussions about outreach, goals and organizing strategies unfolded, the autonomous women's groups recognized the weaknesses of a movement that was majority-Hindu, urban-based, middle-class, upper-caste and highly educated. Movement activists debated what resources they would need to reach out to the mass of women in cities, towns and small rural localities. Some suggested it was just too difficult.

In addition, the focus of the autonomous women's groups on framing non-political 'women's issues' began to seem a shortsighted way to view violence issues of rape, domestic violence and dowry-related murders. Unifying women as a whole around 'women's issues' against the patriarchal state no longer had credibility within the autonomous women's movement, but new strategies for organizing were more difficult to develop. A well-known activist from Maharashtra, Chhaya Datar, concluded that the autonomous women's movement should do what it did best rather than radically change its perspective:

> Autonomous women's groups are made up of professionals. They are more articulate. They can study a particular women's issue thoroughly and write consistently. They should lobby with political personalities, members of Parliament and legislative assemblies. . . . At this stage they should try to gather strength, and project a consistent point of view outside of electoral politics. (Datar 1993: 47)

[1] CWDS 1995. As the organizers of the workshop note in their introduction, almost all of the participants were members of autonomous women's groups from these states.

Datar's point was clear. The autonomous women's groups had not successfully reached women in rural areas, where the greatest number of women lived. Nor could they. In the face of neoliberalism, they should give up on mass politics as a strategy beyond their capabilities. Instead, the autonomous women's movement should pursue a dialogue with the powerful and their gatekeepers. During the 1994 CWDS conference discussions, Datar made a passing reference to the importance of women's mobilization by mass-based women's organizations. Other voices from the autonomous women's groups were less inclusive, and designated leftist mass politics as passé for the Indian women's movement at large (Menon-Sen 2001).

While autonomous women's groups grappled with a crisis of confidence, NGOs enjoyed an explosion in funding from a vast array of sources, primarily external to India. The rise of these NGOs in the 1990s emerged alongside a steady increase in AIDWA's membership; yet the reasons behind these two developments were quite different. The swelling numbers of NGOs were beneficiaries (though not necessarily willing accomplices) of the early stages of neoliberalism's consolidation. The combine of international financial organizations – the World Bank, the IMF and the World Trade Organization (WTO) – had learned by the 1990s to preempt the feminist response to the austerity measures it meted out across the world. 'Women's rights' slid into 'women's empowerment' and both became the bywords for everyone, from the World Bank to the United Nations to mouthpieces of the United States government. NGOs with a focus on women and gender became a critical piece of the neoliberal agenda. The 1991 World Bank report on gender and poverty cited the use of women-focused NGOs as a powerful means to shrink governmental 'interference' in an unconstrained market economy (World Bank 1991). A surge of NGOs that focused on women's issues, sometimes even led by a feminist analysis of gendered relations of power, became a memorable part of the 1990s in India (Bayliss, Fine and Van Waeyenberge 2011).

The same engines of capitalism did not power AIDWA's growing numbers of members, even as they were never wholly disentangled from them. Similarly, the changes for AIDWA stemmed from substantially different concerns from the autonomous women's groups. The worries voiced in the autonomous women's movement were about funding and outreach to the masses of Indian women in rural locations and minority communities (Menon-Sen 2001). AIDWA already had a strong base in rural areas and outright refused funds from sources outside its movement. Its central crisis lay in the increasing isolation and fragmentation of Indian citizens into mutually distrustful camps. With members from all castes, religions, classes and regions, the erosion of solidarity among women was a grave threat to the health of the national leftist women's movement.

Leaders across AIDWA saw the urgency to build stronger connections among its large membership. They recognized the need to develop ideologies that could withstand communal and casteist assaults. The organization as a whole had to educate new and old members about how to demand justice and live out their commitments to equality. And it needed to give their members the courage to develop new methods when old ones failed. AIDWA members faced other challenges. The organization needed to gain the trust of autonomous women's groups without losing its moorings in its leftist allies. It needed to educate its allied leftist mass organizations about the centrality of a gendered analysis of caste, religion and class. It needed to educate its allies in the autonomous women's movement that a single focus on Muslim women or Dalit women was too limited a frame for the issues at stake. Members of AIDWA sought to protect its socialist principles to transform inequitable and oppressive social relations from the grinding battle to just survive. Negotiation and compromise did not always coexist easily alongside revolutionary will.

AIDWA's Politics

Indu came from the small locality of Bandh in Haryana and was a lead organizer at the unit level of AIDWA. Her unit was composed of roughly six women from Bandh, but could also count a handful of non-member sympathizers. Beginning in 1996, Indu's unit fought for the restitution of the locality's common lands previously held and used by landless Dalit families. As a midwife from a Dalit (oppressed) caste, the upper-caste appropriation of common lands meant the loss of her basic economic, personal and political independence. In the process of taking on upper-caste landowners, she lost her waged daily work in their fields. The entire Dalit community faced a year-long social boycott from shopkeepers and dairy owners. They could not buy food or essential commodities, nor could they access scarce water supplies. Indu's brother's handicapped son was badly beaten by upper-caste men when he went to wash clothes one day. After sustained persecution, her husband refused to support her fight; so she continued her campaign without him. In telling her story, she described her political will and ideological commitment to justice in the face of tremendous pressure. She said with focused determination, 'I am not one of those who depends on fate' (Indu interview, 24 June 1999). Her statement reveals the ideological commitment of AIDWA's members. Social mores and entrenched oppressions are not fated. Old habits of inequality can and *must* change. Furthermore, the women who bear the brunt of oppressive relationships will overturn them.

This study attempts to take seriously the work of organizing large numbers of women, and the incredible efforts of women who neither gain recognition for their efforts nor necessarily win their struggles. In the case of Bandh's common lands, Indu and the AIDWA unit in Bandh won the legal rights to the land on 23 July 1998, as well as economic restitution for income they lost in the struggle and the upper castes' work boycott. A year later, after the upper-caste, large landholders' inaction, they won a second ruling on 23 April 1999 that demanded the return of the land to all village members, including Dalits. The land was cleared, but the upper castes continued to hold control over it and refuse its cultivation or use by lower-caste and non-caste members of Bandh. Even with the law on their side, Dalit women and men could not work their common lands.

AIDWA's linkages to the CPM, this study shows, could be enormously helpful when organizing rural, poor, Dalit and Muslim women. In campaigns against casteist violence and untouchability practices in Tamil Nadu, for example, the CPM had an organizational presence that provided a safety in numbers. The Party's other mass organizations, such as the Kisan Sabha (peasant organization), Democratic Youth Federation of India, Student Federation of India and the All India Agricultural Workers Union, provided additional support in mobilizing community members to fight alongside local women activists.

Sometimes the CPM or allied left organizations did not help. In Bandh, for example, the local unit of the Kisan Sabha ultimately withdrew from the struggle for common lands (Jagmati Sangwan interview, 12 July 2005). Members of the peasant organization did not feel that the struggle merited the crippling hardships its members faced as a result. AIDWA at the state level of Haryana and nationally continued to support the Bandh AIDWA unit's case. In 2012, the fight continued to build enough local hegemony to make Dalits' legal rights to the land manifest. They gained a clear legal right to lands held under the often dangerously fluid designation of 'common lands'. Another example lies in AIDWA's organizing against domestic violence and dowry-related violence, and for women's legal rights in marriage and for sexual autonomy. Its networks of women, their institutional supports and legal teams, alongside the local and district units, were built largely from scratch. The CPM did not oppose their work, but the legal centres, and the innumerable struggles to gain justice for women who were raped, abused or divorced, were run wholly by AIDWA's membership. This kind of political independence in the work of AIDWA demands careful assessment.

To fold the women's organizations that have links to political parties into a unified mass is misleading. A central component of each political party is its political ideology. As excellent, fine-grained studies of the women's wings of the communal right-wing have shown, the larger ideological goals are vital to the character of the movement (see, for example, Atreyee Sen 2007). Tanika Sarkar (1991) has stressed the symbolic power of women leaders in the Ramjanmabhoomi movement led by the Rashtriya Swayamsevak Sangh (RSS). Yet the role of women's mass organizations in political parties cannot be flattened into one undifferentiated truth. The women's wing of the RSS, called the Rashtriya Sevika Samiti, as ethnographic work by Paola Bacchetta (2004) details, does not have significant control or autonomy in relation to the RSS. The tasks of its affiliated women's organization are deemed by the RSS to be largely cultural rather than political; yet within this constricted space, women activists fight for a theory of a Hindu nation that sometimes contests the official one. An ideology of reified Hindu womanhood and Indian nationalism structures the role that the RSS's mass organization for women is supposed to play within the movement, even though the women involved exceed these expectations.

For AIDWA, the ideology of socialism sustains struggles on local levels, as well as in policy papers and laws fought for on the national level. Its socialist ideology is central to understanding why the organization continued to grow in the 1990s and 2000s. In the 1970s, when CPM activists raised the need for a mass women's organization, the cross-class character of the group was a site of intense debate (CPI[M] 1981; Brinda Karat interview 24 December 2004). Party members asked whether a mass women's organization that also represented middle-class women would create fissures in the working class between women and men. Early campaigns against sexual violence and the centrality of violence issues within the organization, raised similar concerns that a focus on masculinist sexual violence against women would pit worker against worker in the class struggle. From its inception, AIDWA's ideological framework joined a Marxist class analysis of social change to build a unified working-class and peasant opposition to exploitation and feudal oppression, to a differential analysis of women's lives as gendered subjects, as citizens and as workers (Sivaraman 1975).

The role of activists in this left women's organization is to bring the mass of women into active participation in all of these realms, not just the class struggle (Ranadive 1986). As women changed the conditions of their own lives, founding member Vimal Ranadive argued, they would take greater ownership towards the welfare of everyone.[2] AIDWA's early disagreements with the autonomous women's movement stemmed from this central difference of understanding about women's activism. The focus by the autonomous women's groups solely on gender relations or women's issues was not enough. The masses of women were exploited and oppressed in ways that could not be simply understood by being 'women'. As early leaders of

[2] Ranadive wrote: 'To strike simultaneously at the root of the policies by utilizing different tactics, considering the uneven development of political consciousness, is the task of the mass organizations including women's.' Ranadive 1986: 15.

AIDWA argued, women changed their consciousness about themselves and what could be done through struggle (Mukherjee 1989). This empowered consciousness, they theorized, would strengthen the fight for all people's equality, liberation and a society without classes. Women's emancipation would not emerge after socialism. Instead, women's emancipation was constitutive of socialism as an ideological practice *made possible* through ongoing struggles against women's oppression and exploitation.

In the current configuration, as the next generation of women enters a world with liberalization as its common sense, AIDWA faces new challenges. As the organization turns its attention to the rising aspirations of working-class and lower middle-class women, its ongoing questions around women's sexual autonomy and rights enter a transformed context. In the 1990s and 2000s, AIDWA responded to the powerful shifts in the Indian political economy with alacrity. Its willingness to shed older truths to hone new methods will be vital in the years ahead. Young women are demanding more opportunities and fewer strictures on their choices in their movements, relationships and jobs. AIDWA's organizational focus on neighbourhoods alongside the family will demand creative campaigns to reach these women as they navigate the often empty promises of women's rights in liberalization.

Book Chapters

The first chapter traces the life of a founding member of AIDWA, Pappa Umanath, who lived in Tamil Nadu before and after Indian independence. Pappa's life in the thick of anti-imperialist, working-class independence struggles sheds light on the hidden roots of AIDWA as a national organization. Pappa uses the metaphor of the banyan tree, with its roots above and below the ground, to describe how women's groups forged in the politics of regional states, but linked by their Marxist ideology and their connections to the CPM, gained a national organizational form. The second chapter maps the context of AIDWA's formation during the 1970s and 1980s at the very heart of a regeneration of women's organizing in India. The third chapter details the rise of AIDWA's sectoral analysis and inter-sectoral organizing methods, developed in the 1990s. Activists shifted from a mechanistic analysis of women's issues, one that focused on women as reproducers and workers in more simplistic and essentializing ways, to one that gave a language and politics to other complex gendered realities of caste disempowerment, religious affiliation and class disaffection. The fourth chapter describes the interconnections between campaigns in the 'green revolution' state of Haryana to fight for women's livelihood in their waged work, for their access to land, and to confront feudal practices of patriarchal control of women's sexuality by *khap panchayat* rulings. These three seemingly disparate campaigns gain strength from AIDWA's activist research methods to substantiate its understanding of volatile social justice issues, build its membership and change commonsense ideologies. The fifth chapter analyses how a campaign in rural Tamil Nadu fought against gendered untouchability practices. Again, drawing from activist research, this campaign opens up questions about leadership in the context of movements for social justice. The sixth chapter compares two cases of domestic violence in two cities, one in the south of India, in Chennai, Tamil Nadu, and one in the north, in New Delhi. These campaigns, one conducted in 1991 and the other in 2006, reveal how local activism creates the structure of this national organization. Individual women members' struggles for justice are linked to fund-raising and dues, to membership development, to decision-making, to outreach, and to public perception of AIDWA as part of the Indian women's movement. The seventh chapter details the impact of the United Nations Conference on Women held in Beijing and Huairou in 1995 on leftist, anti-imperialist groups like AIDWA. Transnational feminist networks have largely displaced internationalist women's solidarity as the goal and operating principle to reach beyond national borders and connect women's movements around the world. In neoliberal times, 'women's rights' operates as much like a brand as a political demand. The challenge for an anti-imperialist women's organization like AIDWA is to build and energize channels of communication between similar women's groups around the world.

This book shows how one left-wing women's organization in the global South consistently dared to expose and combat the hardships that neoliberalism wrought on poor and working-class women in rural and urban contexts. Through a focus on its methods and structure, it charts local and national campaigns run by AIDWA from 1991 until 2006 in three locations: Haryana, Tamil Nadu and New Delhi. Activist members use the very techniques discredited as ineffective by neoliberal regimes: mass protests, issue-based coalitions, fact-finding missions, economic independence from outside funders, refusal of government sponsorship, use of democratic governance infrastructure, and the slow but steady building of local units of ten to twenty members into an organization with more than 10 million members across India. These methods are people-centred. That is, they rely on the voices of many women and the power of hearing those voices spoken together with shared goals and combined strength.

Map of India showing state-wise membership of AIDWA

(1 dot = 2,000 members)

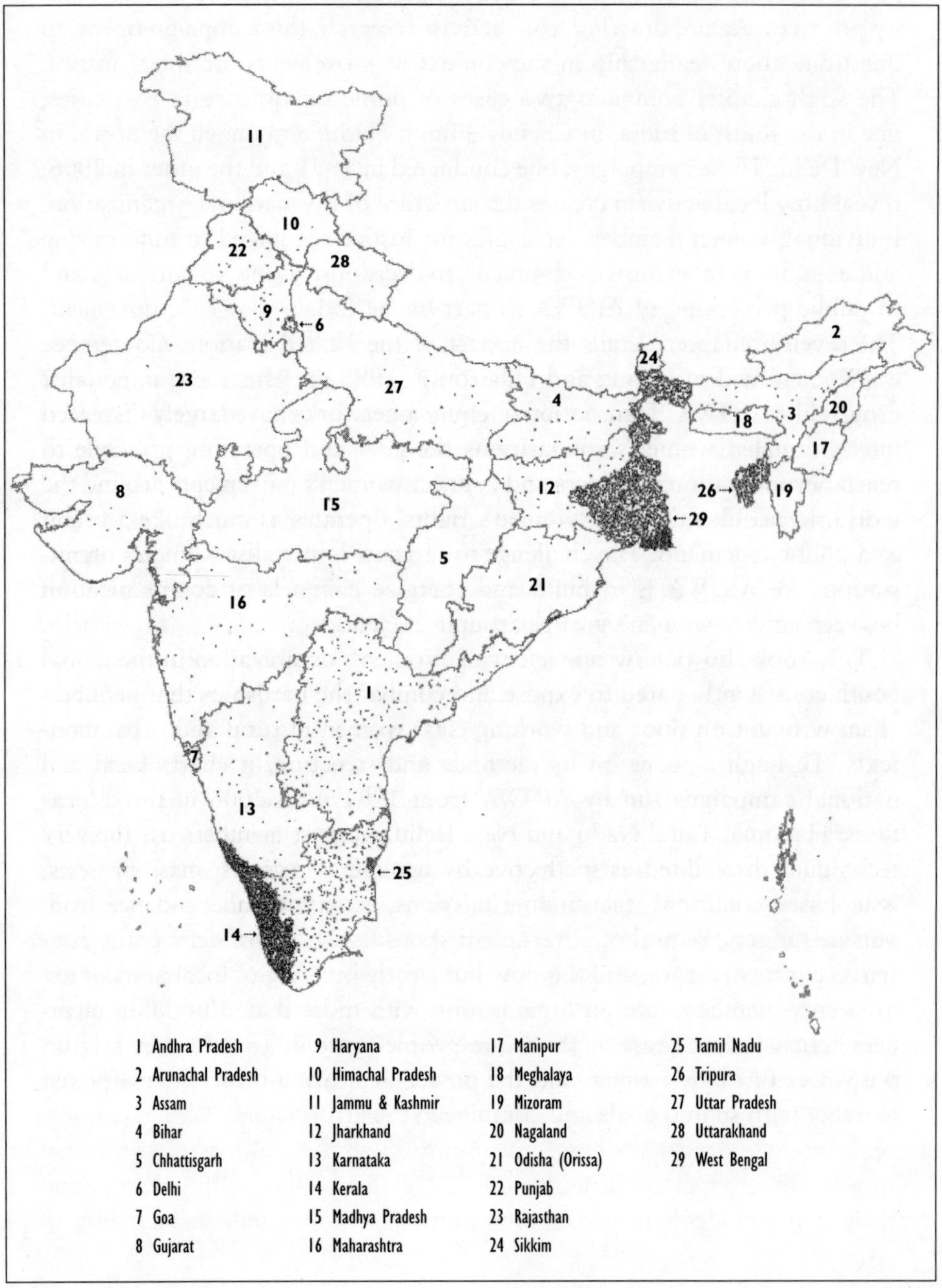

1 Andhra Pradesh	9 Haryana	17 Manipur	25 Tamil Nadu
2 Arunachal Pradesh	10 Himachal Pradesh	18 Meghalaya	26 Tripura
3 Assam	11 Jammu & Kashmir	19 Mizoram	27 Uttar Pradesh
4 Bihar	12 Jharkhand	20 Nagaland	28 Uttarakhand
5 Chhattisgarh	13 Karnataka	21 Odisha (Orissa)	29 West Bengal
6 Delhi	14 Kerala	22 Punjab	
7 Goa	15 Madhya Pradesh	23 Rajasthan	
8 Gujarat	16 Maharashtra	24 Sikkim	

ONE

Origins

The history of the All India Democratic Women's Association (AIDWA) has richly tangled beginnings that drew from anti-imperialist and anti-colonial movements, land and tenant rights movements, anti-casteist formations, as well as from the multivalent demands for women's free and equal participation in the social reform movement. Organizationally, its roots developed early in the twentieth century, when women's groups emerged in various regions, states and localities along different axes of struggle for economic, political and individual rights and autonomy. Pappa Umanath was one of AIDWA's founders who came out of the explosive organizing of twentieth-century India. Hailing from the southern state of Tamil Nadu, Pappa's vision of AIDWA had a regional specificity, but also a national dimension as an office holder in the organization for many years. Her metaphor for the interlocking qualities of struggles and movements across time and location that developed into AIDWA was the banyan tree. 'Like the roots of the banyan tree that spread out as the tree grows, forming many trees that are linked. We formed a national women's organization to fight for the majority of women who face oppression and injustice.' For Pappa, the metaphor of the banyan tree illustrated the regional specificity of AIDWA's national parts. As a national organization, AIDWA joins together state-based women's groups. Some, like the Tamil Nadu Democratic Women's Association (DWA), preceded the national organization by five years or more. Like the banyan tree, with AIDWA it is sometimes difficult to distinguish distinct branches and their roots from the trees that emerge from those roots. AIDWA is a national organization not in a singular sense, but through the multiplicity of regional formations and regional struggles linked together by their national scope and their common ideological vision for women's freedom and emancipation.

Pappa Umanath

Pappa's story of AIDWA's origins weaves together the intersecting movements that shaped her earliest experiences. Her story reveals how these movements nurtured AIDWA's formal inception in 1981 and its growth in subsequent years. Born in 1931, named Dhanalakshmi, Pappa gained her nickname where she spent the formative years of her childhood in Ponmalai, a town near Tiruchirappalli in the southern state of Tamil Nadu, in a railway housing colony called the Golden Rock Railway Workshop. Early in Pappa's childhood her father died, leaving her family destitute. She moved to Ponmalai with her mother, named Alamelu (but called Lakshmi), and two older siblings, to live with her uncle in the railway colony. As a widow, her mother depended upon her kinship ties and her ability to work in order to support her family. Even her ability to work was not always enough since employment options for widows, regardless of their caste, class or social status, were very limited.

Pappa's mother, Lakshmi, survived as part of the informal economy dependent on the railway industry, by selling *idli* snacks to railway workers with the help of her children. Lakshmi shaped her anti-imperialist political commitments to her work's mobility and participated in the freedom movement as a messenger. Pappa described her mother's influence on her own activism with due pride:

> Some [women] were involved in guerrilla struggles, *satyagraha* [Gandhian national independence campaign], going to jail. After independence we fought so that white men's actions would not be repeated. We had to fight against the incoming Congress Party. My mother was not literate, but she taught me to be sensitive to the political issues of the day. During the underground days of the Party [Communist Party of India or CPI], she safeguarded Party letters. She hid the letters in her hair and carried a basket on her head. She could never read the contents of the letters because she was illiterate. Her job was to deliver the letters, to meet Party members secretly, and to deliver food to them so the British authorities would not detect them. I am proud of my mother's work against the British and my own work against imperial rule. (Pappa Umanath interview, 26 March 2006)

Lakshmi's radicalism in the larger context of the railway workers' militancy both before and after India's independence informed Pappa from an early age. She recounted her memories of one critical struggle by railway workers of the South Indian Railways (SIR) to gain fair wages and working conditions through organizing a union, an act declared illegal by the British colonial authorities.

The watershed struggle began in May 1946, and was followed immediately with retribution against union organizers by the General Manager of the Railways, J.F.C. Reynolds ('5000 Golden Rock Workers on Strike', 1946: 7). Railway employees held a one-day strike to protest the dismissal of workers who were organizing for the union. Following the strike, the administration reduced workers' wages and limited their rights to investigate unfair dismissals. The SIR workers dug in their heels. By July, 5,000 workers struck to reinstate the fired workers who had been dismissed for carrying out trade union work. Meetings held in the evenings during the strike brought a surge of support from the larger community, with 12,000 people attending these. Over the following months the strike continued, gaining even more solidarity across the region and inspiring new hopes for anti-colonial and workers' movements throughout the country. In response, the Malabar Special Police was contracted to decimate the SIR strike (Anonymous Labour Organizer 1946: 4). On 5 September 1946, the police force opened fire on the crowd, shot seven people and killed two, one of whom was a Ponmalai communist activist in the volunteer corps of the Golden Rock railway union. After the firing, the police ransacked the railway colony, beating the workers' family members, including women, girls and boys. Four more people were killed in the raid. The violent recklessness of the railway company's actions and the police force's brutal murder of a comrade and other railway workers had profound effects on Pappa, her family and on the militancy of the entire railway colony.

The story of the Golden Rock railway workers' determination and police repression ricocheted through railway colonies across the country as the police sought to curb railway workers' militancy through violence. Yet the death of activists only further galvanized the self-consciously working-class movement among railway workers (Staff Reporter 2006). The railway workers' union activism was not confined to discrete issues of wages or job security, but formed a network for sustained working-class opposition to British rule during the early twentieth century (Krishna 1980). This network crossed regions and states alongside the tracks of the railway to form an opposition that included members of railway workers' families as well as of families in the subsidiary industries that relied on the railway, such as Lakshmi's food business. Pappa mentioned radical women's involvement in guerrilla actions that included armed struggle, *satyagraha* actions guided by Gandhian non-violence, and courting arrest as the militant actions chosen by women to resist British imperialism. Another tactic that Pappa alluded to in her narrative, but did not explicitly name was labour strikes. The centrality of the railway to the British imperial project and revenue, together with its systematic exploitation of railway workers, created a volatile locus for political resistance to the Raj. Tactics such as non-violent *satyagraha* were debated alongside a strike, the method the railway union ultimately chose to pursue in the Southern Mahratta Railway Strike of 1932–33 (ibid.).

The Communist Party of India (CPI) provided important linkages between the residentially-based alliance of the railway's industrial working class and the railway's informal economy, made up of people like Pappa's mother. Pappa joined the radical children's group, called the *Balar Sangam*, when it formed in 1945, which had integral connections to the CPI. She was twelve years old then. In 1948, when Pappa was fifteen, her mother Lakshmi helped to organize women in the railway colony into the Ponmalai Women's Association (PWA), another primarily neighbourhood organization linked to the CPI. The Association functioned in part as a women's committee of the workers' union, to support union strikes, and to fight against police and company sanctions that targeted politically active workers (Parvathi Menon 2004: 110). The PWA also included many women who did not have direct ties to the union, who lived in the neighbourhoods of the Golden Rock railway colony. Pappa joined this group immediately. Because it linked women where they lived as much if not more than where they worked, the PWA addressed more than women's issues within the workplace. It also contested oppressive matrimonial practices, such as child marriage, and fought domestic violence among residents in the railway housing colony.

Many of the PWA's issues in 1948 mirrored the work done by progressive, often communist, women in the national women's organization, the All India Women's Conference (AIWC). During this same time, the progressive forces within AIWC sought to rewrite the Hindu Code Bill to provide women the right to inheritance, property and divorce (Hajrah Begum 1945: 7). The PWA was an organization in its own right, connected to but not a 'wing' of either the labour union or the CPI. It was based in the neighbourhood of the Golden Rock railway colony, and brought women together from across the colony to fight for women's issues that might have otherwise been marginalized as secondary or tertiary issues in the union or the CPI. It sought to build leadership among all women, rather than concentrating primarily on waged women workers.

Pappa described her own childhood reactions to patriarchal control in this context:

> I was a small girl at the time. Everyone in our colony was a member [of the Ponmalai Women's Association]. She [her mother, Lakshmi] began to challenge matrimonial issues and atrocities against women. I hate male chauvinism. Even as a small girl I would ask why women are held in low esteem. Only with that anger can we build a women's organization. Why shouldn't women raise their voices against beating wives? All women are against this. My mother fought against this violence in her time. (Pappa Umanath interview, 26 March 2006)

The basis for women's organizing, in Pappa's terms, is indignation and raw anger against women's subordinate status to men. The strength of the women's movement relies on the impetus of this refusal to accept patriarchal norms and social customs, and needs an independent basis to sustain the power of this rejection. The railway union of her colony and the CPI supported the *Balar Sangam* and the formation of the PWA as kindred political formations that brought more people into the larger goals of their struggle for rights, independence and freedom. Women's and youth groups operated within the locality of Ponmalai's railway housing colony, and alongside (though not wholly within) the national political organizations of the railway workers' union and the CPI. To describe these relationships in current terms, the *Balar Sangam* functioned as mass organization that developed youth leaders and built support for a union led by communists or people closely allied to the Communist Party. The PWA had components of a union women's committee in its overt linkages to the railway workers' union, and of a mass organization as it sought to organize all women in the locality around a range of women's issues, like violence and child marriage. Communists and mass movement activists like Lakshmi and Pappa were outside of the formal waged economy, a location almost certainly not unionized. Their activism created integral linkages between unionized and non-unionized workers in their locality of the railway colony, as well as between the CPI and allied mass organizations. They also provided a valuable spur to remind the union and the CPI of women's issues as workers, and their oppression under patriarchy that demanded specific demands and campaigns to address.

In 1943, the same year Pappa joined the *Balar Sangam*, she also courted arrest by joining a Non-Cooperation movement procession against the British occupation of India.[1] She described her own individual and collective aspirations many years later: 'The judge asked me why I joined the Non-Cooperation movement. I said, "To wipe you all out." The judge asked, "Can you?" I replied, "Yes, I can. That is why I am here"' (Pappa Umanath interview, 26 March 2006). Pappa told of her disappointment when the judge refused to jail her for her activities due to her young age. 'I cried as I lay on my mother's lap. My mother comforted me saying, "That's okay if you could not go this time, you can go another time." She gave me courage. My mother was illiterate, and her words surprised me' (ibid.).

[1] Interestingly, while Pappa clearly links her association with the *Balar Sangam* with her engagement with the Non-Cooperation movement, Sumit Sarkar notes that the Non-Cooperation movement at the national level refused to formalize its ties with the growing trade union movement represented by the relatively moderate, national All India Trade Union Council (AITUC), in the early 1920s. 'The very effective and non-violent, but socially far-reaching, weapon of the political general strike would never be allowed to enter the armoury of Non-Cooperation.' See Sumit Sarkar 1987: 200.

Oral History and Political Organization

Pappa told me how her mother nurtured her own revolutionary resolve with practised ease and good humour, though with a disciplined focus. These were all stories she was comfortable recounting. We met only once in 2006, months into my stay in the southern state of Tamil Nadu where I was researching AIDWA's organizing campaigns as well as their cadre-training methods, spending much of my time in the neighbourhoods of north Chennai, among AIDWA members who depended on the fishing industry for their livelihood. For most of my research I worked alongside B. Padma, a former member of AIDWA, who translated my questions into Tamil and the women's answers from Tamil into English. Soon after the interviews, we would comb through the group and individual interview tapes together, sharpening these quick translations into more nuanced responses. Often, after going over the interview tapes, I would return and interview the AIDWA members again. I had only one opportunity to meet and listen to Pappa Umanath's story. My questions were almost exclusively about origins, of AIDWA and of her own family's three generations in India's Communist Party. I have woven her story of her life and AIDWA's formation into this chapter along the grain of, though not always exactly replicating, her chronology and her information. Many of her anecdotes are supported by existing historical accounts, such as her remembrance of Tania, the Russian anti-fascist fighter during the Second World War.[2] Some retell dominant stories of progressive Indian movements from an unfamiliar perspective.

Oral autobiographical histories are often discounted for chronological inaccuracy and the faulty cracks of memory; yet these same qualities reveal important facets of gendered subjectivity, class and power (Leydesdorff, Passerini and Thompson 1996: 1–3, 8). Much can be gleaned from their structure, as well as the emotional, allegorical and factual meanings that narrators and researchers ask these stories to convey. Narratives that uphold existing relations of power exist more comfortably in the public domain. Memories, like Pappa's, that challenge accepted truths and power are transmitted from a location that oral historians have described as 'from the interstices of society, from the boundaries between the public and the private' (ibid.: 8). Pappa recounted a multilayered story about inter-generational struggle passed from her mother to herself; yet she did not tell me how she had passed her revolutionary commitments to her own politically active daughters. She told me a story of being taught (not of teaching) resolve in

[2] Tania was the name chosen by the Russian fighter Zoia Kosmodemianskaia, who was caught and tortured by the Germans during the Second World War. The Germans executed her at the age of eighteen, on 29 November 1941, after she refused to give her own name or the names of other Russian soldiers. See Krylova 2010: 218–21.

the face of seemingly impenetrable colonial, and later post-colonial, authority. She told this story in Tamil to me, a foreign researcher who speaks no Tamil, through a translator, Padma, whom she had met several times before in the context of their shared political engagement with AIDWA's activism. As I repeatedly asked for stories of AIDWA's origins alongside Pappa's own development as a leader in AIDWA, she seemed perplexed why the same question returned even after she had answered it. She would pause, flick her eyes up impatiently at Padma and then glance at me. In contrast to her flowing historical narrative at the beginning of the interview, she would answer briefly, adding more details with each question.

Women's stories of rebellion, as the oral historian Luisa Passerini suggests, indicate struggles against the social and political order, and simultaneously represent women's gendered constraints and oppression. Oral historians, Passerini urges, should pay attention to a range of meanings in personal narratives, meanings that draw from the present as well as the past, in order to find 'the historical contexts wherein they make sense' (Passerini 1989: 197). Concentrating on a central narrative myth of women's irreverence sheds an important light on Pappa's story of women's inter-generational rebellion as a window into present and past injustice, but also to exemplify the imperative of future struggles. Pappa's narrative of rebellion carries 'its force', in Passerini's words, 'as a utopia of freedom and innovation [that] continues through the epochs' (ibid.: 191). Lakshmi, Pappa's mother, strengthened her daughter's courage to fight colonial power, even as she modelled that resolve in her own activities. Still, Lakshmi's encouraging words to the twelve-year-old Pappa surprised her. Pappa's expressed surprise may refer to her mother's economic vulnerability and illiteracy, or to the extent of her political militancy even as it extended to her young daughter, or perhaps a combination of both these aspects. Lakshmi grounded her commitment to class, gender and national struggles by the dangerous act of passing notes to underground revolutionaries, not through writing or even reading those notes. Lakshmi's support for Pappa's aspirations to do jail time might up-end our own expectations: that the nationalist movement largely was an elite affair, for the literate and well-connected subjects of British India. Many, though certainly not all, histories of anti-colonial movements have taught us that the movement was led by men and their wives, daughters and sons, and not peopled by poor working women and girls. In the tradition of subaltern history writing, Pappa's expressed surprise clears rhetorical space to register how her story overturns dominant assumptions about the Indian freedom movement.

Perhaps Pappa's story of passing her knowledge to her daughters lies within her own story of AIDWA's origins – origins that began with her own political formation as a girl surviving on the margins of the militant working-class railway unions of pre-independence India. She answered my repeated requests for AIDWA's beginnings not with the dates of its founding conference, but through mining her own and her mother's anti-imperialist, communist and feminist past. She also answered by remembering the social reform movements of the nineteenth century for their Indian instigators and for their ongoing importance within the fabric of radical communities, not for the British public's horror at child marriage and widow immolation. Pappa's story, like AIDWA's, is not just a story of resisting British colonialism, but of fighting imperialism as it continued to structure the new nation of India in favour of the wealthy, and against the redistribution of power, land and resources to the organized and unorganized working people. To a foreign researcher from the United States, she emphasized the importance of anti-imperialism to AIDWA's origins: from its earliest glimmers of possibility hidden within the PWA to AIDWA's substantial form as a national women's organization with 9.5 million members at the time of our interview. Pappa's story emphasized the shift in the geo-political order when the imperial mantle has moved from Britain to the United States.

To honour this multiplicity of origins, this chapter tells the history of AIDWA's formation through one primary regional lens, that of one founding member's life in the southern state of Tamil Nadu. Attention to the regional specificity of AIDWA's history reflects national and international movements, ideologies,and solidarities as they impact local organizing. As Vina Mazumdar and Indu Agnihotri remind historians of this period, these local and regional struggles were internationalized in the twentieth century precisely because of their broader resistance to imperialism. 'Confined earlier by locale or limited foci, these [struggles against gendered injustices] now found expression through movements against imperialism, for national liberation and social transformation' (Agnihotri and Mazumdar 1995: 1869). This internationalism powerfully undergirded the local struggles in places like Ponmalai, as Pappa's memories attested to, but a more focused regional lens makes another history visible. What emerges is a story that displaces, sometimes in surprising ways, the master-narratives of India's struggle for national independence in the first part of the twentieth century. India's independence movement seen from localities and regions disturbs the accepted story of educated, elite men as its primary architects. Even more importantly, when trying to understand the rise of women's political activism in twentieth-century India, the regional lens emphasizes how the cutting edge of movements does not reside in a few enlightened, national and female leaders. Instead, it reveals how the demands of committed and wilful participants made these possible. Landless women, rural and urban poor women are the vital centre to women's organizing after independence. These women's stories of organized resistance to violence, exploitation and oppression are the harbingers of the more visible and more celebrated explosion of middle-class women's politics after Prime

Minister Indira Gandhi lifted the suspension of civil liberties in 1977. The regional and local perspective sheds light on how those participants, often undifferentiated by their names or lives in written histories, honed movement tactics, strategies and goals. Each person carries a story larger than herself, and this chapter recounts Pappa's story in its time and place.

AIDWA's Movement Origins

Social Reform and Nationalist Movements

Pappa framed her very local story of organizing women in the Golden Rock Railway Workshop in the years just after Indian independence, as well as her work in cities and towns across Tamil Nadu, through the national movement and well-established social reform movement. Begun in the early nineteenth century, the social reform movement aspired to change the conditions of women's lives in India, particularly of elite women, in caste and class terms, but did not originally boast of many women leaders (Sumit Sarkar and Tanika Sarkar 2007: 1–9). These early campaigns for women's right to education, widows' right to remarry, prohibitions against widow burning, and in favour of girl children's right to wait until adulthood to marry did not end with the passage of British laws. They widened over the nineteenth century to include more women as writers and as political leaders. Women and men in the movement 'took huge and painful social risks. Made outcaste by their families, kin groups and community, threatened by an outraged orthodoxy, they often watched reformist gains peter out in the face of social ostracism and hostility, even when they had been enacted as state laws' (ibid.: 9). The campaigns for social reform were particularly resilient in Bengal, Tamil Nadu, Punjab and Maharashtra, though their institutional support varied – from religious revivalism to colonial bureaucracies to nationalist movements. In the early twentieth century, elite and middle-class acceptance of women's public roles in a range of contexts continued to grow. By the 1930s, social reform campaigns merged with nationalist movements in ways that made them hard to disentangle. Women's rights to public participation and full citizenship galvanized the national independence movement even as it legitimized social reform demands.

For women in the 1930s and 1940s, the political sphere dramatically shifted in a potent combination of what Suruchi Thapar-Bjorkert calls 'the domestication of the public sphere' through the Gandhian ideology and politics of non-violence, and gained critical support through 'the politicization of the domestic sphere'.[3] Lakshmi's and Pappa's lives as waged workers and

[3] Thapar-Bjorkert 2006: 22–24. While Thapar-Bjorkert focuses on middle-class women from northern India in her study, her insights about the shifting norms of respectability for

as politically active women provide ample illustration of Thapar-Bjorkert's insights, though within a distinctly working-class and working-poor context of union and communist movements. Entire families threw their weight behind the movements against British rule, providing a support that sometimes accommodated norms of women's respectability through a personalized politics, such as the home spinning of cloth or *khadi* that maintained women's segregation and confinement.[4] But anti-colonial resistance movements also actively challenged gendered, class- and caste-based norms of social respectability to encourage women's active political engagement in protests, marches and boycotts. National independence movements hailed and trained scores of educated young women in the skills of organizing, many of whom joined the movement while in secondary school and college (Kumar 1993; Liddle and Joshi 1986; Sunil Sen 1985; Ahlawat 1995; Khullar 1997). Bharati Ray identifies a revealing class link between middle-class women's activism in the freedom movement to the emergence of the women's movement. 'The twentieth-century women's movement in India was inextricably bound with the freedom movement . . . the historical point from which feminist consciousness began to be fashioned, arrived with the freedom struggle' (Ray 1995: 177). Ray describes middle-class women's political isolation from poor urban and rural women since the political campaigns inspired by their growing feminist consciousness 'were clearly related to middle-class urban aspirations, their piecemeal schemes of uplifting the rural or urban poor notwithstanding' (ibid.: 210). Nevertheless, as more rural and urban working-class people joined the mass movements against British rule, including poor women, the largely middle-class and elite women's social reform movement gained a corresponding jolt of energy (Forbes 1996: 80–81).

Pappa's story does not tell of middle-class women's involvement in social reform and nationalist movements. Instead, her autobiography emphasizes women activists who were working-class, working-poor and agricultural workers. Her story lies in the interstices, not of public and private exactly since most of these women did not live confined to the domestic sphere, but of the nationalist and women's movements as we think we know them historically. Sumit Sarkar and Tanika Sarkar describe these overlapping and contradictory movements through their historical origins in social reform:

---

middle-class women may synchronized with shifts for women's active involvement in the left and union movements for working-class and poor women.

[4] Scholarship on the diary of a brahmin, middle-class woman who lived in Tamil Nadu reveals how tenuous even the politicization of the domestic sphere was for the public voice of women who supported Indian independence. Both Kamala Visweswaran (1994) and Mythily Sivaraman (2006) trace the faint outline of the anti-British commitment of Subbalakshmi who tersely noted freedom movement books she bought and anti-colonial meetings she attended, but only gave uncoded space in her diary to her nature poetry.

> We can map a trajectory of broadening social and political criticism, if not social change, from the time of reforms. If not directly connected with or created by the reforms, and even when contradicted by the class, caste, and political limits of the early reforms, there were complex, parallel, interanimating movements for rights: for self-determination against colonialism, for social justice for low castes, for the human rights of the labouring poor. (Sumit Sarkar and Tanika Sarkar 2007: 9)

In the historical spirit of the Sarkars' interanimating movements with social reform, Pappa set her description of her own work organizing women in cities, townships and rural localities in the 1940s and 1950s firmly within the context of the social reform movement. She also emphasized the central importance of social reform movements to poor and working-class women today. 'Now women are the majority among waged agricultural workers, and they greatly respect the work of the women's organization which fought for reforms relating to the freedom struggle, against *sati*, for widow's rights, for girls' and women's education and other issues' (Pappa Umanath interview, 26 March 2006). In Pappa's telling, the Indian women's movement in the twentieth century did not simply begin, in a teleological sense, with the social reform movement in the nineteenth century. Neither, for Pappa, did the social reform movement stay within discrete boundaries, with reliable goals and uniform organizing methods. Instead, the social reform movement as it took root in the nineteenth and early twentieth century *made possible* women activists' radical use of social reformist gains for women, of greater personal autonomy, freedom of movement and increased civil rights. She capped her stories about rural Dalit women fighting caste, class and gender exploitation in Madurai and Thanjavur districts in the 1950s and 60s with this insight about agricultural women workers in the present. These women, she suggested, did not inherit social reformist goals, but creatively used these gains to organize toward their own more militant ends. In Pappa's narrative, the separate organization of women into leftist groups like the Ponmalai Women's Association brought social reform demands for women's rights to social and legal equality into post-independence Indian struggles for a more just distribution of wealth and for the social transformation of hierarchies of power.

Women's Committees in Industrial, Informal and Agricultural Workers' Movements

Pappa Umanath's own political initiation traversed the cusp of Indian independence – from 1943 when she first joined the *Balar Sangam* and courted arrest, to 1948 when she joined the Ponmalai Women's Association. K.P. Janakiammal, the first woman to be arrested in south India for her agitation against India's support for the British in the Second World War, was integral to both these organizations, and Pappa's story honoured her importance in her own life and her centrality to the communist women's movement. Janakiammal was already legendary when the British authorities forced her to leave Madurai and live in Ponmalai, when Pappa was a child. Fourteen years older than Pappa, Janakiammal provided another vitally important role model for her (Sivaraman 1992: 14). Throughout her life, Janakiammal defied the norms for girls and women. She joined an acting troupe, the Palaniyappa Boys Company, in 1929 when she was twelve years old. In the all-male realm of theatre, with women's parts played by men, she was known for her skilful acting of male roles (ibid.). At twenty-three years old, she became the Madurai Town Committee secretary of the Congress Socialist Party (CSP); and when she left the CSP a year later, she joined the first Communist Party cell in Madurai. As a teacher in *Balar Sangam*, Janakiammal taught Pappa and other children Tamil folk dances like the *gummi*. She described the Russian revolution, the Indian movements for women's social reforms, and the imperialist reasons for the ongoing famine in Bengal. Pappa described her earliest memories of Janaki's internationalist teachings: 'We learned about a woman named Tania who refused to identify anybody in the resistance movement. As a result, Hitler's army shot her. Many children were named Tania in honour of her actions. As Bhagat Singh was our hero as a freedom fighter, so was Tania' (Pappa Umanath interview, 26 March 2006). From their early days in Golden Rock's children's school as teacher and student, to the ensuing years of shared jail time and political struggle, the two women lived deeply interconnected lives.

In 1948, Janakiammal and Pappa travelled around the state to convince women in railway colonies to join the railway workers' association. They began their campaign to include women on a mass scale in Ponmalai.

> After independence the Congress government came to power. We faced so many attacks during this time, as did all of our comrades. In the Ponmalai Railway Workers' Association there were 5,000 members. Janakiammal, I and other comrades went to each of these 5,000 houses and convinced the women to also join the organization. We replicated our work in Erode, Pothanur, Chennai and other parts of Tamil Nadu. (Ibid.)

Their activism did not end with the enlistment of women's subsidiary help for the predominantly male, unionized railway workers, however. Neither did it concentrate solely on working-class women's industrial labour. Their work building women's committees linked to industrial workers' unions rippled outward to building leftist neighbourhood women's committees connected to agricultural workers' unions. In agricultural workers' unions, women's work and men's work gained an organized voice. Neighbourhood-based women's committees had the potential to foster solidarity between women workers in and around industrial work and women agricultural workers through building their own political group that raised women's issues in their multiple social locations: as women workers in the railways and in the fields, and as women in civil society and within the family.

> We met the women and argued that we needed an organization of our own. When the railway workers' organization held a conference, we conducted a women's conference on one of the days.... Our organization functioned alongside the issues of the railway employees. We were actively involved in the issues of agricultural employees whose wages were very low. Women faced discrimination in the wages they were paid compared to men's. We protested this inequality. We demanded equal wages with men. (Ibid.)

The Ponmalai Women's Association had its place in the Golden Rock Railway Workshop among the women who lived and worked in the colony. It sought to create greater solidarity within railway workers' struggles as well as mobilize this solidarity among all women in the colony to demand basic rights for women workers, such as equal wages to men. Even after the end of formal British colonial power over India, the organization actively built ties around the state, between railway workers' colonies, rural localities and beyond.

Pappa described an important struggle in the 1950s that was led by women agricultural workers in a village named Thuvariman near the city of Madurai.[5] Janakiammal moved to the village and worked in the fields for over a month to better sustain the efforts of the tenant-farming women who fought for better wages and working conditions. The landlords threatened the women, demanding they accept lower wages or face eviction. They defied the eviction order and ploughed the land. 'The landlords' thugs threatened to bring in people from outside the village and give them the right to work the land', Pappa described. 'The women threatened to mutilate the workers' legs. As a result, the people the landlords brought in to replace the women workers ran from the village. After that, the landowners provided employment with higher wages for the women' (Pappa Umanath interview, 26 March 2006). Pappa's story emphasizes Janakiammal's courage to join the struggle when the threat of violence was greatest, not to sweep into the women's lives after the violence was over. Janakiammal, she stressed, faced the danger side by side with the women. What Pappa did not mention directly was Janakiammal's daring confrontation with powerful caste dictates that could denounce a non-Dalit Hindu woman just for standing with Dalit women. Pappa's story of rebellion here is not about her own

[5] The better-known region for the active organization of agricultural women in Tamil Nadu is the district of Thanjuvar. See Velayudhan 1985: 60.

or her mother's, but functions similarly in her own oral history: the brutal caste hierarchy that demanded Dalit agricultural working women and men to submit to their lives of low status also punished non-Dalit Hindus who attempted to change that hierarchy. Rebellion, as a narrative motif, remembers the past as it continues to live in the present, and as it continues to demand struggles to change that injustice.

The courage of these women in the 1950s heralded the struggles in the agriculturally rich district of Thanjavur over a decade later, in a locality named Kilvenmani. As in Thuvariman, the women from Kilvenmani joined the growing leftist women's movement through the principled support of members like Janakiammal of the CPI. In the 1960s, landless Dalit women and men who joined the communist-led agricultural workers' union from Kilvenmani stood up to challenge established traditions of social oppression, labour exploitation and sexual predation (Alexander 1975). In the more well-known struggle in Kilvenmani, Dalit agricultural workers fought the predominantly Brahmin-caste landlords in the region, in the face of violent reprisals against their own lives and their families' safety. Mythily Sivaraman described the instigation of the infamous 1968 Kilvenmani pogrom:

> On December 25, a landlord of Kilvenmani employed labour supplied by the PPA [the Paddy Producers' Association representing the area's landowners] in order to defeat the demand of the local labourers for a higher wage. The area was tense. According to the survivors of Venmani, in the evening, the tea-shopkeeper was kidnapped by the landlords and beaten up for refusing to advise the labourers to join the PPA. The labourers came *en masse* and forced the release of the tea-shop owner. In the clash, Pakkirisami, a landlord's agent, was killed. The *mirasdar*s [large landowners], always used to having the upper hand, planned a massive retaliation. That night, at about 10 pm, the landlords and their men arrived in police lorries and converged on the *cheri* [Dalit neighbourhood] from three different directions, cutting off escape routes and synchronizing their advance through the blowing of whistles. They shot at the Harijans [Dalits] with guns, attacked them with sickles and sticks and set fire to their huts. Several Harijans were hurt, two very seriously. Some women, children and old men ran and took refuge in one of the huts. The murderers immediately surrounded the hut, and set fire to it. Forty-two charred bodies were discovered from that hut the next morning. (Sivaraman 1973: 927)

Mythily Sivaraman visited Kilvenmani after the mass murder and talked to the few women who survived the massacre to understand what had happened. While newspaper reports of the time wrote it off as a labour dispute around wages, Sivaraman discovered that both the landowners and agricultural workers disagreed with this facile explanation, citing rising militance among agricultural workers and their refusal to perpetuate caste-based practices of subservience. Activism after the violent destruction only intensified and spread to neighbouring localities – activism that centred on caste injustice and working conditions among the mostly Dalit agricultural workers. The role of the left women's movement was as critical in Kilvenmani as it was in Thuvariman and Ponmalai. Like the PWA that was linked directly to the railway workers' union, in rural areas around Kilvenmani in the district of Thanjavur, women's committees in the CPI-allied agricultural labour union produced powerful women leaders in the agitations that preceded and followed the Kilvenmani massacre. These same Dalit women active in the agricultural workers' union of Thanjavur created the backbone for the Tamil Nadu Democratic Women's Association (DWA). In the founding convention of the Tamil Nadu DWA in 1974, Dalit women activists from Thanjavur constituted half of its membership of 27,000 women (Omvedt 1975: 41).

The Communist Party of India

The underground CPI played a vital role in the 1940s and 50s in a wide range of movements, particularly through its work organizing peasants' and workers' struggles that interanimated independence and social reform movements. Railway colonies with entire families who depended upon the railways for their employment provided fertile ground for building the communist movement. Pappa's mother, uncle and her immediate family joined the Party in support of the anti-imperialist freedom movement, the militant railway union activities and a class-based vision of democratic self-rule. The Golden Rock railway workers' union was closely allied with the CPI at a time when the Indian government, led by the Congress Party, cracked down on all communist activity with particular ferocity between 1948 and 1951 (Guha 2007: 109–10, 147). Pappa joined the CPI in 1945 when she was fourteen years old. In 1950, when she was nineteen, the police arrested both Pappa and her mother for their communist involvement, as Jawaharlal Nehru's government stepped up its response to domestic political opposition to Congress rule, particularly by the communists and labour unions. Both Pappa and her mother were beaten in the jail so that they would reveal other communists' locations. Both refused to give the Indian authorities any information. When relocated to the Saidapet sub-jail, Pappa and her mother held a hunger strike to demand political prisoner status as communists, a dangerous demand in the political atmosphere of the period (Parvathi Menon 2004: 112–13).

The fight for the designation and redefinition of political prisoner gained new currency under the Preventive Detention Act of 1950, an Act used almost exclusively against communists, particularly those active in the Telengana movement in the neighbouring state of Andhra Pradesh.[41] In the CPI anal-

[6] Ujjwal Kumar Singh writes in fascinating detail about the politics of jail status before and after independence. See Singh 1998.

ysis in the years after India's independence, the prisons were another site for active class struggle, and the hunger strike was one of its most powerful weapons. Under the British governance, political prisoner status was an elite designation within the prison system, with special rights and privileges accorded to many of India's independence activists. After independence, the communists demanded '[t]he abolition of "vindictive class distinctions" and the award of "family allowance for all"' (Singh 1998: 218). 'Political prisoner' in this context became an inclusive category to provide rights to all prisoners, and erode the class and caste distinctions within jails that were encouraged during British rule. The fight for humane conditions for all prisoners had particular resonance for incarcerated women who often lived in a jail within a jail, since the male prisoners gained access to open grounds at their expense. Most of the women in jails were not imprisoned for their political activity, whether communist or communal, or violent offences, but for crimes related to poor mental health and poverty, like sex work, theft and smuggling (Kalyan Chaudhuri 1977: 755).

The hunger strike weakened Pappa's mother; her health deteriorated quickly, and she died on her twenty-third day without food ('11th State Conference Resolve: Further Strengthen AIDWA in Tamil Nadu', 2005: 4). Over the course of her life, Pappa spent many years in jail for her opposition to the government's policies, but her first arrest left her with a 'deep anger' against the system. 'The jailer informed me that my mother had died in jail and asked what I planned to do. I said I would like to see her' (Pappa Umanath interview, 26 March 2006). Pappa described her sadness, incarcerated for her political activity and isolated in another cell, away from her dead mother. 'As the condition to pay my respects to my mother, he demanded that I write a letter resigning from the Party. I could only stare at him. Then I asked him, "Are you human?" I refused to write the letter and returned to my cell.' The cruel manipulation of the guards meant that Pappa last saw her mother's body being taken away through the bars of her cell. Nor was she allowed to arrange her mother's funeral or burial. 'My mother had asked me to bury her with a red flag on her grave when she died, but I could not honour her wishes. Until my last days I will never forget what they did to my mother' (ibid.). The lack of her most basic right to mourn the death of her jailed mother, Pappa said, fuelled her activism in post-independence India.

The repression against communist activists after independence is only briefly acknowledged in dominant historiography; yet, as Pappa attested, the pressures to renounce membership in the Communist Party continued well into the Congress Party's political reign.[7] After the government eased its

[7] After its Second Congress in 1948, the Communist Party took a much more militant line against the Nehru government for failing to demand revolutionary changes in land and

suppression of Communist Party activities in 1951, Pappa was released from jail; but she never forgot the lessons she learned there. The single-party hegemony enjoyed by the Congress Party through the 1950s and into the 60s led to unacceptable abuses of power, even when in the name of national development and integration. Other communist women shared Pappa's renewed commitment for a multi-party democracy where communist dissent could flourish and build political power (Chakravartty 1980: 219–20).

The National and International Women's Movement in the 1940s and 1950s

The repression of communist women in the late 1940s and early 1950s took a similar trajectory in the most overtly political and, by the 1940s, largest national women's organization, the All India Women's Conference (AIWC). Communist members of AIWC in Bengal were expelled from the organization in 1948, and many moved full-time into organizing for the communist women's organization in the state, called the Mahila Atmaraksha Samiti (Women's Self-Defence League, also known as MARS). In the 1930s and early 40s, however, many communist women organized productively within the AIWC (Swarupa Rani 2003: 76). They sought to widen the scope of AIWC goals beyond social reform and charity, to include rural and working-class women's issues around food security and land redistribution. Renu Chakravartty was a Communist Party member, a member of AIWC, and an active member of the radical Bengali women's organization MARS.[8] MARS gained fame in the 1940s, primarily around its famine work of redistributing food, creating work schemes for destitute women, exposing and providing shelter for trafficked women, and for its support of the Tebhaga movement (Mukherjee 1944: 9; Bhowani Sen 1945: 3; Kalpana Dutt 1945: 6–7). *Tebhaga*, or two-thirds, was the share of the crop demanded by tenant farmers, both women and men, in compensation for their agricultural labour on large landowners' farms (Majumdar 2011). This militant movement was most active between 1947, the year of India's formal independence, and 1948, when at least ten women lost their lives to the struggle (Paschim Banga Ganatantrik Mahila Samiti 1993: 22). As a regional for-

---

property ownership and feudal relations. Intense governmental repression followed these pronouncements of direct opposition to the Congress Party government. Gupta 2001: 253.

[8] For example, MARS often contended with the derisory label of being a 'women's wing' or a 'communist front' organization. Tripti Chaudhuri points out that MARS in 1944 had 43,000 members, while the Communist Party in Bengal had 900 members as of July 1943. In March 1943 the Communist Party had only 151 women members. See Tripti Chaudhuri 2000: 312. Radical and communist women played important roles throughout MARS, but the vast majority of women in MARS were not members of a left party – a point ignored by the elitist and sexist smear of being merely a 'wing' or a 'front' for communists with its majority of duped working-poor, indigenous and agricultural women members.

mation in the state of Bengal, MARS valued the support provided by the national reach of the AIWC, even as the AIWC benefited by the political vitality of MARS members (Tripti Chaudhuri 2000: 311).These shifts of political programme and membership in specific regions like Bengal, Kerala, Andhra Pradesh and Punjab had an effect on the generally cautious tenor of the national AIWC's statements (Forbes 1996: 81–83). In 1945, communist and progressive women within AIWC won support for the draft Hindu Code, that sought to provide greater access to divorce, alimony and the right to inheritance for Hindu women (Hajrah Begum 1945). The AIWC conference resolution read: 'This legislation is consistent with modern progressive thought and ensures a healthy growth to Hindu social structure' (ibid.: 7). In 1946, at the 18th session of the AIWC held in Hyderabad, they voted to demand Indian independence immediately and drew up a charter of women's rights to distribute among all political parties ('AIWC Meets: Demands Immediate Indian Freedom', 1946: 10, 12). At the same conference, members fought to resist any ban against communist women's membership in the organization. The instability within AIWC's membership of 25,000 women mirrored a larger contradiction throughout the nationalist movement. Many middle-class women who had been radicalized by the nationalist and anti-imperialist movements were pushed further by the increasing numbers of rural and urban poor activists around the country who joined the political foment, and demanded greater social, political and economic changes in the new nation-state.

The mobilization of rural women in states like Bengal through MARS, in Andhra Pradesh during the Telengana struggle against feudal landlords, and in Kerala in industrial unions and agricultural industries during the mid- to late 1940s created a resounding impact nationally on women's political organization. As a nationalist organization, AIWC was pushed to widen its sphere to support working-class and rural women's activism, considerably beyond its charitable good works among disadvantaged women. The famine conditions in the 1940s that began in Bengal and spread to areas around the country led to AIWC's formation of famine relief work like free kitchens, food distribution centres and health centres, that became foci for mobilizing the women hardest hit by the crisis. In 1943, its extensive famine relief work led to a strongly worded condemnation by AIWC of colonial governance and diversion of food supplies from famine-hit regions to the battlefront of the Second World War (Basu and Ray 2003: 90). A year later, the AIWC intervened in government surveys that affected data collection on the wages and earnings of women, and demanded a national minimum wage for all workers. Also in 1944, it actively sought more detailed information about women's agricultural work and the conditions of their lives (ibid.: 98–100).

Working-class and rural women's activism spurred an important contest within the AIWC around its membership, its political goals and strategies (Sunil Sen 1985: 24). Before independence, the annual membership fees for the AIWC were three rupees, a prohibitively high cost for most Indian women. Communist women within the AIWC led a fight to make the organization accessible to all women through the significantly more affordable dues of four annas (a quarter of a rupee) per year. They lost that fight at the vibrant and most widely attended conference to date, the 19th Session of the AIWC at Akola, held in December 1946 (Chakravartty 1980: 200). Renu Chakravartty recounted other important gains, however: 'the Akola Conference did condemn categorically the repression let loose in most of the Indian states. It went a step further. It condemned the whole system of autocracy. With so many maharanis and begums in its list of past and present presidents and dignitaries, to do this was a great step forward' (ibid.: 211). While its leadership refused to lower dues, the AIWC took an active stand against British colonial repression. As Chakravartty noted, the Indian power elite that had benefited from colonialism took an important step when it actively supported a democratic and independent India.

The spirit of the 1946 conference waned two years later, in 1948, when the AIWC split and its communist members in Bengal had their membership rescinded, even if they could pay the three rupee dues. Communist women like Renu Chakravartty continued to organize with local and state-based leftist women's organizations, such as the Mahila Ganatantrik Samiti in Bengal, the All Kerala Mahila Sangham in Kerala and the Andhra Mahila Sangham in Andhra Pradesh. By 1948, Chakravartty was fully immersed in the Tebhaga movement of landless, mainly Dalit, tenant farmers in rural Bengal. She was one of many communist women who experienced the radicalization of women's activism among the peasantry (Stree Shakti Sanghatana 1989; Mathew and Nair 1986). Expelled from broad women's groups like the AIWC and committed to building socialism in India, these women sought to better shape their activism through explicitly leftist groups that relied on Marxist strategies and ideologies of women's emancipation. In the wake of 1948, these women's groups organized rural and working class women around their economic and social issues – issues largely ignored by the traditions of social reformism, including feminist ones.[9] Thus, even though they were not part of a national women's organization, these activists sought to augment their impact on wider political and social movements for revolutionary change across caste and class.

The impetus to form a national organization reached a special significance in relation to the consolidation of international socialist women into

[9] Some women, like Mridula Sarabhai, who actively sought to radicalize the nationalist movement on working women's issues, chose to leave the AIWC in 1948 due to disenchantment and difficulty in doing their work within the organizations. See Basu 1996: 83.

the Women's International Democratic Federation (WIDF). WIDF formed in 1945 in Paris, after the Second World War. Backed by the USSR, East European socialist nations and communist parties around the world, it sought to rebuild progressive women's movements against fascism. WIDF was one of a handful of new international women's organizations formed after the war, and the only one that made a significant attempt to include women from colonized and newly independent nations (Stienstra 1994: 86). In 1945, two delegates from the AIWC joined its founding conference in Paris, and spoke about the need to condemn imperialism in their fight against fascism. The WIDF delegates passed a resolution in support of all people's right to self-determination. Even with their immediate attention to anti-colonial freedom struggles of women, the AIWC rescinded its participation in WIDF the following year. In 1946, the AIWC leadership barred the Indian delegate elected to WIDF's executive committee from attending its meeting in Moscow because they abruptly decided to join the International Alliance of Women (IAW) instead (Chakravartty 1980: 217–18). As a suffrage organization founded by North American and European women, the IAW supported all women's right to suffrage, including colonized women, but did not voice its anti-imperialist commitments as strongly as the WIDF did (Rupp 1996; Weber 2001). The choice to join the IAW represented a less confrontational means for the AIWC to support a limited platform for women's rights to political equality, without demands for women's rights to economic equality, full democracy or international peace (de Haan 2010).

Left Women's Organizing After Independence

In 1948, two WIDF representatives travelled to India to research and report on the conditions of people under colonial rule, as well as to show their solidarity with colonized women (Chakravartty 1980: 217). Some state-based women's groups, like MARS and Andhra Mahila Sangham, made a different membership choice from the AIWC's, and joined the WIDF after their delegation's visit in 1948. One year later, in 1949, Indian delegates attended WIDF's 'Conference of the Women of Asia' held in Beijing, China. Betty Millard, an American communist and member of the secretariat of WIDF, quotes at length from the unnamed Indian woman's report at this event. The Indian delegate's critique of Nehru's governmental neglect was unvarnished.

> Children from the age of six work 12 and 16 hours a day in factories and on plantations; boys and girls of 10 work in the coal mines. These miserable little ones never know what it is to have a full stomach: 60 per cent of them die of starvation and disease before they reach 14 years. . . . Meanwhile, profits have risen by 159

per cent since the war, and the Nehru government devotes 50 percent of its budget to arms. (Quoted in Millard 1952)

Indian communist women in the late 1940s and early 1950s gained new opportunities to take international leadership in the anti-imperialist and anti-colonial movements thriving across the globe. They gained an international forum for their politics as members of WIDF. In most parts of India, communist women activists held on to their roles in the central national organization, AIWC. Due in part to factions of internal hostility to communist women's activism that gained sway in Bengal with their expulsion from AIWC, they simultaneously built up leftist women's organizations on a regional level. Hajrah Begum, a leader in the CPI and AIWC, and editor of the AIWC journal *Roshni*, remembered a meeting with P.C. Joshi, the general secretary of the CPI, at the first Party Congress in Bombay, in 1943 (Hajrah Begum 1994). She recalled, 'I raised the question of organizing women on an all India basis' (ibid.). She also suggested organizing women from AIWC into the leftist women's organizations. Joshi agreed, but the debate was not settled within the CPI as a whole and continued to unfold during the 1940s into the 1950s.

The National Federation of Indian Women (NFIW), an all-India women's organization affiliated to the CPI, grew out of WIDF's 1953 Copenhagen Conference on Women (Chakravartty 1980: 218). Members who joined WIDF's Conference on Women used the momentum gained in this international forum to constitute a national organization for anti-imperialist and communist women in India. The decision to form NFIW did not occur without a debate, since a mass organization of women was seen by some in the CPI as a divisive move to separate working-class women's struggles from men's. The debate of whether to concentrate on working women's industrial and agricultural organization into unions and *kisan* (peasant) organizations continued to smoulder among left-wing and communist activists even after the formation of NFIW.[10] Many communist women held multiple tasks in unions and peasant groups alongside their work of organizing women into NFIW. In 1954, Hajrah Begum and Charusheela Gupta, both of NFIW, represented India at WIDF's Fourteenth Session Executive Committee meeting. Hajrah Begum was an open communist and author of *Why Women Should Vote Communist*, a CPI pamphlet published in 1962. Her report to the WIDF meeting in 1954 listed a wide range of struggles by leftist activists that sought greater benefits for women from government policies to pro-

[10] These debates quite audibly returned with AIDWA's formation almost thirty years later. A pamphlet published by the Central Committee of the CPM, *On Mass Organizations*, outlines and weighs in on the terms of the debate and the resulting Party decision (CPI[M] 1981). See also, Hajrah Begum 1994.

mote more equitable wealth and land distribution, as well of women workers' struggles (Hajrah Begum 1954). These activities included employment campaigns by rural women in Bengal, Punjab and Travancore; agitations for girl's schools in Punjab; and the fight for better working conditions among cashewnut workers in Mangalore, mica workers in Bihar and plantation workers in Assam, amongst other regional work campaigns. In her report, Hajrah Begum provided a critique and future strategy for these campaigns: 'the issue of employment could have been taken up more vigorously by co-operation with other organizations such as trade unions, refugee organizations, and other women's organizations' (ibid.: 19). She pointed to the need for better coalitional work that spans women's organizations as well as trade unions to bring potential allies to the cause of women's employment issues. She also listed land redistribution campaigns that sought to pressure the government to break up the holdings of large landowners in Andhra Pradesh and Kerala. These campaigns in the 1950s contributed to the passage of the Land Ceiling Act of 1961 (Suhas Chattopadhyay 1973).

Even as Hajrah Begum addressed the international forum in 1954, rural movements, most notably in Kerala, had taken matters into their own hands, with communists deeply involved in land occupation movements across the state. This example in particular reveals that Hajrah Begum's somewhat muted critique of governmental failure in her WIDF report did not support passively waiting for the government to acquiesce to peasant and worker demands. Her report also described more coalitional campaigns around the country, such as the fight against the high price of food. In Hyderabad this campaign brought together fourteen women's organizations. In Bengal, it won a lower price for rice. The leftist women's movement, through the NFIW, took up worker, consumer and agricultural issues across the country. All of these campaigns continued to pressure the Congress Party in the 1950s to live up to the promises it made before national independence, through concerted resistance to governmental inaction.

Renu Chakravartty represented India as an NIFW delegate at the WIDF conference held by leaders of women's organizations in Budapest, Hungary, in 1970. Her brief report spoke in very general terms of the ongoing struggles fought by left women's movements throughout the 1960s. In particular, it referred to the massive land redistribution campaign successfully waged by the left and communist parties in West Bengal during the 1960s and 70s, over a decade after the Tebhaga movement receded:

> There are the general problems affecting women, such as rising prices. We find it difficult to get other women's organizations to support movements which are led by class organizations. The biggest motivating factor in rousing thousands of women is the need of the peasants for land and of the urban poor for jobs. In the great

> struggle for land which we have just conducted, thousands of women participated in action who would never before have thought of coming out in a demonstration, or going to jail. Many have been brought into the movement. We have to bring this lesson home to the middle classes and explain to them what support for this movement means, that it is of no use asking for reforms for women living in the villages unless land and food is assured for them. (Chakravartty 1970)

Organizing women workers and landless women agricultural labourers, the urban and rural segments of the working poor, became the hallmark of what Chakravartty called 'class organizations' for women. These organizations had myriad links to the Communist Party, far greater than to the Congress Party or right-wing political formations. At the time she gave her report in Budapest, Chakravartty had entered electoral politics as a member of the Indian parliament, but her history as a communist woman organizer in MARS gave her words special salience (Sunil Sen 1985: 46). From the earliest years of Indian independence through the 1960s, Chakravartty described the difficulties of forming meaningful alliances across Indian women's groups. This historical legacy of division and isolation continued to mark the political terrain of leftist women's activism in the early 1970s.

In national histories of women's activism in India, the 1960s are often referred to as a time of quiescence, or at least of less vocal resistance to the nation-building project of Congress Party governance that dominated the decade.[11] The Congress Party passed the Defence of India Act in 1962 to curb anti-government dissent during the Indo-China war. This same Act awarded Pappa and Janaki the jail time that inspired them to further formalize their mobilization of women into political activism. The government passed the Unlawful Activities Prevention Act in 1968 and encoded many of the earlier provisions of the 1962 Act into law. As in the case of Pappa and Janaki's imprisonment, these governmental crackdowns could not wholly quell urban and rural peoples' unrest over the severe food shortages in the mid-1960s, or workers' agitations, nor could they expunge the unmet promises for fairer land ownership policies for small farmers and landless agricultural families.

Pappa was jailed several times over the course of her activism in the early 1960s and then again in the early 1970s, while her two daughters were young. One story told by her daughter U. Vasuki locates the origins of the Tamil Nadu Democratic Women's Association to a jail sentence Pappa served in 1962 during the Indo-China war. Pappa and Janakiammal, alongside communist men, were jailed for their opposition to the border war and

[11] Liddle and Joshi (1986: 75–76) denote fully thirty years of women's dormancy, 1947 to 1977, though they contend that the ideas of women's emancipation from patriarchy survived.

for their unyielding promotion of talks between the two nations to resolve the conflict. Vasuki recounted the story Pappa had told her about being one of two women political prisoners. The jailers taunted them, asking why there weren't more women in jail for political causes. The sub-text of their ridicule pointed at their unfeminine, even indecent behaviour that equated their all-too public activism with the other non-political women prisoners who served time for petty theft, sex work or other crimes against respectable womanhood.[12] Dismissing their jailers' sarcasm, Pappa Umanath and Janakiammal asked themselves the same question: 'Why only two women? We can open the doors to a lot of women' (U. Vasuki interview, 14 March 2006). As soon as they were released a year later, in 1963, they began to organize women across the state into their own political organization, one without explicit ties to the union, as were women's committees like the Ponmalai Women's Association. From the 1940s, women's committees had developed in communist trade unions and agricultural unions, and reported strong representation of women at national conferences to take up issues of equal wages, child care and maternity leave.[13] Organizing working-class, agricultural and middle-class women would require a broader lens and a more open range of campaigns, from the cost of food to the sexual violence faced by women.

Tamil Nadu Democratic Women's Association, 1974–1981

During the early 1970s, Pappa Umanath, Janakiammal and many others developed a loose network of women's groups around peasant women's issues in the rural areas, as well as women's labour and consumption issues in urban locations, through a common Marxist analysis of gender oppression and exploitation. Pappa's story of the formation of the Tamil Nadu Democratic Women's Association (DWA) centres on the town of her birth, Ponmalai, and the city she moved to in her adulthood, Chennai, formerly known as Madras. Yet the Tamil Nadu DWA had equally strong connections to rural struggles among landless women who worked other peoples' land as daily waged workers or as tenant farmers. Landless people's issues were shot through with caste oppression, gender oppression and class exploitation,

[12] For a wrenching account of the dangers of women's public participation in political causes, see Mythily Sivaraman's description of her grandmother's diaries and letters as she struggled with her support for the nationalist cause, and her family's disapproval of breaking any norms of feminine and upper-caste behaviour – Sivaraman 2006. See also Kamala Visweswaran's early contextualization of these same diaries – Visweswaran 1994: 142–65.

[13] 'Among Kisan (Peasant) Women', 1945: 2. The report of the All India Kisan Sabha (AIKS) in Netrakona, Bengal stated that of a total 700 delegates, one in ten were women. It also noted that during the 3rd All India Session of Scheduled (Dalit) Castes in May 1945, the AIKS also held their conference for Scheduled Caste women.

since landless agricultural workers often came from Scheduled and Dalit castes. Upper-caste, large landholders successfully dominated a rural locality's political terrain; therefore, rural women's struggles demanded much more comprehensive support than allies within these disparate rural localities could provide on their own. In rural areas, unlike in towns and cities, the Tamil Nadu DWA was particularly important as a state-wide organization for its breadth of resources and allies that strengthened local campaigns in vital ways.

Mythily Sivaraman, who organized women into trade unions in the textile industry in north Chennai in the 1960s and 70s, articulated the political link between these coalitions of women in an essay published in 1975:

> The lack of economic independence of women in our society is reflected in their much publicized docility, timidity and compliance. The negative base of so much of the chastity, virtue, and the proverbial toleration of the Hindu wife – financial dependence on the man – is bound to be brutally exposed with the mass entry of women into productive work. Although the starvation wages given to women workers today help shore up many a marriage, it does not detract from the general validity of the claim that economic independence will trigger off the woman's rebellion in the family. (Sivaraman 1975: 90)

Economic independence or waged work for women formed the critical first step for women's politicization not just as workers, but as daughters-in-law, as wives and as mothers. The chains of familial oppression, as Sivaraman argued, cannot be challenged without women's integration into that peculiarly capitalist freedom: the freedom to sell one's labour power. The women's groups around the country that eventually joined together in 1981 to become the national women's organization of the All India Democratic Women's Association (AIDWA) based their activism, in all its diversity, on a common understanding. But their campaigns were not always union-based or centred on equal pay demands. The banyan tree of AIDWA in 1981 and after took up women's oppression in the family through anti-dowry campaigns, and in the community through campaigns against sexual violence and coercion. But regional campaigns led by leftist women's organizations like the DWA of Tamil Nadu emerged in the 1950s, 60s and 70s before the rush of feminist autonomous women's activism. These regional and local Marxist women's groups took up women's violence issues as well as women's specific work-based issues. In an effort to combine the strength of local groups into a state-wide force, communists like Pappa sought to formalize the ideological connection between these rural and urban 'class organizations' of women with an organizational linkage.

In December of 1973, just one year before Prime Minister Indira Gandhi declared a National Emergency and suspended civil liberties, Janakiammal,

The cover of a Tamil Nadu Democratic Women's Association pamphlet from the late 1970s: *Women in Two Worlds*, by Mythily Sivaraman. The slogan on the banner reads: 'Women's Liberation, Equality, Socialism'.

with Pappa Umanath, founded the Tamil Nadu Democratic Women's Association (DWA). Members of DWA had time for just one convention, held in Tiruvarur in December 1974, before the Emergency rendered all political activism in the country illegal. The DWA, often simply called *Maathar Sangam* (Women's Association) in Tamil, brought together leftist women's groups across the state of Tamil Nadu with the slogan, 'Women's Liberation, Equality, Socialism' (Mythily Sivaraman interview, 16 February 2006). 'Equality' maintains the right of women to hold basic capitalist rights to waged work and citizenship rights to legal justice. 'Women's Liberation' portends aspiration toward lives for women that are richer than simple waged or civic equality, lives only possible in a systemic commitment to their final demand, 'Socialism'. This slogan reflects a more self-consciously leftist organization than does the later, more ideologically inclusive all-India slogan of AIDWA: 'Democracy, Equality, Emancipation of Women'.

Pappa described the debates that swirled around the creation of a national women's organization in the late 1970s, but focused mainly on their outcome:

> Among women activists there were two opinions on how to proceed. Should we invite everyone to join? Or develop aims, policies, goals, etc.? District leaders of the CPI(M) helped to shape our ideas and shape our plans. We asked whether we should link the women's organization directly to the Party or to stand as a women's organization. We decided to run it democratically and as a mass organization. We are not an adjunct to the CPI(M); we are a mass organization of, by and for women . . . that anyone can join. (Pappa Umanath interview, 26 March 2006)

When the Communist Party of India split in 1964 into two main political parties – the CPI and the CPI(M), Pappa joined the latter formation. For six years, the National of Indian Women (NFIW) attempted to unite organizers who were members of both Communist Parties. In states where the organization was strong, such as West Bengal, the effort lasted for all of those six years. In 1970, CPM members from West Bengal started a separate state organization of women called the Paschim Banga Ganatantrik Mahila Samiti that was not affiliated with the NFIW. The loss of their national did not significantly change the work pursued by communist women activists like Pappa who joined the CPM. As in 1948 after communist women in Bengal were expelled from the AIWC, their regional and local organizing continued unabated.

Throughout the 1970s, women and men in the CPM continued to debate how, when and whether to form a national women's organization. A central concern, as Pappa intimated, was whether to become a Party-based women's organization that strictly followed the direction and leadership of the Party, as a 'women's wing'. Another approach favoured an organization for 'the mass of toiling women', that only represented working-class, agricultural, and working-poor women. The first two positions, outlined in CPM documents on the role of mass organizations, feared the liberalizing or reformist aspects of a cross-class women's organization that decided how to frame its campaigns and issues within a large membership. By 1979, AIDWA gained support from the CPM's Central Committee for a mass organization open to all women who wanted to join, regardless of their political affiliations or class background. AIDWA also strengthened the case for all mass organizations linked to the Party to define their issues and campaigns through their members, not by Party direction. One month after AIDWA's first national convention, the CPM published a pamphlet on the debate within the Party about mass organizations, specifically detailing the conflict over AIDWA (CPI[M] 1981). One position criticized in the pamphlet is making AIDWA an organization only for 'the toiling masses of women of all sections' and exclude elite women from it. A related position against a mass women's organization was lambasted in the pamphlet due to its short-sighted fear of feminism. 'Some of these comrades are afraid of a feminist deviation in this connection. Perhaps they identify feminism with fight against feudal customs and the feudal status of women. They forget that the toiling sections of women are the worst sufferers of feudal traditions' (ibid.: 7). The pamphlet issued a declarative support for a mass organization of all women into a CPM-aligned, but not communist-affiliated, organization. The CPM Polit Bureau's position was quoted extensively in the pamphlet. They advocated the importance of Party-based members' role to build hegemony among the larger group of members within mass organizations. They opposed 'the mass organization turned into the appendage of the Party' (ibid.: 6). All women should be welcomed to join and participate since, the Central Committee argued in the pamphlet, all issues that affect women's lives, from violence to high prices, communalism and caste oppression, have class-inflected consequences.

When I asked how AIDWA makes decisions and whether the CPM gives direction to its campaigns, Pappa answered me frankly. 'The Party will give suggestions. Sometimes we overtake the Party in some issues. New sections come into the Party and not all of them are conscious or sensitive to women's issues. We have to accept them and guide them towards progress' (Pappa Umanath interview, 26 March 2006). She inferred, but did not state, that AIDWA does not always follow the Party's suggestions. Her choice of the word 'overtake' suggests a pride in AIDWA's militancy, its willingness to confront the sexism in its allied political party, the CPM. She also centered AIDWA's political development separately from the CPM as a political location to hone AIDWA's own analysis to fight against the exploitation and oppression of women. Pappa's daughter Vasuki added a deeper understanding to Pappa's pride in AIDWA's independent role in relation to the Party. Pappa Umanath was a member both of a political organization, a Communist Party, and of a mass organization, AIDWA. Her daughter, Vasuki, described how Pappa creatively combined her dual political role to build and strengthen AIDWA: 'Even for political work, if she's called to address any public meeting [by a CPM member], her only condition is: "you organize a women's meeting [as well], only then I will come." So she had to wage a great struggle even given the organization, the political organization [the CPM], to start a women's unit' (U. Vasuki interview, 14 March 2006).

Pappa's political will on the state level matched that of other women leaders in the Party at the national level. Kanak Mukherjee was one of AIDWA's conceptual progenitors. She met with other prominent communist women organizers first in 1978 in Trivandrum, Kerala, then in Delhi in 1979, to discuss how to draw together diverse state-based women's groups. As Mukherjee described the process, 'Vimal Ranadive, Susheela Gopalan, Ahilya Rangnekar and myself were the first to meet to chalk out the plans for a new organization' (cited in Parvathi Menon 2004: 38). All of the women had participated in the anti-imperialist independence movement, and all of the women were CPM members. In the 1970s, Vimal Ranadive was the secretary of the All India Plantation Workers'. Susheela Gopalan organized women into the coir workers' union and built Kerala's left women's organization. Ahilya Rangnekar organized the broad-based coalition against high prices in Maharashtra called the Anti-Price Rise Movement as a leader from the Parel Mahila Sangh, which later became the Shramik Mahila Sangh or Working Women's Group (Gandhi 1996: 23–24; Parvathi Menon 2004: 19). Together, they helped to shape the early political and ideological vision to guide an all-India leftist women's organization, one poised to confront the abuse of power and the neglect of women by the Congress government on a national level.

'AIDWA! Our Long Term Wish Will be Fulfilled!' – trumpeted a slogan in the Tamil Nadu DWA's third state convention report in January of 1981. Pappa Umanath was the general secretary of DWA and Janakiammal its president. After seven years as a state-wide organization, the Tamil Nadu DWA's state convention heralded the upcoming convention inaugurating AIDWA, which they would host in Chennai at Hotel Dharmaprakash two months later, in March of 1981. While the national organization was the culmination of tireless effort across the county, as could be expected, state-based business dominated the proceedings reported, with descriptions of Tamil Nadu DWA's activism since their 1978 convention in Madurai. As regional political campaigns dominated the opening conference, examples of national campaigns preceded the coalescence of these women's groups into the national organization of AIDWA. For example, women's groups from Andhra Pradesh, Tripura, Kerala, Tamil Nadu and West Bengal joined together to demand the arrest of Indira Gandhi for illegal offences she perpetrated as Prime Minister during the Emergency. The founding conference report also described state-wide anti-rape agitations carried out in tandem with nation-wide mobilizations against rape.

The pamphlet detailed participation in a national mobilization around the infamous Mathura custodial rape case (discussed in greater detail in Chapter Two) to change India's rape laws. It also described another, less well-known case known as the Nellai Sanganagakulam case in Tamil Nadu, where the Tamil Nadu DWA led a state-wide protest to demand a judicial enquiry into the mass rape case of seventeen Dalit women. It organized concurrent rallies held in Trichy, Salem, North Arcot, Madurai and Chennai to protest the rape of Dalit women by men hired by a large landowner in the rural locality of Nellai Sanganagakulam. The protestors were described in the report as mainly agricultural women from oppressed castes who staunchly refused to be satisfied with the proffered lower-level enquiry and finally won a High Court enquiry (Parvathi Menon 2004: 2, 14–17). At the time of the conference, the Tamil Nadu DWA sought a safer trial location and guaranteed protection for any witness's testimony. These campaigns show how a national organization gave important visibility to old and strong ties of leftist women's activism between states and regions. The breadth of their ongoing politics gave a terse character to the pamphlet's description of AIDWA's mandate: 'This organization organizes all the suppressed and oppressed women from all classes' (Tamil Nadu Democratic Women's Association 1981: 2). Daily implementation of that mandate in rural and urban struggles across the country was in full swing well before the opening ceremonies.

Pappa described the functioning of AIDWA as a mass organization through the difficulty of women's access to protest. In her view, AIDWA is a mass organization by necessity, since even the most minor public acts by women challenge feudal norms. She described AIDWA's organizational process whereby the first step demanded a basic shift in women's consciousness so they could break normative roles delimiting what was acceptable behaviour for women. To gain the courage to join a struggle for a particular issue, women first needed to challenge gendered social norms. Once women breached those ideological boundaries, in Pappa's terms, they began to actively build AIDWA. As she argued, any preconception about who is politically advanced enough to join would deaden the organization as a whole.

> When we began, women leaving their homes was an act thought of as a crime. But when AIDWA grew, women came forward to take up issues they had earlier shunned. They gave more ideas for struggles. We go among women as a united organization without only saying 'Marxism', since we are a mass organization.

This is how we continue to strengthen AIDWA. (Pappa Umanath interview, 26 March 2006)

AIDWA members do not often talk about Marxism in their organizing campaigns, in part because of the reformist quality of many of their local and regional fights for affordable food, safe education and protection from violence. The organization's analysis, however, draws deeply and often quite explicitly on Marxist and materialist analyses of women's gendered oppression and exploitation. Many AIDWA offices I visited in Tamil Nadu would hang photographs of state and local leaders like Janakiammal, alongside framed portraits of Engels and Lenin. Women who join AIDWA often do so because of a specific campaign or service the organization provides, rather than due to their guiding ideology of Marxism and class struggle. Membership in AIDWA, however, does demand an allegiance to the principles in their constitution that share a commitment to the Marxist emphasis on women's work and class-based conditions of survival, as well as class-based visions of women's emancipation. The women who join AIDWA are not expected, even tacitly, to join the CPM or to vote for the CPM's electoral candidates, though AIDWA members do organize in solidarity with other Party mass organizations and often join Party electoral work. Unlike membership in the CPM, women can join AIDWA without a lengthy initiation. Its open membership policy, the freedom of political association by its membership and its affordability define AIDWA, in its own terms, as a mass-based organization.

Pappa Umanath and AIDWA

Pappa Umanath passed away in 2010, with her activism continuing unabated until the end. She was buried in the Golden Rock railway colony in Ponmalai alongside the six workers she had witnessed being killed in the union struggle that she joined as a fourteen-year-old. Pappa was seventy-seven years old when I interviewed her in 2006. When she spoke, she sat upright in a chair with one leg raised on a stool. She had not been well enough to meet with me for several months while I conducted my research in Tamil Nadu. A month before I arrived in Chennai, she broke several ribs when she fell from the podium while speaking at AIDWA's silver jubilee celebration in New Delhi. She finished her speech, she told me with an open smile, but the healing process after the fall took longer than she expected. During the months in Chennai before I met with Pappa, I travelled around the sprawling city to speak with a range of AIDWA members, as well as its unit and district leaders. I attended meetings and training sessions inside the city and beyond. I interviewed members from allied organizations to find out more about the politics of specific localities and the politics in the state as a whole. When we finally met at the end of my research period, my micro-research of AIDWA's campaigns and members in specific areas and towns had gained that wider sweep of vision and hope. Pappa Umanath spoke with confidence about where AIDWA had come during those twenty-five years celebrated at its silver jubilee: from a membership of 1 million plus to almost 10 million, a number she vowed to reach by the following year. Yet her future inspiration was not one of simple numbers, but the character of women's consciousness that had changed. 'Earlier when police came to a neighbourhood, the women ran into their homes', she said at the end of our interview. 'Now that is not true. Women openly confront the police' (Pappa Umanath interview, 26 March 2006). I remain indebted to her for her image of the banyan tree, since it provided a door to understand another forgotten quality of AIDWA: its ability to transform itself in the face of changing opposition and new conditions of struggle. An organization's past is not its future. Yet one quality of AIDWA's past that I explore in the following chapters survives in the banyan tree's mutable resilience.

TWO

Catalysts

The effervescence of post-independence women's activism in India is usually told as a story with two catalysts.[1] The first catalyst was the Mathura case. When Indira Gandhi declared Emergency from 1975 to 1977, she clamped down on basic civil liberties of association and freedom to dissent. Women's organized resistance to state repression exploded within a year after the Emergency ended in 1977. Early in 1978, women in cities around the country protested the Supreme Court's decision on the Mathura custodial rape case first filed in Maharashtra in 1972. Many historians explain this surprising confluence of anger and public outcry for Mathura, an adolescent from a disenfranchised Adivasi or Scheduled Tribe (ST) community, through the suppressed outrage at the abrupt suspension of civil rights during the Emergency (Gandhi and Shah 1992). The other catalyst was a document, *Towards Equality*, that assessed the status of women in India at the request of the United Nations (Khullar 1997). Completed before the Emergency in January 1975, most of the report was not made widely available until after the Emergency ended.[2]

These two catalysts are also important to the formation of AIDWA in the decade before its opening convention in 1981. Many activists like Pappa and Janakiammal, who founded the Tamil Nadu DWA immediately before the Emergency, had to organize underground during this period, and they spent considerable time documenting a range of police abuses in preparation

[1] Maitreyi Chatterjee's regional history of feminism in West Bengal during the 1980s and 1990s that uses these two catalysts to better measure the regional specificities of women's organizing provides one striking example of these two events to even regional histories of the women's movement. Maitreyi Chatterjee 2000.

[2] The report was published in 1975 by two government bodies with slightly different titles. The Ministry of Education and Social Welfare published it as *Towards Equality: Report of the Committee on the Status of Women in India*; and the Indian Council of Social Science Research (ICSSR) published it as *Status of Women in India: A Synopsis Report of the National Committee (1971–1974).*

for when they could file charges against the perpetrators.[3] Police abuse of women and men detainees, as well as police atrocities against those known to be leftist activists – whether Naxalites in West Bengal or communists in Kerala – were an integral part of the political landscape during this period, but under the edicts of the Emergency, justice was on hold. The findings of *Towards Equality* in 1975 probably did not shock the rural and urban activists, like the women in Thanjavur district who fought against casteism in agricultural work, or the women in Maharashtra who organized against increasing retrenchment of women in the textile industry, or women across the country who contested women's paltry rights to own land. It did provide powerful ammunition to substantiate their demands for better distribution of state resources for women and to shift the terms of 'development' towards gender equality. Published by the government, *Towards Equality* was sharply critical of women's exploitation as agricultural workers and equally direct about the remedies.

> The basic solution for the exploitation of agricultural workers lies in redistribution of land, but legislation for this purpose has been grossly ineffective so far. What is worse, some of the land ceiling laws discriminate against women . . . while a major son is entitled to a unit of land outside the family ceiling, no such provision is made for a major daughter, married or unmarried. (*Status of Women in India* 1975: 67)

To focus on these two catalysts alone, however, obscures the centrality of rural women, landless women and urban poor women as the harbingers of the post-independence women's movement in India, and as the core of AIDWA's national membership when it founded in 1981. Campaigns against police repression, specifically sexualized violence against women activists, constantly dogged communist and union-based women after independence. In the case of AIDWA, these catalysts made manifest (rather than instigated) long-standing analyses developed from the activism of state-based leftist women's groups that cohered as a national organization into AIDWA. It grew from a class analysis of women's conditions, an analysis that began with the measure of work, waged and unwaged. Violence against women, by the state and within family relationships, charged this gendered class analysis from AIDWA's earliest beginnings.

After the Emergency ended women's groups and networks continued to press for women's freedom from violence and rights to dignity in the tradition of social reformism, but with an important difference. Vibhuti Patel, an economist who was also active in the non-aligned socialist women's

[3] See also the accounts of feminist women's political activities during the Emergency that focused on the conditions in prisons faced by jailed women activists. Gothoskar, Patel, Patel and Wolkowitz 1982: 101

movement upsurge in the 1970s, refers to the groups involved as 'women's liberation', using a term popular in the United States, Vietnam and Britain, among other countries. Many within these non-aligned socialist feminist groups refer to them as the 'autonomous women's movement' since they eschewed ties to political parties, religious institutions, government agencies and, during this period, any outside funding sources.[4] Patel defines the difference between the two activist periods before and after independence simply: 'Never before had women mobilized around demands related specifically to their gender. In the nineteenth century the reform movement against female infanticide and *sati* (self-immolation of widows), for widow remarriage and the education of women, was initiated and pursued by liberal men' (Vibhuti Patel 1985: 76). Whereas before independence women had been the objects of social reform, Patel argues, in the 1970s women became the subjects of social change. Patel overstates the case for the early and mid-twentieth century, as Pappa Umanath's story illustrates, since many working-class women defied these same social norms to take leadership on a range of issues for their own benefit. Patel accurately pinpoints women's oppression and gendered exploitation as critical nodes for the post-independence women's movement, both for middle-class women who formed the vast majority of the non-aligned autonomous women's movement, and for the working-class, agricultural and working-poor women's movement that fomented the creation of 'class organizations' like the Tamil Nadu DWA.

Organization against women's violent oppression and exploitation in the 1970s, even in the autonomous women's movement, cannot be attributed solely to women's new political consciousness, whether spurred by the excesses of Emergency or the shock of the report on the status of women. Women in the 1970s faced worsening life conditions due to job loss from mechanization in cotton and other industries, and due to land consolidation in many parts of the country. Government programmes to alleviate hunger and ill-health did not begin to tackle the sources of impoverishment, nor did they stem the serious food shortages that devastated West Bengal in the mid-1960s, Maharashtra in the early 1970s and many other parts of the country. Meera Velayudhan adds an important insight to other pressures that precipitated women's immense political agency during this period. Overall, women's work participation rates between 1961 and 1971 declined. Women endured the most precipitous job loss in the industries of jute, textiles and mining.

[4] A range of guidelines to determine a group's 'autonomy' circulated during this period. In West Bengal in the early 1980s, women's groups had to be autonomous from political parties, religious organizations and foreign-funded groups to join a coalitional women's forum. See Maitreyi Chatterjee 2000: 326–27. In Mumbai, activist and women's studies scholar Chhaya Datar describes a more nebulous and therefore wide-ranging definition: 'autonomy of space and organizational form' – Datar, ed. 1995: 4.

But in the states where women's agricultural labour participation rates grew (even as their rates as agricultural cultivators dropped), like Kerala, Andhra Pradesh, Tamil Nadu and Maharashtra, women's militancy in agricultural struggles also rose. That is, as women shifted into working for daily or seasonal wages rather than working on family lands as cultivators, they turned to political agitation to ensure their own and their families' survival.[5] One explanation invokes an intrinsic radicalism to women's conditions: 'Women are the most ready to fight, the first to break through police lines, the last to go home' (Omvedt 1980: 2). Meera Velayudhan offers a less spontaneous explanation for why the 1970s generated such a fierce and widespread surge in women's activism than simply women's newfound consciousness about their oppression. 'The struggles [by women] in the seventies could, therefore, be placed in the context of this *generalized decline* in women's living conditions and social status' (Velayudhan 1985: 58). Women's strengthening political resistance to the violence borne by them during the 1970s is intimately tied to the worsening conditions of their economic survival during the same period.

Towards Equality and the Committee on the Status of Women in India

Towards Equality contained in its title a direct allusion and implicit challenge to the title of the autobiography of India's first prime minister, Jawaharlal Nehru's *Toward Freedom.* While Nehru's title refers to the goal of freedom reached during his lifetime with India's independence, India's success in moving *towards* women's equality, the report's title suggests, is still a work in progress. The Mathura case against custodial rape and *Towards Equality* signify the activism and *the ideology* of two distinct branches of the post-independence women's movement. The political mobilization around the Mathura legal case is usually told as the birth of the autonomous women's movement in India, while the agitation energized by *Towards Equality* often alludes to activism by mainly left-wing, progressive and liberal women's organizations, like AIDWA, that hailed from pre-independence movements (Tharu and Lalita, eds. 1994: 101). Ideologically, Mathura signifies the radical feminism of the autonomous women's movement that saw patriarchy as women's main systemic oppression (Kumar 1993: 109–10). *Towards Equality* ideologically signifies a state-centred analysis of women's exploitation and oppression, as one that sought equal and redistributive rights for women. This bifurcation within the Indian women's movement

[5] Sunil Sen lists the absolute change in numbers of women agricultural labourers rising from 14 million to 20 million in this decade – Sunil Sen 1985: 17.

does not do justice to either of the two catalysts; both rippled outward to inspire a range of ideological understandings of women's conditions. The Emergency and the alarming statistics of women's declining health, life span, education and employment verified by *Towards Equality* gave fuel to campaigns, groups and coalitions in diverse and unpredictable ways.

'We didn't foresee how critical the report would be', remembers Vina Mazumdar, member-secretary of the Committee on the Status of Women in India (CSWI) that researched and wrote *Towards Equality* (Vina Mazumdar interview 2003). In 1972, Vina Mazumdar was teaching political science in Berhampur University, Orissa, when she got an invitation to join the year-old, government-appointed committee, which was labouring to compile existing data on Indian women's lives and struggling to define 'status' for Indian women. At the time that Mazumdar joined the committee, they had completed only one report, 'Women and Law', authored by the feminist Delhi University law professor, Lotika Sarkar. Besides overwhelming stasis in its productivity, the CSWI suffered from other difficulties in its first years, from paying committee members to maintaining a consistent working group of researchers (ibid.). Time was short, and when Mazumdar joined the committee she began the process of defining her research methodology, creating a questionnaire that she sent to women's organizations around the country and conducting tours of states in India. Two of the tours, she remembers, were disasters due to her lack of a methodology. However, the questionnaire yielded results: women's organizations returned 8,000 of them in eight languages, providing valuable substantiation of the committee's hypothesis from their analysis of existing data – that women's conditions had suffered in the years since independence (ibid.). 'Development' as a national discourse of improvement had negative consequences for most Indian women.

Yet, Mazumdar recalls, they still lacked a framework. While touring Himachal Pradesh, she and Urmila Haksar noted that representatives of the state government could not answer their questions about women's status in the state. 'Who runs the Himachal Pradesh economy?' Mazumdar remembers asking Haksar. The answer was simple: men in the plains of a predominantly mountainous region. When Mazumdar began the fifty studies done in one year, she instructed the researchers simply: 'You will talk to *women* in our research' (ibid.). Her edict led to 500 interviews with women from a great range of backgrounds and circumstances that the researchers for the committee conducted across the country. The United Nations required these reports from all member nations in preparation for International Women's Year in 1975, which culminated in the Conference on the Status of Women held in Mexico City. Importantly, however, the reports were not researched, analysed or written by UN representatives, as Mazumdar's experience substantiates (Palriwala and Agnihotri 1996). The prestige of CSWI's findings gained traction because they built their metrics of women's status through their original fieldwork in India. Similarly, Mazumdar describes how they developed their framework from women's rights in the Indian Constitution alongside analysis of women's conditions gleaned from their interviews. In their report, they broke the unitary category 'women' into three sub-groups: '(1) women below the subsistence line; (2) women who move continuously between security and subsistence and often descend below the subsistence line with the disappearance of their means of earning a livelihood; and (3) women firmly above the security (subsistence) line' (*Status of Women in India*, 1975: 4). The committee's framework to assess women's status in India emerged from their assessment of the lives of women they interviewed in light of two measures grounded in the Indian national project for women's equality: one *de jure* and the other *de facto*. First, they considered the conditions of women's lives in relation to the encoded constitutional provisions for women's equality. Second, they assessed how women benefited from existing governmental policies, laws, programmes and infrastructure, those 'measures which would enable women to play their full and proper role' (ibid.: 1). Given their attention to the specificity of India's legal and constitutional commitment to women, their findings were even more devastating.

Towards Equality documented the severe inequities women and girl children continued to face even two decades after India's national independence from British rule. Women and girl children had civil and economic rights on paper, but they were still measurably hungrier, lived shorter lives, faced more violence and enjoyed fewer rights than men and boy children. Many historians of the India's post-independence women's movement do not emphasize the effects of the UN conference itself, though some credit the conference in Mexico City for the nascent formation of a network of non-governmental organizations. *Towards Equality* was a powerful document on its own terms, since it provided unassailable, government-sponsored evidence of the discrimination and overt misogyny faced by women of every class and caste, in every state of the nation. Its governmental purview was also the report's weakness, Mazumdar noted, since even sympathetic ministers expressed concern that it would be buried (Vina Mazumdar interview, 10 January 2002). As Vina Mazumdar crisply noted in a later essay:

> The CSWI had certainly been appointed by the Government of India, but neither its mode of investigation, nor the report had any influence on the government. Nor did it lead to any serious State action until the 1980s – when it took place under pressure, from a coalition of national women's organizations – the 'Rights Wing'. (Mazumdar 2000: 7)

AIDWA was an integral part of these organizations that used *Towards Equality* to demand structural changes for women.

The Mathura Case

The edicts of the Emergency could only dam but not contain the widespread anger over the disturbing trends across India, such as the decline in the sex ratio, the death of women in their in-laws' homes and startlingly high rates of illiteracy among girls and women. By 1978, women and men regained the rights to protest injustice, rights they claimed with enthusiasm (Agnihotri and Mazumdar 1995: 1870). Many histories cite the Mathura case (*Tukaram v. State of Maharashtra,* 1979 SCC[Cr] 381) as *the* case that galvanized the widespread organization of newly political women into groups, coalitions and, ultimately, a coherent post-independence women's movement.[6] Mathura was a minor, fourteen years old, from an Adivasi community in rural Maharashtra. One afternoon she was picked up by the police for questioning, taken to the station, held overnight and raped by two police officers. Mathura, with the support of her family and her community, lodged a case against the police officers in 1972. The Sessions judge ruled in favour of the police officers. The Nagpur branch of the Bombay High Court overturned the ruling and charged the men with rape and sentenced them to jail (Forbes 1996: 244–45). The case hinged on whether Mathura had consented to sexual relations, not to whether sex had occurred. Seven years later, in 1979, the Supreme Court reached its verdict on the case. Again, the previous ruling was overturned; and again, the police officers were deemed innocent of forcible rape. The Supreme Court reversed the guilty verdict on the grounds argued by the defence: that the sex was consensual, not coerced. It ruled that Mathura's physical injuries did not sufficiently prove she was raped. The judgment described the alleged intercourse as 'a peaceful affair' (quoted in Gothoskar, Patel, Patel and Wolkowitz 1982: 94). The Court also supported the defence's position that the young woman could not be raped since she already had a boyfriend and thus was a loose woman (Mathur 2004: 60). The text of the Supreme Court verdict went further in the basis for its opinion: 'Since Mathura is a tribal girl, there is no question of her being violated' (*Tukaram v. State of Maharashtra*, 1979, SCC [Cr] 381).

Lotika Sarkar, a former member of the CSWI, and three other prominent lawyers publicly protested the decision and demanded a review in an open letter to the Chief Justice (Baxi *et al.*, 'Open Letter to the Chief Justice of India', 1979, 4 SCC [J] 17). From local injustice to national spotlight, Mathura's legal case was transformed into a rallying cry of women across the country. In February of 1980, the lawyers' letter galvanized the Forum Against Rape, a

[6] See Shah and Gandhi 1992. The authors' unabashed overview of the autonomous women's groups in the post-independence women's movement as *the* contemporary women's movement begins its history with the Mathura case and does not mention the publication of *Towards Equality* (ibid.: 36–37).

women's group in Bombay, to act. They demanded that the case be reopened. Women's groups affiliated to left parties as well as unaffiliated women's groups joined forces across the country in support of this demand, convening two large public meetings and signing petitions to change the rape law (Gothoskar, Patel, Patel and Wolkowitz 1982: 95). On International Women's Day, 8 March, 1980, women's groups marched and rallied to demand a retrial in cities and towns such as Mumbai, Delhi, Nagpur, Pune, Ahmedabad, Bangalore and Hyderabad (Kumar 1993: 129–30). 'In effect, this was the first time that feminist groups came together across the country to coordinate a campaign' (ibid.: 129). In this assessment, Radha Kumar points to the national character of the organizing around Mathura's case, a scale of mobilization that led to changes in the nation's rape law in 1983.[7]

The Mathura case in 1979 certainly spurred a more national integration among autonomous women's groups around the country, and even built ties among long-standing leftist women's groups, but the agitation was not the first of its kind in the 70s. One overview of the Indian women's movement written in the early 1980s cites the Mathura case as exceptional: 'Despite the fact that in the past no organization or political party had taken up the issue of rape, this issue has built up enormous protest' (Gothoskar, Patel, Patel and Wolkowitz 1982: 94). The record of post-independence women's organizing still lacks a careful account of regionally based cases against sexual violence by agents of state authority that precede and even guide the national organizing around the Mathura case. Custodial rape of detainees by police officers is central to understanding the post-independence women's movement in India. Custodial rape was an early locus for drawing middle-class and elite women into the burgeoning upheaval of women's political engagement. Attention to pre-Emergency organizing by women shows that campaigns against custodial rape stem from early agricultural women's militant struggles, women industrial workers' fights against retrenchment and poor women's movements for affordable food from the early decades of independence onwards. Custodial rape cases were not simply an autonomous women's group issue as a contestation of the state and, by extension, the patriarchal family, but were class issues for socialist women's groups.

A case of custodial rape fought in 1976 in Kerala, over three years before the nation-wide coordination of women around the Mathura case, was intimately linked to the widespread political activism of working women in that state. The Kerala Mahila Sangham (KMS), one of the groups that folded into AIDWA in 1981, fought for justice in this case. Many of the state-based women's groups that founded the national organization had a strong commu-

[7] Radha Kumar, from her perspective as a feminist agitator based in New Delhi who was active in the campaign, gives a detailed recounting of the debates, campaigns and actors leading up to the 1983 change in rape law. See Kumar 1993: 133–36.

nist membership. Women's groups connected to the CPM developed a measurably different organizational model than the later autonomous women's groups used to fight for women's issues. Groups like the Tamil Nadu DWA built their strongest links to agricultural and working-class women in towns and cities, though they also actively encouraged middle-class women to join. Importantly, these women's groups also drew upon an array of organizational support by other communist mass formations, such as agricultural workers' unions and peasant movements, communist unions and the Communist Party itself. They sought, to different degrees, to maintain their separate identity from other communist mass formations and from the Party, mainly through the issues they raised, the campaigns they fought and their open membership to all women. Leftist and working-class women activists did not give up on building alliances with middle-class and elite women's organizations. Neither could they rely on their solidarity.

Kerala Custodial Rape Case, 1976

The coir industry, one of Kerala's two primary industries, witnessed impressive mobilization of women workers for better wages, against the retrenchment of women workers and for on-site child care facilities, beginning in the 1960s – a mobilization that gained particular force in the early 1970s. The Kerala Mahila Sangham (KMS) first formed in 1968 and was very active among women in the coir industry (Mathew and Nair 1986: 139). Susheela Gopalan was an important member of KMS, a communist who also worked as the president of the Coir Workers' Centre in 1971 (Parvathi Menon 2004: 126). Gopalan grew up in the midst of militant union activities in the Alappuzha district since she, along with her mother and sister, lived with her uncle who was a union leader in the coir industry during the 1940s. Through the Coir Workers' Centre, Gopalan launched campaigns to gain better wages for women. Women in the Coir Workers' Centre fought alongside women in the CPM-affiliated CITU (Centre of Indian Trade Unions); and both groups of women were very active in the general strike of 1971 that stopped coir products from entering the warehouses. As a result of these activities, in 1972, the daily minimum wage for women in the coir industry almost doubled, from Rs 1.75 to Rs 3.30 (ibid.).

The wages rose just as another crisis confronted the workers: mechanization of coir manufacturing. The threat of mechanization was particularly damaging to the entirely women work force who beat the retted coconut husks. These women were most vulnerable to the machines. One study conducted in the late 1970s showed that an experienced worker could defibre between 70 and 75 husks a day (Gulati 1981: 136–63). But the locally developed husk-beating machine, operated by only ten workers, could defibre over 8,000 husks each day. Women's wages for husk-beating were very low, even after their wages were doubled in 1972. In this study set outside of Thiruvananthapuram in Kerala, women's wages were roughly one-fourth to one-fifth of men's wages in the industry. The women huskers made roughly half of what women agricultural workers in the same region made. Yet women in the coir industry could stay employed for 300 days of each year, an improvement over women agricultural workers in the area who worked an average of 160 days per year, even though for a higher daily wage. Husk-beating machines were installed across the state of Kerala from 1965 to 1973, and by the end of this period there were as many as 400 machines in operation (ibid.: 151). Coir workers successfully fought off the machines, and by 1973 the husk defibering machines were officially banned from Thiruvananthapuram, Kollam, Alappuzha, Ernakulam and Thrissur. In their campaign, however, a 51-year-old coir worker named Vazhamuttathil Ammu was killed (Velayudhan 1985: 59). The KMS organized widespread solidarity actions in her honour. In May of 1973, coir workers formed a procession that began at the martyred woman's memorial (Parvathi Menon 2004: 127). Their protest march snaked its way across the coir-producing areas of Kerala as they walked during the day, while by night the workers met and discussed the issues they confronted in their jobs, their communities and their families. By 1974, the localized struggles against these threats to job security coalesced into a state-wide strike of women and men to fight for bonuses not only from the public coir sector, but also in the much more ruthless privately owned coir companies. At the end of the strike, private and public companies promised a yearly bonus of Rs 25 for the coir-spinning division, an occupation that employed two of every three women in the industry (ibid.). In 1974, just months before the Emergency suspended all political agitation, women coir workers, with the support of men also working in the industry, won a significant concession regarding land redistribution policies that survived the central government's crackdown.

Women in the land grab movement in rural Kerala matched the militancy of labour struggles by women in Kerala's coir industry. Rural women active in the land grab movement of 1972 sought to reveal 'surplus' land to the government; that is, land consolidated by one family over and above the legal land ceiling (Mathew and Nair 1986: 139). 'In their raising slogans and in their enthusiasm, the women left the men far behind', described one newspaper account. 'It was as if they had taken over Alleppey [Alappuzha] for the day. It was impossible to estimate how many participated but half of them were women and most of them wore red blouses [signifying communist affiliation]' (quoted in Velayudhan 1985: 58–59). Two hundred thousand people pushed the state to redistribute 175,000 acres of land. Another powerful state-wide strike led by women in 1972 fought against the rise in the costs of basic food commodities. After the Emergency ended, KMS also organized against the growing problem of dowry. Dowry at marriage, or the transfer of cash and commodities from the bride's family to the groom's family, had become an increasingly insistent demand among Christian communities and upper-caste Hindus. Women suffered from a rise in violence and even murder at the hands of their husbands and husbands' families due to dowry expectations and demands. Anti-dowry campaigns, like struggles against sexual violence, became a signature campaign that united all parts of the post-independence women's movement.

Police arrest of protestors, whether coir workers or housewives, exacted an additional penalty of sexual violence while in detention. In 1976, two girls active in political protest were raped by police officers in Kerala while under detention. After their release, they committed suicide. KMS coordinated a protest across the state in front of all the police stations to protest the rape of these two girls. Unlike the Mathura case, women's groups across the nation were not involved in this protest. Rather than spreading its support across the country and nationalizing the pressure through press coverage and other tactics, KMS chose to build its coalitions and its public pressure primarily within the state. Similar to campaigns run by the Tamil Nadu DMK during this period, it linked variegated groups, such as different women's groups, trade unions, agricultural workers' unions and communist parties, across the densely populated state. This coalition, led by KMS, won a significant policy change in police procedure across the state: they forced the police to release any girl or woman they detained before nightfall, whether she was an activist or not. The importance of violence issues for KMS did not supplant struggles in the late 1960s and early 1970s against price rise and retrenchment, or for industry-based day care facilities and equal wages. For groups like the Tamil Nadu DWA and KMS, sexual violence was another tool to terrorize women into accepting the status quo, and the fight against it was integral to their founding principles for women's equality and freedom. For most of the leftist women's organization from around the country that coalesced into AIDWA in the early 1980s, campaigns against sexual and physical violence against women and girls preceded the rise of autonomous socialist feminist groups in India.[8] Their struggles against violence in the 1950s, 1960s and 1970s cannot be lumped into pre-independence workers' campaigns that fought British rule, or a colonial holdover in a post-colonial

[8] Mary Fainsod Katzenstein epitomizes this kind of backhanded dismissal in her article about the Indian women's movement in the 1980s, though she mis-states the actual date of AIDWA's formation. She writes, 'the All-India Democratic Women's Association (AIDWA) formed in the 1970s under pressure from the newer women's movement. The national organization has been less active than particular sub-units such as the Janwadi Mahila Samiti in Delhi whose protest against dowry deaths and whose work in slums is well known.' Katzenstein 1989: 55.

country (Mathew 1981: 27–29). Instead, early campaigns against dowry violence and rape were integral to women's and men's class struggles seeking a more just distribution of the nation's land and wealth. The class analysis of gendered violence that motivated these campaigns also supported the drive that visibly began in the late 1970s to consolidate state-based, leftist women's groups into AIDWA as a national organization.

In 1975, the general secretary of the CPI(M), E.M.S. Namboodiripad, published an article called 'Perspective of the Women's Movement'. This article illustrates the growing recognition within CPM leadership of the importance of organizing women through their own mass organization. Namboodiripad provided critical support for the emerging consensus among women activists in regional groups to create a national mass women's organization allied to the Party (Parvathi Menon 2004: 52). Brinda Karat, the general secretary of AIDWA through much of the 1990s, credits Namboodiripad with the understanding of women's exploitation and oppression that continues to guide AIDWA; an analysis built as much from the politics of his natal state of Kerala as from Lenin's speech for International Women's Day in 1921 (Brinda Karat interview, 28 December 2004). Namboodiripad described women's oppression as three-fold in character: the oppression of women as women, of women as workers and of women as citizens. In his article, he emphasized women's unpaid reproductive labour in the home and raising families; women's unequal wages, work and working conditions; and women's inequality in legal and civic status, as constitutive elements in the struggle to gain women's emancipation. Namboodiripad argued that within left and communist movements, however, women's emancipation is not contained within its mass organization or as one segment of the revolutionary movement, but that the entirety of movement's success rests upon its commitment to fighting for women's equality. These two features of Namboodiripad's analysis recur in AIDWA speeches and documents, as well as CPI(M) resolution documents. First, women's emancipation and liberation must be central to political work in the CPI(M) and all the mass organizations led by communists. Second, 'women' are not a homogenous section of the population and face distinct, though overlapping forms of oppression and exploitation.

Namboodiripad also raised the dangers of feminism to communist-led organizing of women: 'we have to carry on a relentless struggle as much against bourgeois and petty-bourgeois "feminism" as against male chauvinism' (Namboodiripad 1975: 7). The critique of feminism gained momentum in AIDWA's publications during the 1980s about the Indian and international women's movement. Feminism also became a contested category of identification and politics by activists not linked to the organized left, activists like Madhu Kishwar who founded the women's publication called *Manushi* in the late 1970s. In 1990, Kishwar published her widely read piece, 'Why I Do Not

Call Myself a Feminist'. She wrote: 'feminism, as appropriated and defined by the west, has too often become a tool of cultural imperialism' (Kishwar 1990: 3). Kishwar argued that feminist ideology comes predetermined far from the history and conditions of women's activism in India – that feminism 'inhibit(s) and stunt(s)' understanding women's lives in India (ibid.). The heat generated by the debate over 'feminism' had roughly two sides. One side negatively characterized 'feminism' through its class limitations (that is, as 'bourgeois' in Namboodiripad's terms), its reformism and its adherence to imperialist tenets. The other side advanced an equally impassioned defence of feminism as the truly radical means to eradicate patriarchal oppression in the family, civil society and the state. Feminism, as a positive ideology, pushed the Indian left to face up to its own dismissal of the woman question within its political parties, its organizing and its analysis.

Namboodiripad's characterization of feminism was an opening salvo to this polarizing debate:

> The other [bourgeois feminism] however appears on the surface to be more 'radical'; it adopts a 'leftist' and 'revolutionary' garb; it is therefore even more dangerous to the integration of the women's movement for their equality with men, and the common movement of the working people for ending all forms of pre-capitalist exploitation and, along with it, liquidating capitalism. (Namboodiripad 1975: 7)

He contended that feminism will hamper the 'integration' of organized women into the revolutionary movement. His phrasing suggests another worry: that men will not be integrated into the movement for women's equality. What is hidden in his words here becomes much more explicit in future AIDWA publications: that feminist demands will divide the working-class movement by pitting women against men. As one example of a feminist misdirection, he cited the demand for abolition of the family. The elimination of capitalism and pre-capitalism (sometimes called semi-feudalism in AIDWA and CPI[M] pamphlets) demands a 'common movement'.

AIDWA's opposition to feminist conceptions of 'patriarchy', that emerges most visibly in the late 1980s, echoes the logic of this passage. Patriarchy alone, without a systemic critique of capitalism, divides the revolutionary movement of working women and men. A feminist movement that organizes women as a homogenous group, regardless of class, caste status or religious differences, creates an analysis and thus campaigns that jeopardize working-class unity. Namboodiripad's denunciation of bourgeois feminism also reveals a damaging slippage between communists' imperative to build unity between working-class women and men, and their recalcitrance in challenging violence and inequality in the family. The vexed site of the family, particularly as it shaped the debate on patriarchy, continued to shape

AIDWA's early political formation. Even Namboodiripad's example for an ideal campaign carries stabilized assumptions about the family.

> Equal wage for equal work between men and women among the workers and middle-class employees, for instance, not only raises the status of the women in society, but directly adds to the joint income of the whole family. . . . Jobs for women, equality of wages, a general raising of the level of wages and working conditions – these therefore are the common demands. (Ibid.: 6)

For Namboodiripad, the common demand of equal employment and wages for women did not divide the working-class movement by emphasizing the specific inequities faced by women; instead, it produced a goal that benefited all workers. As a gendered class issue, equal wage for equal work contests ongoing protests within the CPM that a national women's organization enervates union-led demands. Namboodiripad also argued that women and men benefit from a 'women's issue'. Yet his logic depends upon the stable family unit, a unit left unchallenged for its internal oppressions around women's wages and their independence.

The growing polarization around terms like 'feminism' and 'patriarchy' was not just about ideology, but referred to other differences in the forms of struggle as well as campaign issues. Where AIDWA preferred mass mobilizations of women around issues, such as the anti-dowry protests in the mid-1980s, autonomous women's groups used targeted delegations over marches. AIDWA sought to include issues like food affordability and world peace into coalition platforms, while many autonomous women's groups saw those issues as dilutions of women's central concerns around violence in the family. The formation of AIDWA as a national organization promised a stronger voice in Indian politics as a whole, empowered by its most powerful regional formations in Kerala, West Bengal and Tamil Nadu, all states with high rates of landlessness and agricultural workers. As an organization that aspired to a multi-class membership, the bulk of its members mirrored the vast majority of women workers in India (over 80 per cent of all working women): rural, landless and surviving from informal agricultural work. The ensuing furore over feminism and patriarchy had its context in AIDWA's ideological precepts, its organizing strategies and issues, its history, *and* its membership. Alongside these disagreements, AIDWA built powerful coalitions with a wide range of autonomous and older women's groups, particularly in the anti-dowry struggles of the 1980s.

All-India Politics in the 1980s

At their inaugural conference held for two days in Chennai, Tamil Nadu in March 1981, AIDWA formally configured a national whole from its cache of small rural and urban women's groups. Most of these groups were already connected within their state or across neighbouring states, and linked to other communist mass organizations as well as to the CPM. Many others relied upon even more local networks of groups within a district or at the smaller administrative level of their *taluk*. As a national organization, AIDWA activists sought to build units in states largely hostile to the organized left and women's political activism, in places like Haryana and Uttar Pradesh in north India. One report lists the initial membership of AIDWA at 1,100,000 women; another describes membership coming from sixteen of twenty-seven states around the country (Tamil Nadu Democratic Women's Association 1981). Members pledged their support for AIDWA's constitution adopted at the conference. The constitution listed aims such as the struggle for women's civic and legal rights, to fight against 'social evils and feudal legacies' of dowry, child marriage and polygamy; and to fight casteism and communalism (*Aims and Objects Programme Constitution of All India Democratic Women's Association*, 1981). Members agreed to seek solidarity through 'united actions with all other women's organizations who stand for the struggle against social injustice, for equal rights and opportunities and for economic independence for women', as well as solidarity with working-class people and peasants, and with international people fighting neo-colonialism and exploitation. Its programme stressed mass struggles and 'continuous propaganda campaign' around dowry, equal rights in divorce and the rights to own land, and for protective legislation for women workers like equal pay for equal work and unemployment relief.

Vina Mazumdar, former member-secretary of the CSWI, opened the conference with a moving inaugural address. She ended with a vision of AIDWA and the role for the wider post-independence women's movement:

> Women's organizations can help to stimulate and activise women's collective consciousness outside their family and their class, because there are experiences, problems and deprivations which they share. Articulation of their varying needs, aspirations and understanding; planning to overcome their fears through interaction, comparison and sharing of knowledge and exerting pressure at different levels of society to change its structures, values and institutions so that it can function without exploitation, within and outside the family, are the goals of the Women's Movement. If it does not succeed, the people's desire for social justice also will not. A non-exploitative, just society cannot be built on the exploitation of women. (Mazumdar 1981)

Mazumdar's vision of building a movement that could lead women to cross class and familial communities, and develop a collective knowledge about women's shared concerns, also inspired the role AIDWA hoped to play. She recognized the profound difficulty of this prophecy through her mention of women's varying needs and hopes, and of the many facets of social struggle reconfiguring ideologies and structures. This women's movement made large demands on its role for the emancipation of women, but also, Mazumdar reminded the 300 conference delegates, held the future success of all movements for social justice in its aims. Mazumdar's logic echoes Namboodiripad's from 1975. She targeted exploitation within the family as well as outside it as central to a gendered analysis of working-class women's issues. She also reinforced the importance of integrating all justice movements into the demand for women's emancipation. Like Namboodiripad, she stated that the women's movement must not be a movement segregated from other movements to end exploitation and oppression. Mazumdar also echoed Namboodiripad's reminder that a separate women's organization will not disrupt class unity but will strengthen the revolutionary movements' goals to end exploitation. Five years later, AIDWA continued to attract new members. At its national conference in 1986, it reported a growth of 700,000 members to a total membership of 1,880,591 women from seventeen states ('AIDWA's Growing Path', 1987: 14). By far the largest AIDWA state unit was West Bengal with 1,250,000 members; the smallest was a new unit in Rajasthan that had 2,130 members.

As AIDWA solidified nationally, the well-documented division between leftist organizations like KMS in Kerala and the Tamil Nadu DWA in the one camp, and autonomous women's groups like the Forum Against Rape in Bombay on the other, sharpened in the late 1970s (with some important exceptions) and continued to calcify in the early 1980s.[9] Unlike earlier struggles with women's organizations like the All India Women's Conference (AIWC) around dues and mass membership, later differences within the women's movement centred explicitly on ideology as it shaped groups' strategies and organizational structure. All too palpably, the debate to change AIWC's dues did have a significant ideological component for a women's movement, of who should organize and lead women. But unlike the debates in the 1940s and 1950s, in the 1970s the divides around activists' analysis of women's issues, their vocabulary to describe that analysis and their disagreements over movement strategies began to cleave wider gulfs between activists committed to building women's political organization. The new currency of the term 'patriarchy' provides a powerful example of one highly contested difference between AIDWA's vision for a mass women's organization and the smaller, often urban-based autonomous women's groups that mushroomed

[9] Brinda Karat, the general secretary of AIDWA from 1993 to 2002, reflected that the divisions between the left and autonomous women's groups eased only in the devastating aftermath of the anti-Sikh riots in 1984, and in the coalitional campaign among women's groups over the Muslim Woman (Protection of Rights on Divorce) Act in 1986. Brinda Karat interview, 29 December 2004.

in cities and towns across the country after the Mathura case in the early 1980s.

Vimal Ranadive, AIDWA's vice-president from 1981 to 1992, wrote a pamphlet in 1986 entitled, *Feminists and the Women's Movement* on behalf of AIDWA. Here, Ranadive points to the stark differences between the two political visions; she sharply disagrees with autonomous feminists' systemic analysis of patriarchy, which she described in the following way: 'the exploitation of women in society is because of patriarchy in the society and unless we fight men, women will not achieve emancipation. What is the way out? Women of all classes should come together to fight against men' (Ranadive 1986: 3). 'Patriarchy' became a shorthand term in Ranadive's pamphlet for the feminist analysis that pitted women against men, no matter what the struggle, context or short-term goals. Patriarchy, conceptually, mirrors the CPM's critique of feminism as a movement that undermined class unity between working-class women and men. Ranadive compared AIDWA's understanding in equally pithy terms. 'Once the causes of inequality, domination by the feudal tendencies and discrimination are removed by abolishing the private property relations, the way for the emancipation of women is opened' (ibid.: 8). Emancipation of women and a socialist revolution, she argued, would be impossible with the absolute autonomy of women's activism from men's, since private ownership of property underpins women's oppression in seemingly cultural structures like the family. In the early 1980s, most AIDWA activists used the term 'male chauvinism' in place of the systemic term 'patriarchy', since capitalism in its historical specificity, not patriarchy, is the source of women's exploitation.

Ranadive's pamphlet became a critical document for many autonomous women's activists to enumerate their differences from AIDWA, and other socialist women's organizations allied to left and communist political parties. Kumari Jayawardena and Govind Kelkar responded to Ranadive's charges against feminism in the *Economic and Political Weekly* (Jayawardena and Kelkar 1989: 2123–26). The left, they argued, had to 'understand and come to terms with patriarchy in its historical setting and its complex and problematic relationship with dominant relations of production' (ibid.: 2123). They defined feminism in contradistinction to Ranadive's charges that feminism solely fights patriarchal systems of oppression: 'Feminism is thus related to the fundamental restructuring of society with a women-centred approach, something that challenges the basic structures of oppression and inequality' (ibid.: 2126). The differences between left-led groups like AIDWA and the socialist feminist groups in the autonomous women's movement did not result from a simple miscommunication. AIDWA sought to strengthen the work of the communist movement, by mobilizing and educating women to struggle against their own exploitation and oppression as part of a larger class struggle against capitalism and imperialism. Autonomous feminists sought to organize women outside of the communist movement, to reform its collaboration with patriarchal relationships, albeit towards common goals of equality, justice and empowerment.

The Research Centre for Women's Studies based in Mumbai's SNDT Women's University collected important articles in the debate raging during the 1980s, including the article by Jayawardena and Kelkar, and Vimal Ranadive's pamphlet in its entirety (Krishnaraj, ed. 1990). In 1990, the Centre hosted a debate on the question of the women's movement, with the collected essays sent to the participants beforehand. The essays became a photocopied volume that was widely circulated, with an extensive introduction written by Maithreyi Krishnaraj who encapsulated the discussions at the meeting. Krishnaraj also included Ilina Sen's rejoinder to Ranadive's pamphlet, entitled 'Feminists, Women's Movement and the Working Class', first published in *Economic and Political Weekly* (Ilina Sen 1989: 1639–41). Sen's response continues to be published in volumes about the post-independence women's activism, even while Ranadive's original argument has vanished from the debate.[10] Sen demolishes Ranadive's understanding of patriarchy. 'To define it as "fighting men" is both malicious and ridiculous' (Krishnaraj, ed. 1990: 71). Instead, she suggests that patriarchy is a more malleable concept that both guides and emerges from Indian feminist politics: 'analysis of patriarchy and the structures of patriarchal dominance has developed through feminist practice, but once again details and precise positions vary depending on positions the feminists take vis-à-vis the rest of society' (ibid.). Sen deflects the criticism of 'patriarchy' as an imported concept, arguing that it is not a rigid doxa among autonomous women's groups, and does not create a homogenous movement analytically or politically.

For communists organizing working-poor and agricultural women, patriarchy could not explain landless agricultural women who faced myriad avenues of oppression and exploitation, patriarchy being only one of them. Dalit landless agricultural workers, men and women, could not be organized around such a concept. Nor could contestation of patriarchy alone build support for industrial working women's issues, who were a demographic minority in factories and mines, and in the unions that represented these workers. The illustrative difference comes around some of AIDWA's most successful struggles in the 1970s around 'price rise', or the precipitous increase in basic foods and supplies. This campaign, centred in Maharashtra, managed to unite working-poor, working-class and middle-class women around the

[10] Two revealing examples of this elision are Nivedita Menon, ed. 1999, and Maitrayee Chaudhuri, ed. 2004. Neither collection concedes any space for publication by women's groups affiliated to left and communist parties, a revealing lacuna, even while several articles malign their role in Indian women's movements.

common goal of food affordability. This cross-class alliance was a rare strategic victory after independence, given the deep class divides among women. Chhaya Datar, an early member in Mumbai's Forum Against Rape, in one commonly heard argument during the 1980s, contemptuously discarded price rise struggles from the post-independence women's movement. Datar writes: 'the anti-price rise agitation conducted just before 1975, cannot be said to be a part of the new movement. It belonged to the earlier movement since its ideology about women's place in society and the functioning of the leadership originated from the independence movement' (Datar 1995: 5). Autonomous women's groups in the 1980s often refused to work in coalition around anti-price rise campaigns, contending that price rise was not a women's issue (Palriwala and Agnihotri 1996: 508).

Kanak Mukherjee, AIDWA's vice-president from its inception until 1999, published a less overtly polemical book titled *Women's Emancipation Movement in India* in 1989, three years after Ranadive's pamphlet. In some regards, Mukherjee's attack on Indian and western feminists did not carry the same heat as Ranadive's in its tone, but her position and her language were strikingly similar. Rather than focus solely on trends within the Indian women's movement, Mukherjee wrote about feminist organizations in the US, specifically the National Organization for Women (NOW):

> Now the imperialists are also throwing a challenge to the healthy democratic women's movement. . . . These feminists, though of various views, pose the woman's question as opposed to men's and hold the patriarchal system of society responsible for the exploitation of women. Thus they try to divert the class struggle into a struggle between men and women. This breeds hatred in the family, conjugal life and social life, and leads to the isolation of the women's movement from the mainstream of the people's movements. (Mukherjee 1989: 103)

Mukherjee cited NOW's theory of patriarchy as an example of neo-imperialist divisionary tactics within the Indian women's movement. Not only are women's groups within India divided, a problem less troubling to Mukherjee, but the strength of 'people's movements' is sapped. Patriarchy as the primary problem faced by women at work, in social relationships, in dominant cultural practices and hegemonic ideologies creates a movement, AIDWA organizers like Mukherjee and Ranadive contended, that shrinks women's issues to culturalist problems alone. In addition, patriarchy as the focus for women's politics, potentially segregates struggles led by women from gender-mixed people's movements; particularly movements where men are in the majority, like the trade union movement. Sen's contention that Ranadive overstates the divisiveness of patriarchal analyses of women's oppression and exploitation is also short-sighted, though the divisions caused by the debate were exacerbated by the stakes of what should be women's issues, women's struggles and women's goals in their movement. The limited understanding of patriarchy from this period allowed many autonomous activist groups to devalue, reject or simply ignore AIDWA's most successful struggles, such as their mobilization against the high cost of basic commodities in urban areas, regional campaigns against women's unequal wages and poor working conditions, and their fight against endemic landlessness among rural, agricultural women.

More recent assessments of the patriarchy debate between the aligned and non-aligned segments of the women's movement, by activists on both sides of the debate, rue the acrimony it intensified and the divisions reified by these semantics, however grounded in significant differences. In an interview from 2005, Brinda Karat, the general secretary of AIDWA from 1993 to 2004, reflects on the debates about patriarchy from this period in AIDWA's history. She suggests that AIDWA activists' refusal to use the word 'patriarchy' was misplaced.

> But of course we were also looking at it [patriarchy] – now when I look back on it we did have a certain notion that to use the word patriarchy, as opposed to using the word 'male supremacy' or 'women's subordination' . . . would somehow be giving in to the feminists . . . because they were posing patriarchy as an autonomous system and our objection was precisely to that. (Brinda Karat interview, 29 December 2004)

From the perspective of a supporter of non-aligned feminists, Mary John also suggests another confluence between these two trends of the late 1970s and 80s, since they shared the same target in many of their campaigns. 'However critical the institution of patriarchy was to become in the self-understanding of the women's movement, especially among autonomous groups, the Indian state has been the movement's most constitutive site of contestation' (John 1999: 108). Brinda Karat and Mary John look back at the distrust within the women's movement and the coalitional politics it stymied, but do not wholly conflate these lost opportunities with substantive differences of analysis, politics and members that existed between groups across the spectrum of women's political organization.

The fierce debates over theories of organizing women did not entirely prevent coalitional work between autonomous and left-allied women's organizations in the early and mid-1980s. One prominent example was the formation of the Dahej Virodhi Chetna Manch (DVCM – Anti-Dowry Awareness Raising Forum) in 1982, a coalition that included thirty women's groups from across Delhi to protest increasing incidence of dowry murders in the nation, and the legal and governmental indifference to the crimes (Mathur 2007: 4–5). Indu Agnihotri and Vina Mazumdar credit DVCM with giving national visibility to the issues of dowry-based violence against women through a march of hundreds of women through the capital city of Delhi (Agnihotri and Mazumdar 1995: 1871; see also Kelkar 1992: 75–99). Dowry was launched as a national women's issue, one that gained international resonance through skilful use of media and visual public representations of a previously privatized violence. An important early coalitional document from DVCM in 1982 states that dowry is not an 'isolated phenomenon'. Instead, it is

> linked with the entire gamut of inferior female condition. Its increasing incidence is symptomatic of the continuing erosion of women's status and devaluation of female life in independent India. It is equally related to the worsening socio-economic crisis within which structural inequalities have accentuated and black money power grown to fuel greater human oppression. (Document cited in Palriwala and Agnihotri 1996: 506)

Patriarchy is not stated in their document, but its contours are explained through terms like 'women's status' and 'devaluation of female life', and their grounding in capitalist exploitation as a 'fuel [for] greater human oppression'. Men are not the primary perpetrators, indeed many dowry murders were linked to violence by the mother-in-law of the woman's husband's family. While patriarchy could have explained women's complicity in dowry violence, this DVCM document blames the 'human oppression' of women on the rise of capitalist acquisitiveness where a woman's dowry enriches the entire family of the husband.

Ranadive and Mukherjee also agreed about the organizational vision for AIDWA. AIDWA allowed women to gain consciousness about immediate issues they faced, such as the high costs of electricity, and fight for changes in those issues, such as a city-wide demonstration against electricity price increases or a delegation to city or state minister. They sought to politicize women through these local struggles around national issues, such as the campaign to increase government budgets for social services. These national campaigns should ideally continue to widen and include more issues, ones not necessarily in the immediate orbit of each woman member of AIDWA, such as the campaign for a bill outlawing dowry murder, the struggle for Muslim women's rights, and the agitation for landless, Dalit women's right to own land. Ranadive described the goal of AIDWA to reach beyond the women's movement, to make women political actors within political parties: 'women's organizations will try to mobilize women on the urgent issues concerning women with the object to politicalize [*sic*] them so that they can join the mainstream of the democratic movement' (Ranadive 1986: 9). She visualized this mainstream through their opposition to the bourgeois state: 'the common object of each mass organization, students, women, Dalits, etc. is to fight the reactionary policies of the state, the effects of which they all experience in their day to day life, such as molestation and rape on women, increase in fees of education or meagre wages for agricultural workers' (ibid.: 15). In an interview conducted twenty years later, Kanak Mukherjee described a similarly tiered vision for AIDWA's politics.

> The main objective of AIDWA when it was first set up, according to Kanak, was to uphold the democratic rights of people, women in particular, against Congress authoritarianism. The second was to link and give an all-India character to women's movements for democracy in different states. An all-India organization also made it possible for the left women's movement to intervene in issues arising in the states, like the Shah Bano case, the Ujan Maidan mass-rape case, and instances of communal violence. (Parvathi Menon 2004: 38)

AIDWA's activism moved from its national aim against the Congress government to its campaigns against anti-women, anti-people agendas and policies of state-based governments. The local campaigns, in Mukherjee's description, took up specific issues that may or may not have had a specifically national resonance as they impacted communities and localities within each state. Mukherjee outlined another series of overlapping circles, this time geographic in scope, where the smaller regional campaigns fed the state-based demands of AIDWA units, in terms of consciousness of its members and numbers of participants. These state-wide actions then culminated in a national resistance against the Congress government that ruled India for much of the 1980s. As schematic as these descriptions may sound, AIDWA's activism in the 80s was dynamic, creative and anything but predictable.

AIDWA launched a series of overlapping national campaigns throughout the 1980s. State units around the country conducted ongoing campaigns against dowry murder, custodial rape, female infanticide and familial-based violence against women. But the organization also responded to the rising violence of communalism. In 1984, after the assassination of Prime Minister Indira Gandhi, Sikhs faced organized riots against their property and their lives. Prominent AIDWA activists, like Lakshmi Sahgal, met rioters in the streets, forcing them to retreat away from her medical clinic in a densely populated neighbourhood of Mumbai. AIDWA activists, alongside progressive people and activists, joined together to provide relief, medical care, shelter and safety after the attacks on Sikh houses and businesses subsided. Relief work after such huge losses demanded ever more vigilant attention to the rise of communalism, both anti-Sikh and anti-Muslim. All women active in the progressive and left-affiliated women's movement in the mid-1980s critically assessed past analyses and strategies to develop more effective organizing methods against communal bigotry as an organized political force. Communalism as a women's issue shattered any easy assumptions about women's natural unity, reflected Brinda Karat, an AIDWA leader active in New Delhi after the riots, since women also supported and participated in the violence (Brinda Karat interview, 28 December 2004). In addition, rigid autonomy from gender-mixed groups became an unaffordable luxury during this period. One constitutive ideal of autonomous women's groups, their unequivocal separation from all representative politics and political parties, lost favour during the state-supported anti-Sikh riots.

Local Politics Nationalized

Pappa's banyan tree provides a powerful visual metaphor of AIDWA's interconnected local, state and national politics, and the eclecticism of its historical precursors. But the movement, the flow of ideas, campaigns, leadership and ideology within this agglomerated mass is harder to illustrate. AIDWA's history is not one of linear political movements seamlessly connecting to each other. Even with shared temporality, AIDWA's regional politics maintain a tenacious connection to the *place* of those politics. Social movement scholars of AIDWA often collapse the structure of decision-making in the organization, in many locations a form of democratic centralism, to the interactive relationship between AIDWA as a national organization to its state-based units (Ray 1999; Basu 1992). Raka Ray insightfully attends to the regional differences in AIDWA's politics with her research in Mumbai and Kolkata, but gives only cursory attention to the national character of the organization in relation to these states. For Ray, AIDWA is structured more like an (imitative) ladder:

> The structure of the women's organization closely approximates that of the party [CPM]. At the grassroots level there are primary units, and the task of these workers is to maintain day-to-day contact with women at the grassroots and also to mobilize them for demonstrations. Above them are local, district, state and national committees, in that order. (Ray 1999: 60)

Leaders within AIDWA have posed a slightly less mechanistic understanding, though equally static in their terms. Kanak Mukherjee's, discussed earlier in this chapter, provided another explanatory rubric of AIDWA's organizational model: AIDWA fights for women's equality at a national level in their state-based groups, through regional and local issues. Additionally, Mukherjee stated, at the national level AIDWA provides the stability and organizational strength to states and localities so they can maintain their commitment to issues as they unfold. Neither of these descriptions attends to AIDWA's distinctive strength of local and regional leadership that substantiates the national organization. This strength, of meaningful leadership from state-based grassroots struggles, is also its weakness at a national level, since AIDWA's membership continues to be very high in states with a long history of women's activism, such as Kerala, West Bengal and Tamil Nadu, and

The cover of a pamphlet of the All India Democratic Women's Association in Tamil Nadu from the late 1980s, titled *We are Being Consumed by Fire, Let the Volcano Erupt!*

organizationally weak in states such as Gujurat, Haryana and Orissa. Each active state *mahila samiti* or women's group has a distinctive history, a different date of formation and particularly important struggles that animate its politics.

Many states have their own publications distributed in regional languages that do not replicate AIDWA's national publications, *Women's Equality* published in English and *Stree Samya* published in Hindi. The Ganatantrik

Mahila Samiti in West Bengal has published *Eksathe* since 1968 to spread the word about their activities and develop discussions about important issues of the day. In Kerala, AIDWA's publication is called *Tulyata*. In Tamil Nadu, the DWA publication began in the mid-1970s called *Ulaikum Magalir Mathayadu Sinthanai* or *Monthly Magazine of Working Women's Thought*. In January 1986 it became simply *Magalir Sinthanai* or *Women's Thought*. A comparison of the articles and struggles represented in the inaugural issue of *Women's Equality*, October–December 1987, and those in *Magalir Sinthanai* during the same period allows a more vibrant look at the relationships between AIDWA as an all-India organization and its state and regional character in Tamil Nadu, the state of Pappa Umanath's involvement.

In 1987, *Magalir Sinthanai* carried a description of its role in the organization: '*Magalir Sinthanai* supports noble causes and should reach women across the spectrum. We need to widen our audience and our sales and our annual subscriptions. We must discuss these issues when we collect subscriptions. Our magazine is an important campaigning tool for our organization's work' ('Magalir Sinthanai', 1987: 3). As a campaigning tool, the regional character of the magazine alongside the national issues it covered allowed AIDWA in Tamil Nadu to reach literate women who may have fallen outside their neighbourhood-based units, and become a means for group discussions among predominantly illiterate members. With its signature wry sense of humour, this article also described *Magalir Sinthanai* in contrast to standard women's magazines.

> People think if a magazine takes up women's issues it has cooking tips, beauty tips, housekeeping tips, how to save and how to please the husband. Only these important issues are covered in a women's magazine. Social evils, the poor status of women are ignored. They are strangers to price hikes and how unemployment affects women. They feel these evils against women are not worth covering. They do not raise women's awareness about national unity or world peace. (Ibid.)

Their articles usually centered descriptions of the women's lives in their campaigns. Authors made sense of these women's stories alongside a contextual or systemic view of the issues at stake, but each issue began with local campaigns fought across the state by AIDWA. In February 1987, the issue recognized how different their stories were from commercial women's magazines – yet the editors' admission of their focus on deep social, economic and political problems turned immediately to a Dalit woman active in an AIDWA-led campaign to annul her husband's second marriage.

> Some say that we only report atrocities in *Magalir Sinthanai*. If you feel like this reading the magazine, imagine how the people feel who experience these things in their lives. We introduce you to Emina who like thousands of women has been

subjected to atrocities in her life. Emina is a poor woman from the scheduled castes. ('Introductions', 1987: 3)

Finally, editors of *Magalir Sinthanai* did not aim for the publication to be solely agitational or informational, but sought to sustain links between local and regional campaigns and national issues fought by AIDWA. As a publication linked to a women's organization, it also aspired to raise women's consciousness and radically change typical ways of understanding the world:

> Women's problems and social hierarchies are relational. Women must care about these problems in our country and the atrocities done by the rulers. *Magalir Sinthanai* explains these issues through articles and real incidents to overcome superstitious thinking and come to full consciousness and knowledge about our lives. We have a doctor's column for advice about your health; we have a world events section; we carry poetry, but not like other publications. We do not tell women how to act for men's pleasure. Our poetry links social evils of dowry to women's larger issues. We detail how dowry burning and harassment cannot be understood as women against women violence [mother-in-law against daughter-in-law], but our magazine shows the gaps in that argument to show how the system discriminates against women. ('Magalir Sinthanai', 1987: 3)

The campaign against dowry inspired wide sections of the women's movement beginning in the 1980s. In the inaugural issue of AIDWA's English-language publication, *Women's Equality*, lawyer Kirti Singh challenged the weakness of the 1961 Dowry Prohibition Act, arguing that there are 'hardly any successful prosecutions under this Act owing to the glaring loopholes in the Act itself' (Singh 1987: 19–20). Her article looked at successive amendments to the Act that did little to address the gaping holes and inconsistencies in the law. She applauded one new clause, Section 498-A, a clause won by hard-fought agitation by the women's movement, that places the burden of proof of not taking or demanding dowry on the husband's family. Yet she ended with a demand still ignored, for 'equal legal rights for women in matrimonial property and inheritance', and a reminder of the length of the fight still to go (ibid.: 20). The issue described the Roop Kanwar case in Deorala, Rajasthan, of a young woman celebrated by the Hindu rightwing for immolating herself on her husband's funeral pyre. It held more general articles on the upsurge in communalism, on the movement for peace, and one article on the politics of water, of drought and flooding, and the related inequities in food distribution. The issue provided statistics, suggestions, legal advice and a large section about AIDWA struggles carried on in the states. It did not suggest specific kinds of campaigns around dowry, yet gave valuable information to spur the process of organizing against it.

The creativity of regional responses to these issues is better revealed in regional publications. An article by R. Chandra, 'It is our Great Fortune to be Born Women...?', illustrates an early example of AIDWA's signature means to develop local, regional and national campaigns to build a systemic understanding of the issues at stake. Chandra began the article on the low status of women and burgeoning female infanticide, a disturbing trend she linked to dowry.

> In Madurai district, Usilampatti taluk, 300 families belong to the Kallar community. Most of them are small agriculturalists, some women among them are agricultural labourers. Men and women are working equally hard. To eradicate the burden of dowry, they are killing girl babies when they are born. Their hearts are hardening like the hard work they perform each day. (Chandra 1986: 30)

She asked why these women and men kill their girl babies, not beginning systemically or economically with the severe hardships they face, but with their own knowledge. 'How do they kill their own children? We can only know from their own words.' Chandra transcribed her interviews with women who killed their girl babies, detailing their ages, their villages, their number of children.

> Paraipatti Annamma responded in tears saying, 'In my community dowry harassment is more intense. I killed my three first children, all daughters, after they had grown. How can I afford to search for a bridegroom? My fourth child was a boy. After him, I delivered four more girls, but those I did not kill.' She wiped away her tears as she showed me the graves of her first three daughters. (Ibid.: 4)

But Chandra refused to end her report with the women's words, their analyses of female infanticide, and a condemnation of dowry and girl babies' murder. She described how she took her report to the doctors of private hospitals that dominate many areas like Usilampatti, as well as the area government hospital. They all agreed with her assessment. One social worker gave her additional information: 'Last year 600 girls were born in the government hospital. 570 of those girls were killed. In the last ten years 6,000 girl babies born in the hospital were killed' (ibid.). These testimonies, by mothers, fathers, doctors and social workers, Chandra took to the state minister Hande and the Madurai district collector, Varadarajulu. The minister denied knowledge of the statistics and the district collector responded that it was difficult to punish the perpetrators.

Chandra ended with a state-wide and nation-wide call to action from her very localized research of the issue in a caste-homogenous area of agriculturalists and agricultural labourers in Madurai district:

> Our research shows that these murders often happen without anyone knowing about them. To deter the killing of girl children we must fight for the eradication

> of dowry more powerfully. Mothers must be taught how to use contraception. The struggle for women's emancipation must be strengthened. To revalue women, not only women, but also progressive men, must come forward to wage ideological battle. Only a united protest can lead the way, otherwise children will be buried before they even open their eyes and see the world. We will all fight against this evil! (Ibid.)

Chandra's report on female infanticide illustrates an early example of AIDWA's presently widespread use of research to instigate and formulate their campaigns, methods and demands. It also reveals a very different model for how AIDWA acts as a national organization. Chandra's findings are cited in academic articles about AIDWA and women's activism against dowry and female infanticide. They are also woven into the description in the 1994 National Conference reports to illustrate growing national strategies employed in Tamil Nadu and Haryana specifically, to counter female infanticide (AIDWA 1994: 35). AIDWA did not simply provide national support and knowledge to regional or local campaign issues, in Mukherjee's formulation, though Kirti Singh's and others' articles from *Women's Equality* show that relationship of the national organization to its parts. AIDWA's publications also analysed why rising social trends had economic and political dimensions.

Chandra's article on the rising death of girl children developed a complex understanding of how women's declining status and the rise of dowry demands across all class, caste and community backgrounds in all regions exacerbated female infanticide. It condemned governmental inaction and created a vision for future campaigns. In short, Chandra's profoundly local research in the Madurai district of Tamil Nadu unearthed national strategies for AIDWA. Her research also developed a means for AIDWA to explain the structures that link skewed sex ratios, high infant mortality of girls and the rise of dowry murders to the economic and social relationships that fuel those crimes. Chandra's attention to women's consciousness about their murder of their own infant girls did not lend itself to easy answers for any political organization. In the terms of praxis, the individual women's stories allowed an organization to build towards social and economic change of the problem that began rather than ended with solving the individual problem of its grassroots member; a very different model than dictating structural changes from above.

The organizing around the issue of female foeticide in Tamil Nadu in the 1980s, like dowry murders in north India, were coalitional campaigns. Many women's organizations joined the work at numerous sites, keeping in touch with other groups and coordinating joint actions. The unorthodox methods AIDWA members used to develop their politics, like canvassing members, conducting wider research around an issue and actively bringing women most affected by the issue into the leadership did not create divides between autonomous women's groups and the left-allied women's groups. When working on an issue in coalition, the different analyses of the issue did not necessarily reinforce divides between activists and their organizations. Instead, the linkage between the composition of groups' memberships and their ideology has produced friction and even an inability to work together. In the case of AIDWA, its methods of activist research to shape its analysis and political response are directly linked to its mass membership from the rural and urban poor. The analysis of family and gendered community norms that many of the most contentious disagreements in the 1980s hinged upon demanded a sharpened understanding by the entire women's movement in the 1990s and 2000s. 'Patriarchy' as a conceptual framework for intra-familial and intra-community violence against women may have crossed borders within the Indian women's movement. But 'patriarchy' alone could not confront complexities of neoliberal trends of women and violence that sharpened the imperatives of hierarchical community boundaries. The nascent coalitional work within the women's movement during the 1980s would become critical to the movement's own survival in the decades that followed.

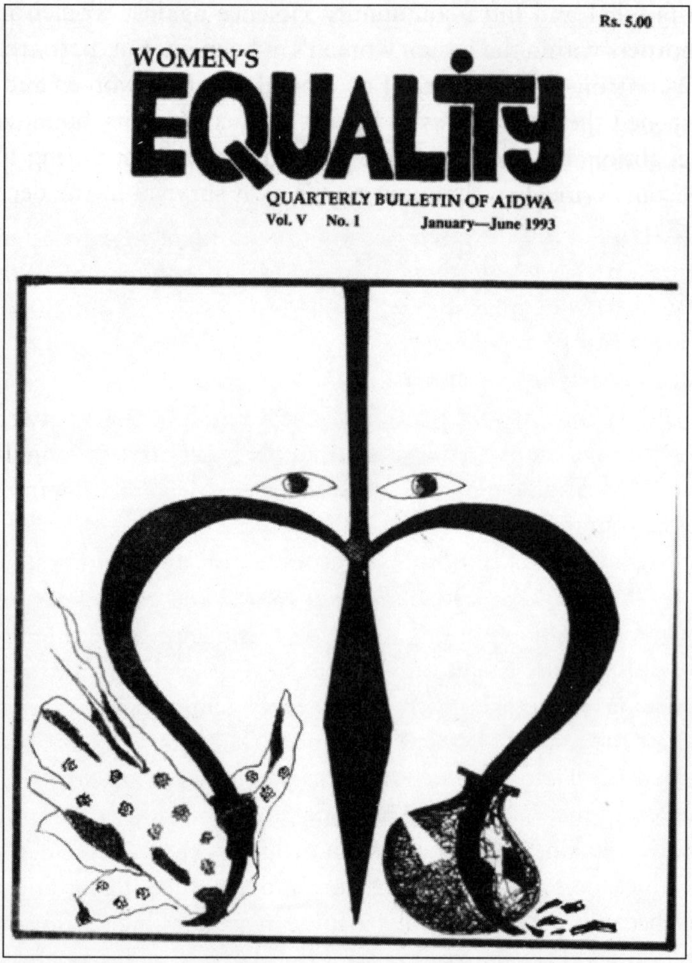

Cover of AIDWA's English-language bulletin, *Women's Equality*, vol. 5, no. 1, January–June 1993.

THREE

Inter-Sectoral Praxis

The All India Democratic Women's Association held its Fourth National Conference in Coimbatore, Tamil Nadu in 1994. It assessed the grimly historical quality of the three years between 1991 and 1994, since the last conference held in Jadavpur, West Bengal, at the end of 1990. 'We could not at that time have imagined that the next three years would arguably rank as the worst since independence, for the mass of the people in this country' (AIDWA 1994: 3). The Coimbatore conference was attended by 785 delegates, with each delegate representing approximately 4,800 members. AIDWA's total membership was tallied to just over 3,768,000 women. Thirteen years had passed since AIDWA had been founded, and the Fourth Conference opened with a profoundly different context for its organizing, its strategies and, particularly, its members. The three short years between 1991 and 1994 witnessed an explosive growth in the power of communal politics to mobilize Hindus against non-Hindus, the pace of neoliberal retractions of government programmes for vulnerable people, and the ferocity of casteist campaigns against redistribution of resources or opportunities from the dominant to dispossessed castes. Women lived at the cutting edge of all of these trends in the Indian polity. The women's movement, in different ways, responded with alacrity to all of these crises.

These national trajectories, with their deeply gendered effects, shaped the politics across the Indian women's movement. The internal debates between feminist, liberal and leftist women's groups that choked the early years of the 1980s receded in the wake of virulent challenges outside of the movement. While debates remained, coalitions with groups within the women's movement and allies in other movements around communalizing and casteist campaigns became a critical tool to forge new possibilities for women's movement politics. This chapter explores the changes configured by AIDWA between the mid-1980s and early 1990s as it developed a sectoral analysis of particularly marginalized women, and an inter-sectoral organizing strategy to counteract the rising power of communalism, casteism and neoliberalism. These methods were often spoken about by regional leaders using the terms 'sectional' or 'sectoral' interchangeably. In the crucible of these difficult challenges, AIDWA gathered its experiences across the country to identify, slowly and with careful thought, the following sectors for particular attention: rural women, Muslim women, Dalit women, Adivasi (indigenous) women and women in the informal economy.

AIDWA members at the state and national levels combined their focus on specific women's issues with inter-sectoral organizing between these often porous and inter-related groups of women. For example, many rural women were also Dalits and tended livestock in the informal economy; and specific campaigns might reflect aspects of some or all of their sectoral issues. In localities, AIDWA members raised campaigns around land, employment, violence, casteism and communalism in ways that kept the women most affected by these issues at the forefront of a campaign's mobilization, leadership, goals and strategy. Sectoral and inter-sectoral organizing also sought to develop, at every level of the organization, movement leaders from oppressed and marginalized sectors out of local and regional campaigns.

The development of AIDWA's sectoral analysis and inter-sectoral organizing methods seemed to flaunt accepted wisdom about building unity among diverse groups of women through common campaigns that all women could relate to through their own needs and experiences, such as campaigns for affordable food or domestic violence campaigns. In fact, unity was critical to AIDWA leaders' thinking about how to build a stronger women's movement against the intensifying divisions of caste, class and religious bigotry, but it was a unity reconceived. Brinda Karat, the general secretary of AIDWA from 1993 to 2004, described this method in more detail as 'inter-sectoral, inter-class and crossing', to explain their seemingly risky campaigns that linked women's political activism across class, religious and caste lines within the organization's membership. Karat explained:

> For example, if you were taking up Dalit [oppressed caste] women's issues, could your movement organize upper-class women in support of Dalit women? Then you would say, 'Yes, this is women's unity, this is sisterhood.' Unity would be of some meaning if it was unity on an aspect which is usually divisive among women. . . . So could you organize women who would normally not be eating in a Muslim household to come out in support [of Muslim women], to defend Muslim women against the state? Not their own fundamentalists, but against the oppression of the state? . . . Are you prepared to go to Hindu localities and tell Hindu women that they are utterly wrong? And that is what women's unity is and must be. (Brinda Karat interview, 26 December 2004)

Unity demanded that AIDWA members directly confront discrimination from within their own class, caste and religious location. Rather than ask members to memorize an organizational position on communal harmony, Karat laid out a more difficult vision where women from the dominant religion, in her example, confront the state (and its often explicit alliance with citizens from dominant castes, classes and religions) alongside women from the minority religions who waged allied but differently positioned struggles. The parts of this unity were incommensurate to each other but attuned to the specific changes that differently located women could demand. The unity sought to bring these parts together in a complex whole to shift the very ideologies that enabled a communalized, competitive and identity-based polity.

AIDWA began in 1981 with a three-part analysis of how to organize women, credited to E.M.S. Namboodiripad, the CPI(M) general secretary between 1977 and 1992. He configured women's differential positionality: as workers, as citizens and in their gendered social roles as women (Namboodiripad 1975). Yet even as AIDWA's political activism in the 1980s seemed to adhere primarily to women as citizens, it also revealed the overlapping and complicated way women experienced these three roles. The best of their campaigns worked creatively on multiple locations of women's positionality. As exploited workers, women drew on their solidarity as producers in the work place and their civic rights to equal wages and fair working conditions. As gendered beings in patriarchal and feudal relationships, women sought the autonomy afforded by their legal rights to land and property to combat abusive relationships. Yet, seen alone, these three spheres mask the inter-subjectivity of women's religious, caste-based, sexuality-based and class-based identities. In the communal and class-divisive landscape of the 1980s and 90s, this silence could damage AIDWA's activism.

In the 1980s, AIDWA leaders began to clarify ways to build unified campaigns to counteract divisive identity politics. They began to explicitly weave those facets of women's lives into their organizing methods *and* goals. Inter-sectoral organizing allowed AIDWA members to confront the oppressive relations of power, whether feudal, patriarchal or capitalist, that rent (and, as Karat suggests in the quotation above, potentially unified) its members in myriad ways. Inter-sectoral organizing, she argues, sought to build this complex unity among its members to strengthen its campaigns against rising caste, class and religious sectarianism. AIDWA members did not frame these campaigns as a charity to others, or othered members of AIDWA, but as legitimate aspects of struggle for all its members, whether they enjoyed middle-class, dominant caste, majority religion status or not. The fight for an equitable, secular and just social fabric was a fight for everyone to win.

Inter-sectoral organizing had an important second component for the structure of AIDWA. State and national leaders sought to foster AIDWA's future leaders from within these historically marginalized communities, and to build an organization that took their leadership to its campaigns and analysis. Subhashini Ali, a founding member of AIDWA and the president of AIDWA between 2001 and 2010, described this component as an inter-sectoral organizational concern. She said: 'We also want to develop leaders from all these sections, and not just say, okay, since you have got a correct understanding, so therefore anybody can represent anybody, anybody speak for anybody' (Subhashini Ali interview, 22 July 2008). An AIDWA member's ideological clarity on issues of caste or communalism was not enough to speak for the women marginalized within these sectors. AIDWA, Ali stated, must build leaders within the organization among disenfranchised women to lead the organization. These two components, of building inter-sectoral solidarity among women for specific women's issues and of strengthening its own leadership from among particularly disadvantaged communities of women, grew from the powerful lessons AIDWA learned in its battle against communalism, casteism and neoliberalism beginning in the 1980s.

AIDWA developed its analysis about these sectors of women most fiercely affected by communal politics and market forces during the 1980s and into the twenty-first century. AIDWA continued to strengthen its ties with allied left organizations and its coalitions with the women's movement over this period. Inter-sectoral organizing allowed it to grow astonishingly quickly during these difficult times: from 1,880,591 members in 1986 to 2,400,000 members in 1994, to almost 6 million in 2001. By 2010, AIDWA had 15 million members, many of whom were from these sectors of women: rural, Muslim, Dalit and informal sector workers. They still sought to consolidate their membership among Adivasi women, and raised powerful campaigns for land rights, sexual dignity and autonomy and community control.

Anti-Sikh Riots and the Indian Women's Movement

In 1984, Prime Minister Indira Gandhi was killed by her Sikh bodyguards at her residence in New Delhi. Her assassination was political, linked to the tensions in Punjab around the demands for an independent Sikh state, and the government's violent suppression of the movement in the Sikhs' most sacred site, the Golden Temple in Amritsar. Immediately following Indira Gandhi's murder, Congress(I) forces directed their retribution against the entire Sikh community through well-coordinated terror. In New Delhi and other cities across north India, mobs targeted Sikhs for attack, murder, displacement and destruction of their homes and businesses. The anti-Sikh violence was particularly brutal in the nation's capital city, and after four days, the rampaging mobs killed 2,400 Sikhs, mostly men and boys. Activists in the women's movement and the nation at large were taken by surprise at the speed, ferocity and systematic execution of the riots. After the four days of violence abated on 3 November 1984, the ruling Congress(I) government refused to alleviate the suffering of displaced Sikh families, a breach filled by ordinary citizens, civic and political groups that created makeshift relief camps, procured food, clothing and medical supplies for a traumatized Sikh community. In the wake of the anti-Sikh riots, women's movement activists across the country recognized the rising centrality of communal politics to their own activism. The communal, state-abetted character of these targeted killings, beatings and looting foreshadowed the surge of organized, political violence against Indian minority groups, particularly Muslims, but also Christians and Sikhs, that stained the decades after 1984.

AIDWA members threw themselves into relief work for Sikh victims of communal violence without an explicit theory of organizing, only the desire to give solace and aid. They drew on a longer history of relief work that dated back to the Bengal famine in the early 1940s, when leftist women organized brigades to distribute food and supplies to the millions of starving rural people in the state.[1] By 1985, an analysis began to emerge within AIDWA out of its members' anti-communal activism that gave conscious attention to the specific needs of vulnerable groups of women and actively sought their political leadership. Indu Agnihotri, a scholar and an AIDWA member who lived in New Delhi during this period, remembered the impact of relief work on AIDWA's members and its activism. 'In 1984, we went immediately into those areas where the Sikhs were directly attacked,' she recalled, 'and also to ensure that Sikh women in those areas where we had a membership, that they should feel secure, that we are with them' (Indu Agnihotri interview 2008). She defined their work in three stages: first, of providing relief work in areas most affected by the devastation; second, reaching out to Sikh members of AIDWA to provide reassurance and support; and third, tending to the ideological fabric of AIDWA to ensure a strong basis of internal support for anti-communal work. Agnihotri described AIDWA members' general relief work in predominantly Sikh neighbourhoods as their first priority. She also mentioned the particular attention AIDWA activists gave to the Sikh women who were members of AIDWA. After the anti-Sikh riots AIDWA sought 'to ensure that the fundamentalist propaganda and the religious divide did not affect our own organization. . . . We told our activists, "You have to be there, you have to stand up for these women, make sure that they feel safe, that they should not feel insecure." I think our activists did that' (ibid.). AIDWA's third task was an ideological one that proved critical in the years ahead: to counter a powerful rhetoric of divisions between increasingly communalized religious groups, and to shore up unity between women in AIDWA.

[1] The relief work in Bengal, like after the riots in 1984, provided vital services to people left behind by an indifferent state, and created an infrastructure staffed by activists from a range of supportive political groups and movements. See Tripti Chaudhuri 2000.

The Communal Crisis and the Indian Women's Movement

After the assassination of Indira Gandhi, her son Rajiv Gandhi took over the leadership of the government. Under his watch, state support for secularism as a national ideology of multi-ethnic, multi-faith unity faced further erosion. In 1985, the Supreme Court ruled on the divorce case of Shah Bano, a Muslim woman seeking maintenance from her husband after their divorce. The Court recognized her right to monetary support to avoid destitution using Section 125 of the Criminal Procedure Code, a right that bypassed the Muslim personal laws due to her poverty. The Supreme Court ruled on the Shah Bano case in 1985 with a judgment that supported her right to a monthly sum for her maintenance to be paid by her former husband. Prominent fundamentalist Muslims protested the ruling on the grounds that it interceded on the jurisdiction of Muslim personal laws.

Kirti Singh, a lawyer and active member of AIDWA, outlined the scope of personal laws. 'Personal laws in India deal with marriage and divorce, maintenance, guardianship, adoption, wills, intestacy and succession, joint family and partition, and can broadly be characterized as "family laws". These laws are basically divided along religious lines, whether or not they are based on religion' (Singh 1994: 378). Hindus, Muslims, Christians and Parsis all have specific personal laws – laws that, Singh argued, share a common anti-woman bias. Relics of the British colonial administration, these personal laws have resisted significant change, with the exception of some changes in the Hindu Code. After independence, the Indian Constitution's guarantee that the state will not interfere in religious practices further shielded these laws from progressive reform. In Shah Bano's case, Muslim fundamentalist leaders argued that her successful use of the Criminal Procedure Code (a code that governs all Indian citizens and is not tailored to codified religious custom) subverted and in effect overruled the Muslim personal laws.

Rajiv Gandhi's Congress (I) Party was stung by conservative Muslim leaders' criticism of the Shah Bano verdict. In 1986, the Congress(I) government proposed the Muslim Women's Bill only months after the Supreme Court's ruling on Shah Bano. The Bill denied Muslim women's right to use Section 125 of the Criminal Procedure Code to secure maintenance in the face of destitution (Hasan 1990). Zoya Hasan linked the government's decision to reverse its earlier support for the Supreme Court's ruling in Shah Bano's case to the electoral losses the Congress (I) Party sustained in December of 1985 (Hasan 1989a). In response to its perceived alienation from Muslim voters, Hasan argued, the Congress(I) government proposed the Muslim Women (Protection of Rights on Divorce) Bill. Despite widespread protests even from Muslim leaders within his own government, Rajiv Gandhi forced the Bill's passage in record time. In an inflammatory reaction to the instatement of the Muslim Women's Act, the Hindu fundamentalist political party, Bharatiya Janata Party (BJP), raised a counter-demand. They supported a Uniform Civil Code (UCC) that would demolish all personal laws, including the Muslim personal laws.

Three months before Rajiv Gandhi passed the Muslim Women's Act, on 1 February 1986, his government unlocked the gates to the Babri Masjid, a fifteenth-century mosque in Ayodhya, Uttar Pradesh. In this instance the government buckled to pressure from Hindu fundamentalist forces, specifically the Vishwa Hindu Parishad (VHP) (Noorani 1989; Hasan 1990). The VHP launched the Ram Janmabhoomi (Ram's birthplace) campaign in 1984, claiming the mosque's location as the original site of Ram's birth (Hasan 1989a). The VHP campaign demanded that the ancient mosque's grounds be opened to Hindu worshippers of Ram, something the government had previously refused to do. In 1986 Rajiv Gandhi's Congress(I) government complied and one government official reported that Rajiv said 'it was tit for tat for the Muslim Women's Bill' (Noorani 1990: 2461). By 1989, the Ram Janmabhoomi campaign united three powerful Hindu fundamentalist forces that called its alliance the *Sangh Parivar.* These Hindutva forces included the ideological leader of the group, the Rashtriya Swayamsevak Sangh (RSS), its political party the Bharatiya Janata Party (BJP), and its international outreach organization, the Vishwa Hindu Parishad (VHP).

For the Indian women's movement, the Shah Bano case and the Muslim Women's Bill incited immediate debate and organizing. The effects of the decision to unlock the gates to the Babri Masjid were not immediately apparent, and thus among women's groups there was little public outcry about the government's decision. Women's groups supported the Supreme Court's decision on Shah Bano since the ruling allowed Muslim women, and other women governed by their religious personal laws, greater flexibility to secure their own futures after divorce. The ruling also confirmed that Muslim women had recourse to the universal laws governing the country in the Criminal Procedure Code. Over the next two months, AIDWA drew on their Muslim members to develop a wider understanding of Muslim women's position on the ruling, and on their evaluation of the Muslim personal laws. In concert with these forums organized by AIDWA, and more quickly than the women's movement at large, progressive Muslim leaders – both women and men – responded to the reactions of conservative Muslim forces after the Shah Bano ruling. They countered the rhetoric of an embattled Muslim faith and a *de jure* Hindu government by opening a public debate on Muslim women's rights that drew from Muslim women's experiences. They sought to reveal the fissures and multiple positions within the homogenized grouping of 'Muslim' by responding to both Muslim fundamentalist leaders and the Congress(I) government.

To counter the antagonistic and distortive response to the ruling, progressive Muslim leaders formed the Committee for the Protection of Rights of Muslim Women (CPRMW). On International Women's Day of 1986, the Committee delivered a memorandum about the Shah Bano ruling to the prime minister signed by prominent Muslim women and men. Their memorandum did not seek to overturn personal laws in favour of a Uniform Civil Code. Instead the CPRMW advocated extending the widest possible legal interpretation for the equality of rights to all women. The memorandum stated:

> Regardless of the rights and privileges that Islam may have conferred on Muslim women, they should not be denied the rights guaranteed by the Indian Constitution based on the recognition of equality, justice and fraternity of all citizens. It is imperative in a secular polity like ours to go beyond the rights conferred by various religions in order to evolve laws which would provide justice and succour to all women, irrespective of their religious beliefs.[2]

The early interventions by CPRMW and other liberal and progressive Muslims to counter conservative Muslims' accusations of an imperilled Islam did not slow the introduction of the Muslim Women's Bill into the Lok Sabha in March 1986.

During the Bill's introduction in parliament, women activists blocked traffic outside of the parliament building for several hours to protest the proceedings. The civil disobedience spread across the country, culminating in a large rally in New Delhi in April 1986. After significant organizing by AIDWA, groups of Muslim women across the city debated the Bill to determine its effects on their lives. By April, a joint statement from progressive organizations, including AIDWA, argued that the Muslim Women's Bill did not represent the will of Muslim women at large. AIDWA continued to actively organize signature campaigns of Muslim women to support that contention. They gathered the signatures of 100,000 women, with 20,000 of those signatures from Muslim women (Singh 1994: 385). On 5 May 1986, the day of the Bill's passage, 100 women chained themselves to the parliament gates to symbolize their protest (Palriwala and Agnihotri 1996: 516). Soon thereafter, the Hindu fundamentalists won a significant victory when the gates of the Babri Masjid, a mosque in Ayodhya that they claimed as the birthplace of the god Ram, were unlocked. The simultaneous victories, of Muslim fundamentalists and of Hindu fundamentalists, are linked in many women's movement activists' accounts of the Shah Bano and Muslim Women's Bill campaigns.

2 'Memorandum by Committee for Protection of Rights of Muslim Women', submitted to the Prime Minister on 24 February 1986; quoted in Engineer 1987: 218.

Feminist activists who had long supported the Uniform Civil Code to govern laws on marriage, divorce and property equally for all women, regardless of their religion, found an unwelcome ally in the BJP. In 1975, the Committee on the Status of Women report *Towards Equality*, had demanded a Uniform Civil Code as a way to change these discriminatory personal laws that directly affected women's lives. Feminist activists were not deceived by the BJP's support for a UCC. Many activists interpreted its demand for a Uniform Civil Code 'as a convenient whip against Muslims and . . . a uniform civil code that in their understanding probably meant a Hindu civil code' (ibid.: 385). Communalism had politicized women's issues in ways that demanded great care on the part of the women's movement to articulate its analysis of the issues and its political demands. 'Women's organizations had to tread a delicate line,' Rajni Palriwala and Indu Agnihotri noted: 'in order to separate clearly and unambiguously their opposition to the Muslim Women's Bill from that of the Hindu fundamentalists with their new found and short-lived "concern" for women's rights' (ibid.: 513). What the women's movement came to terms with during the frenzied months of organizing between the Shah Bano verdict and the Muslim Women's Bill was its own understanding of secularism as a women's issue. Through coalitions, conversations and debate, activists from the women's movement had to balance the communitarian rights of women and men in minority religious groups with their own abstracted, and therefore often Hindu by default, definition of 'women's rights' (Sunder Rajan 2003: 147–73). The movement's commitment to 'women's rights' became a topic for self-critical debate given their class and religious privileges. Women's groups began a difficult self-examination of their own Hindu-dominated membership, and their lack of ties to working-class neighbourhoods or women from the minority religions.

Several 'bitter lessons', as Radha Kumar characterized them, were drawn from these struggles by the women's movement at large (Kumar 1993: 169–71). First, fundamentalist forces envisioned 'women' as an important site for hegemony: as a site to shape gendered roles and as a group that must remain under religious control. Second, the state easily buckled to communalist demands, even in the face of sustained agitation by women's groups and their allies. The third lesson Kumar and other feminist scholars emphasized was the lesson of representation, or how a majority Hindu women's movement could lead a struggle against Muslim fundamentalist interpretations of Muslim women's rights, without being conflated with majority Hindu fundamentalists. One aspect of this last bitter lesson is that of public perception, in the media as well as by Muslims: the Indian women's movement was a Hindu, middle class, and upper caste women's movement in all but name. Activists across the spectrum of the women's movement sought to clearly distinguish their positions on Muslim women's rights, on personal laws and on the UCC from both Hindu and Muslim fundamentalist positions. Yet other more troubling questions remained unanswered by this difficult work alone. In what ways had the women's movement in India reinforced the unequal power and class relations between majority Hindus and minority Muslims through their blindness to religious inequities and differences? Activists within the women's movement asked where prominent Muslim women leaders were in the Indian women's movement. They questioned how Muslim women's leadership in the women's movement as a whole had been neglected. The women's movement debated these concerns alongside the dangers of tokenizing Muslim women at the crux of overtly communal politics.

AIDWA did have ties among Muslim women activists and had organized in localities with large Muslim populations. However, in these localities and in units with strong representation by Muslim women, AIDWA members did not necessarily organize around specific religious or community issues of Muslim women (Indu Agnihotri interview, 29 July 2008). As Brinda Karat noted, 'What struck me was that in our movements the voice of Muslim women was not that strong, or not that heard' (Brinda Karat interview, 26 December 2004). AIDWA activists were able to act quickly alongside the upsurge of Muslim women's groups who supported the Shah Bano ruling (Hasan 1989a: 45). AIDWA members also worked closely with the Platform in Defence of Muslim Women, in part because many of its members were also AIDWA members. In Karat's assessment, the Platform in Defence of Muslim Women was one critical, early site for AIDWA's development of their inter-sectoral organizing strategy (Brinda Karat interview, 26 December 2004). Out of this powerful experience, AIDWA members began to develop a sectoral analysis of Muslim women's issues and lives, with religion as a central axis of their understanding. AIDWA leaders also began to envision how to foster Muslim women's leadership within the organization. AIDWA's sectoral analysis emerged alongside its organizing strategies developed before and after independence. It projected its strongest critique against the communalizing state, rather than on the sites of inter or intra-community fundamentalism.

AIDWA launched the inaugural issue of its English-language magazine, *Women's Equality*, in October of 1987 amidst the tumultuous organizing of its secular campaigns. The magazine's editor was Susheela Gopalan who was also the president of AIDWA between 1981 and 2001. She also wrote the lead article, titled 'The Challenge Before Us', which framed the campaign against the Muslim Women's Bill as a struggle against a communalizing and disenfranchising state. Similarly, the article described a government that exploits rural women workers, 90 per cent of whom are agricultural workers. This government, which was 'fanning and fostering communal forces, the ideological forces of reaction . . . are a clear example of this attempt to break our unity and strength'.[3] Gopalan described these national campaigns as ones against a communalism fuelled by a state that sought to increase its own power by dividing the masses of people against each other. She provided a mandate for AIDWA as a women's organization. AIDWA can strengthen economic struggles by and for the workers who seek to shape better government policies. AIDWA, she argued, could accomplish this goal by bringing more women into active political participation through a range of struggles. These women, in Gopalan's words, will 'give more militancy, courage and strength to women to participate in the struggle for an equal position for themselves in society' (Gopalan 1987: 5). Economic and political independence go hand in hand since the state is controlled by the big capitalist, feudal and propertied classes. Women's joint struggles with allied organizations of students, labour, youth, agricultural and peasant organizations were the key to women's mass organization. Gopalan also stressed the importance of organizing the largest number of women to join political struggles for women's equality. 'It is political parties which take policy decisions in this country. If women fail to join political parties and make an impact within them . . . women's problems cannot receive proper consideration. This is the real challenge before the women's movement.' She exhorted, 'Let us take up the challenge' (ibid.: 6). The political import of Gopalan's vision was twofold. First, bring the largest numbers of women into active struggles around issues that most affect their lives. Second, foster the means for these masses of women politicized by the women's movement to challenge and transform the state itself.

Gopalan's emphasis on AIDWA's and the entire women's movement's need to struggle against the state hearkened back to the previous three decades of women's activism in India. Anti-imperialist women demanded a liberated and liberating state in the fight for national independence. These women, many of whom took up leadership positions in AIDWA during the 1980s and 1990s, continued their work towards the state's full and equitable representation of women. Muslim women's rights and all women's fight against communalism, as Susheela Gopalan articulated them, are struggles to build a better unity among women, and to heal misleading and harmful divisions of religion and caste. With a stronger unity, then, women in AIDWA can more effectively work to transform the state.

Inter-sectoral organizing and sectoral analysis did not directly contradict AIDWA's founding strategy and analysis, but added new sites for intervention. Inter-sectoral organizing did not solely fight against communal politics

[3] 'Editorial', Equality, October–December 1987: 2. The magazine's name was soon thereafter changed to *Women's Equality* and was registered under the latter title.

on the terrain of the state, though the state played a centrally important role. Subhashini Ali described the changing process of organizing against communalism at this time. 'This is something that we have become very conscious of since then, the way in which women's issues, for example, the issue of rape, is used for very narrow political gains, because either the religious communities involved are two different communities or the castes involved are two different castes' (Subhashini Ali interview, 22 July 2008). With the rise of caste and religious tension, a women's rights case of rape is used to stoke communal feeling and retribution. To remain ignorant about the wider context, AIDWA understood, undermined the very unity that common women's issues of violence were supposed to engender. Ali distinguished AIDWA's response to the Shah Bano and Muslim Women's Bill campaigns from other women's groups as one that recognized how communal all women's issues had become.

> AIDWA, out of all the organizations at that time which took up the Shah Bano issue and that were against the laws being changed for Muslim women, was the only organization which did not echo the demand for a common civil code. . . . We said we are not interested in equality between all religions being reduced to one thing, we are interested in gender equality within each religious group. (Ibid.)

AIDWA's answer to the communalized debate of women's rights around marriage, divorce and custody was a complicated one that sought women's equality in the law, but a differential equality that shifted the realm of struggle from the state to the community and religious boards that governed the personal laws.

Out of these insights, AIDWA developed a position it called 'Equal Rights, Equal Laws'. In December of 1995, AIDWA held a two-day conference that described its position. The conference resolution stated AIDWA's commitment to the 'cardinal principle of the Indian women's movement of equal rights for women of all communities in every sphere, economic, social, political, legal. It reiterates the need for common laws for all women based on equality' (AIDWA 1998: 1). AIDWA voiced its discomfort with the Uniform Civil Code as a code that flattened differences between communities through the pretence of abstract equality, even as it inflamed the divisions between them. What AIDWA sought in its position was a differential unity among women in favour of equal rights. This strategy sought to transform community-based personal laws from within, alongside its work to develop common laws around less communalized issues that affect women. Brinda Karat described the slogan's intent: 'The movement must fight for common laws, applicable to all sections of women, on individual issues' (Karat 1993: 5). The state was only one site for AIDWA's activism, a conclusion it learned from the experiences around Shah Bano and the Muslim Women's Bill.

Organizing around the Muslim Women's Bill had to be inter-sectoral, but also led by Muslim women. Further, the minority and majority communities themselves were sites to build progressive values and political changes. The state could support some progressive measures to dampen communalism, but laws on their own could become a weapon for communal political ends. The inter-sectoral organizing strategies targeted the state, and worked to challenge communal ideologies within and across religious groups.

The Hindu communalist forces sought to use the demand for a Uniform Civil Code as a means to universalize the Hindu code to all Indian citizens. AIDWA developed its own understanding with its 1995 'Equal Rights, Equal Laws' conference, and articulated its position in contradistinction to the Hindutva logic. 'This convention holds that the BJP demand for the uniform civil code is nothing but a garb for imposing a Hindu code on all the religious minorities in line with its commitment to establishing a Hindu *rashtra*' (AIDWA 1998: 3). In this context, AIDWA had to address not just the state and the ruling government as purveyors of communalist, divisive and discriminatory politics. It also addressed inter and intra-community rifts on issues of women's rights, rifts that had different religious trajectories and histories. For Shah Bano, as a Muslim woman in north India, and for Mary Roy, a Christian woman from the southern state of Kerala who instigated a spate of progressive changes in Christian personal laws, the campaigns for women's rights in marriage, to own property, to gain divorce and to keep custody of their children, among a range of rights, remained embedded in the different religious personal laws. Brinda Karat characterized AIDWA's strategy developed from 1985 and 1986 as two-fold: 'forming coalitions with those sections within the community who are committed to reform within their personal laws on the one hand, as well as simultaneously launching campaigns for equal laws in individual areas where women of all communities are equally affected, on the other' (ibid.: 9). In her article 'Uniformity vs. Equality, On the Uniform Civil Code', she detailed more specific areas for common action that mirrored AIDWA's 1998 national convention demands. She listed three areas in Indian law to rebuild 'the foundation, the expansion of the concept of social "uniformity", equal rights between men and women as reflected in the legal framework' (Karat 1998: 44). The 1998 Convention for AIDWA also listed three specific changes to this end: the compulsory registration of marriages; a law on joint property rights in marriage; and a comprehensive law against domestic violence that would cover the rights and security of all women in their families (AIDWA 1998: 7–8). These common grounds of registration, property rights and domestic violence law fostered new possibilities for secular laws that apply to all women. They also changed the legal impetus of 'women' in law as a means to engender equality between women and men, rather than invoke protection for women or safeguard gendered norms of tradition. As its slogan declared, 'Break the present uniform code of patriarchy through equal laws!' (ibid.: 9). AIDWA imagined a multi-faceted movement that sought a more equitable legal basis for women's rights in Indian secular laws, alongside the important but necessarily piecemeal campaigns to reform personal laws for Hindus, Christians, Parsis and Muslims.

The 1987 Deorala *Sati* Case of Roop Kanwar

The Indian women's movement took centre stage in national debates around communalism during the 1980s in three struggles that confronted the gendered aspects of religious and civic rights. The first was the Shah Bano case in 1985. The second, the Muslim Women's Bill in 1986. The third struggle did not centre on Muslim women's rights or Muslim fundamentalism, but on the spread of upper-caste practices among non-brahmin Hindus, and the rise of Hindu fundamentalism in rural and urban areas. The 1987 *sati* case in Deorala, Rajasthan, involved an upper-caste, Hindu woman, Roop Kanwar, who was from a wealthy Rajput family, as well her husband's family, local officials and politicians (Sangari and Vaid 1999). The women's movement joined the debate over the nationally publicized case of *sati* worship, or widow immolation. Roop Kanwar was a young, married woman who had been recently widowed. She burned to death on her husband's funeral pyre. Her death was witnessed and widely celebrated by thousands of Hindu devotees as a manifestation of purity and as a victory for traditionalist Hinduism. When the celebration of her *sati* was cut short by the state as an illegal practice, they mobilized their opposition to ending *sati* as a defining Rajput community practice. The women's movement's campaign against Roop Kanwar's immolation on her husband's funeral pyre, and its celebration by Hindu communal forces, revealed another deeply entrenched weakness in it between urban, upper-caste and middle-class women (scornfully designated '*baal kati*' or 'short-haired' by detractors), and rural women. Rural women of all religions, classes and castes held a numerical majority, but lacked the education and access to public participation of urban feminist activists. Rural women lived in the context where feudal relationships between women and men, upper castes and oppressed castes, Muslims and Hindus, landowners and the landless met the market forces of capitalism that profited from these same divides in the agricultural economy.

Organizing against widow immolation, like organizing against religious fundamentalism in Shah Bano's case and the case of the Muslim Women's Bill, raised similar issues, since they were all civic as well as religious and ideological campaigns. As civic campaigns, many women's groups worked for legal remedies like the 1987 Anti-Sati Act that banned *sati* and its glorification. In ideological campaigns about religious values, the women's movement sought to shore up women's rights to equality and their lives within a secular value system. The Indian women's movement successfully lobbied for a law against *sati*, though the terms of the Act made the widow's marital family abettors to her crime of immolation. The law also gave precedence to the most conservative interpretation of religious custom, in this case to Hinduism, which angered many activists, including members of AIDWA, who sought to redraft the bill before it was passed ('AIDWA Memorandum to the President of India on Sati Bill', 1988: 21). As an AIDWA editorial explained: 'The issue is not whether any religion sanctions *sati* or not, but whether society will tolerate the murder, torture and degradation of widows in the name of religion' ('Anti-Sati Bill and the Women's Movement', 1988: 18). Activists in the women's movement also successfully demanded that the chief minister of Rajasthan condemn Roop Kanwar's murder, though their demand for the state governor's resignation was not won.

At local levels government officials did nothing to end the immolation, nor stem the tide of supporters. Ideological campaigns tried to shape social consciousness and value systems in favour of a secularism that supported women's rights and equality. Indian women's groups struggled to maintain their agility against historically and ideologically embedded foes who wielded the powerful language of tradition – specifically that of a majority religion, Hinduism – to bolster their cause. The opening editorial of *Equality*, written months after the Deorala campaign, demanded just this kind of ideological and political assessment from the women's movement. Women's oppressive relations, it claimed, are rooted in 'the contradictions within Indian society. Secondly, the movement has to gear itself to meet the ideological challenge of the forces of reaction . . . the women's movement has to necessarily define its own political positions vis-à-vis the contradictions and the social classes representing these' ('The Deorala Tragedy', 1987: 8). Contradictions between feudal landed relationships and capitalist agricultural economies, the editorial highlighted, also shape the context for women's rights. Atrocities against women, like *sati*, are not timeless, traditional or inevitable, but the women's movement had to develop clarity about the range of issues at stake.

AIDWA was better prepared for organizing in rural areas than many groups in the women's movement, since it had a long commitment to organizing outside urban centres, among poor and working-class women. Yet AIDWA was not satisfied with its attention to rural women's issues. The 1990 AIDWA Conference report published in *Equality* was deeply self-critical. 'Our failure to focus on the problems of rural women was pinpointed. . . . It is necessary that programmes aimed at social transformation of the agrarian sector be given priority on the agenda. Along with this it is necessary to fight oppression and its ideological impact on the lives of the mass of rural landless women' ('Third AIDWA Conference: A Report', 1990: 3–4). By 1990, rural women became another central sector of AIDWA's analysis. By the time of its 1994 convention, AIDWA began to share its conclusions.

AIDWA linked its organizing against the rise of Hindu fundamentalism and against communal divisions to India's gradual shift to a global market economy. By 1994, AIDWA had directly linked the lessons of the Roop Kanwar agitations in 1987 to their analysis of neoliberal and religious fundamentalism. AIDWA's convention paper, 'Women and Regressive Ideology', stated:

> Roop Kanwar's 'sati' (or more appropriately, murder) and the uproar in favour of asserting one's religious beliefs and customs in the last decade is a pointer to the above. Many studies of the Deorala incident have convincingly shown that it had more to do with the business and political interests of a caste community. The commercialization of the event showed that it was 'big business'. As several studies have pointed out, sati became a way of regaining lost political and economic clout for the Rajput community. Religious belief had little to do with it. Sati was a custom created to avoid having to give the widow a share in property. (AIDWA 1998: 32)

Local economies of wealth and of status, according to AIDWA's position paper, played a central role in Roop Kanwar's immolation. Here, AIDWA represented its organizational lessons in about religious conservatism or fundamentalism, economic power, ethnic identity and caste fealty that learned from the Deorala national campaign against *sati*. As a tangled web of community, family and self interest, the murder of Roop Kanwar demanded a much more nuanced understanding of rural politics than simple models of anti-woman violence could effectively counter. Feudal and capitalist economies produced the atrocity of *sati*; the women's movement had to consider these forces carefully in its own responses to the violence.

Jayati Ghosh wrote with disarming clarity about the rise of bigoted, community-based identities in the globalized world, whether communal identities based on region, caste, religion, race, language or ethnic group. She noted that this rise of religious and other violent identity formations should not inspire so fulsome a surprise from pundits. 'For it is possible to identify links between them, not least because the actual operations of integrated and "globalized" markets do not necessarily unify and homogenize the world (except in the most trivial sense) but instead tend to aggravate and perpetuate inequalities' (Ghosh 1999: 108). Her point was illuminatingly simple: the economic polarization of neoliberalism is mirrored in social relationships around the world. Since neoliberal economic disparities of wealth and poverty are lived in people's localities and regions, these cleavages of insecurity occur along established borders of difference in an area, for example, by caste and religion. Importantly, these cleavages simultaneously occur along older fissures of systemic inequality like gender and class, even as they reinforce and reconfigure those hierarchies. Neoliberalism as a universal ideology of free market fundamentalism spawns area-specific cultures of inequity and distrust that are both old and new again.

Liberalizing the Economy, Communalizing the Polity

Out of the Roop Kanwar case against *sati*, yet with less national attention from the larger women's movement, AIDWA took up rural women's issues as a critical sector for organizing. With the effects of agricultural mechanization, agricultural work-days for women shrank. As land reform goals receded from the horizon of public policy, women depended even more on highly exploitative and underpaid waged agricultural work. As men migrated out of their rural localities looking for work in cities and more prosperous agricultural regions, women workers became the backbone of the rural, agricultural economy. Rural and urban poor women's work in the informal economy also emerged during this period, as women lost paid agricultural work and the numbers of small landholdings decreased in the countryside. Women's informal work dominated poor women's work lives, and included home-based work, livestock tending, day labour and individual selling of goods.

In 1989 and 1990, casteist tensions took national stage over the central government's decision to enact one of the recommendations of the Mandal Commission's report, to reserve a percentage of government job openings for designated backward class or lower-caste applicants. Indu Agnihotri described strategies within AIDWA in the wake of these protests. 'We had several discussions around the Mandal agitation, around issues of caste within the organization, in our state committees, with our activists in the resettlement colonies where our membership is from those castes who would be directly affected' (Indu Agnihotri interview, 29 July 2008). The widespread protests of dominant-caste students across India against the Mandal Commission ebbed by the early 1990s, but remained simmering below the surface of national news coverage in the rising number of local caste atrocities committed against Dalits (Viswanathan 2005; Frankel and Rao, eds. 1989; Srinivas, ed. 1996; Mendelsohn and Vicziany, eds. 1998).

By the mid-1990s, the effects of the Mandal Commission policies enacted in 1989 began to cement gains by non-Dalit, exploited castes, designated by the government as Other Backward Classes (OBCs). As rural landowning and village structures reacted to these changes in power, caste atrocities against Dalits rose in intensity and number. In this climate of brutal suppression of Dalit and Adivasi demands for livelihood and dignity rights, AIDWA began to seriously pursue its analysis and organizing among Dalit women. AIDWA's focused assessment of Dalit women's issues was a process that gained traction in Tamil Nadu, a state particularly racked by extreme violence against entire Dalit hamlets and neighbourhoods in the 1990s. Local activists gathered research about untouchability practices across the state, noting regional specificities and state-wide commonalities of caste oppression and anti-Dalit violence. They held regional conventions of Dalit and non-Dalit AIDWA members to circulate their report findings and to listen to the testimony of Dalit women about how untouchability practices assailed them in daily and life-threatening ways.

The Rise of Two Fundamentalisms: Religion and the Market

The virulence of three forces – communalism, casteism and liberalization – powerfully converged between 1991 and 1994, with lasting effects on the Indian women's movement and on AIDWA. The conditions for the ascendance of religious *and* market fundamentalisms began in the 1980s under the governance of Indira Gandhi and, after her assassination, of her son, Rajiv Gandhi. The New Economic Policies (NEPs) began under Rajiv Gandhi's Congress(I) government with limited loans from the International Monetary Fund (IMF), amounting to $220 million. Indira Gandhi softened her position towards the IMF in the early 1980s. Later, Rajiv Gandhi took some loans and enacted minor changes in the Indian economy to gain favour with the IMF. After Rajiv Gandhi's death, by 1991, the Indian government threw its support behind economic liberalization and the IMF/World Bank loan conditionalities linked to the first economic stabilization loan to cover the interest and capital payments on the Rajiv Gandhi government's debt. Utsa Patnaik published an article in *Women's Equality* in 1991 that predicted the much larger loans to come (Patnaik 1991). She described the devaluation of the rupee by 25 per cent in early 1991 in the context of the meeting scheduled in July of 1991 between the Indian government and the IMF. The government's support for IMF loan conditionalities grew into an enthusiastic embrace of the more wide-reaching structural adjustment policies (SAPs) by subsequent governments in the 1990s and into the 2000s.

In July of 1991, Finance Minister Manmohan Singh signed a loan agreement with the IMF after discussions in Bangkok, Thailand. On 4 July 1991, Prime Minister Narasimha Rao declared on national television that 'complex maladies call for drastic remedies', describing India's new agreement with the IMF. The crisis was indeed grave: the foreign exchange reserves fell to the equivalent of two weeks' imports (Ghosh 1998: 108). To tide this balance of payments shortfall, the government air-lifted 47 tons of gold to London as security against a short-term hard currency loan of $400 million from the

Bank of London. India turned to the IMF. In November 1991, Manmohan Singh said that 'negotiations with the IMF were difficult because the world has changed. India is not immune. India has to survive and flourish in a world we cannot change in our own image. Economic relations are power relations. We are not living in a morality play' (quoted in Seabrook 1992: 10). Faced with certain 'realities', the Indian government had little to bargain with. The negotiations enrolled India into the club of nations who took loans under the Structural Adjustment Facility.

In 1992, the United Nations characterized this facility thus:

> The IMF has exerted a strong influence over developing countries by setting stiff conditions on the loans it offers. This conditionality has generally been monetarist and deflationary, obliging governments to reduce their demand for imports by curtailing overall demand – cutting back on both private and public spending. These cutbacks have often reduced consumption, investment and employment – and stifled economic growth. (UNDP 1992: 75)

The IMF's cure for a low growth rate, in the description of the United Nations Development Program (UNDP), resulted in low growth.

Political scientist Mustapha Pasha locates this year as the end of the period he calls the first phase of liberalization in India (1980–91), and the beginning of the second 'most dramatic' phase of liberalization (1991–95) with privatization of public services, reduction of import substitutions and devaluation of the rupee (Pasha 2000). Primary education funds were slashed 15 per cent, and funds for the social safety net dropped by as much as 25 per cent in some areas (Vibhuti Patel 1994). The newly elected Narasimha Rao government's NEP began its assault on the public distribution system (PDS) that distributed and set the prices for basic food supplies such as rice, wheat and pulses at subsidized rates. Forced up to market price levels, the cost of these staple foods rose 85 per cent in a space of four years (Bidwai 1995). The effects on rural and urban poor women and men during this first phase of Indian neoliberalism were immediate and devastating.

After Rajiv Gandhi's assassination, communalist rhetoric also intensified. In mid-1991, leaders from the BJP and the *Sangh Parivar* launched their underwhelming bid to national relevance, the *rath yatra*. The *rath* or carriage (complete with Hindu deities and speaker system) rolled through rural and urban India to meet small, disorganized knots of people, attempting to stir up support for their Ram Janmabhoomi campaign that had gained its last victory in 1986, with the opening of the gates of the Babri Masjid to Hindu worshippers. This time the *Sangh Parivar* sought to tear down the Babri Masjid and build a Ram temple on the land. Throughout 1991 the Hindu fundamentalist campaign met only sporadic success, even in the vaunted Hindu-belt of north India. Organizers had difficulty bringing out significant numbers of people to welcome the *rath*. By 1992, however, the campaign had gained traction among a wider swath of people – men and women; rural and urban; elite, middle class and poor. On 6 December 1992, mobs led by the VHP and RSS attacked the Babri Masjid and dismantled the ancient mosque stone by stone over the course of six hours, with the police force sometimes joining the siege. Riots against Muslims spread from Ayodhya across the country to cities like Mumbai, Ahmedabad, New Delhi and Surat. Property owned by Muslims was destroyed. Muslims were forced to flee from their homes, businesses and land. Muslim women were targeted for rape and sexualized humiliation, and thousands of people, mostly Muslims, were killed in a matter of days. Secularism itself, the core ideology of a tolerant, independent India, an ideology that hailed India's multi-lingual, multi-ethnic and religious diversity of faiths as the nation's strength, came under siege (Sangari 2002).

The *rath yatra*, as a means to stir up support for the Ram Janmabhoomi campaign, was a carefully planned political move by Hindu fundamentalist organizations and the BJP. Communal politics attempts to establish a civic, public sphere irreducible from religious control. But communalism, as Tanika Sarkar persuasively argues, cannot be reduced to the cynical mobilization of religion for political gains, since it also configures a modern religious movement. 'Communalism', Sarkar wrote, 'is part of a process in which modern political concepts draw many of their valences from the realm of sacred meaning' (Tanika Sarkar 2001: 272). In this sense, communalism draws its strength from traditional binaries of public/private spheres, even as these sites gain new political resonance. The public and private roles of women *within* the Hindu fundamentalist movement could not be discounted by the women's movement as nominal or simply coerced. Women actively supported even the most violent tendencies of the Hindutva movement. Women increasingly took on visible leadership roles in the *Sangh Parivar*, though its women's groups primarily supported Hindutva edicts rather than shaped the *Sangh*'s positions (Bacchetta 1996; Basu, Datta, Sarkar, Sarkar and Sen 1993). Women who were not formally part of communalist groups gave tacit or open support to violent actions against religious minorities (Atreyee Sen 2007). More insidiously, women from the majority religion interpolated their Hindu faith as a more central component of their self-conception, even as bigoted Hindutva ideologies absorbed competing definitions of what 'Hindu' meant in a secular nation. Increasingly during the 1990s, to be Hindu meant to be not-Muslim, and in some regions, not-Christian (Mathur 2008). The effects of seemingly subtle ideological changes in the national fabric had important resonance as the women's movement came to grips with the changing political terrain of the late 1980s and early 1990s (Agnes 1995).

Throughout the 1980s, the women's movement debated the quality of women's political unity. Characterized as the difference between the autonomous women's movement and the left women's movement, groups argued whether unity of the women's movement resided in women's shared biology and experiences of patriarchal oppression, or whether it was a goal to achieve through political struggle that attended to class and caste discrimination as well as gender oppression (Shah and Gandhi 1991). The 'autonomous' wing of the women's movement, Flavia Agnes argued, mobilized upper-caste Hindu iconography of Durga and Kạli to hail this unified group of 'women'. Their strategy backfired when Hindutva forces coopted their symbolism with greater effectiveness to mobilize women in favour of an anti-Muslim platform (Agnes 1995: 141). Agnes illustrated how the Shiv Sena in Bombay was able to turn feminist slogans against patriarchy into communal slogans against Muslims, such as the women's movement slogan: *'Hum Bharat ke Nari Hain; Phool Nahin Chingari Hain'* ('We are the women of India, not delicate flowers but smouldering embers') (ibid.). She described autonomous women's groups' creation of feminist icons that relied on majority religious iconography. 'The intention of using the symbols from the dominant religious culture was not to propagate Hindu ideology', Agnes wrote. 'But since the movement did not have "secularism" as one of its prime objectives, no conscious efforts were make to evolve alternate symbols' (ibid.: 139). Without any careful analysis of those identities and social forces of religion and caste, in this case, the autonomous women's movement drew on contradictory symbols to build an undifferentiated women's unity.

To ignore rising communalism and casteism, argued an emerging consensus in the women's movement, 'would only mean to be either swept aside or coopted by it. From the position of seeing women as sufferers and victims of caste/community violence we began to see that this violence structured the definition not only of women but of community, caste and nation' (Kannabiran and Kannabiran 1995: 121). This more dialectical view of violence moved away from addressing rape and domestic violence outside of their context of casteism and communalism. Also, communal and casteist violence became a women's issue for many women's groups after the Babri Masjid–Ayodhya riots. Agnes argued that women's issues and minority issues became linked after Ayodhya. In addition, women's groups showed greater vigilance that the general political category of 'women' did not implicitly reflect majority religion, dominant caste, or middle-class women's interests and perspectives.

As a part of the left women's movement, AIDWA adamantly refused to rest its politics on any naturally unified category 'woman', in its conceptions of allies, issues, goals and political campaigns. For example, AIDWA supported coalitional work with progressive allies like trade unions that included men, fought for issues of international peace and framed campaigns against the high cost of basic necessities as important issues for the women's movement to address (Brinda Karat interview, 24 December 2004). Autonomous and leftist women's groups agreed after the Babri Masjid–Ayodhya riots that women's unity had not been strong enough to withstand the Hindutva assault on secularism and its stoking of women's majoritarian communal identities (Agnes 1995: 151). Unity among women, for AIDWA, even in a communalist social fabric was not impossible. Unity, in part, meant shielding women's rights from internecine battles between casteist and communalist political forces, so that coalitions of women can unite to support Muslim women's rights. Unity also included an understanding of what women's groups can work to gain from the state in the form of progressive laws and policies, and what women's groups must build ideologically among minority and majority communities to support women's rights and equality.

Finally, in AIDWA's assessment, after the devastating anti-Muslim riots in 1992 and 1993, unity could not assume homogeneity or the erasure of lived differences even among women who hold common goals or common membership in an organization. Unity was as hard-won within AIDWA, by and for its members, as it was outside AIDWA, in coalitions among allies or in the vibrant, multiplicitous communities where its members live and organize. While women's groups, including AIDWA, addressed the rising conflicts among women, they also celebrated acts of women's solidarity in the face of those divisions. Communalism had not achieved a complete victory over secularism. Activists attested to numerous stories of Hindu women sheltering Muslim neighbours and strangers in their homes during the worst of the rioting in Mumbai, Ayodhya, Surat and New Delhi, in the face of potentially violent consequences to themselves.[4]

After Ayodhya, AIDWA maintained its emphasis on class-specific issues, such as the rising costs of basic commodities, to build a bridge between middle-class and working-class women's interests. It also continued to frame its political strategies through its common target for critique, the negligent and discriminatory state. What shifted within AIDWA was the recognition that these common sites for building women's unity, of cross-class survival issues and state-based demands, could not counter the fragmenting forces of casteism and religious communalism alone. AIDWA did not concede the importance of building coalitions with women and men in allied left movements. If anything, their reliance on these allies intensified during the 1990s. As AIDWA activists became more directly involved in anti-casteist struggles against Dalit oppression, anti-communal struggles, and fights for women's rights to land, equal wages and sexual autonomy, the danger their activists faced rose precipitously. These alliances among activists on the left became

[4] Both of AIDWA's investigative reports – in 1992 (Surat, Bhopal and Ahmedabad) and 2002 (Gujarat) – give ample evidence of women providing shelter or disguises of *saris* to protect Muslim women. However, by 2002, the report also records Hindu women's fear to admit to their actions to protect Muslims.

increasingly vital to the well-being of AIDWA activists, members and supporters in townships and rural areas.

In the mid-1980s, AIDWA's strategy to confront communalism kept a close eye on the tactics of the communal movement, worked alongside progressive Muslim women and men, and organized activist Hindu women to confront majority Hindu fundamentalism. But even with these contentious methods, AIDWA could not dam the surge of communal tension. The force of the Ram Janmabhoomi campaigns in the 1990s produced organized pogroms against Muslims across the country and fuelled violence against other religious minority communities as well. These campaigns had a deeply embedded gendered ideology of sexualized violence against women and girls. The communal riots from December 1992 in Ayodhya, Surat and Ahmedabad continued into January 1993 in Mumbai. Communal pogroms against minority religious communities continued in the 1990s in more regionalized and sporadic forms. They intensified in 2002 to the state-orchestrated murders of Muslims across Gujarat. AIDWA's methods allowed for some constructive campaigns to build a stronger secularism and to support women's rights in areas where their membership was strong. But the politics of countering communalism, by necessity, was often a politics of reaction to atrocities committed in its name. AIDWA's early use of activist research, as in the Deorala *sati* case, became a powerful tool in the fight against communal brutality. During the 1990s and 2000s, AIDWA launched fact-finding missions even before the communal violence had abated. It worked in coalition with other women's movement groups to interview affected women, to check reported facts on the causes for the riots and the losses inflicted, to detail crimes committed and to demand justice.

Communal Riots and Targeted Violence against Minority Women

AIDWA members were part of the Joint Women's Delegation to Bhopal, Ahmedabad and Surat. They met with almost 500 women who were directly hit by the violence between 6 and 9 December 1992. The group of seven women visited two months after the attacks, between 16–19 February 1993, and collected testimonies from Muslim and Hindu women.[5] They wrote up their report with extensive recommendations for progressive social movements, the women's movement, and for the local, state and national government. The stories they reported tell of violence that crossed religious communities. But Muslim women and girls, by far, were the most likely targets of sexualized humiliation and violence such as stripping, sexual assault and

[5] The other women's groups represented were National Federation of Indian Women (NFIW), Centre for Women's Development Studies (CWDS), and Mahila Dakshata Samiti (MDS).

rape. They detailed the complicity of 'criminals in police uniform' in the murders and rapes, emphasizing the role of the media in spreading misinformation and fuelling the communal hatred. The report had a stated goal alongside disseminating direct testimony from women survivors, and sometimes perpetrators, of the violence. It also sought 'to assess the effectiveness of official measures for their relief and rehabilitation, especially of families which are now headed by women' ('Report of the Women's Delegation to Bhopal, Ahmedabad and Surat', 1993: 1).[6] It detailed the gendered character of sexualized violence that targeted Muslim women and girls, but also emphasized the importance of listening to women's narrations of events and of the gendered after-effects of the pogroms. The report's recommendations for the government stressed all of these aspects, and included attempts to destabilize the patriarchal, traditional local leadership bodies through the inclusion of women members from both religious communities.

They developed four specific areas for recommendation in the report. First, they advised collecting information about the violence more carefully with attention to women, including through judicial enquiries and independent research organizations with assistance from the state bureaucracy. Second, they recommended the formation of peace committees based in the neighbourhoods involved, both Muslim and Hindu. These committees, the report stressed, should include substantial numbers of women. Third, they demanded the state produce 'an effective system of communication' (ibid.: 11) that directly informs women-headed households of their rights, state enquiries and restitution, since many Muslim women whose husbands were murdered in the violence had no information about government action against the crimes. The fourth recommendation was related, since they repeatedly found in their discussions that women's testimonies were silenced or refuted by men from their communities. They argued that riot-affected women needed separate meetings with officials, with the active participation of local women's organizations and other credible secular groups. The report's recommendations, given the deeply disturbing stories they quoted in detail, were materially connected to the circumstances of the three cities the group visited.

The report, and the substantial information about the riots that the delegation collected, gave power to AIDWA's campaign to demand state accountability for the rise and growth of communalism after Ayodhya. AIDWA's position after the demolition of the Babri Masjid and the month-long violence in Mumbai stressed the monumental shift communalism played in the Indian polity. AIDWA members lived on the frontline of anti-communal resistance: in New Delhi they were a central organizing force behind the

[6] From a personal copy of the report. It was also published in AIDWA's magazine *Women's Equality*, 5, no. 1 (January–June 1993): 10–22.

march on 7 December 1992, only one day after the Babri Masjid demolition and during ongoing communal violence. They joined relief work and actively protected women targeted by mobs in Mumbai and New Delhi. As a part of the Rashtriya Ekta Samiti coalition, AIDWA did survey work of the violence, facilitated fair distribution of government relief goods and helped victims of the violence to fill in compensation forms. In Mumbai, the second wave of riots in January 1993 brought the public distribution system (PDS) to a standstill. AIDWA members distributed PDS food supplies and 'helped to normalize the situation and draw people out of their houses' (Gill 1993: 25). AIDWA was one part of a much larger secular movement that sought to provide immediate aid, longer-term relief and justice against the perpetrators of the violence, and that sought to build a stronger secular polity. Its actions after the riots in December 1992 and January 1993 mirrored its work in New Delhi after the anti-Sikh riots in 1984.

AIDWA's Central Executive Committee (CEC) released a statement in March 1993 that outlined its position in stark terms. 'Fighting the communal danger is now not just another issue – it has to be seen as the crucial question in the struggle for women's rights which has to be linked to every other struggle' (AIDWA CEC 1993: 2). The CEC's analysis included women's secular consciousness as critical to AIDWA's fight to counter Hindutva ideology. 'The strongest and most widespread ideological and political battle is required to ensure that women not only reject the backward platform of so-called Hindutva, but come forward as committed votaries of secularism' (ibid.: 4) During the decades after the Muslim Women's Act, AIDWA wove its commitment to building secular values into its campaigns for women's rights and equality.

AIDWA's fight against fundamentalism, particularly Hindu fundamentalism, did not wane even in the face of the BJP/Hindutva combine's increasing consolidation of power. In the 1998 elections to the central government the BJP won a majority of the seats, to form a coalition government called the National Democratic Alliance (NDA) that ruled between 1998 and 2004. Also in 1998, the BJP won state control in Gujarat. Under Narendra Modi's leadership in Gujarat, the BJP set the stage for anti-Muslim carnage organized by the Hindutva *Parivar*, that murdered over 2,000 Muslims. Most of the murders occurred between 28 February and 3 March 2002, but the violence continued sporadically across the state, with particular ferocity in rural areas, for the following three months. Muslim women and girls were targeted routinely for sexualized violence against their bodies; afterwards they were burned by mobs of attackers. Only a week after the horrific violence, between 10 and 13 March, AIDWA and the CPM sent a delegation to Gujarat to report on the BJP–VHP–RSS–Bajrang Dal-led atrocities. The violence, their report concluded, could not be explained as a spontaneous reaction to the torching of a railway car filled with Bajrang Dal *kar sevaks* (religious volunteers) and unrelated passengers in Godhra. 'In Gujarat,' the report countered, 'the events are the bloody harvest of years of the systematic spread of communal poison and hatred against minority communities, both Muslim and Christian, by the constituents of the *Sangh Parivar* in the implementation of the political slogan of Hindu *rashtra*' (CPI[M]–AIDWA 2003: 2). Tanika Sarkar, a member of the Concerned Citizens Tribunal, spent two weeks in May 2002 collecting extensive interviews with violence survivors. She emphasized the absolute centrality of the state and central governments in the most political assertion of Hindu fundamentalist violence to date, as the BJP combine captured every level of the government from political offices to schools to hospitals (Tanika Sarkar 2002).

The genocide of Muslims in Gujarat, as the CPI(M)–AIDWA report emphasized, targeted women and girls with conscious savagery. Women and girls were gang-raped, then sexually tortured and beaten for hours before their bodies were burned, often while they were still alive. Foetuses were cut from women's bodies and burned before the mothers' eyes. Sarkar summarized the 'pattern of cruelty' against women and children in Gujarat, linking it to the violence against women during the attacks investigated by AIDWA in 1992 in Surat, Ahmedabad and Bhopal. 'One, the woman's body was a site of almost inexhaustible violence, with infinitely plural and innovative forms of torture. Second, their sexual and reproductive organs were attacked with special savagery. Third, their children, born and unborn, shared the attacks and were killed before their eyes' (ibid.). Sarkar detailed the meanings of gendered torture, a sadism that she argued sets the violence in Gujarat apart from previous Hindu fundamentalist terror.

Rape of women signifies dishonour of the entire Muslim community and through sexualized violence symbolically takes Muslim men's virility. But Sarkar's analysis is more specific:

> to physically destroy the vagina and the womb, and, thereby, to symbolically destroy the sources of pleasure, reproduction and nurture for Muslim men, and for Muslim children. Then, by beatings, to punish the fertile female body. Then, by physically destroying the children, to signify an end to Muslim growth. Then, by cutting up the foetus and burning it, to achieve a symbolic destruction of future generations, of the very future of Muslims themselves. (Ibid.)

The brutality of these reports defied rational strategies to address the wrongs committed. Fact-finding groups sought to hold Narendra Modi's government in Gujarat accountable for its crimes. They sought to hold the BJP-led NDA coalition government accountable for its willingness to accept Modi's protestations of innocence. They sought to renew the state's duty to protect all Indian citizens and redress the fury it unleashed against Muslims.

AIDWA's Inter-Sectoral Organizing Strategy

Brinda Karat opened AIDWA's Fourth National Conference in 1994 with a speech that assessed what the organization had learned over the previous thirteen years. She provided an example of how socio-economic class position cut across discrete women's issues differentially, even those within one sphere.

> On some issues, like communalism, it would be possible in this category [women as citizens] to cut across class, while on other issues like access to civic facilities or education and health, class differentiation would mean that such issues would be of real concern to only poorer sections of women. In other words, on an issue such as communalism, both the daughter of a mill worker and the daughter of a senior government servant may be directly and equally concerned, but on the issue of the rights of slum dwellers, the two could be in opposition. (Karat, 'On the Occasion of AIDWA's Fourth National Conference', n.d.)

As general secretary, Karat articulated for AIDWA's membership the methods they were all actively producing in their regional and local campaigns. Inter-sectoral organizing directly confronted those potential sites of opposition to weave them into the fabric of the organizing methods: who organized whom, how activists embodied their ideals, who they targeted and the larger aims they sought. The answers to these questions, as Karat's example above suggests, were deeply contextual to the contours of the struggle, the women involved and the goals they developed. Karat's description of AIDWA's inter-sectoral organizing had wider implications that she linked to AIDWA's allies on the organized left: the Kisan Sabha or peasants' organization, the Agricultural Workers Union, the Centre of Indian Trade Unions (CITU), the Democratic Youth Federation of India movement, the Student Federation of India movement and the CPM.

Karat positioned AIDWA as a 'left-oriented women's organization', one that does not simply seek to solve women's social oppression through the future horizon of socialism, but also actively struggles against this oppression every day. She invoked simplistic dismissals from the organized left that women's issues of dowry, rape and domestic violence were 'diversions' from the most important battle of class struggle. Instead, Karat answered AIDWA's left critics directly:

> Just as the question of upper-caste oppression cannot be brushed aside when it is practised by upper-caste workers in any particular instance, in the name of workers' unity, so also the specific demands and problems of workers or peasant women in relation to male family members cannot be ignored or considered diversionary or as breaking class unity. On the contrary, mobilizing both men

> and women of the oppressed sections against such practices . . . in their own lives becomes an important part of the struggle for an alternative society. (Ibid.)

Karat's speech repeated arguments that have important ramifications for AIDWA as a mass-based, leftist women's organization. Within AIDWA, inter-sectoral organizing directly shaped the methods it developed throughout the 1990s to mobilize women against the rapidly growing forces of communalism and free market globalization. Among AIDWA's allies on the left, inter-sectoral organizing could potentially transform organizing against women's oppression and for women's equality within all the mass-based groups as well as cadre-based political parties like the CPM. Inter-sectoral organizing, as Karat's 1994 speech suggested, could make the struggle against anti-women violence, among other distinctly gendered issues, an integral part of the wider class struggle.

Karat stressed that AIDWA's shift in its understanding of globalization, alongside communalism and religious fundamentalism, changed its campaigns profoundly, as well as its analysis. Perhaps more importantly, AIDWA's shift to inter-sectoral organizing sharpened the independence of the women's organization from its allies among left-oriented organizations. She said:

> we found that just a flat critique in a generalized way of how globalization impacts on women was doing injustice by ignoring the far more nuanced experiences related to the different levels of cruelty and savagery that these processes visited upon women; and we started this basically with our work among rural women . . . [before] we just accepted the given critiques that were relevant in the literacy of peasant organizations or workers' organization. We went along with that, mainly. (Ibid.)

AIDWA, through inter-sectoral organizing, began to more sharply represent the voices of the vast numbers of its members from rural areas of the country. Karat described AIDWA as a left-allied organization that began to gender its campaigns against globalization in ways pushed by the experiences of AIDWA's local units.

The campaigns that emerged over the following two decades allowed AIDWA to continue to raise consciousness among Muslim women and among Indian women as a whole. For example, among Muslim women, AIDWA mobilized around signature campaigns on four issues: polygamy; immediate, unilateral divorce (saying '*talaq*' three times); equal custody and guardianship rights for both parents; and equal rights to property and inheritance held in a marriage (Subhashini Ali interview, 22 July 2008). These campaigns have also built much stronger representation of Muslim women leaders within AIDWA. Subhashini Ali describes leadership development as a place where AIDWA must actively constitute its own ideals.

> In the beginning there was resistance that, 'Oh, are we becoming casteist? Are we having a kind of tokenism that we bring people up and promote them?' But now there is an understanding that it's not a question of promoting, but a question of developing leaders and activists. It is the responsibility of the organization to equip them so that they can develop their innate strengths, without having the advantages that middle-class, educated women have. (Ibid.)

The development of leaders from within the sectoral campaigns on Muslim women's issues has its parallel process among agricultural women and Dalit women. U. Vasuki, the general secretary of AIDWA's Tamil Nadu unit, credits Brinda Karat with this organizational change in AIDWA:

> That is another contribution by Brinda [Karat]. She always says that we must see the leadership's social composition. It's not that like bourgeois parties we give representation. It's not like that. But in a particular district [where] Dalit population is the highest, that should be reflected in your leadership: membership *and* leadership. (U. Vasuki interview, 14 March 2006; emphasis hers)

For AIDWA, the independence it sought within the women's movement and the left movement reflected this shift in its own membership and leadership. Its own strength and the strength it could offer to their alliances depended on nothing less.

By 2004, AIDWA's strategy had clear contours and careful planning with regional focus on specific issues, such as casteism (particularly in rural areas) in Tamil Nadu and Haryana, informal labour and cash-cropping in Andhra Pradesh, and religious fundamentalism in Maharashtra, Gujarat, Orissa and New Delhi. The inter-sectoral strategy developed from the organizational weaknesses that AIDWA assessed in the crucible of a time of trouble in the late 1980s and early 1990s. The strategy threaded across its most ambitious, creative and generative organizing. Inter-sectoral organizing, by many AIDWA activists' accounts, began with the organizing in the 1980s around rural women's issues and Muslim women's issues, and then Dalit women's issues (Brinda Karat interview, 26 December 2004). Karat characterized the most significant aspect of this period as follows: 'We turned our faces to the village, turned our organization to the village, and tried to organize from the village level' (ibid.).

This process began in the late 1980s with conferences for agricultural women workers to discuss their issues within the organizational framework of AIDWA, not as part of the Kisan Sabha or the Agricultural Workers Union (ibid.). Paradoxically, given its roots in agricultural women's working lives, AIDWA's inter-sectoral organizing work left women's struggles as workers in the informal economy richly studied, but only sporadically organized into local and national campaigns. The reasons for this lacuna are all the more surprising because AIDWA had a strong ideological commitment to addressing women's work issues in the informal economy. It did not have the same strength of organizing in what U. Vasuki called 'class issues', or that third aspect of women's lives: women as workers. In 2006, Vasuki talked about AIDWA's own understanding of its role in organizing around working women's issues: 'Over a period we were able to shape the thinking among AIDWA women that it is our work to take up class issues also. But then other fraternal organizations haven't really done that seriously enough, so the thinking of other fraternal organizations needs to undergo a change' (U. Vasuki interview, 14 March 2006). In the national context, AIDWA leaders like Vasuki suggest that a shift within AIDWA's allied organizations is a necessary, and constantly evolving, first step towards organizing women as workers.

AIDWA's state leaders do not suggest that the problem of organizing unorganized, informal work based in homes or in fields can be simplified to recalcitrance by its allied trade union, the Agricultural Workers Union, or peasant organizations to organize these women workers. As AIDWA's own hard-won research reveals, these women's lives in the informal economy militate against their organization *as workers*. Subhashini Ali characterized this problem using the metaphor of identity for the large number of Muslim women in home-based labour and Dalit women in agricultural work: 'More and more, because of communalization and so on, the primary identity may be of being a Muslim woman. Similarly, because of strengthening of identity politics, maybe a Dalit woman's primary identity would be of being a Dalit woman, and not of a worker or of an agricultural labourer' (Subhashini Ali interview, 22 July 2008). Communalism and casteism tore at the very basis for women's solidarity as women with a common citizenship or a common status in the class system. Instead caste, religion and ethnic identification became the sites for women's commonality, not their roles as exploited producers in work places and in the fields.

Scholars who have studied women's role as workers in the neoliberal economy of globalized production since the late 1970s argue that the problem of how to effectively organize women workers in the formal and informal economy is *the* critical, unanswered problem of neoliberal times. Patricia Fernandez-Kelly published ground-breaking work on women as the new international proletariat, and about the feminized character of waged factory work more generally, in her 1978 dissertation research on *maquiladoras* (factories) opening in Mexico (see Fernandez-Kelly 1983, the book that drew from her early research). Thirty years after her initial research, she wrote: 'at both ends of the geopolitical spectrum has been the absence of viable workers' movements aimed at curtailing some of the noxious effects of economic internationalization' (Fernandez-Kelly 2007: 510). The next two chapters of this book detail, historically and ethnographically, the tangled connections between the gendered issues of caste, class, religion and locality for the AIDWA activists who powered these campaigns. These chapters reveal how AIDWA connects women's specific issues of caste, minority religion and community oppression to the class issues of women's work.

AIDWA's relationships to its allies in the women's movement, as well as to left allies in trade unions, student, youth, peasant and agricultural workers' organizations, underwent important shifts during the 1980s and 1990s. Their analysis and campaigns connected the intensified violence against women in rural areas to a range of issues: drastically reduced employment for women and men in globalized agriculture, increased food insecurity, increased migration of women and men from distressed rural areas, greater commodification of women, and the abandonment of rural services by the state and central governments. The class contradictions AIDWA identified in 1987, in relation to Roop Kanwar's murder in rural Rajasthan, sharpened the caste, religious and ethnic identities refracted by her immolation on the funeral pyre of her husband. As AIDWA 'turned its face to the village' in the late 1980s and early 1990s, even its units in the cities or their campaigns against casteism and communalism would never be quite the same.

Map of Haryana

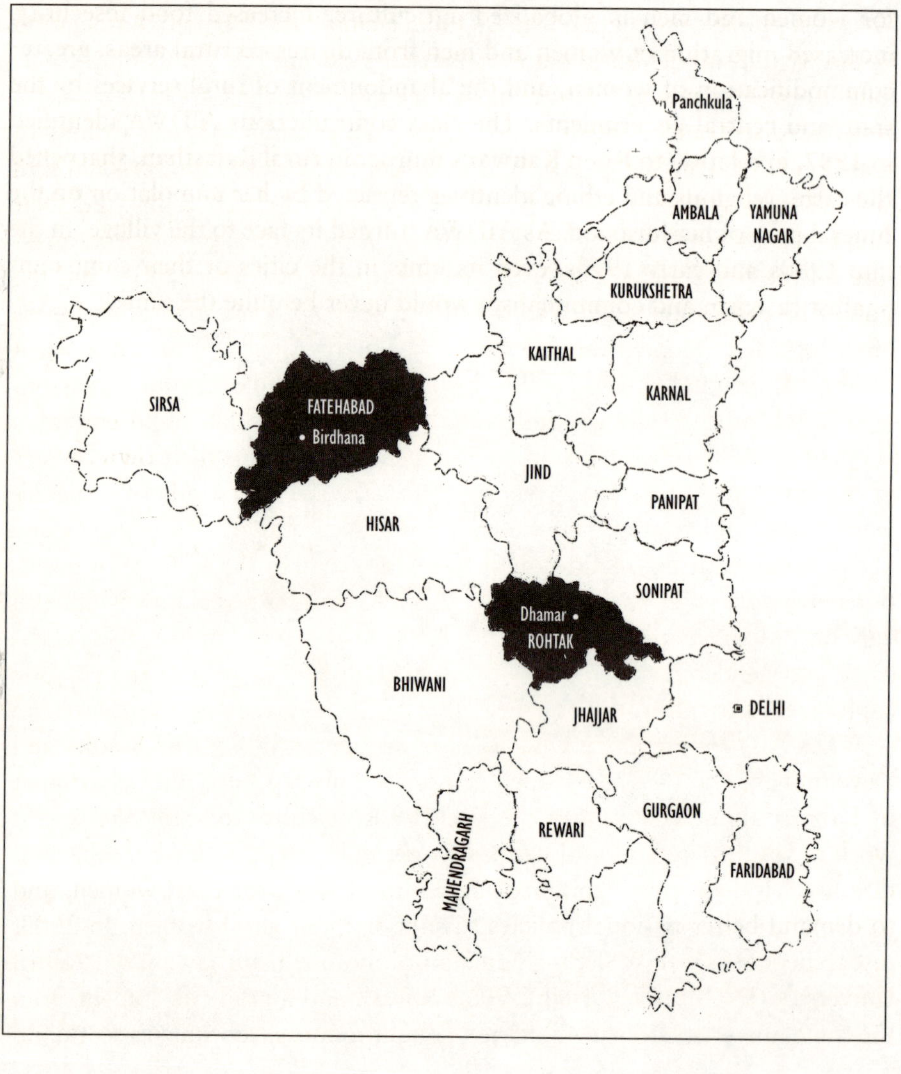

FOUR

Activist Research in Haryana

The most public campaigns of the All India Democratic Women's Association in the wealthy agricultural state of Haryana during the 1990s and 2000s fought powerful vested interests in two seemingly distinct areas of women's systemic disenfranchisement: land rights and community/caste values. In both kinds of campaigns, AIDWA members took enormous personal and familial risks to demand greater access of women to their rights and their dignity. They mobilized the legal system, held public hearings and put pressure on the people and structures that held power in the localities and the state. The campaigns seemed to operate in very different spheres and were often reported independently of each other by the media. Where one set of campaigns demanded land rights – both access to land and land ownership – for land-insecure women and men, the other sought to build equitable gender and caste rights for women and men to determine their own choices in marriage and in personal relationships. Yet the two kinds of struggles were deeply interrelated, and the resource and capital allocation embedded in the struggles around land cannot be seen outside of the cultural contestations of gender and caste hierarchies. AIDWA's politics reveal how neoliberal agricultural policies introduced in the 1990s also sparked upheavals in class, caste and gender hierarchies as forms of domination in Haryana's highly capitalized, agricultural political economy.

When AIDWA's research wing, the Indian School of Women's Studies and Development (ISWSD), developed its research proposal for the Department of Labour about Haryana in the late 1990s, it chose to study the waged work of landless agricultural women workers. It sought to lay bare the conditions of India's most capitalized agricultural work for rural women, and to demand better national policies to support poor rural women. In 2003, researchers for the ISWSD, including an economist from Jawaharlal Nehru University (JNU) in New Delhi, Vikas Rawal, and a graduate student from the same university, Keya Mukherjee, sought to measure women's work and property in the much-vaunted 'green revolution' state of Haryana. With the strengths of a modest grant from the Indian government and AIDWA's membership in Haryana of 20,000 women, they began to map the effects of neoliberal agricultural policies on landless, agricultural women workers in two villages of Haryana: Dhamar in the southern part of the state near Rohtak, and Birdhana on the far western edge of the state near Fatehabad. The small-scale research project initiated by the ISWSD and AIDWA in rural Haryana challenged the presumption of social scientists and supra-national research bodies like the World Bank and United Nations Development Program (UNDP) that studying rural women's work could not shed light on the larger picture of agriculture. The study adhered to standard economic survey research methods through random sampling, but departed in one significant respect: in the ways it involved the knowledge of agricultural workers who were AIDWA members. Unlike individual academic researchers, even those with strong political commitments among the community members they studied (such as Bina Agarwal who wrote the landmark study, *A Field of One's Own: Gender and Land Rights in South Asia*), Rawal, Mukherjee and other researchers did not approach the study wholly outside of the community members they sought to study.[1] This quality set the study apart from not only the government's census data collection and international non-profit researchers like the Mahbub ul Haq Development Centre, but also ethnographic studies about Indian rural lives that value the researchers' distance from the data collected as much as the objectivity of that data itself (Mahbub ul Haq Human Development Centre 2002; James and Rajan 2004: 659–63; *India's Villages*, 1955). The Haryana study showed that a general analysis of agricultural production requires careful analysis of its gendered effects on women and men. Even on its small scale of research data analysis, the study was able to formulate reasons for why the growth rates in employment in rural areas had fallen from 1.36 per cent in 1988 to 0.67 per cent in 2000 *because of* its attention to women's waged work (National Sample Survey data cited in Ghosh 2001: 101).

Caste and gender-based violence were not an explicit focus of the study, yet its analysis of wages, work and property among landless women revealed the honed edge of violence in the fields of neoliberal agriculture. The epistemology of the field on landless women workers rests on a structural analysis as well as the knowledge sought, the analysis derived from the data and where that analysis is situated. Politics bleed into every part of knowledge production. This chapter explores why the ISWSD chose to study landless women's wages and property in Haryana when neither of AIDWA's central

[1] Agarwal describes her affiliations with her academic study in the field of economics alongside her political connections to the women's movement in rural areas primarily as inspirations for her own study of women's land rights. Agarwal 1994: xv.

struggles in this region, around land appropriation and community-sanctioned violence against women, seems to gain obvious direct benefits from the knowledge produced by this study. This chapter also details how a left-wing, activist women's organization could challenge the terrain of statistics gathering by the Indian census and the National Sample Survey Organization (NSSO). It looks at whether AIDWA's commitment to enfranchising rural women generated new possibilities for data collection and analysis, and at the effects of this focused study on the dominant conversations about agricultural work, gender and neoliberalism.

Land and Violence: Women's Activism in Haryana

During the mid-1990s, upper-caste landowners in Bandh, a settlement of 5,000 people near Panipat in Haryana, appropriated 137 acres of common or *panchayat* lands, one-third of which was reserved by the government specifically for scheduled caste members of the locality. Without this shared land, the mostly Dalit (also identified as scheduled caste) landless women and men of Bandh had no place to graze their livestock. Neither could they grow food to supplement the diet their wages could buy. Additionally, they lost a place to relieve themselves, an enormous loss of daily independence and dignity. But local women in AIDWA did not accept the loss of land. 'I am not one of those who depends on fate', stated Indu, a midwife and leader of the AIDWA unit in Bandh (Indu interview, 23 June 1999). She and other AIDWA members fought to regain the lands, first through their *sarpanch* (the head of the *panchayat*, an elected local governing body with seat reservations for women and Dalits), a sympathetic Brahmin woman named Laxmi Devi. Because of her support for the landless women's cause, Laxmi Devi was banished from her caste and suspended from the *panchayat* by the local *khap panchayat* (a non-elected, community-based governing body, also called a caste *panchayat*, with no representation of women or Dalits). Next, AIDWA filed a case in the courts. In coalition with the All India Agricultural Workers Union (AIAWU), it used the media, demonstrations and sit-ins to publicize the court's inaction on the case, and the upper castes' often violent social boycott against the landless women demonstrators and their families. It won the land case in court on 23 July 1998.

AIDWA's fight to enact the verdict did not end with the court case. In the seizure of communal lands by large landowners, the landless women and men lost any economic independence from upper-caste landowners who controlled not only land, work and commodities in the locality, but also access to credit. One AIDWA member active in the struggle described their land as a means towards economic independence; with the seizure, 'that road was closed' (ibid.). With a lock on all levers of power and self-sufficiency, the village upper castes even gained control over the political independence of landless women and men. Without physical access to common lands to buffer their own survival, landless – mostly Dalit – women and men had to vote for caste Hindu candidates; otherwise they faced another social boycott. AIDWA's coalitional campaign with AIAWU won them the legal rights to the common lands, but not the use or the benefits facilitated by those lands. It did not break the back of the social control by upper-caste landowners.

AIDWA's campaign in Bandh to push back land encroachment was one of many similar cases they fought during the 1990s and 2000s. States across India passed laws designed to erode the commons, evade the Land Ceiling Act and reverse land reform policies of the past (Rao and Storm 1998: 236–37). The structural adjustments of the early 1990s in India predominantly focused on trade, currency and industrial policies rather than agricultural policies (Jha 1996: 69). But by 1996, after the Uruguay Round of the General Agreement on Trade and Tariff (GATT) talks were signed in 1994, the Indian government's agricultural policies adhered more strictly to liberalization demands, even in the heartlands of the green revolution.[2] This attention on agriculture as a site for neoliberal reforms meant the loss of subsidies for fertilizer, power and seeds, the scaling back of employment programmes for rural waged workers like the Jawahar Rozgar Yojana, the slashing of budgets for subsidized food and price supports for food grain, and the erosion of state-sponsored credit programmes for poor farmers (Vashishtha and Mukherjee 1996: 34). AIDWA's activism and its analysis of its politics in Haryana refuted two simplistic explanatory models for the rise in caste and gender violence during this period. The first is that the fault lies solely with the insecurity created by liberalization for middle-income farmers and low-income agricultural workers. The change toward neoliberal agricultural policies, however, did not create caste violence, gender discrimination and unequal legal protection suffered by landless women agricultural workers in Haryana on its own. Second, women's struggles in Bandh fold into narratives of timeless caste brutality, narratives marked primarily by religious beliefs and the will to power rather than globalization. But, as AIDWA activists showed, these determinants need to be seen in a dynamic relation with each other. Simply choosing one catalyst – of outside economic dictates or age-old hierarchies – oversimplifies the changing terrain of rights, and the forces that forge old and new weapons in specific localities to perpetuate even as they refigure gender, caste and class hierarchies.

Under neoliberalism, the guiding watchword of efficiency in farming launched an ideological assault on previous governmental agricultural poli-

[2] The Indian government cut development expenditures from 13.2 per cent of the GDP between 1985–90 to only 7.8 per cent between 1991–93. See Utsa Patnaik and Prabhat Patnaik 2001.

cies in India.[3] Efficiency meant phasing out the redistribution of land through land reform since proponents argued that large-scale farming, whether corporate or family-run, produces higher agricultural yields with greater productivity by workers and machines. The demand for efficiency also meant a scaling back of rural employment programmes by the government since corruption dogged their implementation and siphoned off funds from jobs for the rural poor. This criticism of inefficient corruption also eroded programmes to provide access to fair credit terms for landless agricultural workers and cultivators of small plots (Ramachandran and Swaminathan, eds. 2005). The push towards corporate and large landholding farms continued apace, and export-driven agriculture took precedence over locality-driven food crops and subsistence agriculture. The economics of cash-cropping put more money into high-yield, patented seeds, machinery, fertilizers, pesticides, and power generation for irrigation, and less money into hiring women agricultural workers for wages (Sheila Bhalla 1989: WS67–WS73, WS75–WS78). The productivity rates of agricultural workers rose with the higher mechanization of farming (Prabhat Patnaik 2011: 172–76). Simultaneously, their wages fell as the number of agricultural jobs decreased in an area, and decreased overall due to the high numbers of migrant workers dispossessed from their land and in search of paid work (Reddy and Mishra 2009). The logics of efficiency naturalized the agrarian crisis for land-insecure rural workers who faced starvation, debt and itinerancy as a regrettable necessity of market growth and agricultural productivity. Hopeful commentators imagined growth in the informal sector, or self-employment, as a means to catch agricultural workers abandoned in the new economy, a vision that did not materialize for the vast majority of people, women or men (Ghosh 2004; Deshpande and Prabhu 2005; Chandrasekhar and Ghosh 2003). The neoliberal agricultural economy is a jobless one for agricultural workers.

The Triple Burden and Neoliberal Agricultural Economies

Caste violence and gender discrimination travel along circuits of neoliberalism in complicated ways, described by AIDWA as the 'triple burden' of caste and class oppression of women (AIDWA, *The Triple Burden*, 1999). Landless rural women experienced the tightened strictures of caste and gender violence both when they lost their access to common land and when

[3] Many of these debates raged between the early to mid-1990s in prominent publications like the *Economic and Political Weekly* and media outlets across the country, but also in policy centres and conferences around the world. For book-length articulations of these positions, see Gulati and Narayanan 2003; Hanumantha Rao 2005; Bhagwati 1993; Joshi and Little 1996; Das 1998). Terence Byres also provides a helpful overview of the Indian context for economists' debates about stabilization and liberalization policies. See Byres 1997.

they fought that encroachment, as the struggle in Bandh starkly illustrated. AIDWA's conference report from 1998, 'AIDWA Experiences in Struggles Against Violence', described the spike in violence seen by organization members between 1994 and 1998. 'The largest number of sexual assault cases (both reported and unreported) has been against women agricultural workers and rural poor women who have no alternative but to put themselves in the same vulnerable situation every day because of their dependence on the landlord employers for survival' (AIDWA, *Women and Violence*, 1999: 38). The effects on women's lives of precarious livelihoods, increased physical and sexual vulnerability, and increased dependence on large landowners exacerbated long-term hierarchies of caste and gender relations in ways that flowed directly into AIDWA's activism in Haryana as the policies of neoliberal agriculture were implemented during the mid-1990s and 2000s.

The second area of AIDWA's activism in Haryana against community-sanctioned violence against women also demanded careful attention to how caste and gender dictates met changing class relations in rural areas. During these decades, AIDWA's campaigns included an influx of cases against 'honour killing', the name given to murders of women and sometimes men who married outside their caste communities, within their *gotra* (sub-caste), or behaved in ways deemed unacceptable for girls and women. The woman's family usually, but not always, perpetrated humiliations and murders against the woman or girl in the name of community or family honour. In the international context, honour-based crimes against women are assumed to occur in Muslim-majority regions; in India, these violations have a regional association with north India rather than a religious one (Chakravarti 2005). In Haryana, these crimes target caste Hindu women, Sikh women, Muslim women, as well as women of oppressed castes for their failure to conform to community standards of gendered and sexual propriety (Chowdhry 2007).

In 2004, AIDWA organized a day-long convention against honour killing, excoriating the prevalence of community-sanctioned violence and murder of women (Rajalakshmi 2004b). A booklet published a few years later, *In the Name of 'Honour': Let Us Love and Live*, detailed the influx of cases fought in Haryana. Jagmati Sangwan, AIDWA's state president in Haryana, recounted the difficulty of organizing against honour-based crimes and in favour of the women and men violated, and traced AIDWA's analysis of the upsurge of these crimes to the prominent Darshana Ashish case in Jhajjar district of Haryana in 2000 (Sangwan 2010). The couple, married for two years with one child, had their marriage nullified by the *khap panchayat* (a local, caste-based governance body) for marrying within their *gotra*.[4] The

[4] For a detailed description of this case in its larger context, see Chowdhry, 'Redeeming "Honour" through Violence'.

The cover of *In the Name of 'Honour'*, published by AIDWA in 2010, containing its analysis and activism against the so-called 'honour' crimes.

woman was physically harassed and forced to tie a *rakhi* bracelet around her husband's wrist (to signify his brotherly status). When the AIDWA delegation met with the leader of the *khap panchayat* in this case, he provided a surprising insight. Jagmati reported:

> his response was an eye opener for the deep thought and understanding it gave us of the mentality that foments such heinous crimes. We were taken aback at his categorical statement that this was a result of the seed that Nehru had sown by giving property rights to women/daughters. We realized that this was not a stray incident, but the result of organized thinking and opposition to democratic rights for women. (Sangwan 2010: 73)

The unrepentant *khap panchayat* leader linked his aggressive reaction to women's legal rights to property ownership rather than women's sexual uncontrollability or violation of their community's honour. In a time of shifting property relations around land, agricultural produce and capital, women's honour had a distinctly material value, which the *khap panchayat* leader sought to maintain through intimidation and violence.

Jagmati described how AIDWA's campaigns shifted in response to this insight, to openly build consensus and field debates about women's rights. They did so to link in explicit ways how community values and property values constitute women's rights. AIDWA members began registering these cases as a crime with the local police, itself an often conflictual process. They then developed a committed group of people within the community who could withstand community pressure to pursue the case in court and in public perception. Only then did AIDWA members call for the community group to meet with the *khap panchayat*s to demand a dialogue about the case.[5] Public visibility and sanction against honour-based violence through naming and discussing these actions as crimes, Jagmati emphasized, was a powerful weapon in AIDWA's many campaigns to hold *khap panchayats* accountable. Jagmati described one debate in Rohtak regarding an honour-based crime where AIDWA members sought to build common ethics around issues of women's rights such as opposition to the abortion of girl foetuses and violence against women (Sangwan 2010: 76). She described how AIDWA members sought to resolve honour-based disputes between *khap panchayat* members and aggrieved community members around women's basic rights to dignity in ways that addressed underlying land, capital, labour and resource contestations.

Land-based and honour-based cases in Haryana around the turn of the twenty-first century, both illustrate the complexity of women's triple burden

[5] For a description of one such community hearing held by AIDWA in the Rohtak district of Haryana in 2004, see Rajalakshmi 2004b.

of caste, gender and class. More visibly, the struggles of landless agricultural women for land and dignity traced the historical exclusion of women, and Dalit and oppressed caste people, to property ownership. Community-sanctioned violence against women revealed less obvious linkages to land and property issues, and caste, class and gender oppression. In a prescient article for AIDWA's publication *Equality* in 1988, Zoya Hasan suggested systemic linkages between caste Hindu women and Dalit women of Haryana, and between these two seemingly disparate fronts of AIDWA's activism:

> Again it is the green revolution which has contributed to the marginalization of women because it has led to a massive reduction in the availability of jobs. Women have been relegated to part time and seasonal jobs in farms where mechanization is taking place. In some areas, much of the specialized work like wheat grinding, carding and spinning earlier done by women is now mechanized.
>
> The inequality of women has been compounded by the prosperity generated by the green revolution, especially in the case of women belonging to upper caste and intermediate caste households who have been withdrawn from agricultural work and confined to the house. The new productive system confines women to the domestic sphere, where they have limited access to resources and decision making. This is what their newly acquired 'social status' supposedly demands. (Hasan 1988: 3–4)

Hasan describes the perverse effects of the green revolution in the agricultural economies of states like Haryana, Punjab and to a lesser degree Andhra Pradesh, where the Indian state poured resources into building up the infrastructure of roads, irrigation and electrification, as well as the science and technology of seeds and other inputs, to increase agricultural productivity. One well-documented outcome of the green revolution was higher agricultural yields between 1965 and 1980, with diminishing returns as the chemical fertilizers, pesticides, tractor use and continuous cropping depleted the soil reserves (Glaeser, ed. 1987; Kusum Nair 1979; *Seeds of Plenty, Seeds of Sorrow*, directed by Manjira Datta, 1992). Another less heralded effect was the growth of inequality that cleaved industrial agricultural economies, dividing poor farmers and workers from rich farmers and landowners, Dalits from caste Hindus, and women from men, with greater disparities of wealth, wages and resources (Chowdhry 1994: 143–204; Ahlawat 1988; Frankel 1971). If the green revolution depended upon the largesse of the Indian state's policies, the neoliberal transformation of agriculture demanded a reliance on private capital over public support. Neoliberal agriculture still requires the Indian state to enforce privatization of land and agricultural products, as well as maintain vital infrastructural resources such as roads, power and irrigation. Yet policies that support increasing marketization and privatization also demand an elision of the state's role of monitoring or facilitating the allocation of these resources, as well as the state's control over capital flows such as price supports for agriculture or credit programmes for low-income farmers. Hasan's insight about the disparate effects of income and wealth polarization for women across classes and castes reveals important connections between rural women's lives on the neoliberal landscape. The challenge for a class and caste-inclusive organization like AIDWA is to build bridges between those differential struggles for women's empowerment and enfranchisement.

The Turn to the Village

AIDWA's turn to the village in the late 1980s precipitated its need for a greater depth of information about rural women's lives and their survival. By 1990, AIDWA's movement leaders began to develop their idea for a research centre with independent standing as a non-governmental entity that was also linked to their regional activism (Shakti Kak interview, 18 June 2003). This centre, they imagined, would produce regional reports about specific issues and industries, use regional comparisons to map national trends in agricultural economies, build AIDWA's membership in rural areas with a long-term vision for women's emancipation, and educate about pressing issues faced by multi-class, multi-caste coalitions of rural women (ibid.). In 1995, the Indian School of Women's Studies and Development (ISWSD) began as a hub for activists to collect, assess and distribute information about under-researched aspects of women's lives. Woven into the needs and resources of AIDWA's activism, this research centre did not function as part of a university or inter-governmental research agency, though it maintained similarly rigorous methods of information gathering and assessment. In contrast to university-based research centres, ISWSD drew heavily on AIDWA's membership for researchers and knowledge producers.

The ISWSD's first report analysed the impact of using aquiculture to produce cash crops on women's agricultural work in Andhra Pradesh and Orissa (ISWSD and Janaki Amma Trust for Welfare of Women and Children 1998). Its second report looked at landless women's agricultural work in Haryana in two rural localities, one near the southern city of Rohtak and the other near the western city of Fatehabad. AIDWA's turn to the village demanded a complex analysis of gender as it structured rural relations, an analysis it framed as 'a triple burden' of gender, class and caste oppression. Studies about the impact of neoliberal agricultural policies on landless agricultural women workers were rare in the 1990s.[6] Even rarer was research that attempted to

[6] Two well-known exceptions are Bina Agarwal and Vandana Shiva who have published extensively on these issues. See Agarwal 1994; Shiva 1998; Shiva 1999: 35–38. See also Chowdhry 1993: A135–A137; A140–A148.

understand how the oppressed caste status and gender status of agricultural workers compounds their economic exploitation (Kak 1994a; Kak 1994b). The activist research methods and findings of ISWSD researchers in Haryana during the summer of 2003 reveal valuable experiments in data collection, and the ongoing assessment process of their methods, research tools and findings. Their research report, titled 'Women Workers in Rural Haryana: A Field-Based Study', verified what AIDWA activists already knew about the ongoing loss of women's employment in waged agricultural work since the all-time high in the late 1980s.[7] The report highlighted the dearth of *any* studies that 'examine the impact of decline in overall employment availability in the 1990s on the nature of employment of women workers' (ISWSD 2003). Its findings about landless women's days of employment exposed the tenuous conditions of these women's survival. The report gave specificity to National Sample Survey data which showed that rural employment had decreased from 2.03 per cent between 1987–88 and 1993–94 to only 0.58 per cent between 1993–94 and 1998–99. It provided more accurate count to the Indian census data from 2001 which revealed that the number of waged workers who received less than 183 days of work per annum increased in the work force by about 2.5 times during 1991–2001 (from 3.3 per cent to 8.7 per cent). Landless women agricultural workers from these two localities, according to the ISWSD data, had an average of 40 days of paid work (in cash or in kind) per year, a precipitous drop from the mid-1970s when women in Haryana had an average of 66 employment days per year.[8] The Indian census threshold of 183 days of work per year was a high bar in Haryana even during the green revolution. Women agricultural workers' cataclysmic loss of one-third of their working days was rendered invisible by the census calculations.

The ISWSD report also detailed how widely varied methods of control were exercised against landless women workers in the two localities. In Dhamar, in the southern part of the state, the report found that a shift from hourly waged labour to piece-rate labour for women allowed employers to avoid minimum wage laws and gender parity laws for agricultural workers. Migrant labour was also an important disciplinary regime in Dhamar, since local wages further eroded in the face of competition from more desperate workers from Rajasthan and Bihar. In the western Haryana locality of Birdhana, piece rates also prevailed for women's work in particular, but rather than migrant workers driving down wages, a form of tenancy farm-

[7] C.P. Chandrasekhar and Jayati Ghosh cite National Sample Survey data that emerged from 1993 onwards about the loss of jobs for this sector in their book *The Market that Failed*; see Chandrasekhar and Ghosh 2000: 141–46.

[8] Ahlawat 1988: 93. He cites the Rural Labour Enquiry statistics, 1974–75 to support his claims.

ing with bonded labour characteristics, called *siri,* dominated other forms of waged agricultural work. In particular, for women workers who were not formally part of a *siri* labour contract, their husband's contract usurped women's and girls' labour from his family into waged and unwaged work obligations to the landowner (Rawal 2004). Women were not signatories on *siri* contracts, but their labour was bound by the agreement nonetheless. *Siri* workers received a portion of the final crops, between one-fifth and one-twelfth, in exchange for their labour, the costs of any paid labourers, and all cash inputs such as seeds and fertilizer. The landowner provided the land, high interest loans, irrigation and machinery usage. The ISWSD report on these very different contexts emphasized how agricultural economies of women's work both intensified decades-old systems of oppression, through driving down wages by outside competition as well as older bonded labour forms, but also shifted those systems to neoliberal ends (Ahlawat 1988: 102; Patnaik and Dingwaney, eds. 1985).

Caste oppression continued to determine rural people's lack of access to land. Women's rights to own land were still in jeopardy due to gender discrimination. Yet the character of these truths had shifted on the neoliberal landscape since the knife-edge of survival had grown ever sharper with fewer working days, more precarious social safety nets, and more contested access to *panchayat* and other common lands. The neoliberal logic emphasized 'efficiency of resource use' over the older capitalist logic of 'investment as the key to growth'. India's green revolution demanded concentrated amounts of capital and state resources to build up the transportation system, electricity grid and irrigation system, and to provide buffers to the unpredictability of farming through price supports and other policies that fostered growth in grain production, employment and the economy. The shift to 'efficiency of resource use' in the 1990s had immediate effects on the lives of agricultural workers, a majority of whom are Dalits and women (Patnaik and Chandrasekhar 1996). Rather than invest in workers' greater potential through better nutrition, or greater access to health care and education, or even through job training, the stripping down of current resources became the key to economic growth. Gender and caste oppression weakens the ability of the majority of agricultural workers to demand fair wages and working conditions. These hierarchical systems of domination thus become another resource to utilize 'efficiently', to keep the labour cost of agriculture down to its bare minimum and increase labour productivity.

The turn to the village sharpened AIDWA's assessment of women's triple burden on this changing neoliberal terrain of their relationship to land, labour and economies of survival during the 1990s, but also the organization's own political strategies and tools to build alliances that could withstand these assaults. Questions of casteism, land ownership, work participation and anti-women violence took radically different forms in each locality even as they shared basic structural features of women's lower wages, their lack of control over working conditions and wages, and their decreased days of work.

Statistical data about women's sharply decreased days of yearly employment in the ISWSD report helped to 'give teeth', in the words of an AIDWA activist from western Haryana, to the organization's demand that the government of India should actively foster rural women's employment and empowerment opportunities (Veena Rani, Fatehabad AIDWA group interview, 13 June 2003). The report also bolstered the importance of land distribution policies, a post-independence promise still unmet in Haryana where many holdings far exceed the national ceilings for maximum amounts of land that can be amassed by one entity. It documented how close to starvation huge numbers of rural women, and by extension their families, were in the richest agricultural heartland of the country. The report directly opposed the move to create a public distribution system of subsidized food that targeted food-insecure people by assigning different levels of need amongst them, over a universal system of fair-priced food.

The study of women's agricultural wages allowed AIDWA to highlight the lives of some of the poorest and most disenfranchised rural women. By setting the study in Haryana, it could address the effects of neoliberal agricultural policies in one of the more capitalized agricultural states, one most able to accommodate the emphasis on the promised benefits of cash crops, intensified agricultural methods, and the reduction of tariffs and trade barriers to agricultural products. If women agricultural workers in Haryana shouldered the costs of liberalizing agriculture at the forefront, then the rest of the country could expect similar if not more extreme experiences. Struggles for women's rights and for Dalit people's rights, as AIDWA's activism and ISWSD's research showed in Haryana, met at the crossroads of the changing economic conditions of a liberalizing economic and political arena. To study wages, as ISWSD proposed to do, allowed AIDWA to understand survival in Haryana of the 1990s and 2000s, at a time when women's individual rights to marry became that much more policed and contested within their families and by their communities.[9] The study opened the door to Zoya Hasan's observation that prosperity bound women differently than did poverty, but in systemically correlated ways. As she observed about the green revolution in 1988: 'The new productive system confines (intermediate caste and middle class) women to the domestic sphere, where they have limited access

[9] Prem Chowdhry cites lawyers in Chandigarh who assert that the Punjab and Haryana High Court 'receives as many as fifty applications per day from couples seeking protection. This is a staggering tenfold rise from about five to six applications a day, five years ago.' See Chowdhry, 'Redeeming "Honour" through Violence'.

to resources and decision-making' (Hasan 1988: 4). A community's and a family's caste and class status rested on women's seclusion and conservative, gendered social norms. Yet the polarization of wealth and poverty fostered by the green revolution and intensified by neoliberal agricultural economies also created a crisis in the standing of middle income and intermediate caste rural families. Women's roles as workers and as reputable family members in a range of class and caste locations were a locus for the effects of this increased sense of vulnerability. Not only landless women or Dalit women felt the pressures of neoliberalism's cultural effects. The ISWSD's report measures the ever-shrinking days of women's agricultural employment, a loss that did not directly affect landed, caste Hindu families. However, the report provides a palpable example of the widened gulf between economically secure rural classes and the poor. These differences in rural women's disenfranchisement were deeply linked, a linkage that AIDWA continues to mine in its activism across the state as it seeks to build cross-class and cross-caste alliances among women, even as it grounds its analysis and its activism through the lens and with the leadership of the most disenfranchised people.

Land and Landlessness in the 1990s

Since it was founded in 1981, AIDWA joined and often incited national debates about agricultural women's wealth and wages. Its struggle for the inclusion of women in land reform initiatives of the 1980s rephrased the left movement's rallying cry, 'Land for the Tiller!', since tilling is almost always considered a man's agricultural task. AIDWA replaced it with a women-inclusive demand: 'Land to those who work on it!' (AIDWA, *The Triple Burden,* 1999: 7). Across the country, AIDWA sustained regional struggles for women's rights to land and fair wages. Yet the right to joint-owned *pattas* (land ownership documents) gained legal legitimacy, and several states promised concerted efforts to register land in both women's and men's names. Except in West Bengal and Kerala, these campaigns rarely amounted to significant changes in land ownership. Land reform during the 1990s became an impossible dream rather than the cornerstone of a newly independent nation (Avinash Kumar 2011). For landless women, the precipitous loss of employment days drove many more women and their families into destitution. The push to enforce minimum wage laws held little meaning for the piece-rated, time-rated, casual agricultural work open to women.

In 1988, the government released *Shramshakti: Report of the National Commission on Self Employed Women and Women in the Informal Sector,*[10] and provided a bombshell of damning information about the lives of rural

[10] The title of the report, *Shramshakti*, translates as 'The Power of Work'.

poor women. Ela Bhatt, the respected leader of the Self Employed Women's Association (SEWA), wrote an 80-page preface to the report, a preface that excoriated governmental development projects, the absolute inattention to the Equal Wage Act, and the active marginalization of women from governmental training programmes women most needed. The report drew on census and NSS reports, and commissioned an additional forty-nine studies (Spodek 1990). Of one million questionnaires sent around the country, agencies and activist groups returned 150,000. Researchers visited seventeen states to interview officials in government agencies, leaders and staff in nonprofit groups, as well as self-employed women themselves. Given the difficulty of studying women's informal work, including home-based, part-time and agricultural work, the report gave teeth to struggles to change women's lives in rural areas of India. Brinda Karat lauded much of the report for the voices it carried, and the recommendations it pushed. 'A graphic picture emerges of the tremendous burden of work shouldered by these women and the deplorable conditions and circumstances in which they struggle for survival', she stated (Karat 1988: 22). 'Between 20 and 60 per cent of the women interviewed in all age groups were the main bread-winners of the family' (ibid.). The report had an important effect on policy and administration. One of its central recommendations was to set up an Equal Rights Commission at the central and state levels. While the Equal Rights Commission remained mired in politics around the bill to reserve one-third of the Rajya Sabha electoral seats for women, the demand for a national and state-level body to adjudicate on behalf of women's equality gained traction. Three years later, in 1991, the National Commission for Women and State Commissions for Women were instated across the country. But, Karat argued, the report disappointed since it did not attempt to answer the central question its own findings lay bare regarding the immiserization of waged agricultural workers and the subsequent rise in unorganized workers in the informal economy. For this reason, Karat raised the demand for land reform as an essential addition to the report. She argued:

> While the oppressive conditions are given, the institutional setting under which such conditions exist are not spelt out. Clearly the growth of the unorganized sector is linked with the general participation of the peasantry. Therefore the crucial question of land reform needs to be raised. . . . Because of the lack of such an analysis the report is unable to answer why an increasingly larger number of women are being forced into this sector. (Ibid.: 23)

Brinda Karat returned to this question when she wrote about the Agricultural Workers Bill proposed by the Central Labour Minister in 1997 to allay the crushing poverty among the rural poor. In a newspaper article on the Bill, she exhorted policy makers to understand why agricultural work is a women's issue: 'Popular perception identifies the agricultural worker as being male even though India is witnessing a growing trend of feminization of the agricultural work force' (Karat 1997: 14). Karat asked why in the decade of 1981–91 the numbers of women agricultural workers increased disproportionately higher than men agricultural workers – an increase of 36.15 per cent for women in comparison to an increase of 31.18 per cent for men. She directly countered the Bill's subtle attempt to gloss these differences while describing increased women's agricultural work as 'a direct benefit of the new economic policies of the government . . . concealing the reality that it reflects both an increase in levels of poverty among agriculture worker families as well as an increase in levels of exploitation and profit-making of the landlords' (Karat, 'Agricultural Workers Bill', n.d., personal copy).

Women workers are overwhelmingly employed in the agricultural sector of rural work (Vepa 2007). By 2008, 80 per cent of all women workers were agricultural workers. The turn to the village, AIDWA saw as early as 1988, grew from a central question of why agricultural work has become women's work. The corollary to that structural question requires research like the *Shramshakti* report conducted: what has agricultural work become? When ISWSD researchers in concert with AIDWA members in Haryana initiated their small-scale research project, they sought to clarify what statistics had measured and what activists in the state already knew: landless women faced the brunt of feminized agricultural work in lost wages, shrinking work days, vulnerable working conditions, and increased work for food or fodder rather than cash. The study sought to measure women's wealth and wages as a window into these conditions as they structured women's lives. The researchers framed the survey to answer questions AIDWA uncovered through concerted political struggle in rural areas across the country, about the effects of shifting from local economies of rural agriculture to cash crops like flowers and shrimp farms, and of the spreading hegemony of dowry and dowry-related violence against women even among castes and communities that had little historical connection to these practices. AIDWA's national president in this period, Subhashini Ali, framed the connections clearly between the rise in atrocities against women and Dalits, and the agrarian crisis:

> Now, after tremendous crisis in the agrarian sector, the whole issue of agricultural labourers' wages has really taken a beating, because if the whole sector is in crisis, the peasant is only able to squeeze labour. He is not able to get cheap water, he is not able to get cheap seeds, he is not able to get cheap electricity, cheap fertilizer, so the only factor of his production that he can squeeze is the worker, and the wages; so the increase in the number of agricultural women workers is directly in proportion to the decrease in wages. So wage struggles are much fewer whereas

atrocities are much greater, because that's a way of keeping the wages down. (Subhashini Ali interview, 22 July 2008)

A study of wages and wealth, in Ali's words, sheds light on the social and ideological weapons used 'to squeeze the worker' in the new agricultural regime. Agrarian crisis for small and middle-level farmers travels to the workers on those farms, a caste and gender-structured labour force. Both of AIDWA's research methods, struggle-led and discursive activism, closely tie the changes in rural economies to the intensification of violence along lines of caste, gender and religion. As Ali's vivid language conveys, the beating on wages actively relies upon caste intimidation, coercive patriarchal norms, as well as overt forms of violence against women.

The ISWSD Haryana Report, 2003

Dhamar and Birdhana, the two localities researched in the ISWSD study, had significant differences between them. Different castes in each area dominated the landowning and politically connected families. Jats held the largest amounts of land and power in Dhamar, though they were only 2 per cent of the locality's population. Households from the Mehta and the Bishnoi castes owned the largest amount of land in Birdhana. Disparities of wealth and land were high in both places, but Birdhana had a shocking level of landlessness, with 77 per cent of the residents without land, whereas Dhamar to the south of the state had a landlessness rate of 50 per cent (Rawal and Mukherjee 2006: 186). The relative size of landholdings was also markedly different. In Birdhana the largest landowner held 100 acres of irrigated land, while in Dhamar the largest landowner owned 40 acres of irrigated land. Different forms of work predominated in each area, with casual work rather than long-term work contracts shaping Dhamar, compared to three predominant forms of work in Birdhana: short-term casual work, debt-bonded tenancy work called *siri,* and least commonly, the work of long-term, fixed wage farm servants (ibid.).[11] Also, the landless workers were from a number of different castes, designated Backward Class (BC), Other Backward Class (OBC) and Scheduled Caste (SC) by the government. Their crops were different, as was their land distribution and average farm size. Yet these differences also emphasized the commonalities between the two localities, partic-

[11] The difference in landlessness between the two localities may be linked to the growing reliance on *siri* labour contracts, though other factors such as migration of labourers, landholdings size and irrigation must also be taken into account. Utsa Patnaik predicted an increase of debt bondage labour arrangements like *siri* contracts in conditions of greater immiseration for agricultural workers. See Patnaik 1999: 198–206.

ularly for agricultural women workers who sought enough work to survive. Most landless women worked for wages or for exchange; all landless women saw their annual wages shrink as well as their days of employment; and they all faced a dearth of non-agricultural jobs (ISWSD 2003: 1–3).

The ISWSD researchers used random sampling, standardized questionnaires and rigorous mapping of village houses within settlements and in the fields. Their final report provided illuminating answers to the problem of disappearing waged work spurred by liberalization of the agricultural economy. Through an attention to women's agricultural work, ISWSD's report departed from reports led by the World Bank, the International Monetary Fund (IMF) and their sometime facilitators in the United National Development Program (UNDP) (NCAER 2003; Mahbub ul Haq Human Development Centre 2003). The opening of the ISWSD report demarcated startling gaps in research of Haryana: about employment trends of all women workers, of how women participate in rural economies, and how land, caste and gender shape poor women's employment (ISWSD 2003). The report addressed the critical question of 'the impact of the decline in overall employment availability in the 1990s on the nature of employment of women workers' (ibid.). In its discursive activism, AIDWA, as a left-wing, activist women's organization, joined ISWSD's social scientists engaged in measuring work, to add caste and gender questions into a usually homogenous designation of agricultural employment. Significantly, the report did not seek to amend the standard category 'work' to include women's non-waged domestic and reproductive work. 'Work', however, did include any in-kind of payment in its measurement, such as work for fodder and fuel, and work for debt repayment.

The report's answers to gendered questions about the agrarian crisis allowed AIDWA to sharpen its ongoing national campaigns for the right to work for equal wages, the right to food, and for fair distribution of land and resources. These campaigns for basic necessities sustain ongoing campaigns against violence. AIDWA's local campaigns in Haryana during the 1990s and the period of the study equally focused on the vicious cases of sexualized violence, community-sanctioned violence against women and men who crossed caste barriers in their relationships. The study allowed AIDWA activists to clarify how their anti-violence campaigns were linked, though sometimes in subtle ways, to campaigns for more equitable food distribution to widows and women's access to government food-for-work schemes. In 2011, Subhashini Ali gave a speech about AIDWA's analysis of Haryana's upsurge in community violence that tied land and labour issues to gender and caste rights movements. She linked the *khap panchayat* rulings against unsanctioned relationships to wider economic controls.

> The panchayat decisions are couched in the vocabulary of protecting honour and tradition and they receive wide social sanction from the dominant, landed castes which correctly recognize them as a mechanism for preserving unequal land relations, hegemony over the poor and scheduled caste labourers, and controlling young women and their sexuality. (Ali, 'Survival in a Time of Violence', 2011.)

As the ISWSD study gave teeth to AIDWA's activism, AIDWA's commitment to structural social change generated new possibilities for ISWSD's data collection and analysis. Their collaboration in this study threaded struggle-based knowledge throughout the research process and methodology.

Mass Struggle and Knowledge

In the winter of 2002, ISWSD's survey questionnaire was adapted by Vikas Rawal, Shakti Kak, the director of ISWSD, Brinda Karat, the general secretary of AIDWA, and AIDWA's state activists in Haryana.[12] In March, Keya Mukherjee joined Rawal in Rohtak to further refine the form in consultation with local AIDWA members. Two months later, Mukherjee and Rawal went through a similar process for the second village Birdhana, outside of Fatehabad, to understand the specificity of women's agricultural work in the area and best measure its changing worth. They added sections on animal husbandry and domestic work that generated income to their questionnaire. They also expanded the questions around long-term work contracts for Birdhana because contracted labour arrangements called *siri* were so common in the village (Vikas Rawal interview, 14 June 2003). In addition, they surveyed 1,000 of 1,600 households in the village to list all landless households, sometimes returning to households to check the accuracy of their findings. In Birdhana, 882 of those 1,000 families they sampled were landless. From these 882 landless households, they randomly chose families to interview through a computer programme designed for that purpose.

The research teams initially consisted of AIDWA members from Rohtak, many of whom were landless women workers. With the perimeters of the research project set, the insights these women could bring to the process allowed ISWSD researchers to ask more pointed questions to assess some of the challenges faced as well as solutions derived by women most affected by structural adjustments. Having research team members who were already deeply invested in the political landscape of the area destabilized the value of objectivity for experts in the field. Training landless women workers to ask

[12] They adapted the questionnaire used by V.K. Ramachandran in his long-term study of gender and agriculture in Gokilapuram, Tamil Nadu. See Ramachandran 1990; Ramachandran, Swaminathan and Rawal 2002: 445–72.

questions and record answers from the people they interviewed was not necessarily less objective than geographically disconnected researchers, but it could change the answers given by the respondents, both in their detail and the qualitative character. The ISWSD model overturned aspects of standard assumptions of who can know the facts, and refigured the experts in the field. It implied the methodological values of active knowledge as alternatives to the imperative of objectivity. Credibility for government census takers, as much as academic degree holders, rests in part on maintaining an emotional and structural distance to shape a discrete object of study. ISWSD proposed another kind of study, one subjectified through the lived knowledge held by the same people who negotiate the gendered relationships of wages and property every day. Their data collection methodology knit the political economy of agriculture and its gendered reproduction into the fabric of ISWSD's investigation.

Keya Mukherjee talked about the difficulty of this new process. 'Many of the women had small children, and those who did not live in Rohtak but came from surrounding villages or towns, could not leave them for more than one or two nights at a time' (Keya Mukherjee interview, 13 June 2003). The research itself was gruelling. Interviews with women and their families could last as many as three or four hours. At most, one research team could accomplish two interviews in a day. The interview form was complex and had many pages, so the training process was at least a week long – too long to create continuity among the high turnover group of researchers in Rohtak. As Mukherjee stated frankly, 'the women were very committed to the project, and picked up the knowledge and interview process quickly, but the constant dislocation of researchers was ultimately too much' (ibid.). After Rohtak, the research group changed to a largely student-based group, most of whom were women – some from Haryana and some from New Delhi (Vikas Rawal interview, 14 June 2003).

The disintegration of all women, all AIDWA-member research teams did change ISWSD's initial methodological challenge because the researchers did not necessarily have close knowledge of the data they collected. But the experiment in the process of knowing still gave prominence to landless women's agricultural expertise. Landless women's insights still shaped how questionnaires framed 'women's wealth and wages'. Landless women activists in AIDWA helped to develop the extensive 'assets list' on the form, which measured the goods a woman brought as dowry. Animal husbandry gained greater attention since increasingly women survived decreased waged work by work and income from raising goats and buffaloes (Keya Mukherjee interview, 13 June 2003). In this way, both 'wages' and 'wealth' gained a gendered specificity in the regionally sensitive questions the researchers asked. Yet who asks the questions and the context of those questions shape the answers as well. What happens when the researchers are no longer activists directly experiencing and involved in landless women's struggles? Does the knowledge collected become suspect, objectified by lack of authenticity in its collection process? Or does the construction of the questionnaire formalize landless women's subjective knowledge?

'*Sadda Haq, Aithe Rakh*' ('Our Rights, Put them Here'), or The Local Knowledge of Reports

AIDWA members from the Fatehabad area were not represented in the research teams, yet their support for the research and the findings was strong. They pointed away from asking who gathered the material toward how that knowledge was produced (arguably in the creation of the questionnaire form), and what it substantiated in the knowledge gained, policy and politics. AIDWA activists saw the research project in a range of ways. First, they saw it as a means to sharpen local campaigns against joblessness and hunger. Veena Rani, the general secretary of the Fatehabad AIDWA, wanted a clearer idea of what the new government policies of 'targeted' ration cards meant for poor women. She said the information would help AIDWA 'fight for their right to government poverty schemes' such as food for work and food policies to aid widows (Veena Rani, Fatehabad AIDWA group interview, 13 June 2003). This collection of information (as much as the final report), she argued, could help AIDWA members further hone their campaign demands relating to the government's public distribution system (PDS) for food, newly revamped along IMF stipulations.

The process of gathering information as well as the final report, AIDWA members in Fatehabad argued, could also build local support, media recognition and pressure on the government for ongoing campaigns in Haryana against gendered violence (Fatehabad AIDWA group interview, 13 June 2003.). Additionally, the research focus on gender and agriculture could strengthen links between organizations such as the All India Agricultural Workers Union (AIAWU) and progressive local elected officials, particularly around *siri* labour and its consequences for women. Jatinder Kaur was a member of AIDWA and an elected member of the *zilla parishad* that represented Fatehabad and thirty-one villages surrounding the city. She talked about these bonded labour cases and AIDWA's activism. The report, she said, would give teeth to the organization's protests. As its slogan said, '*Sadda haq, aithe rakh*' ('Our rights, put them here') (Jatinder Kaur, Fatehabad AIDWA group interview, 13 June 2003). Jatinder talked about the sexual abuse and violence faced by women in bonded labour arrangements with landowners. A recent example was the torture inflicted by the employers of Bachan Singh and Rani Kaur in 2001 (Rajalakshmi 2001). The couple had worked on Sukhdev Singh's farm for twenty years, never realizing their labour was bonded. They began working there after Bachan Singh's father borrowed money from Sukhdev Singh. They had worked since then for sporadic wages of cash and clothing, under the assumption of debt repayment. Rani worked in the landowner's house and collected cow-dung for fuel for 10–15 hours a day. Neither she nor Bachan was allowed to leave the farm without Sukhdev Singh's permission, and when Bachan left for his niece's wedding on 30 June 2001, the punishment brought the couple's bondage into the open. The AIAWU was contacted by Rani Kaur's parents after Bachan Singh returned from the wedding on 3 July. Sukhdev Singh and his family members brutally beat and chained Bachan, forcing him to work with his left hand chained to his left leg. Rani, who was not allowed to see her husband, fled to her parents' house. The Democratic Youth Federation of India (DYFI) and AIDWA joined the campaign to release Bachan Singh and charge Sukhdev Singh under the Bonded Labour (Abolition) Act, 1976 and the Scheduled Castes and Scheduled Tribes (Prevention of Atrocities) Act, 1989.

If not for AIDWA and its coalitional campaign, the local authorities could have easily ignored the complaints Rani and her family lodged with the police. Registering the case against Sukhdev Singh was even more difficult despite the political pressure, and took several days. Jatinder Kaur argued that a report like this one could provide authority to *siri* workers' struggles for justice. 'We can shout slogans,' she said, 'we can hold rallies, if we have these facts. . . . We must snatch these things, facts help us snatch them' (ibid.). The details of *siri* work in ISWSD's report brought to light the bonded aspects of *siri* contracts over their tenancy aspects, such as the presumption of an entire family's labour rights, the loss of daily waged work to supplement the crop percentage, the usurpation of women *siri* workers as domestic labour, as well as the sexual predation on these women. Jatinder suggested that a research report like this one that both documented and generalized the individual abuses faced by *siri* workers, particularly because it was funded by the Indian government, could strengthen activists' fight to successfully register cases against *siri* labour contracts. The report also emphasized the lack of control women had over even casual waged work. In their own words, they were called by the landowners to work, but that call did not come to them directly but to the men in their families. Women worked in groups for physical safety in the fields, but they were also paid as a group and thus had no say over their working conditions and labour, nor any control over the final wages they earned. The facts of women's working conditions opened the door to changes such as the demand for time-rated and piece-rated minimum wages over daily wages; the very enforcement of these changes depended upon knowing the way women worked and were paid. For activists who lived in and around Fatehabad, the report could bolster their demands to charge powerful people with crimes committed, but also support the policies they lobbied to pass through local, state and federal agencies.

Shakti Kak, the director of ISWSD, elaborated on another possible consequence of its research projects. She drew on past experience to argue that the projects provided a chance to strengthen AIDWA's profile in the region and guide ongoing campaigns in the region studied. As she stated, 'when you talk to women, they become aware' (Shakti Kak interview, 18 June 2003). This awareness and the contacts researchers develop, she suggested, helped to build new AIDWA groups in the areas studied. She cited studies already completed by ISWSD and AIDWA members in Tamil Nadu, Orissa and Andhra Pradesh to support her point. Kak said the idea for ISWSD in the early 1990s came from every level of AIDWA's activism. ISWSD filled a 'gap felt by activists about the information they needed to draw wider conclusions and comparisons between regions . . . to help them understand campaigns in a structural manner' (ibid.).

Rani Kaur, Jatinder Kaur and Shakti Kak describe instrumental reasons, although at different levels, for research on landless women's wages and wealth in agriculture. They primarily address AIDWA's short and long-term campaigns. They mention a use for facts to prove women have an especial and often neglected need for government poverty alleviation programmes and work programmes as married, unmarried and widowed women. ISWSD's research provides more detailed information about the gendered role of *siri* work in relation to neoliberal policies, and women's decreased access to waged agricultural work. ISWSD's information collection builds consciousness, accuracy and support for AIDWA's activism. ISWSD's final research report provides a tactical weapon for AIDWA's struggles. In this sense, we can understand activist methodology and research as instrumental tools in ongoing campaigns. In the case of the Haryana report, AIDWA's activism took up several campaigns related to its findings: the fight for fair distribution of government-subsidized food and government work schemes to women, particularly Dalit and Adivasi women, the Right to Food coalition to fight for a universal public distribution system of food, and better protections for women under the National Rural Employment Guarantee Act (NREGA).[13]

[13] Rajalakshmi 2008; AIDWA, 'Memorandum to the Parliamentary Standing Committee of the Ministry of Rural Development on the National Rural Employment Guarantee Bill, 2004', 15 February 2005, personal copy; AIDWA, *For a New Food Policy*, 2003; Karat 2003. For an excellent overview of AIDWA's national and regional campaigns around women's right to food and work, see Agnihotri 2009.

Violence and the Possessive Investment in Masculinity

Community-sanctioned violence against women who challenge caste boundaries and transgress accepted behaviours, the so-called honour killings, in AIDWA's analysis, had deep material connections to land, wages and wealth in the changing political economy of Haryana during the 1990s and beyond. Tradition was a guise that disenfranchised women from oppressed castes, and their class and caste communities, of land and wages. Similarly, sexual violence and the threat of physical intimidation of women, as ISWSD's research project showed, structured every part of women's waged work. From their inability to extract themselves from *siri* labour contracts of their families and their lack of say in the waged work employers gave them to their lack of control over their own pay, women's sexual vulnerability structured their lower wages, their working conditions and the character of women's work in the fields. Sexual intimidation was a lived reality that had no public recognition or legislative protection.

Shakti Kak emphasized that ISWSD's research methodology allowed it to pursue the information *it* felt was important, not just provide data dictated by the grant donor. Even when given a government grant to carry out the research, ISWSD had methodological independence in what questions it asked, how it framed its study and how it assessed the data. ISWSD would accept grants from the United Nations and the government of India, Kak clarified, but not 'outside donors', in order to ensure this level of independence.

The ISWSD report on Haryana addressed issues of women's wages and wealth, but also asked questions not wholly part of those categories: about changes in the government's food distribution system, about sexual violence perpetrated on women by their employers, about non-waged domestic labour, and about dowry costs and dowry-based wealth – all struggle-led questions in support of AIDWA's ongoing campaigns and experiences in the area. Who asks for information, then, matters. Kak emphasized another aspect of ISWSD reports: they produce a long-term analysis of current conditions to ask where these trends lead, and perhaps even help to predict how to win greater gains for landless agricultural women.

The ISWSD study on Haryana drew unusual connections between agricultural women's loss of wages, their increased vulnerability to sexual violence and the erosion of women's social value. Two overlapping questions attempted to build a database of women's non-waged domestic work for employers (particularly prevalent in *siri* labour) and women's sexual exploitation. Question four of the questionnaire had several parts under the heading 'Freedom of Employment'. The third question asked, 'Does any woman in the family provide unpaid/underpaid labour service to the employer of a male worker of the family or to the person who employs the family on piece-rated contracts?' This question allowed the ISWSD survey to measure women's non-waged 'productive' work (called *begar*), such as cleaning paid for in kind by employers, or sweeping for water rather than wages (in the case of one woman interviewed), or work performed by women in return for leaves to feed the buffalo calves they raised. Non-waged productive work also included jobs like the three years of unpaid domestic work done by Risik Kaur, who worked on the landowner's promise to take care of her eldest daughter's wedding costs. 'It may not be for the dowry,' Risik speculated, 'but they may pay for the wedding tent' (Risik Kaur interview by Keya Mukherjee and Vikas Rawal, 13 June 2003.). The seventh question in this section of the questionnaire seems at first to merely restate this query: 'Has any member of your household been coerced to work for an employer? Coerced by any person the household is indebted to? Any instance of extra-economic coercion or threat? Give details.' Although coded enough so that 'rape' and 'sexual harassment' are not mentioned by name, unpaid domestic work is distinguished from sexual violence by the term 'coercion'. Several of the women researchers emphasized how the question allowed the women they interviewed to talk directly about *chherkhani*, so directly in fact that they used the word for sexual harassment rather than merely implied it (ISWSD research group interview, 13 June 2003). The answers to these questions revealed that often girls were not sent to government schools for fear of elopement and sexual violation, and that women would only take group work in fields such as wheat harvesting to protect themselves from attack. Even women working in the fields as part of larger non-familial groups, as in paddy harvesting, faced sexual harassment from other workers to pressure them against taking scarce daily waged work (ibid.). Under these conditions, Vikas Rawal reported, 'women have virtually stopped going to the fields' (Vikas Rawal interview, 13 June 2003). The value of women in times of decreased women's work, these initial findings suggest, rests even more tenaciously on their sexual status. Women's jobs in unprotected work conditions, however badly needed, must be sacrificed for the sake of the woman's, the family's or the community's honour.

Questions about increased vulnerability to sexual violence in the study, as well as the costs of dowry, all shift how we currently understand women's wages and wealth in the neoliberal regime.[14] The ISWSD report reveals how decreased agricultural work is driven by factors in addition to increased

[14] Feminist academics such as Bina Agarwal, Gita Sen, Maithreyi Krishnaraj and others fought to change how the Indian census asked land ownership questions from the household as a unit to the gender-differentiated members of the household. Critics also fought to measure women's unpaid domestic work as well as paid work, a struggle that successfully changed the National Sample Survey Organization and then the Indian census questions. See Agarwal 1994; Gita Sen and Chiranjib Sen 1994; Maithreyi Krishnaraj 1990.

mechanization. The survey questions allowed compounding gender and caste factors into the report's understanding of decreased agricultural work for women.[15] The questions showed how endemic was the sexual predation of girls and women who worked in agriculture for wages and as debt-bonded labourers. Because of its limited scope, the report does not generalize about all landless women agricultural workers in Haryana. Its results are written as a spotlight understanding, with attention to the localized specificities of landless women's intensified insecurity in neoliberal India. However, Vikas Rawal argued, the report can be used to draw generalizations about how waged work disappears for different reasons in specific localities, yet diminishes to a similar degree, as in the two very different localities of Dhamar and Birdhana in Haryana.

As landless women lose waged work, the ISWSD report showed, gendered labour practices and larger social relationships also change (Vikas Rawal interview, 14 June 2003). In terms of the report's long-term instrumental value, the struggle-led questions about widows' right to government food subsidies, food distribution, dowry and sexual violence cannot predict how activists will gain governmental support. They do not overtly untangle how to reverse or stall the stark contraction of the government's role in poverty reduction schemes. Neither does the report itself speculate about how a gendered understanding of *siri* labour will sharpen the fight against bonded labour in the Fatehabad region. The use of the report, in other words, does not stem from the questions asked or even the report's own conclusions, but from the social movements that use it in their local and national campaigns. Shakti Kak and others in ISWSD and AIDWA believe that those answers will develop from a re-energized activism this report can engender.

Activist Methodologies

The research adhered in several ways to mainstream and feminist academic/public policy standards. It used basic random sampling techniques from economic surveys of income and wealth. It asked questions only about women's income-generating labour, bracketing off debates about the value of unpaid domestic work for their own families. In this sense, the report did not take advantage of the victory won by prominent feminist economists like Gita Sen to compile Indian census and NSS data on women's unpaid reproductive labour for their own families. As the grant proposal clearly stated, 'the study does not aim to examine the time spent on and economic significance of the domestic work done by women' (ISWSD 2004: 2). However, ISWSD's report does reveal other hidden venues of women's non-waged work for employers

[15] The lead researcher Vikas Rawal pursued these aspects in more detail in a subsequent article on unfreedom and *siri* work. See Rawal 2004.

(or potential benefactors as in the case of Risik Kaur), possible in part, perhaps, because of the increased legitimacy of measuring the value of domestic labour. The ISWSD report used the powerful methodological point made by another feminist economist, Bina Agarwal, to understand gendered questions of land ownership and dispossession. Rather than measure women's access to waged work within the family unit as a whole or by separating out the women in the household from the men, the survey individualized each family member in terms of property, wealth and employment, to disaggregate the complexity of landless women's conditions from a more simply gender-marked household unit (Agarwal 1985).

In addition, the researchers maintained a methodological distance from activist groups in the area like AIDWA as they conducted their interviews. They made no reference to ISWSD or to AIDWA when interviewing the women, though some information about both these organizations travelled within the village. Vikas Rawal recounted an interaction he had with one interviewee the day before, who wanted to know who would use the survey. 'He asked, "Will communists use it? Communists should use it"' (Vikas Rawal interview, 14 June 2003). The researchers did not promise campaigns to change the women's obvious destitution, or material support towards their survival. Bluntly put, they recorded the women's answers and left. A notable incident occurred during the research project in Birdhana, when the daughter of a *siri* worker reported the abuse of her father. The daughter was a member of AIDWA, and news of AIDWA–AIAWU's successful intervention in her father's case revealed to everyone in the locality how strong were the connections between the ISWSD researchers and politically active groups in the region like AIDWA and AIAWU. As AIDWA and AIAWU members in the region attested, their daily work in the area included a steady stream of cases to stop abuse of *siri* workers. The only worthy demand, in their assessment, was to abolish *siri* altogether (ibid.). Nevertheless, at the level of data collection, the instrumental reasons for the report in support of AIDWA's activism, including its innovative research methodology, remained all but invisible. The report filled gaps of knowledge about particular agricultural women's lives, and began a data-bank for other researchers to complete. The analytic practice of AIDWA's long-term strategy for this report is more difficult to grasp. The focus on the wages and wealth of people most marginalized in the agricultural economy by their gender, their caste and their class comes back to AIDWA's challenges as a multi-class, multi-caste organization. AIDWA was deeply involved in Haryana's intensified violence directed against women in the middle classes and intermediate castes, as well as upper classes and castes. How can AIDWA build a movement that connects the powerful energy of activism against that violence to the lives of working-poor, oppressed-caste women in the same localities? How can women in these movements cross caste and class boundaries to support economic and cultural changes in women's value?

This research powerfully centers on how sexual violence is never marginal to economic violence. The questions probe how neoliberalism intensifies economic relationships of sexism, often caste-specific, that are not lived in 'timeless' or 'traditional' but in profoundly modern ways by landless agricultural women workers. In this sense, the report illustrates Lourdes Beneria's argument that the polemical divide between women's economic struggles, what she calls 'economic justice' issues, and 'gender justice' issues around sexuality and citizenship is 'artificial and misleading' (Beneria 2003: 27). Beneria gives an example: 'domestic violence against women has been linked to problems of poverty and unemployment among men. Consequently, campaigns against domestic violence should focus both on the social construction of gender that shapes men's and women's attitude and behaviour and on the root economic justice aspects of the problem' (ibid.). Her example interweaves the causality of economic and gender justice issues. Yet ISWSD's report on landless women's wealth and wages takes Beneria's point a step farther. It provides evidence that sexual violence, in part, determines the lived character of the economic violence faced by disenfranchised women.

The ISWSD report achieves its most powerful epistemological insights when its adherence to scholarly protocol meets the openly political subjectivity of its knowledge. Women's survival as landless agricultural workers has become more tenuous after the economic and political consolidation of neoliberalism.[16] Women have fewer waged jobs in neoliberal fields, and those jobs that remain receive smaller wages. Whether due to casualization of work as in Rohtak or due to landlordism as in Fatehabad, women's agricultural work faces severe contraction (NCAER 2003; Mahbub ul Haq Human Development Centre 2003: 26.). Even when women find daily waged work, sexual harassment hampers their decisions to take these jobs, if it is not woven into the very demands of the job. As a long-term strategy to tackle neoliberalism, then, AIDWA does not overlook the reciprocal struggle against gendered violence. Dowry, 'honour killings,' domestic violence and rape are also the economic and political struggles of women and men disenfranchised by neoliberalism. In Haryana, AIDWA's politics squarely faced the increasing retribution against inter-caste marriages and intra-*gotra* marriages, and cases of rape and dowry-related violence. For AIDWA, gender and caste atrocities cannot be thought apart from the agrarian crisis. The findings of ISWSD's report stayed close to its data, and its generalizations are better seen in AIDWA's politics around the right to food

[16] See the essays on current conditions of land and survival in Alice Thorner, ed. 2001. Particularly relevant to this discussion is Bina Agarwal, 'Disinherited Peasants, Disadvantaged Workers: A Gender Perspective on Land and Livelihood', ibid.: 159–201.

and PDS policies, around the fair distribution of land, and employment generation policies like the NREGA. AIDWA's explicit gendering, in its politics and its research, of seemingly ungendered hardship – hunger, employment and landlessness – complicates both simple class unity and undifferentiated sisterhood among all women.

AIDWA's Organizing through Activist Research

Subhashini Ali characterized AIDWA's organizing strategy in 2008 for landless women in the face of a worsening rural economy in these words: 'first of all, demand work, then get work, then ensure their wage payments, and also see that onsite facilities are made available' (Subhashini Ali interview, 22 July 2008). The connections between AIDWA's 2003 study in rural Haryana and its active intervention in the implementation of the NREGA are not hard to see.[17] Women's employment in agricultural work had shrunk to forty days of waged work per year, in stark comparison to landless men's employment of 100 days per year (ISWSD 2004). The research found that men also faced similarly decreased work-days in agricultural work, equalling roughly forty days of paid agricultural work. Landless men's additional 60 days of work was due to their access to non-agricultural employment. Landless women had very little access to wages in non-agricultural work, unlike landless men. Also, landless women had no access to jobs through public work schemes, since those primarily involved digging – considered men's work. AIDWA's intervention during the drafting of the NREGA in 2005 responded directly to these findings. It demanded that women be given priority for 30 per cent of the work offered in rural areas by NREGA, even as the Members of Parliament they lobbied argued that women would not take the work (AIDWA, 'Memorandum to the Parliamentary Standing Committee of the Ministry of Rural Development on the National Rural Employment Guarantee Bill, 2004', 2005). Ali stated the evidence of AIDWA's intervention: in 2008 women held 42 per cent of NREGA jobs (Subhashini Ali interview, 22 July 2008).

The vibrancy of AIDWA in rural areas across the country also gave the organization another view of India's economic globalization in the 1990s and later. The links AIDWA drew between access to basic resources like water and land, and employment, derived from its leftist analysis of the roots of women's exploitation and oppression, but also from its focus on rural localities. Caste oppression inflected the gendered violence faced by women during the consolidation of neoliberal agricultural policies. Neoliberalism

[17] Not least because ISWSD researchers authored another field report on precisely this topic: ISWSD 2006.

transformed the agricultural economy from one defined by small-scale farming as well as the highly capitalized, national farming in Haryana beginning in the late 1960s. It shifted the national horizon of producing enough food grain to feed the country's populace to a globalized commodity industry with food grains priced by the global market, farming inputs like fertilizer and seeds priced by multinational corporations, and an infrastructure for irrigation and well-paved roads that overwhelmingly benefited large-scale farming operations. In a competitive global agricultural economy, every cost is weighed to maximize profit or 'efficiency'. In agriculture, like most other industries, human labour costs take the largest hit since, in the language of free market economics, the production costs of labour are the most flexible. AIDWA measured the consequences of these changes for the women erased and forgotten even in critiques of global agriculture: landless agricultural women workers, regardless of their caste or religion. Yet, through inter-sectoral organizing, AIDWA's drive to build membership and organize landless women workers did not erase these community and caste specificities. AIDWA showed that among landless, often Dalit agricultural workers, women workers most dramatically felt these blows to their earning power: they worked for fewer days and smaller wages as jobs previously gendered as 'women's work' became mechanized and disappeared (ISWSD 2004). Women remained in the village, at least during the 1980s and 1990s, as men migrated in search of waged work to the cities. Migration rates began to include larger and larger numbers of women after the 1990s, as small farming operations and waged agricultural work failed to support families even with the cash contributions of male family members' out-migration.

At the heart of this chapter is AIDWA's means to instigate and consolidate inter-sectoral activism; its membership-led and struggle-led research. AIDWA's research, surveys, reports and lists of demands produced by its members across the country have given urgency and clarity to the inter-sectoral campaigns AIDWA members address at the local, state, regional and national levels. One component of AIDWA's activist research is struggle-led: that is, this activist research has animated AIDWA's turn to the village as it built its organizational knowledge, drew new members, developed more leaders, and sought new inroads against the systemic oppression and exploitation women face. The other important component of AIDWA's activist research is a discursive activism with one eye to changing how social scientists and policy makers, nationally and internationally, view rural women in relation to rural development politics, and another to the economic stakes of food security, government employment guarantee schemes and land distribution policies. Both the struggle-led and discursive activisms of AIDWA's research rely upon a strong class analysis that makes gender and caste oppression inseparable from an understanding of what must be done.

FIVE

Anti-Casteism in Tamil Nadu

Changes in India's agricultural economy begun in the 1990s overwhelmingly favoured the landed and caste Hindus over the landless Dalit and other agricultural workers. AIDWA witnessed the effects of these economic changes as it focused its attention on the specificities of rural women's lives through its campaigns in Haryana around land appropriation, wages, and *khap panchayat* rulings against behaviour deemed transgressive of gender and caste norms. AIDWA documented in its writings and activism that these changes in rural economies fuelled intensified hierarchies of caste and gender, and placed Dalit and Adivasi women in positions of increased vulnerability. The organizing of Dalit women in rural and urban areas, and AIDWA's campaigns against untouchability practices across India in the late 1990s, were an important catalyst for changes in AIDWA's organizational vision and analysis. Sectoral issues such as Muslim women's issues of communalism, Dalit women's issues of dignity and untouchability practices, Adivasi women's issues of landlessness, and rural women's issues of unemployment formed the backbone of AIDWA's focus on inter-sectoral organizing campaigns and strategies.

The transformation of caste politics across India after independence reverberated from demands made by Scheduled Caste (SC), Scheduled Tribe (ST), and Other Backward Class/Caste (OBC) citizens and groups to hold the government to its promises of caste-based equity in education, jobs and land (Jaffrelot 2003: 411–12; Hasan 1989b).[1] Beginning soon after independence, the government reserved access for SC and ST members to education, legislative seats, government jobs and land redistribution. These people were part of the Backward Classes (BC), since SC and ST people had a range of religious

[1] The 'Other Backward Class' (OBC) designation is a mutable one that includes backward castes and communities defined through their social, economic and political disadvantages. The term 'Backward Class' refers to Scheduled Caste (or Dalit), Scheduled Tribe (or Adivasi) and OBCs as a whole.

Map of Tamil Nadu

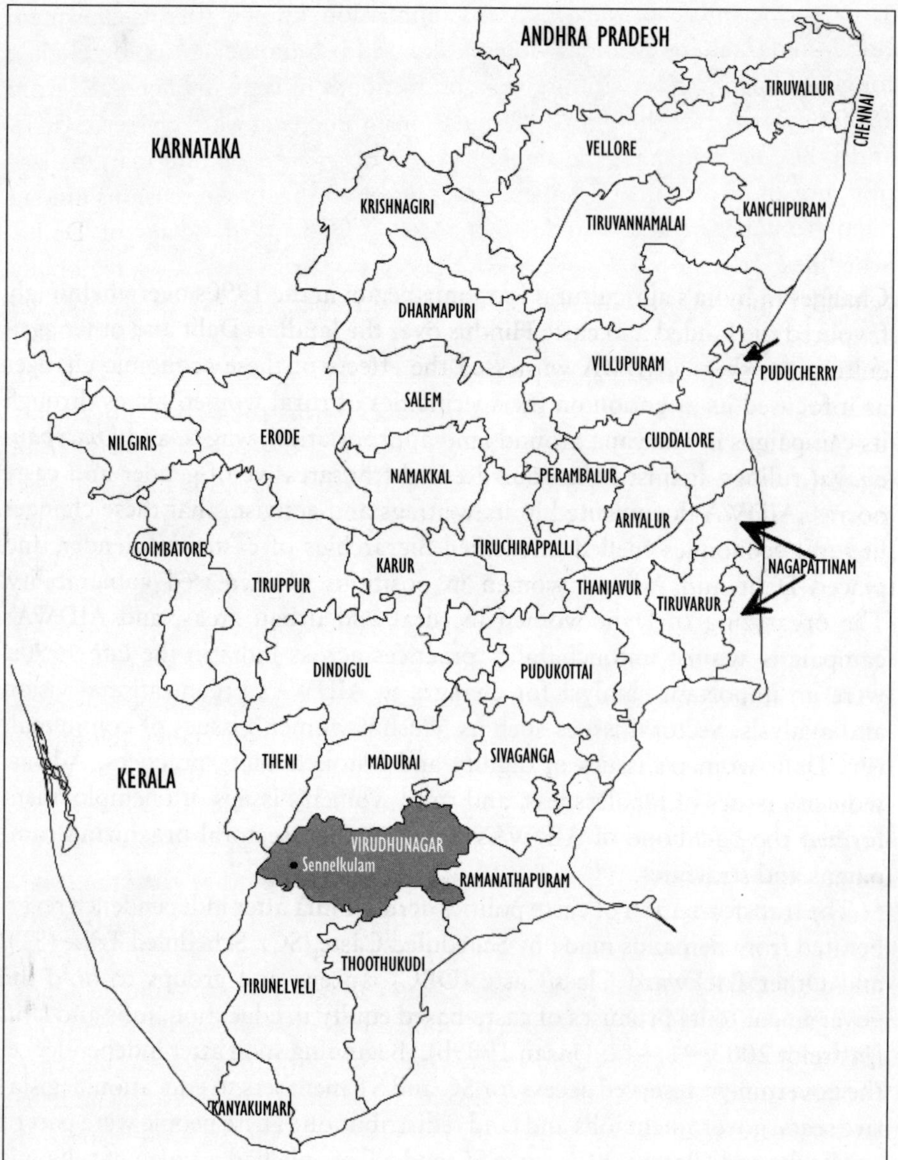

backgrounds, including Muslim, Christian, Sikh and Buddhist. Other historically dispossessed lower castes, sometimes designated by the short-hand of Shudras, did not receive reservations to these governmental resources. This group was called Other Backward Classes, beginning in 1953 when the First Backward Classes Commission was created (Yadav 2002: 4495). In 1979, the Second Backward Classes Commission, known after its chairman, B.P. Mandal, as the Mandal Commission, added another grouping eligible for governmental reservations; its recommendations were implemented from 1989 onwards. Yet these three designations in the backward classes, SC, ST and OBC, do not share the same histories of oppression and marginalization, nor of governmental remediation, and have historical tensions among them from before the Mandal Commission. Scheduled Castes or Dalits, Scheduled Tribes or Adivasis, and Other Backward Classes – a regionally defined group of socially, educationally and economically disadvantaged people, largely held together in support of the Mandal Commission's report in the wake of the fierce backlash by upper castes against the report's recommendations (Omvedt 1990a: 2195). In places with strong caste movements like Tamil Nadu, the OBCs had already gained access to reservations from the state for land, government jobs and entry into educational institutions. Yet even within the OBCs in Tamil Nadu, the coalition faced internal strains since a small number of OBC-designated castes in that state had received a far greater share of the benefits of reservations (Panini 1996: 58).

Beginning in the 1970s, alongside the implementation of reservations for OBCs, upheavals in land ownership patterns and political power in rural areas in Tamil Nadu shifted from the hands of Brahmins and upper castes to OBCs (Hasan 1989b; Gough 1973; Mendelsohn and Vicziany; Teltumbde 2011). Much of the caste conflict that racked the southern state of Tamil Nadu for ten years, between 1995 and 2005, was anti-Dalit violence perpetrated by dominant OBCs in rural localities around land, wages, dignity and an end to *begar,* or unpaid caste-based work, such as beating the drum at funerals (Viswanathan 2005; Gorringe 2005; Human Rights Watch 1999: 82–126). The rise of anti-Dalit tyranny in the 1990s was linked to lower and middle-caste landowners who responded violently to Dalit demands for dignity, and the end to untouchability practices of separate temples, different cups at tea-stalls and restaurants, the right to sit in the presence of caste Hindus, and the right to sexual autonomy and control. The temple entry campaign in the hamlet of Sennelkulam in the central district of Virudhunagar, Tamil Nadu, began in 1998 when Dalit youths attempted to worship at their local temple. They were met with violent opposition from OBC and middle-caste members of their locality. The conflict continued until a resolution that unlocked the temple doors and opened the temple to all was reached in 2003. The temple entry campaign in Sennelkulam contains the strategies of alliance and coalition that AIDWA mobilized to build inter-sectoral campaigns against caste oppression across Tamil Nadu, and developed in other states across India.

Activist research played a hidden, yet paramount role in the temple entry campaign in Sennelkulam. R. Chandra, an AIDWA leader in Tamil Nadu, systematically gathered evidence from localities across the state to understand the breadth of untouchability issues faced by rural and urban women. While Chandra led the efforts in Tamil Nadu, she did not gather evidence alone. Through her research methods, she sought to break down casteism among its caste Hindu members in AIDWA, and build solidarity for Dalit women's issues across the caste lines of its members. AIDWA's activist research mobilized its own members across a district or zone to gather information about untouchability practices in their own localities. Chandra trained the researchers and often developed the questionnaires, but produced an organizational membership made up predominantly of the most active members of a research team who could map social injustices on their own terrain. For AIDWA's inter-sectoral organizing strategy, activist research allowed the voices of the most oppressed rural women to define the problems they faced and become the leaders they sought. Activist research also forced prominent members, in terms of their local caste and class status, or in the upper levels of AIDWA's leadership, to listen. At its best, AIDWA's activist research aided in the devolution of leadership to the level of AIDWA's units, its smallest formal body of members formed in neighbourhoods or localities. Activist research spurred the increases in and strength of AIDWA's membership through hard-fought campaigns to gain justice.

Sectoral Issues and Inter-sectoral Organizing

AIDWA's local organizing campaigns that fought casteism and practices of untouchability reshaped its own coalitional models of organization – between local women's groups, left allies and other sympathetic groups. These campaigns fostered clearer articulations of what sectoral organizing meant for AIDWA, in this case around Dalit issues and Dalit women. AIDWA's political work in the 1990s and 2000s around issues of Dalit women and against caste oppression relied on three primary (and sometimes overlapping) alliances. It worked with left allies, Dalit rights groups and women's organizations in ways that garnered important stability from the allies' strengths, but also pushed their weaknesses. AIDWA's campaigns led its left allies – such as the All India Agricultural Workers Union (AIAWU), the Democratic Youth Federation of India (DYFI), the Centre of Indian Trade Unions (CITU) and the Communist Party of India (Marxist) (CPI[M]) – in its attention to building a class unity that pays close attention to caste, religion and gender particularities among workers and citizens. AIDWA's coalitional work with Dalit rights organizations around the country, such as the All India Mahila Adhikar Manch, created multi-caste organizing efforts against caste oppression. AIDWA also built a network between local, regional and national women's organizations, and drew on the resources of the National Women's Commission and State Women's Commissions to support its campaign goals.

AIDWA's sectoral model of organizing against casteism differed from separatist ideologies of Dalit unity or women's unity; that is, theories of unity built upon oppressed caste status and experience, or women's gender oppression and exploitation. In the 1990s, AIDWA put into practice the difficult lessons learned from debates in the 1980s about communalism and women's rights. The hardest and most powerful coalitions and campaigns, as AIDWA's own literature and movement practices attested to, were ones that created solidarity between caste, class, gender and religious constituencies, with movement leadership from the most oppressed and exploited members. Equally important to AIDWA's practices of sectoral organizing was its focus on changes *within* the organization around members' own caste, class and religious prejudices, even as it sought to transform those ideologies in the communities at large through organizational pressure.

In December 1998, AIDWA held its first National Convention against Untouchability and Dalit Oppression. Over 1,000 Dalit women from states across north India joined the convention. Reports of anti-Dalit violence from seven states included personal testimonies by women, many of whom were AIDWA leaders from their localities, about fighting local instances of untouchability practices. Shyamali Gupta, the president of AIDWA, welcomed participants as part of a working conference to develop strategies 'to mobilize all sections of women against the caste system' (Moghe 1999: 8). AIDWA speakers also reiterated that the convention actively contested the notion of a unified sisterhood that unproblematically joined all women in their struggles for justice, dignity and equality. Bela Malik, a middle-class AIDWA member from New Delhi, emphasized women's casteism as one target of the gathering. 'Upper-caste women are often among the perpetrators of oppression. In this general environment, the significance of . . . an exclusively Dalit women platform seems only natural', she wrote (Malik 2005: 103). Malik also drew the connections between Dalit women's oppression and their class exploitation as dispossessed women forced to survive in rural and urban localities on low-paid manual labour. 'Given the nature of oppression, a struggle for a better life for Dalit women cannot, perhaps, be divorced from a wider social emancipatory agenda' (ibid.). Malik's overview of the political stakes of AIDWA's conference emphasized questions of women's unity that the conference raised, alongside a more complex understanding of Dalit oppression as not simply a social, religious or cultural discrimination, but at its core, an economic one.

AIDWA sought to build women's unity through the conference by recognizing that complexity of anti-Dalit crimes. The women's unity they asserted demanded alliances across women's particular caste and class locations. The conference declaration made explicit their inter-sectoral analysis:

> The Conference asserts that the slogan of women's unity and sisterhood has meaning only if it is based on the struggles against systems and cultures of caste apartheid and economic and social inequality. There is undoubtedly a commonality of gender-based oppression which all women face. However, that cannot be the shield for a so-called homogenous identity which ignores the pain, the suffering and the exploitation of the vast majority of poor women of this country. We believe in women's unity against untouchability, women's unity against the caste system, women's unity against class and social exploitation. (AIDWA, 'Resolution, Declaration, Demands Adopted at the Dalit Women's Convention', 1999: 46)

Unity as a goal cannot rely on shared injustices experienced by the movement's members. Unity demands an ideological commonality, one that seeks to dismantle the entire system of caste hierarchy, class exploitation and patriarchal social oppression. The outlines of AIDWA's strategy for inter-sectoral organizing emerged through the convention's focus on Dalit women's issues, with its concerted attempt to engage Dalit women members in the conference proceedings, and its emphasis on hearing their stories and their demands for justice. The convention provided a platform to local and state-based AIDWA campaigns against untouchability in Haryana, Punjab, Rajasthan, Himachal Pradesh, Uttar Pradesh, Bihar and Madhya Pradesh, but also showed how far the country and AIDWA had to go in their commitment to eradicate untouchability practices.

Sectoral issues in AIDWA highlighted the specificity of particularly oppressed women. As a strategy, inter-sectoral organizing methods refused to allow the political answer to be segregated by caste, class or religious affiliation. One technique to build caste, class and gender unity suggested in its organizational literature was to wage anti-casteist struggles framed through common goals, such as the fight for access to water. Water access and water use is a deeply caste-riven issue in rural areas, since a mainstay of untouchability practices is separate and unequal water facilities in localities – with one well for caste Hindus and another for Dalits. Water is also a scarce resource with moneyed interests, such as industrial producers, large landowners and powerful families, gaining the lion's share. An anti-casteist struggle against untouchability practices of separate and often inferior wells can also raise the rights of all locality members to adequate water supplies.

'Unity' in this declaration emphatically did not stand in for 'likeness' or 'homogeneity'. Instead, AIDWA's notion of unity reimagined what a caste or religious identity means for women when they struggle against bigotry within their social, religious, ethnic and cultural communities. U. Vasuki talked explicitly about changing the language of non-Dalit participants in Tamil Nadu's conferences against untouchability crimes, from a language of 'them' to a discourse of 'us'. She said:

> When non-Dalit women speak, even if they are [AIDWA] activists, they will say 'we' and 'you'. They just sympathize with them or empathize with them. . . . We have noticed this, and when the state leadership now addresses all these activists, we say, 'Even when you talk about Dalit women's issues, you should say "we" and "our". Identify these issues as yours, as the issues of the organization. You are not an individual, you represent an organization.' (U. Vasuki interview, 26 March 2006)

Unity, here, demands that women cross their own parochial identities in solidarity with Dalit women, that is, to enact inter-sectoral politics in their commitment to social change. But inter-sectoral organizing means non-Dalit women must struggle against and within their own communities against casteism. Unity against Dalit oppression is not for 'them' but for a reconceived 'us'. Yet non-Dalit women's participation should be one of taking leadership from Dalit women's analysis and experience of untouchability.

The risks of inter-sectoral organizing, made especially visible as AIDWA embraced Dalit women's issues and the fight against untouchability at a national level, did not just challenge the women's movement or the Dalit movement. Inter-sectoral organizing of Dalit women intensified AIDWA's understanding that just as 'women' do not have an internal coherence, neither does 'the working class'. The strategy of inter-sectoral organizing, Brinda Karat argued, began with AIDWA's turn to the village and attention to the issues faced by rural women. AIDWA took on questions of rural women's unequal wages and their inability to gain access to government work programmes; they fought domestic violence faced by rural women, their inability to gain schooling, the rise of dowry demands for all castes (and religions) of women, and female foeticide and infanticide. Rural women's issues included their informal working conditions, the inaccessibility of resources like land and water, as well the dearth of non-agricultural work for women. A sectoral approach to rural women's issues brought class-based struggles of wages and working conditions into AIDWA's immediate purview, and challenged their left allies in rural localities, particularly the Kisan Sabha, the Agricultural Workers Union and the CPM.

In the sectoral work of AIDWA, women's issues were palpably class issues.

Left mass organizations allied to AIDWA that explicitly addressed work issues keenly felt their failure to address the class exploitation of women AIDWA's activism represented. Karat described:

> I remember first raising the issues of agricultural women workers in the late 1980s, and there were discussions on this and a certain hesitation among both sections of the organization [AIDWA] and among the fraternal organizations: 'Why should you be able to do it?' And we had to fight that, as it was linked to a very narrow understanding of class by many of our fraternal organizations. (Brinda Karat interview, 26 December 2004)

The left allies resisted AIDWA's activism as their territorial loss. Out of AIDWA's agricultural women's conventions, the issues of Dalit women's caste oppression emerged as a central factor among a majority of agricultural women's workers. 'There were so many different aspects that came that have to be included in any movement of agricultural women workers', Karat explained. 'Caste, of course, was a very, very big issue; land was a big issue' (ibid.). By the time of the Convention against Untouchability and Oppression against Dalits in 1998, AIDWA had amassed the research and organizing experience that entwined Dalit women's issues inextricably with rural women's issues. In her keynote address to the convention, Karat said: 'There can be no struggle for liberation which does not specifically address and fight against caste oppression' (Moghe 1999: 8).

Caste Politics after the Mandal Commission Report, 1989

In 1989, V.P. Singh's government accepted a central recommendation of the Mandal Commission Report on caste when it declared 27 per cent reservation of all government jobs for citizens designated OBCs. The Commission Report had sat dormant for nine years before the central government acted on any of its recommendations, and a number of explanations have been given for why V.P. Singh's government chose that moment to pay attention. Many commentators have linked his decision to the departure of his deputy minister Devi Lal, who was a powerful Jat leader, a caste designated as OBC (Srinivas 1991: 834). The V.P. Singh government's attempt to counter the Bharatiya Janata Party (BJP), who made significant gains from this defection, led to its selective embrace of the Mandal Commission Report. The government ignored recommendations to enforce land reform policies and distribute land to OBCs, focusing instead on what Zoya Hasan calls 'socio-political issues' over economic issues of caste inequality (Hasan 1989b: 195). The response was immediate and vociferous with widespread protests, student self-immolations, and opposition party demonstrations erupting across the country in 1990. V.P. Singh's decision was stayed by a legal challenge until 1993 when the Supreme Court upheld his ruling with one exception, to withhold reservations from 'the creamy layer' of economically and socially more privileged OBCs. The coalition government in power in 1993, of the Samajwadi Party (SP) and Bahujan Samaj Party (BSP), both with strong Backward Class constituencies, and enthusiastic supporters of the proposed quotas, implemented the policy immediately with one addition. It added a 27 per cent reservation for OBCs in medical, engineering and management colleges (Jaffrelot 2003: 374). The sting to upper-caste power barely registered in 1993 and the amendments took effect without public opposition. One factor that contributed to its ease was that as liberalization gained steam, the power and economic gain of government positions ebbed in favour of jobs in the private sector, an area untouched by caste-based reservations. Upper castes and upper classes moved into the privileges of private sector jobs away from the public sector, the reason some give for the resounding lack of response to job and university seat quotas in 1993 (Jaffrelot 2003: 367; Venkatesan 2006). The Secretary of the Mandal Commission, S.S. Gill, lamented years after their Report about the failed potential for lower-caste alliances against casteism. Gill had hoped that Dalits and OBCs would 'join hands and form a powerful alliance to secure political power and wield it to improve the lot of their historically disadvantaged castes. But the pursuit of narrower personal ends has produced just the opposite results' (Gill 2003). The quotas expressly for OBCs created the potential to consolidate gains made by landowning OBCs in the towns and cities of India – gains made on the backs of Dalit agricultural and urban workers rather than in coalition with them (Chowdhry 2011: 369–411).

Caste in contemporary India gains its salience though relatively recent changes in rural land ownership due to post-independence land reform and subsequent 'green revolution' policies that dismantled the interdependence of the *jajmani* caste system, and created a proletarian class of Dalits surviving through waged work alone, without upper caste patronage. 'The displacement of upper-caste landlords from villages, enrichment of a section of the Shudra caste cluster [traditional farming castes] through this programme and the consolidation of the populous shudra castes into a powerful political constituency changed the entire socio-political fabric of the country' (Teltumbde 2010: 11). The shift from power and land concentrations in the hands of upper-caste landowners alone, particularly felt in the rural areas of Tamil Nadu, created a new caste divide. Anand Teltumbde characterizes this caste division in stark terms: 'These caste dynamics reduce caste to the divide between Dalits and non-Dalits' (ibid.). For Teltumbde, caste in contemporary India can be reduced to two castes: Dalit and caste Hindu. Any distinctions within the caste Hindus, he argues, are negligible in the current social, economic and political context.

For many scholars of Indian politics, the protests against the Mandal Commission propelled the issue of caste and caste violence into urban social movements, including the Indian women's movement (Rao 2005: 1–47). Uma Chakravarti argues that the virulent attack by caste Hindus against the Commission's Report in 1990 instigated the feminist movement to directly address caste issues. She marks a double failing, of feminist analysis and feminist politics, during the late 80s. Chakravarti writes candidly: 'no feminist viewpoint based on a *feminist* understanding of the caste system appeared in the course of the debates. Feminists failed to intervene and decisively shape the debates' (Chakravarti 2003: 3). She provides a historical narrative for feminist analysis of caste that is markedly different from the political development articulated by AIDWA leaders from this period. In fact Indu Agnihotri, a feminist scholar and member of AIDWA, argued that it already actively negotiated issues of casteism within its membership by 1990, due to its rural organizing work. She marked the differences of class and locality that shaped AIDWA's experience of Mandal Commission politics in contrast to the rude awakening experienced by predominantly middle-class women's organizations in cities. The protests against Mandal were based in the perceptions of the middle class, and middle to upper castes, of unfair advantage for OBCs. Middle-class women joined and organized protests against Mandal, surprising feminist groups with a more homogenous, predominantly middle-class and urban membership. Agnihotri noted that anti-brahmanism was only one aspect of AIDWA's response to the Mandal protests, since AIDWA faced a complex range of caste-based discrimination in rural areas: 'We were also aware, on the basis of our membership amongst rural communities, of the divides within the so-called lower castes' (Indu Agnihotri interview, 29 July 2008). Unlike more urban feminist groups, Agnihotri argued, AIDWA's activism among working-poor, rural women impelled its drive to better understand the majority of women who lived and worked in rural areas. The issues of caste and religious inter-marriage and status consciousness had permeated not only the campaigns AIDWA addressed in the early and mid-1980s, Agnihotri contended, but also as issues *within* AIDWA as an organization that recruited the widest possible membership.

In 1998, the year of their national convention against untouchability, AIDWA faced criticism from feminists that they were class reductionists in their struggle against women's caste oppression. As Sharmila Rege wrote, 'the left party-based women's organizations collapsed caste into class' (Rege 1998: WS43; Thorat 2001: 12). AIDWA also contended with assumptions that it rebuffed Dalit women's organizations, like the National Federation of Dalit Women, as caste-sectarian. Kiran Moghe, a leader of AIDWA in New Delhi, was interpreted to have argued that 'Dalit women's organizations faced the threat of being "autonomous from the masses"' (Rege 1998:

WS44). Critics further charged that AIDWA members opposed or felt threatened by Dalit women's organizing separately because it drained energy from class-based struggles for land, resources and employment.

AIDWA's own documents support a more nuanced understanding of Dalit women's organizing. A 1998 convention paper stated: 'We view the movements and demands of Dalit organizations with sympathy and solidarity. Our approach toward Dalit organizations is necessarily different from an approach to other caste-based organizations, as the former are fighting the reality of continuing untouchability and caste oppression' (AIDWA, 'Fighting for the Rights of Dalit Women', 1999: 56). Moghe's own article about the 1998 convention articulated the issue of Dalit women's organizing very differently. She referred to an AIDWA leader's report, a woman named Nirmala Devi who was a Dalit woman and an elected member of the Chandauli district *zila parishad* (district-wide government body). Nirmala Devi's report criticized the Scheduled Caste party in the northern state of Uttar Pradesh, the Bahujan Samaj Party (BSP): 'The BSP leaders had mobilized Dalits on the basis of their caste but had never once given a call for land struggle' (Moghe 1999: 8). In AIDWA's analysis, the demand for equal rights to land is both a caste-based and deeply gendered class issue. To organize as Dalits, or to organize as Dalit women, did not change the class-based anchors of the caste system, nor did it necessarily separate Dalit women from class struggles, depending on how the fight against the caste system was waged. The BSP, Nirmala Devi contended, opportunistically mobilized Dalits without attention to these central class components of Dalit oppression.

Dalit Women's Organizing for Temple Entry in Sennelkulam, Tamil Nadu

When AIDWA members from Sennelkulam, in southern Tamil Nadu, tell about their long struggle to open the Kaliamman temple to the entire Dalit community, they openly celebrate their victory. 'We were not very friendly [with the caste Hindu, Thevar community], we did not worship the gods together' – stated one woman from the caste-segregated colony of Sennelkulam who was active in the fight, and joined AIDWA because of the struggle. 'They would not let us enter into the temple. They pushed us out from the temple. It was a problem at that time' (Sennelkulam group interview, 13 February 2006). The story of the struggle for dignity and equal access to a place of worship by members of the Dalit caste has a reassuring clarity of purpose, though the tale has many actors. This woman told the story through the efforts of AIDWA and Dalit women like herself who lived in Sennelkulam. 'Five years after the young men tried to worship at the temple, we wanted to open the temple', she said about the first unsuccessful attempt to enter the temple; 'so we went to AIDWA to tell them we wanted to open it. We asked for their help. With AIDWA's help, we have opened the temple' (ibid.). This woman's story is one strand of a remarkably unified struggle against one of many endemic practices of untouchability in rural Tamil Nadu.

In 1998, young men from the Dalit community in Sennelkulam, armed with an education and a keen appreciation of their rights, attempted to worship at their local temple (ibid.). The police, at the behest of the Thevar members of the hamlet, locked the temple doors. On 22 August, an agreement was reached between the Dalit youths and the two Thevar families who held exclusive control over the temple: the doors would be unlocked and the temple would be open to everyone. But the doors remained locked for another five years (Vasuki 2004: 45). An attempt to build a temple for Dalit families was also stymied by the two Thevar families and local officials when they refused to give a permit for building on public land (Sennelkulam group interview, 13 February 2006). In 2002, a CPM member and worker in an NGO in the colony heard about the fight that had been lost, won and lost again. He brought the news of the stalemate to the CPM unit in nearby Rajapalayam, and the Party decided to take up the case. AIDWA also joined the struggle at this point. As U. Vasuki, general secretary of AIDWA in Tamil Nadu remembered, 'The Party felt that if a women's organization takes up [the temple entry issue], the opposition will not be that much' (U. Vasuki interview, 26 March 2006). Negotiations between CPM and AIDWA organizers, Dalit families, Thevar families and officials yielded no results. Sugonthi, an AIDWA state secretary for Tamil Nadu who hails from the largest city in the district, Virudhunagar, was actively involved in the campaign. She recounted, 'They [Thevars] said that "so far Dalits have not entered the temple, and they will not enter it even if the DC [District Collector] demands"' (Sugonthi interview, 13 February 2006). On 4 July 2003, Dalit members of Sennelkulam and local CPM members attempted to forcibly enter the temple. They were rebuffed by a police force led by the District Superintendent of Police. Ten men were arrested for disturbing the peace, all of whom were CPM activists who did not live in Sennelkulam (Sennelkulam hamlet group interview 2006). The temple remained locked.

The larger settlement of Sennelkulam has roughly 200 houses owned by upper-caste families, mostly from the Maravar caste, a historically dominant caste in the area. The segregated colony outside of Sennelkulam consists of roughly 100 houses, of which all but two are owned by Dalit, or Scheduled Caste (SC), families. David Mosse defines the term 'Dalit' historically and politically:

> The label 'Dalit' implies the conscious assertion of socio-religious and political iden-

> tities which are separate from the dominant Hindu (often conceived as Brahmanic) culture. In doing so, *Dalit* leaders draw on the 'counter-cultural' discourses of Jyotirao Phule (in Maharashtra), E.V. Ramaswami (Periyar) (in Tamil Nadu) and most particularly of B.R. Ambedkar. (Mosse 1994: 101; see also Zelliot 1996 and O'Hanlon 1985)

This challenge to untouchability practices launched by Dalits of Sennelkulam takes on the symbolic and economic dimensions of untouchability described by David Moss as constitutive of higher-caste and low-caste identities, though in markedly unequal ways. Whereas caste Hindus gain status through the dependency of lower castes; Scheduled Castes are 'principally *defined* by dependence and service' (Mosse 1994: 73). The ritual exclusion of Dalits from worshipping at the hamlet's temple underscored their subordination and secured the local caste hierarchy. The campaign for temple entry launched by AIDWA and the CPM challenged a specific instance of caste oppression, opposed the stability of the unequal caste hierarchy, and also named the oppressors. In this case, as in many violent clashes over practices of untouchability in Tamil Nadu, the oppressors were caste Hindus, yet from a caste only marginally higher than Dalits in the caste order. The remaining two houses in the colony were owned by families from the Thevar caste, designated one of the Other Backward Classes (OBC) or sometimes Most Backward Caste (MBC) by the government. Importantly, in Sennelkulam, almost all of the Dalit families owned some land, between 0.5 to 5 acres, giving them a modicum of economic independence from caste Hindu landowners. In comparison, caste Hindus in Sennelkulam owned as much as 300 acres of land.

Hugh Gorringe describes the proximity and material power of Other Backward Castes, like Thevars, to rural Dalits. 'Backward Castes tend to be better placed in administrative authorities, local politics and the police', he writes. 'Whether they want to apply for a government loan or scheme, to set up a shop in the village . . . or to instal electric lights and paved roads in their part of a village, therefore, the Dalits are forced to turn to them' (Gorringe 2005: 127). These groups have also responded the most viciously in Tamil Nadu to Dalit assertions of equality and dignity, as they are in the most direct competition with them for status as well as resources. S. Viswanathan, a reporter who covered the wave of anti-Dalit violence in Tamil Nadu in the 1990s into the 2000s, describes the best way, in his estimation, to understand the horrific levels of violence between 1995 and 2004. He argues that BCs did not simply act due to feeling threatened by Dalit resistance or Dalit empowerment, but decided 'to test their newfound authority on those below them' (Viswanathan 2005: xii). Rather than explain the violent repression through an age-old practice of the *varna* caste system, Viswanathan, along with other scholars of caste in Tamil Nadu, take pains to document that caste hierarchy in Tamil Nadu, unlike in northern India, is a relatively recent incursion dating back to the fifteenth century.[2] Scholars of caste violence and caste hierarchy mark the current context of casteist repression to the period after the 1950 constitutional protections of independent India, a distinct (yet not wholly discontinuous) break from the colonial systemization of caste from the early nineteenth century. The consolidation of BC power after Indian independence, from caste reservations and government affirmative action policies, forms the contextual basis to understand the rising violence against Dalits and Dalit assertions of full citizenship after 1950. In Tamil Nadu, the benefits offered to OBCs by the Mandal Commission in 1989 set in motion the unprecedented wave of intimidation, lootings, beatings, rapes and murders against Dalits that swept the state in the mid-1990s (Mendelsohn and Vicziany 1998; Human Rights Watch 1999: 37–39).

The caste-segregated colony of Sennelkulam, in the agriculturally fertile southern district of Virudhunagar, with its Dalit and Thevar residents, is separated by a fair expanse of fields from the upper-caste village of Sennelkulam with its mostly Maravar residents. In the evening, when I arrived, the distance between the two localities was great enough that the two parts of Sennelkulam were not visible to each other. As is often the case of violent reprisals against Dalits who assert their rights, this story about a struggle to enter the Hindu temple does not overtly concern actions by members of the upper-caste area in Sennelkulam. One reporter succinctly described the complexity of anti-Dalit reprisal:

> The forward castes, including Brahmins, seem to stay aloof from the 'low caste' attack on the Dalits, and often press for 'peaceful' solutions and compromises in local conflicts. Mythily Sivaraman has observed that the plea for communal 'peace' results in 'persuading' Dalits to surrender their just claims. (Surya 2003)

In Sennelkulam's caste-segregated hamlet, Thevar men controlled the temple's use. In concert with local government officials and law enforcement, they refused to allow Dalit women and men to use the temple. Like so many of the violent clashes against myriad practices of untouchability in Tamil Nadu, this dispute directly involved the government, as well as BC communities and Dalit communities. After every dispute, authorities formed 'peace committees' that never honoured the resolutions they brokered. Sivaraman's

[2] Mythily Sivaraman cites the scholarship by K.R. Hanumanthan, particularly his book, *Untouchability* (1979). Hanumanthan agrees with scholarship that locates the entry of Vedic-Brahmin religion and untouchability in Tamil Nadu only after the fifteenth century as the hegemony of Buddhism and Jainism in the area waned. He cites Burton Stein's work (Stein 1995) on the historic dimensions of the alliance between Brahmins and non-Brahmins between the thirteenth and nineteenth centuries to decimate Buddhism and Jainism.

characterization describes how these committees concealed the active hand of upper-caste residents of Sennelkulam in the temple entry struggle.

AIDWA members and Dalit women from Sennelkulam continued the struggle after the arrests of CPM cadre in July 2003. Ramalakshmi was a leading figure from the hamlet who refused to acquiesce, a Dalit woman who joined AIDWA in the course of the struggle. She described their next actions to wring justice from local officials: 'First we went to the rural development officer, nothing happened. Then we went to the collector and nothing happened. . . . First Balabharathi [a state-level AIDWA leader], then Vasuki came to our meeting. Then we went outside the collector's [district collector or DC] office with a petition' (Sennelkulam group interview, 13 February 2006). She described a petition to the DC that AIDWA members delivered to counter his press statement that there were no untouchability practices in the district. The petition detailed specific untouchability cases, and the DC promised action. Nothing happened. Even a Pongal demonstration staged by women outside the Kaliamman temple brought no action. Sugonthi credited Vasuki and Balabharati with breaking the stalemate by bringing in Vasanthi Devi, the chairperson of the Tamil Nadu State Commission for Women, and Poornima Advani, the chairperson of the National Commission for Women. On 27 October 2003, AIDWA successfully managed to call enough attention to caste issues in Tamil Nadu that Vasanthi Devi and Poornima Advani organized an official hearing, held in the district's largest city of Virudhunagar, on discrimination against Dalit women and ongoing untouchability practices in eight southern districts of Tamil Nadu.

They summoned witnesses, examined their statements, and demanded further documents to study the cases regarding violation of Dalit women's legal and constitutional rights. Local police officers and regional officials attended the hearing – the same people who had stymied all attempts to open the temple. AIDWA organized the testimony by Dalit women of seventeen crimes, ranging from humiliation to overt violence (Surya 2003). Twenty-five Dalit women from Sennelkulam travelled over an hour to attend the meeting in Virudhunagar. Among other stark atrocities, they testified to being coerced to remove their slippers in the presence of caste Hindus, to being forced to eat human excrement because a Dalit woman asked for loan repayment, and to unpunished rape by a physical education instructor of a fourteen-year-old Dalit girl in her school. All these were active AIDWA campaigns in the area. Sometimes it had to struggle just to register the crime with the police, who refused to recognize any wrong done. The cases filed fell under the Prevention of Atrocities (POA) Act. Vasuki elaborated on the POA – in her words, 'a very good Act'. The POA, she described, 'has all the three components. One is punitive, giving punishment. The other is civil, that is compensation to the victim, and providing women the means to come to court as witnesses, since otherwise they lose a day's wages. . . . The third is proactive measures like setting up monitoring committees' (U. Vasuki interview, 15 January 2005). AIDWA used the Dalit women's testimonies to record the violations, talk to other witnesses and create the proof necessary to give teeth to the laws against untouchability practices. Yet in most of the cases, the law was a tool rather than the final authority; it signified Dalit rights to full citizenship as much as a means to wrest justice.

In the temple entry case in Sennelkulam, the chance to testify before a jury of nationally respected judges and officials gave the women the leverage they needed. As Vasuki reported in *Women's Equality*: 'The jury told the Superintendent of Police of the district to open the temple the next day itself so that the jury panel too could worship the goddess Kaliamman, along with the Dalit sisters from Sennelkulam. Hell broke loose' (Vasuki 2004: 45). The DC opened the temple, and though the two Thevar families would no longer use it, Dalits worship at the temple and have completed building the second temple as well. AIDWA grew as a result of this campaign: 75 women from the 100 houses in the colony joined AIDWA. They tell this story with pride, and even after a full day of work in the fields three years after the struggle, most of the hamlet joined a meeting to describe what happened. As soon as Ramalakshmi finished her narration of the temple entry struggle, a man in the crowd began clapping with tears in his eyes. 'Her husband', a person beside me explained. A number of women described their relationship to AIDWA. Said one woman in her forties: 'After the temple entry and guidance by AIDWA we feel courage and are not afraid of anything and can face

Pictures of national and regional leaders hanging in AIDWA's office in Virudhunagar, Tamil Nadu. *From left to right*: R. Kasturi, an agricultural worker activist from a Dalit family in the Madurai belt; Susheela Gopalan, a national leader and one of AIDWA's founders, elected three times to the Lok Sabha; Leelavati, a revered leader in the Madurai region who was murdered in a struggle over access to water; Viṃal Ranadive, a national leader and one of AIDWA's founders; Janakiammal, one of the founders of the Tamil Nadu Democratic Women's Association in the mid-1970s, which joined AIDWA at its formation in 1981.

all the problems'. Many of them mentioned the travel made possible by their membership in AIDWA: 'After we joined AIDWA we travelled to so many places in Tamil Nadu. That has given us a greater awareness. Now we want to strengthen AIDWA.' They discussed the possibilities for future action; a young woman stated that her goal was to open a library in the hamlet. She said simply, 'I want a public library to learn more.' (All quotations are from the Sennelkulam group interview, 13 February 2006.)

Left Allies, Leadership, and Coalitions in Tamil Nadu

Mythily Sivaraman, a state-level AIDWA leader, wrote in moving terms about the fight against anti-Dalit violence as itself a success against acquiescence: 'Absence of open conflict is not an indication of real amity and peace. If smouldering discontent is suppressed, it can only be the peace of the graveyard' (Sivaraman 1999: 5). Winning entry into the Kaliamman temple required a coalition to succeed. The narratives pieced together to tell this story include Dalit young men, women and men from Sennelkulam, AIDWA members from Virudhunagar, Rajapalayam and across the state, and CPM members from all three localities. The narratives often overlap, contradict each other, invert the order of events and protests, and place different emphasis on the importance of different actions or actors. The leaders of this coalition shift depending on who told the story and which part of the struggle they related. At times, women activists from Sennelkulam phrased their position as petitioners to AIDWA who asked for help. They named particular state leaders of AIDWA as pivotal actors in their victory. At other times they gave their own leadership credit and appreciate AIDWA's 'guidance'. Women from Sennelkulam who joined AIDWA talked about the organization as a vehicle to open their world view and make their own aspirations possible. Often, they figured AIDWA as a collective organization that provides them the strength to follow through on their own convictions.

When a local CPM cadre described the campaign, he largely obscured the role of AIDWA and the women from Sennelkulam, and emphasized the actions led by the CPM there as well as the court case proceeding against him. When asked about this erasure of AIDWA and the local women's leadership, Vasuki described another process that shaped the campaign from 2002 onwards. She told me the rationale of the local CPM for pushing AIDWA to the forefront of the temple entry struggle as a means to go forward and avoid the grievously violent reprisals that mark many similar campaigns for Dalits' dignity across the state. Yet, as she elaborated, the lines of leadership again blurred:

> See, usually, in rural areas it's not that one organization takes up issues. There

> are very few people. AIDWA cadre will participate in DYFI [Democratic Youth Federation of India] activism, and DYFI people will come here. That's a kind of mixed thing. Immediately the information goes to the Party. And the Party unit will start guiding them and intervening. So it will be simultaneous. But the role of AIDWA was very prominent and decisive [in Sennelkulam]. (U. Vasuki interview, 15 January 2005)

Many of the AIDWA leaders involved in the Sennelkulam case, like Vasuki, were also members of the CPM; yet in my interviews, they explicitly framed their actions as AIDWA members. Here, Vasuki argued that AIDWA, as a distinct organizational entity, made important contributions to the campaign.

A coalition with the DYFI, a youth mass organization also allied to the CPM, has a different character than a coalition with another women's group or women's non-profit organization; different not just because DYFI has members who are both girls and boys, but also because of their ideological affinity and organizational ties to the CPM, a communist political party. R. Chandra, another state-level leader in AIDWA, recollected her own recognition that the Kisan Sabha (peasant organization) and Agricultural Workers Union should join AIDWA's campaigns against caste violence, particularly those that take up upper-caste landowners' employment boycotts of Dalit women agricultural workers who demand their rights (R. Chandra interview, 17 March 2006). She also described a particularly volatile case of inter-caste marriage between a Dalit man and a caste Hindu woman, a Chettiyar woman, in Pudukottai district. 'We thought the Party [CPM] should intervene because women alone cannot go and fight these caste Hindus', Chandra argued. 'And especially when you have demonstrations against landlords, we felt that at least indirectly from the back stage, the Party must be there to support us, otherwise just AIDWA alone cannot fight it out. Because sometime they even kill you, caste feeling is so strong' (ibid.).

These coalitions share common ideological moorings and political affinities; however, as is often the case, the organizations in the coalition are not commensurate political formations. They have different compositions, different histories of struggle and different bases for functioning. The CPM is a cadre-based party with strict membership guidelines. Both DYFI and AIDWA are mass organizations that any youth, in the first case, and any woman, in AIDWA's case, can join if they commit to the organization's charter, attend meetings and pay minimal dues. Like any coalition, the organizations that work together have different leadership and must develop a common agreement for unified actions. Unlike coalitions that AIDWA joins among women's movement groups, in coalitions with left allied groups the leadership can overlap, particularly between the Party and the mass organization. In R. Chandra's case, because of her work on Dalit women's issues and the close linkages with the Kisan Sabha that her work engendered, she is now active in the Kisan Sabha at the state level as well as in the CPM (ibid.). In the case of inter-sectoral work fighting Dalit women's caste oppression in rural areas, AIDWA members describe two especially salient reasons for working with left allies. First, the basis for Dalit women's empowerment lies in employment, including land ownership, and in access to resources like water and food. These allies, like the All India Agricultural Workers Union (AIAWU), might have AIDWA members since their interests in rural areas overlap. Chandra states the second reason bluntly: activism against casteism is very dangerous, even life-threatening work. AIDWA, Chandra says, trusts the backing they receive from the Party and left allied groups as they confront entrenched and powerful forces. With so few organizational allies in rural areas, Vasuki concurs, AIDWA depends on these coalitions to gain a real peace for Dalit women, of equity and dignity, rather than the silenced peace of the graveyard.

When AIDWA members talk about the relationship of AIDWA to CPM they dispute one prevalent characterization of AIDWA as a 'women's wing' of the Party. They often cite their independence and democratic functioning as a way to refute the demeaning assumption that AIDWA merely follows Party directives. In a careful assessment of AIDWA's inter-sectoral organizing strategy, two factors are particularly salient to understanding how 'leadership' configures a campaign like temple entry in Sennelkulam. One component that muddies clear lines of leadership is ideological, since these coalitions among left allies share a common, though not always identical, analytic understanding. A 'decisive' intervention by AIDWA in this case, what I call its intellectual leadership, is its analytic clarity on Dalit women's positionality in the localized and national context, without conflating the two arenas. As an organization, AIDWA has honed its analysis of Dalit women's issues, not in complete disregard of Dalit men's and youth's oppression, but with a clear assessment of the specific oppressions faced by Dalit women, and by the gender-specific cultural practices and legal tools at hand. AIDWA uses the phrase 'triple burden' to analyse Dalit women's position: 'today the most oppressed sections in India are Dalit women who bear the triple burden of caste oppression, class exploitation and gender discrimination' (AIDWA *et al.* 2000: 66). Even when AIDWA joins coalitions with gender-mixed organizations of left allies, this analysis of the particularity of Dalit women's discrimination holds paramount. The other intellectual leadership AIDWA visibly provides is its strategy of activist research about Dalit women's oppression across *taluk*s (state-regional designations), to develop its inter-sectoral political campaigns.

In the case of the Dalit community's right to enter their local temple in Sennelkulam, AIDWA's systemic analysis was clearest during the hearing they successfully agitated for by the State and National Commissions for Women. Temple entry is not clearly gendered as an issue or as a goal (though practices of worship have gendered aspects). Yet in the hearings, Sennelkulam's campaign was only one injustice among many aired that specifically targeted Dalit women for humiliation, degradation and sexualized violence. In this limited sense, then, temple entry in Sennelkulam became a women's issue. When the chairpersons of the State and National Commissions for Women joined the fray, a wide range of Dalit women's issues from the area were publicly aired, and continued to be fought under the aegis of AIDWA. The coalition of left allies responded to the stalemate produced after the attempt on 4 July 2003 to forcibly enter the temple. They broke the impasse, with minimal overt violence, by framing the case as a women's issue with local Dalit women and AIDWA in the lead. In this sense, the leadership was about visibility of women activists, about the articulation of discrimination against Dalits as a women's issue, and of mobilizing state and national resources, the Commissions for Women, to bolster their cause.

One other question about AIDWA's ideological leadership in its coalitions with left allies remains however. How successful was AIDWA in integrating throughout its coalition allies its own analysis of Dalit women's particular oppression? Did the local Party unit adjust its understanding of Dalit women's activism in Sennelkulam through a gendered, as well as caste-based and classed analysis? Did the Party come to regard the position of Dalit women as specific in character and intensity through specifically gendered violence, like the systemic sexualized aggression that targets Dalit girls and women; and as the gendered effects of a prejudice more acutely borne by women, who have the highest rates of illiteracy, hunger and other deprivations? A report from the CPM Tamil Nadu State Conference suggests that AIDWA's analysis and methods permeate Party activism on caste oppression, particularly regarding specific demands for Arunthathiyar sub-caste reservations, and their organization of anti-untouchability conferences around the state and one national convention (CPI[M], 'Tamil Nadu State Conference, "Extracts from the Political-Organizational Report"', 2008: 6–12). Most significantly to this study, they are questions produced by AIDWA's analysis of Dalit women's triple burden, since in AIDWA's formulation caste is not analogous to class, nor is gender merely an added identity qualifier.

For Brinda Karat, the general secretary of AIDWA until 2004, inter-sectoral organizing demanded greater independence for AIDWA, as well as greater leadership from local levels of the organization. She described the changes AIDWA underwent in the 1990s: 'You had to ensure your direct links with your membership, and you had to ensure that the voices of that membership were heard loud and clear' (Brinda Karat interview, 26 December 2004). In part Karat described a process of training local activists to become leaders of the organization, to respond to the local conditions of rural poverty, caste violence and gender oppression. But she also described this process of building local AIDWA leaders in rural areas that had few other political allies, as Chandra also stressed. Karat argued that the shift to the village demanded a more tightly run organizational structure,

> that is a process of strengthening democracy in the organization. . . . We have to hold committee meetings more regularly, there cannot just be one person doing it, you have to have a collective, you have to have a record of discussion, and monitor how far you're able to implement these decisions and discussions. (Ibid.)

She called all of these aspects of AIDWA's increasing 'democracy'; of local women taking leadership, defining their own issues to fight, and raising their voices in wider levels of AIDWA's organizational structure, from the local unit to the taluk and district levels, to the state and the national levels of discussion and decision-making.

Even with her frank assessment of the CPM's active role in the Sennelkulam temple entry struggle, Vasuki argued that AIDWA did not play the supporting role of a women's wing to the Party, that is, of simply following its guidance or taking its lead. Instead, she described AIDWA's work as 'prominent and decisive'. Activist research methods honed by AIDWA have had important effects on the CPM and its left allies, and have allowed AIDWA to further devolve leadership within its membership ranks. Activist research pursued by AIDWA on rural women's issues, agricultural and informal sector women workers' issues, and Dalit women's issues has fuelled the power of inter-sectoral organizing. As R. Chandra stated, 'This kind of taking up research, and looking at these problems in detail, started after the sub-committees for each specific area were formed, and one office bearer was put in charge of a sub-committee [on rural women, Dalit women, Muslim women, etc.]' (R. Chandra interview, 17 March 2006).

Activist Research in Tamil Nadu

The surveys on untouchability practices in Tamil Nadu began in 1998, the same year that AIDWA held their national conference on Dalit women in New Delhi. The research conducted beforehand mobilized AIDWA activists and local Dalit women for the conferences. As R. Chandra described in an article for the CPM weekly paper, *People's Democracy*, these conferences had wide-ranging effects:

> These conferences provided a platform for women, for Dalit women in particular, to share their experiences of oppression as well as their strategies of struggle. These conferences promoted their solidarity. They brought out numerous instances of

cruel oppression, especially those related to the crime of untouchability. Following these conferences, the AIDWA launched a series of agitations and struggles. Taking stock of the overall experience, the AIDWA state committee decided to conduct zonal conferences, with delegates from several districts, to deliberate on how to carry the struggle forward. (Chandra 2002)

Chandra says the technique of surveys began because of the request for more specific information from sympathetic officials (R. Chandra interview, 17 March 2006). Yet, when she launched her first survey in five districts – Dindigul, Thoothukudi (Tuticorin), Pudukottai, Theni and Cuddalore – in rural areas of Tamil Nadu in 1998, she did not know in advance what issues she might uncover, but sought to build solid evidence of the ongoing criminal practices of untouchability. In April 1998, AIDWA sponsored a one-day anti-untouchability convention in the village of Karambakkudy in western Pudukottai to raise two instances of casteist injury uncovered during the organization's research: the urination by an upper-caste Hindu into the Dalit community's well, and the two-glass or two-tumbler system at tea-stalls in the area.[3] In the first case, it targeted the deputy superintendent of police (DSP) for refusing to investigate the well case and castigating the women who insisted on filing the case. AIDWA's demands were direct: investigate the case, charge the guilty and clean the well. The two-glass system crosses the state of Tamil Nadu whereby Dalits and caste Hindus have separate glasses for the tea they buy at the stall (Sainath 1999). Dalit customers' glasses are of inferior quality to the caste Hindus'. Often, they are forced to wash their own glasses and pay without touching the cashier. The system is a multi-glass system in some locations, with up to four different caste statuses policed by four different grades of glasses and sets of practices. The two-glass system has become a national symbol of ongoing caste oppression.

After a year of agitation, in May 1999, the district collector (DC) 'denied the well-substantiated claims of AIDWA' (Athreya and Chandra 2000). AIDWA responded to the DC's dismissal with a protest of the multi-glass system organized the following year in another village in Pudukottai, called Kulattur. These events were organized during an extremely volatile period; as Chandra characterized it, 'that was the time when the atrocities against Dalits . . . was actually peaking, you could say it was reaching its peak' (R. Chandra interview, 17 March 2006). Brinda Karat, then the national general secretary of AIDWA, attended the rally, and challenged casteist assumptions about AIDWA's activism and commitment to communal harmony. 'The dis-

[3] Sivaraman 1999: 5. Mythily Sivaraman, the article's author and an AIDWA office bearer in Tamil Nadu, stated that the article was also published in the Tamil language press: Mythily Sivaraman interview, 17 February 2006.

trict administration accuses us of creating a law and order problem and communal disturbance by demanding an end to the multi-glass system', she said to the crowd. 'In fact, it is they who are creating such a problem by refusing to take action against a clear case of violation of the Constitution and laws relating to untouchability. There is, after all, a simple way to maintain law and order. The upper classes have to accept that the Dalits are equal to them' (quoted in Sivaraman 1999: 5). Through the public attention to untouchability practices it received, including coverage from the BBC, AIDWA was able to ensure that local authorities cleaned the well, and local tea-stalls served their beverages in the same cups to everyone.

After the success of these early surveys in 1998 and 1999, R. Chandra coordinated the surveys for a series of regional, or 'zonal' in her terms, conferences based on survey work done by local AIDWA members beforehand. She began with a regional conference held in Pudukottai district in 2002, with research gathered from six adjacent districts and attended by 202 women delegates. After Pudukottai, AIDWA held three other zonal conventions in rapid succession between 2002 and 2004. One zonal convention, in the western district of Coimbatore, covered nine districts including Salem and Erode. The next, held in Theni district, included research from eight neighbouring districts. The third was held in the district of Villupuram, with research from a total of seven northern districts. AIDWA's research challenged assumptions that casteism predominated in the southern districts of the state of Tamil Nadu, where some of the most violent attacks against Dalits took place in the 1990s. Untouchability practices had regional variations, like the refusal to provide adequate burial grounds for Dalit communities in western districts. Some practices, like the multi-glass system, crossed all regions with differences in their prevalence.

Vasuki, who attended all the regional conferences, noted that the participants also differed in their approach to fighting casteism. In the first three zonal conferences, as well as the district conferences, many speakers raised issues of casteist violation of their social dignity. As they related stories of their humiliation, and the targeting of their families and friends for violent humiliation, they wept. The third zonal conference, held in Theni, had a markedly larger number of participants, amongst them Arunthathiyar women from the lowest sub-caste (or *jati*) of Dalits. Arunthathiyar women and men are commonly assigned jobs of scavenging, cobbling shoes, and removing human excrement from houses, drains and public facilities. Vasuki noted a change of issues, from dignity issues to resource issues. 'Most of them came with petitions. They said, "we want water, we want civic amenities." Apart from that, nothing about untouchability because that is not the issue if you don't have water' (U. Vasuki interview, 26 March 2006). In the fourth zonal conference she also noted a change of tone, from '"we are suffering, you have to help us"', to Dalit women's 'assertion and confidence' as they spoke (ibid.)

Activist research developed through these zonal conferences in several ways. Chandra emphasized the increased quality and amount of research local members were able to collect. She described their improved protocol for the second zonal conference in Coimbatore:

> We had a meeting, prior to the collection of the data, that I attended, and I called all of them and told them how to go about it, how to cross-check the data and so on. Just don't simply come away with whatever they say, cross-check whether it is true or not. And see that you don't take more than five samples from one village, try to cover as many villages as possible. So a one-day training kind of thing we had. I would read out the questionnaire and how to fill it up to all the leading activists who would go to the field to collect the information. So that way about 490 questionnaire forms were filled for that convention. (R. Chandra interview, 17 March 2006)

Chandra described her care with what AIDWA activists found in their research surveys, and how they verified the information. She sought qualified information to include in her reports for specific regions. The more specific the information, she noted, ongoing campaigns advanced through helping them to formulate clear demands. Accurate findings in different zones also allowed the organization to draw generalizations about untouchability practices in particular regions, rather than assuming that Dalits in the state of Tamil Nadu faced undifferentiated casteist abuse. The conferences where the reports were presented allowed members to discuss the reports, recruit Dalit women and sharpen the politics of their own membership – both Dalit and non-Dalit. At all of the conferences sponsored by AIDWA, leaders and members sought to educate their membership about their own caste prejudice. Chandra described this process:

> We targeted about 200 delegates, and we said that 30 per cent of the delegates must be non-Dalit women, we insisted on that. . . . Because even among our women, at least in the rural areas, they are very conscious of the caste to which they belong. . . . So we took a conscious decision that if they bring ten delegates from one district at least three or four should be non-Dalit women. We need to sensitize our own women and let them hear the harrowing experiences of these women. (Ibid.)

Vasuki shed light on the connection between activist research, Dalit women's leadership at local levels and the transformation of AIDWA as a whole, at every level. She targeted the bottleneck for casteism within the organization at the level of the area – *taluk*. She described two organizational shifts: first, to change activist members' recruitment of Dalit women involved in local campaigns against untouchability practices as well as other issues; second, to build leadership among Dalit women activists at the middle levels of the organization. In the past, Vasuki asserted, activists had not always sought Dalit women's membership after taking up issues of caste discrimination. 'Previously our women activists will go to many places and take up issues, conclude them, like civic issues and all that. So Dalit women will thank them and they'll happily come away' (U. Vasuki interview, 26 March 2006). Yet after the central leadership of AIDWA developed a series of questions for local units about their members recruited from campaigns, the numbers of Dalit women who joined AIDWA rose. Vasuki described the new standard: 'Take up issues, membership, organizational consolidation, unit-level leadership. Automatically they [Dalit women] become the unit secretary and president because in Dalit areas they become the unit secretary' (ibid.). Units are the smallest parts of the organization, rooted in their localities and led by the most active members. Members culled from struggles in segregated Dalit neighbourhoods will be Dalits, and the leadership of units formed from these members will reflect this. The *taluk* level includes a number of units in its purview, and is the next organizational level. Vasuki then described the next step in AIDWA's development of inter-sectoral organizing that sought to break down social hierarchies and segregation at the level of the *taluk*. She said:

> When *taluk*-level and district-level conferences take place, the person from the higher committee . . . will ask this question: 'You've done really well in that area, how many Dalit women will you include in the *taluk* committee?' It took us nearly thirty-three years to reach this position. . . . So only when the *taluk* conference takes place and the *taluk* committee is being elected, if there is some kind of pressure and understanding, realization, then they [Dalit members] will come into *taluk* committees. Then it's much easier to come to district committees and state committees. (Ibid.)

Breaking down local hierarchies of caste discrimination and caste segregation, as Vasuki described, meant finding ways to actively foster Dalit women's leadership at this mid-level of the organization. Only when Dalit women unit leaders have risen to the level of *taluk*-level leaders, Vasuki found, did the district-level Dalit women leaders, state-level leaders and national-level leaders also rise. *Taluk*-level committees were usually desegregated from local units' caste and class exclusivity, and had units from a number of different class and caste locations. If those *taluk*-level committees promoted Dalit women's leadership, and organizationally had to listen to the leadership of Dalit women's units, the hidden casteism within its own organizational matrix also had to be confronted directly. As scholars like Chowdhry and Gorringe show through their analyses of Haryana and Tamil

Nadu, the most pernicious relations of caste oppression are deeply localized as they reflect those relational struggles over resources and status.[4]

Yet significant quandaries remain intrinsic to AIDWA's inter-sectoral organizing strategy; particularly about the stasis of sectoral categories themselves. Both Chandra and Vasuki wrestled with one particularly disturbing atrocity thrown up by the activist research on Dalit women in Tamil Nadu: systemic intra-caste rape. The endemic sexual exploitation of Arunthathiyar women by men from other Dalit sub-castes mirrors upper-caste men's sexual exploitation of Dalit women. Arunthathiyar women sought sectoral organizing methods to address the sexual violations they faced within the Dalit community. On 29 December 2003, AIDWA held its fourth zonal anti-untouchability conference in Villupuram, a northern district. Three hundred women attended the conference from all seven districts surveyed: Vellore, Tiruvannamalai, Tiruvallur, Kanchipuram, Cuddalore, Villupuram and Pondicherry (Chandra 2004). Surveys went out to AIDWA activists beforehand and the report from the conference records numerous crimes against Dalits (Chandra, 'Fourth Conference on Eradication of Untouchability: Research Paper'). The report discusses specific instances of the two-glass system in at least six of the villages they surveyed. It describes caste humiliations of being called derogatory caste names, being forced to stand at the bus-stop and tea-stall, being refused a hair-cut, and being forced to stand in garbage when receiving an offering of food. Another section of the report details the encroachment on Dalit graveyards, so that bodies must be buried in layers on top of each other. The report quotes a woman named Alagammal who said: 'We bury the bodies in Pennai River sand. If there is water in the river it causes a problem', since the bodies emerge from the sand (ibid.). The report describes three other central crimes faced by Dalit women: of unfair land distribution, of barred entry into temples and of sexual abuse. The surveys found endemic sexual abuse of Dalit women: 'In Villupuram, Cuddalore and Vellore [three districts surveyed], women, whether they were married or not, are forced to have sexual intercourse with upper-caste men. . . . Dalit school-going girls are subjected to eve-teasing [sexual harassment] at large' (ibid.) The report gives updates on ongoing AIDWA cases against sexual assault and harassment of Dalit women. It records that women who testify about sexual harassment in their neighbourhoods has decreased due to the organization's vigilant intervention.

The report, delivered at AIDWA's fourth zonal conference against untouchability, incited an unexpected, yet vehement request from women belonging

[4] In particular, see Chowdhry's essay first published in *Modern Asian Studies* in 2009, titled '"First Our Jobs then Our Girls": The Dominant Caste Perceptions on the "Rising" Dalits', in Chowdhry 2011: 369–411; Gorringe 2005.

to the Arunthathiyar caste. They sought their own conference, for violations against Arunthathiyar Dalit women in particular. Chandra described their intervention: 'They asked me and Vasuki, "Will you organize a separate convention?" . . . They were telling us how badly they were harassed by other Dalits' (R. Chandra interview, 17 March 2006). The fierce discrimination faced by all Dalits, one marked by the sexual control of Dalit women by caste Hindus, lies at the heart of AIDWA's campaigns against untouchability practices by upper castes. Chandra explained the difference:

> If they are harassed by upper-caste men it is a different thing, we can go and have demonstrations, or we can go and meet the officials, collectors, or whoever it is, and take action. But here is a case where they are harassed by their own men and women, so it is a different thing. (Ibid.)

Yet Arunthathiyar Dalit women faced a similar oppression at the hands of other Dalit men from higher sub-castes. Their request for a separate conference for Arunthathiyar women complicated the efforts to challenge caste Hindu repression. In Chandra's words, 'This is a community [Dalits] which is oppressed and exploited, and within this community you see one section trying to . . . [her ellipsis]. Then Arunthathiyar men are also harassed, not just the Arunthathiyar women alone. Arunthathiyar men are also suffering' (ibid.). While Chandra did not specify the types of harassment faced by Arunthathiyar men, she did not signify that it was for sexual availability to upper-caste men, but the more general caste humiliations suffered by everyone from the sub-caste. She concluded without settling the issue, merely stating her opinion: 'You cannot organize separate conventions I feel. Maybe we can talk to them, and we can negotiate specific problems' (ibid.). Ultimately AIDWA and later CPM organized a rally to spotlight Arunthathiyar struggles as part of the coalition that began in 2007, called the Tamil Nadu Untouchability Eradication Front (TNUEF). After the rally, coalition members held events across the state of Tamil Nadu, and through this momentum successfully pushed for a 3 per cent reservation within the SC reservations marked for Arunthathiyars.

The Triple Burden, Activist Research and Inter-sectoral Organizing

At the 27 October 2003 hearing led by the State and National Commissions for Women (NCW) in Virudhunagar, a formal letter was sent to Poornima Advani on letterhead paper, topped with the names of AIDWA's state president, Sudha Sundararaman, and general secretary, U. Vasuki. The letter lists ongoing forms of untouchability in Tamil Nadu:

> Ban on cycling, not permitting Dalits to stand in the queue with others in rations shops or in the tea stall, usage of a double tumbler system in tea shops, not allowing them to draw water from the common pond, ban on wearing chappals, refusal to provide chairs to Dalit panchayat presidents, etc. (Letter to Poornima Advani, 2003)

The letter also describes why AIDWA has such detailed knowledge of specific untouchability practices: its ongoing regional conventions around the state against untouchability. These conventions included between six and nine districts, informed by considerable legwork gathering data. 'Village-level surveys preceded the convention. Dalit women who came to the conventions narrated issues from untouchability to denial of civic amenities, land *patta*s [documents of ownership], etc.' (ibid.). AIDWA submitted a list of ten demands to the NCW chairperson based on its experiences of holding anti-untouchability conventions and its local activism on the issues that emerged. The demands utilized all three aspects of the POA Act that Vasuki elaborated: punitive, civil and proactive. Many of the demands sought better governmental protection of Dalit civil rights and freedom from violence through frequent performance reports by state agencies and police; district-level advisory committees that included Dalit groups' representation as well as representation from women's groups; Dalit women's assured attendance at local governmental meetings; special courts to address anti-Dalit violence; and strict disciplinary action against officials who deter Dalit rights. The third demand concerned the triple burden carried by Dalit women:

> Dalits are often unable to stand up due to their economic dependence on the upper caste. Hence, *panchami* [common] land meant for Dalits should be taken over and returned to them. Either individual *patta*s to women or joint *patta*s in the name of husband and wife should be distributed. Minimum Wages Act should be strictly implemented. (Ibid.)

Citing the authority of its careful research of untouchability and its activism against anti-Dalit violence, AIDWA framed its demands to address the structures that cement inequitable power relationship among Dalits and caste Hindus in rural areas. All the demands to the NCW sought justice from the state. Some demands relied on local and state governance policies, both proactive and punitive. Others, like the ninth demand, rested on constitutional promises of equality: 'Basic civic amenities, house *patta*s, etc., must be ensured for Dalits to enable them to lead their lives with dignity as enshrined in Article 21 of the Constitution' (ibid.). Dignity, here, resides in equal access to basic resources provided, where necessary, by the government. Both the third and the ninth demands reached beyond law enforcement as they sought to shape public policy, and change the very conditions of Dalit women's discrimination.

After the hearing, AIDWA followed up on the 2003 letter submitted to the chairperson of the NCW, Poornima Advani. In a letter dated 22 May 2004 signed by U. Vasuki, she thanked Advani for her support and offered additional clarification for AIDWA's demands based on their survey work. Specifically, this letter responded to the NCW's request for further information. Vasuki listed men's and women's wages in fifteen villages from one area, Tirukoyilur *taluk*, in Villupuram district, to clarify their third demand about enforcing the Minimum Wage Act. Listing wages that ranged from Rs 15 per day to Rs 30 per day, Vasuki's letter offered proof that all the women agricultural workers they surveyed received wages that were below the government-mandated Rs 45 per day. She explained the complexity of AIDWA's analysis and politics: 'Agricultural wages for women are much less than the minimum wages. We did not mean to convey that other women get minimum wages and only Dalit women are discriminated [against]. Since most of the agricultural workers are Dalit, we had added that demand' (Letter to Chairperson, National Commission for Women, 2004). The confusion of the NCW implicit in Vasuki's clarification was that agricultural women workers are not usually configured as caste-based, let alone caste-typed workers. Yet AIDWA frequently cited the connections in their reports about the triple burden of caste, class and gender that Dalit women face. Fully 20 per cent of the population of Tamil Nadu are Dalits. Among these, almost 80 per cent live in rural areas. As a sectoral issue, then, Dalit women's issues are palpably rural women's issues. Dalit women in Tamil Nadu comprise 70 per cent of agricultural workers, but only 5 per cent of the cultivators, a census category for those agricultural labourers who work their own land.

The rest of the letter detailed five cases where officials neglected to act on anti-Dalit atrocities. They named the woman and her residence, the date of the offence, the official and the official's role – whether *panchayat* president, police officer or district educational officer. The last case of inaction around the attempted rape of a married Dalit woman described the cascading violence that spreads beyond the original injury to include the whole family or the entire local Dalit community. The incident was listed as follows:

> Mari, an upper-caste youth, attempted to rape her on 2.8.03 in her house, but escaped seeing someone coming home. She was injured in the process. Next day, when she went and complained to his mother, his relatives assaulted her and her husband. When she complained to the police, DSP Jayachandran called her a prostitute and humiliated her using caste name, threatened other witnesses. On 15.8.03, her father-in-law Rasu, who is the panchayat president, was slippered when he tried to hoist the national flag. Later, police arrested 4 persons *but did not take Mari into custody. Still he is at large. No action against DSP Jayachandran* [emphasis hers]. (Ibid.: 3)

Like its demand to enforce minimum wage statutes, AIDWA revealed a nuanced understanding of how anti-Dalit violence unfolds. Even in the relatively brief overview of this case, it included the attack on the woman's father-in-law as directly connected to her attempt to press charges of attempted rape against an upper-caste man. The sexualized violence of rape targeted the Dalit woman directly, but her refusal to drop the issue created a spiral of violence and violation. Another case included retributions that shut off water and electricity to the entire Dalit hamlet. The specificity of AIDWA's charges and its refusal to simplify the complexity of anti-Dalit violence bolstered its more transformative demands even as it showed its resolve. AIDWA pushed the ambit of the NCW in taking up Dalit women's issues, seeking to widen its understanding of sexualized violence against Dalit women to include the ramifications for the entire Dalit community. It also sought to frame Dalit women's issues as class issues, about land ownership and employment, not simply caste and gender issues.

Gender, caste and class configure a triple burden in these stories of AIDWA's activism in the southern state of Tamil Nadu and the northern state of Haryana. What they reveal is the complexity, even within one region or state, of how these factors operate in different localities. AIDWA's activism revealed the complexity of crafting a politics that remains sensitive to the ways caste and gender inflect the political power of land, in the case of social boycotts led by dominant castes in a locality. AIDWA's attention to the ways gendered oppression meets class and caste oppression raised more difficult tensions among Dalits. Intra-Dalit violence against women destabilizes mobilizations against anti-Dalit violence, as the case of Dalit men of higher caste status targeting Arunthathiyar women for rape revealed. Yet the challenge of how to proceed effectively, while not easily answered, also proved AIDWA's success in listening to some of the most vexed problems.

All of these specific campaigns and organizational challenges in Tamil Nadu simultaneously targeted the vast epistemological violence of caste and gender-blind analysis and public policy. The women's movement in India in the twenty-first century remembered what it sometimes overlooked during the 1980s: that caste, religion and class cannot be disentangled from patriarchal gender relations. AIDWA's experiences of sectoral organizing since the mid-1990s identifies rural women's issues, Dalit women's issues and Muslim women's issues as inter-related sites for analysing and acting to change the particular meanings of caste, religion, class and gender in emancipatory ways. AIDWA's organizing techniques, including its strong relationships with allied left organizations, may not translate to different political formations within the women's movement, but its analytic insights, drawn from their politics, remain an open resource for activism, discussion and reflection.

SIX

Anti-Violence in New Delhi and Chennai

New Delhi newspapers proclaimed the winter of 1991–92 one of the coldest winters in twenty years. The temperatures dipped below zero degree Celsius with startling regularity. In the north of the country, at least thirty people on record died of exposure. These treacherous conditions coincided with other phenomenon often described as similarly unpredictable and uncontrollable: the slow but steady enactment of economic policies that we now commonly refer to as neoliberalism. 'There is no alternative' or TINA encapsulated Margaret Thatcher's approach to UK's downsizing and privatization policies in the 1980s. The Rajiv Gandhi government in India designated its related economic shift in the mid-1980s using a less draconian description: the 'New Economic Policy' or NEP. 'Loan conditionalities' and 'austerity measures' in late 1991 and early 1992 were buzzwords for the onset of globalization in India.[1] In the summer of 1991, the Indian government paid for old IMF (International Monetary Fund) loans with a new, bigger loan – one that was larded with structural adjustment demands on Indian monetary policy, governance, and spending priorities.

Subsidized milk was the government's first visible casualty in New Delhi. Long lines of mostly women and their children wrapped tightly in woollen shawls formed across the city, snaking down the streets from empty and shuttered shops. The foggy morning air in that cold winter penetrated the most tightly woven shawl, for even an average Delhi winter is cold. For several days the public milk supply simply disappeared, and the women waited

[1] 'Loan conditionalities' refer to the terms of the International Monetary Fund (IMF) and World Bank loan agreements entered into by national governments. The details of these terms were not revealed to the nation's citizens, but were the source of conjecture and deduction as changes to the banking system, for example, or to the nation's global currency value, or the government's programmes for affordable food, education and health care emerged in the months and years after the loans were signed. 'Austerity measures' refer to the governmental rollback of services, infrastructure and wages, as well as tighter monetary policies that benefit global capital at the expense of national publics.

in vain. When the government-subsidized milk returned in December, newspapers reported that the Delhi Milk Supply (DMS) scheme had increased the cost of a one-litre pouch of milk by one rupee, from Rs 5 to Rs 6 ('Housewives Express Shock, Anger', 1991: 3). One woman interviewed, Ram Kali of Trilokpuri, wondered 'how she would feed her baby. "My husband works as a labourer and I supplement the family income by cleaning and sweeping in a few houses in the neighbourhood", she said in grief' (ibid.). That one-rupee rise in the price of government-subsidized milk tipped the balance for many poor families. A man named Dev Kumar described his dilemma for a newspaper interview. '"*Pet bhookha ho to jitna bhi teza ho, pet to bharna hai; nahin bharte to marte.*" If one is hungry and has an empty stomach to fill, one has to fill one's belly however high the prices may skyrocket; if we don't, then we die' (Mohapatra 1991: 5). In the same article, two married construction workers who made a combined total of Rs 60 per day were also interviewed. The man noted that with his three daughters the increased cost of milk meant a complete loss: 'I am not able to give milk to my children' (ibid.). One side of that rupee coin of subsidized milk's increased cost was government savings to repay its loans. The other side measured how close poor working people were to nutritional lack since that rupee increase was weightier than their fragile budgets could absorb.

Over ten years into a liberalized Indian economy, in late December of 2004, Chennai, the capital of Tamil Nadu in south India, faced the destructive impacts of nature's force. The tsunami that devastated islands like Aceh in Southeast Asia hit the southern and eastern shores of India only an hour later. Fishing communities in Chennai who lived closest to the impact of the waves' devastation faced the greatest immediate losses of homes, lives and livelihood. For six months after the tsunami, the fishing industry in north Chennai, as in many parts of the state, came to a standstill. Rebuilding among these communities revealed changed priorities of the government, as some areas became open terrain for land speculators. Other tracts of land became earmarked for government development projects that ignored their ongoing importance to the livelihood of people within the fishing industry.

The effects within fishing communities, like those in north Chennai, revealed other fissures of inequity (Armstrong 2006). In restitution and recovery programmes, the gendered maldistribution of aid for lost livelihood vastly under-rated the losses faced by women fish traders. In workers' collective representation, it showed the punitive effects of gender segregation and exclusion, since only men were allowed into most of the collective bodies that sought governmental and charitable aid to rebuild. In both of these periods – at the beginning of neoliberalism in India in the early 1990s, and during its consolidation in the mid-2000s – from north to south India, AIDWA's daily anti-violence work among women took into account the political economy of its individual neighbourhood campaigns as both deeply localized and inextricably globalized in character.

The term neoliberalism includes loan conditionalities and the ensuing austerity borne by poor and middle-class people, but much more besides. Neoliberalism is a doctrine, an economic model, an ideology, and a set of governing policies only minimally tailored by negotiations with particular nations (Harvey 2008). All of these aspects of neoliberalism have discontinuities between an ideal model and specific actions, discontinuities that produce integral contradictions that effect how we understand it as our dominant form of capitalism from the late twentieth century onwards. This chapter looks at two cases of domestic violence addressed by AIDWA units, one in a predominantly Dalit neighbourhood in New Delhi, the other in a fishing people's housing compound in Chennai. These cases bookend the consolidation of neoliberalism in India: the case in New Delhi unfolded in 1991 and was resolved in 1992; the case in Chennai took place between 2005 and 2006, after the devastating tsunami washed away the neighbourhood's infrastructure and livelihood.

AIDWA's strategies to fight for women's right to live without violence are primarily reformist in character: they demand the rights of abused women to their legal protections and state-mandated restitution. But their strategies exceed these reformist means as they attempt to transform an area's acceptance of domestic violence and produce new actors to combat that 'private' intra-familial violence. Perhaps most strikingly of all their organizing campaigns, in their domestic violence work, AIDWA has developed its strategies independently from its left allied Party, the CPI(M), and its mass organizations. When they draw on the resources of these allies, it is to direct their appropriate action to strengthen a particular case, not to seek advice or permission. Local units direct their own cases to fight violence cases brought by women – what they consistently report is the wide class background of women who draw on their support, legal advice and activism. Many of AIDWA's members have joined the organization because of effective organizing against violence in their lives, or in the lives of sisters, daughters, mothers and friends. The New Delhi units in particular emerged from the anti-violence organizing in the late 1970s and early 80s. Their strategies of centering the woman's demands and needs alongside negotiation and consistent follow-through with the accused parties developed during this early period. In addition, members in New Delhi, most notably Kirti Singh, have been at the forefront of writing and passing laws to protect women from violence and give them the legal teeth to gain justice.

The inter-sectoral praxis that marked much of AIDWA's organizing over the mid-1990s through the 2000s, on the surface, has not significantly changed the model of its anti-violence work. Domestic violence happens inside familial boundaries, and within class- and caste-segregated neighbourhoods – its focus is more within established community formations than across community boundaries. While all women, regardless of caste, class or religion, face violence, it is not an issue that easily builds those cross-community bridges of solidarity. In fact, the universalism of gendered violence against women can also reinforce communal divides rather than span them, whether through class-preferential resources for battered women, or assumptions about the primordial, insurmountable violence of lower-caste men. Creating the possibility for supportive community ideologies against gendered forms of violence was a mainstay of AIDWA's organizing against violence, but not its outer limit. Those internal values, in the context of inter-sectoral praxis, were the critical beginning. The difficult and inter-sectoral part of this work lay in forging those ties to gendered issues that were more overtly divisive in the wider social polity, such as struggles against gendered abuses marked by caste affiliations, religious beliefs and class hierarchies.

Legal Aid Centres

Legal aid centres, run by AIDWA members, are integral to AIDWA's anti-violence work across the country. These centres are often open one day or evening a week, and provide free counselling about violence, dowry and child custody issues to anyone who attends them. The AIDWA members and lawyers involved in the legal centres also mediate agreements between women and their husbands' families and follow through with the parties to enforce these agreements. The legal centres may also be the location where women take their weekly or monthly maintenance payments, or where men and their families face reprimand for failure to comply with the terms of the agreement. The New Delhi legal aid centre, open on Saturdays in 2005, was where I witnessed the sheer range of ongoing cases, services and methods employed by the women who ran the centre. Family members from middle class to working poor people came to the centre, often for many Saturdays in a row, to resolve disputes and keep their financial promises of maintenance. In addition, information about rallies and marches was disbursed. In the summer of 2005, AIDWA organized a rally of several hundred within days to protest the sexual harassment of a young woman attending Delhi University who was attacked on the campus.

AIDWA's legal centres have built up a reputation as a reliable, disinterested and affordable advocate for women in matters of divorce, physical safety, sexual autonomy and independence. Their integrity gives the organization standing among the middle-class and working-class women, and their natal families who use their services. The centres' reputation for honesty makes them an attractive alternative to the formal legal system. Members in

New Delhi recounted numerous cases where women or their natal families brought their case to court only to be advised by the judge that they could find better, faster and less expensive results for the women through AIDWA's legal centres (Ashalata interview, 2 July 2005). What the judges themselves stressed was the fearlessness of these legal centres in the face of influential people charged with violence. As the women's movement has laid bare, violence is not an issue confined to one class, caste or ethnic background – for any court to take anti-violence laws seriously demands the willingness to confront accused parties who wield power and resources.

AIDWA's legal centres have also become a warehouse for finding out about other locality struggles. In the neighbourhood of Inderpuri, New Delhi, in the mid-1990s, a father's inquiry to the legal centres to help his daughter regain custody of her children from her estranged husband led to a neighbourhood fight against the fair distribution of milk. The successful resolution of that local milk racket, in turn, brought in other neighbourhood members with their own struggles against intra-familial violence. The legal centres provide a visible, stable meeting place where the neighbourhood units, with their daily work on common issues of affordable food and adequate infrastructure, can fill in the more individualized needs of women in their personal and affective relationships.

Since the 1980s, AIDWA's anti-violence work has countered the facile critique that as a leftist women's movement organization, it refused to take seriously internal familial conflict. Violence against women within the family, in its analysis, is a multi-class issue, which cannot be considered free of class constraints. But violence is also handled as a deeply personal as well as inter-personal issue, and the desires of the woman who brought the case guides the process and outcome of the case. AIDWA's legal aid centres give material form to its ongoing activism against dowry murders and inter-personal violence, as well as its aid for divorce and women's right to child custody. Anti-violence organizing builds AIDWA's membership, can develop leaders and provide basic justice to women in trauma. It also opens an avenue for educating women about the interconnections between intimate, familial relationships and the political economy of gender.

The legal centres operate as a parallel legal system to the federal and state courts, another facet to the legal pluralism that includes the patriarchal *khap panchayat*s in north India. AIDWA's legal centres are anchored by a fierce commitment to women's rights to live without violence, to have custody of their children and to receive maintenance after divorce, and, importantly, a woman's right to determine her own goals for the outcome of her case. The legal aid centres are only one aspect of AIDWA's anti-violence work for individual women, with unit- and district-level activism being the other important site. AIDWA's daily activism within local units for individual women and their families often provides services to members and non-members, like a registered non-governmental organization (NGO) or religious charity group. Yet AIDWA's legal centres and its anti-violence work, while deeply individualized, have a collective edge. Like its work against structural disenfranchisement of oppressed castes and religious minorities, AIDWA solidifies its collectivity out of domestic violence cases when it seeks to build its membership from the parties involved in specific cases. The organization gains members because of its reputation for providing fair, thoughtful and satisfying remedies for the women who seek their help, and for strengthening the democratic fabric of the entire neighbourhood.

AIDWA Membership and Dues

AIDWA's membership dues are one rupee per member, per year. Membership is renewed annually; each year new and old members alike pay one rupee. The dues in 1991 were the same as they were in 2006. Each rupee is split up between the organizational centre in New Delhi, the state, the district, the local committee and the unit group. If additional funds are needed, mass collections are initiated locally towards specific goals, such as a new well or to pay for a banner. As a member-sustained organization, AIDWA is one of the only nation-wide women's groups in India that operates without funds from any sources outside its power-building project, including the Indian government. An AIDWA member explained its policy in the following way. While AIDWA categorically refuses government and institutional funding on all organizing projects and campaigns, they would not refuse government funds for their research. Thus far, however, the only research that received government funding was conducted by AIDWA's research-based non-governmental organization, the Indian School of Women's Studies and Development (ISWSD). Another AIDWA member said that AIDWA would take government funds, but their combative relationship to the state meant that this possibility was neither likely nor forthcoming.

AIDWA's membership imperatives, and its membership dues, also affect its understanding of localized struggles against domestic violence in the larger frame of women's intensified insecurity due to structural adjustment policies. AIDWA's ideology determines how its one rupee dues produce specific forms of value for its activists and members. The organization's values and goals of 'democracy, equality and women's liberation' circulate alongside and against neoliberal monetary values. This contentious relationship to neoliberalism strengthens an organization that does not promise wages to most of its activists nor discrete monetary incentives for its members to stay in the organization. If membership is about ideology, then how does AIDWA address the issue of women's violence through its stated goals of 'democracy, equality and women's liberation'? Women's violence issues include, for AIDWA, individual and familial cases of violence against women, as well as the violence of the state and neoliberalism itself as these structures disregard or oppose women's demands for equality. AIDWA directly challenges women's increased worthlessness in the terms of neoliberalism and women's destabilized market value. Exchange values of women as cheap (as workers) or worthless (as women) contrast to AIDWA's ideological battle to demand and create respect for women's worth on an individual level, and in women's relationship to the state and the market. To understand the ideology of dues demands an answer to three questions. First, what is the value of an AIDWA membership for its members? Second, what is the value of an AIDWA membership to its most active members (women I call 'organizers', though very few are paid for their activism)? Third, what is the value of its membership policies to AIDWA as a collective women's organization? AIDWA, in the fifteen years between 1991 and 2006, grew dramatically in its membership, and sustained itself primarily by its membership dues during a period marked by the increasing dominance of neoliberal policies, economics and values. Its goals have been shaped by this context, but the horizon of the organization's aims still envisions radical change.

AIDWA, in these ways, has developed an organizational means to address the patriarchal, familial character of violence against women by their partners and their partner's families. AIDWA leaders also see these local and individual cases as an integral part of their larger mandate to create the conditions for socialism. Domestic violence cases demand a fight for much more than women's basic right to live without violence in their own homes since they are predicated on the goals articulated in AIDWA's slogan: democracy, equality and women's liberation. But this slogan precedes the economic and political shifts that mark the long decade of neoliberalism in India, that formally began with the structural stabilization and adjustment of the Indian economy in 1991. How do AIDWA's reformist struggles across the country to fight domestic violence, struggles that contain socialism as their horizon, thrive in the context of neoliberalism? As the state recedes from guaranteeing basic survival to its citizens, the demands for services such as mediation, legal aid and law enforcement increase. As economic policy favours private profits over public welfare, the daily costs of survival also rise. AIDWA's legal centres, which span the country, provide free legal advice, counselling, mediation and the means to enforce negotiated agreements.

AIDWA is a large mass organization with units around the country, and its members pay dues if they agree with the organization's basic tenets. The coin of membership in AIDWA, according to U. Vasuki, the general secretary of AIDWA in Tamil Nadu, is rights and duties (U. Vasuki interview, 26 March 2006). The cost of one year's membership in AIDWA between

1991 and 2006 was one rupee. A closer look at the rupee in this period reveals within it the measurable changes wrought by neoliberalism. It also provides a means to envision the social and historical relations coterminous to neoliberalism, relations that are harnessed, transformed and discarded by neoliberal policies and economies. One rupee is surprisingly mutable in this regard, but it also has an unchanging character: it represents the value of exchange for goods, services, property and work. The rupee coin measures those worldly relationships in profoundly human ways.

During the fifteen years between 1991 and 2006, the rupee's measure of value also shifted dramatically. In a time measured by the absolute exchange value of the rupee, fully afloat on the sea of international currency market speculation, what do AIDWA's dues mean for their members, their organizers and the organization itself? Its refusal to depend on donor largesse or to curtail militant demands on the state suggests that AIDWA's rupees have specific values as well as an abstract, exchange-based one. Monetarily, AIDWA retains its independence from powerful, moneyed organizations, governments, corporations and people. The organization's strategies, tactics and goals are its own, but it cannot escape from the rupee's dramatic devaluation during this period. Internationally it lost over half its value.[2] In India, one rupee no longer bought the same quantity of goods in 2006 as it did in 1991. Vasuki, AIDWA's Tamil Nadu general secretary in 2006, described the logic of its dues and its organization with deceptive simplicity. 'We link up membership dues with our slogan for changing society. That is, "democracy, equality and women's liberation." There is a linkage between the goal and membership [dues]' (U. Vasuki interview, 26 March 2006). The cost of an AIDWA membership, she stated, bears a direct relationship to its radical demands for women's equality and women's liberation. But how does the rupee signify equality or liberation for women? What value must this rupee measure and what values does it aspire to upend or create?

Vasuki revealed another set of values for AIDWA's unchanged dues in this period. She connected AIDWA's goals and ideologies through the affordability of its membership.

> You need a real group strength to achieve that change. To get the strength means you bring in more women into the fold of the organization. You just can't speak to any woman on the road about democracy, equality and women's liberation, so the first step is to enter the organization. To travel towards the goal, membership is the first step. To achieve that kind of strength and membership, we feel that financial commitment should not be an obstruction. So an amount that is easily affordable by a majority of women should be fixed. (Ibid.)

---

[2] In 1991, one US dollar had the official market value of 20.90 Indian rupees. In 2006, that rate hovered between 44 and 48 rupees to the dollar.

Membership dues provide an opening to speak to women about daily concerns and a means to address those problems. Affordable dues allow more women into that conversation. In this regard, AIDWA, like many women's organizations, works to provide services for women and gain reforms in women's lives. Yet their affordable dues support much more than the services they are known for, like legal aid workshops, counselling, municipal and federal lobbying, and conflict resolution.

Vasuki described a more ambitious hope for an organization with dues affordable to the majority of Indian women. With inexpensive costs to enter AIDWA, Vasuki suggested that all women would join the organization and its local struggles for justice, learn about the seemingly abstract values of women's equality and emancipation, and then fight for more radical visions and struggles. AIDWA, as a large organization that represents women *en masse*, could support more than simply reforms; it could also raise systemic changes to support 'democracy, equality and women's liberation'. In AIDWA's 2005 Tamil Nadu state report, many activists noted how difficult it was for rural members to find the one rupee to renew their membership (Vasuki, 'Further Strengthen AIDWA in Tamilnadu', 2005). As seed costs, fertilizer costs and other agricultural input costs rose, and the worth of crops on the increasingly open, international market shrank, fewer agricultural women could find even one rupee a year for their AIDWA membership. Farmers lost money even with bumper crops. The reports of mass suicides of farming women and men in the neighbouring state of Andhra Pradesh since 1998 began to include wide swathes of Maharashtra and Tamil Nadu by 2000. Even in a state as agriculturally fertile as Tamil Nadu, one rupee dues were not universally cheap, and the stakes of those dues for members' survival chances also rose.

Structural Adjustments in a Cold Winter

During New Delhi's cold winter of 1991–92, the city's large population of working and underemployed poor people immediately felt the impact of Prime Minister Narasimha Rao's extension of Rajiv Gandhi's New Economic Policies. Governmental policies around expenditure on public welfare shifted immediately after Manmohan Singh, the Finance Minister, signed the IMF loan agreement in July 1991. The first measure dictated by the IMF was stabilization, a provision that affected the country's fiscal policy, and worked to tighten the circulation of currency and reduce the nation's borrowing. Stabilization policies, while predominantly affecting the government's monetary policy, set the groundwork for decreasing public expenditure on social services and goods, such as health care and education. This decreased public expenditure, among other policies, is a critical component of the second phase of IMF-restructuring demands, called structural adjustment. In late 1991, the cost of staple foods on the open market rose dramatically, without government intervention to soften the blow. When food costs rise above people's ability to pay, they could normally turn to the food stores held by the Food Corporation of India (FCI), the agency that bought and held for public distribution a substantial percentage of harvested grains. This year the balance shifted. Without any warning from the Ministries of Food and Agriculture or the FCI, the shelves of 'fair price' stores were almost bare.

Government-subsidized goods in fair price stores were part of the universal public distribution system (PDS), a system that did not target its supplies to those who demonstrated extreme need but was open to anyone with a government-issued ration card. When the stores emptied, Prime Minister Rao expressed outrage at the lack of food, citing the misdeeds of hoarders and distribution warehouses as the culprits (*Hindustan Times*, 14 February 1991: 1). Government economists blamed 'proxy' farmers for the rise in costs of essential commodities. As one economist explained their reasoning: 'Traders were using the farmers as a "proxy" to stock large quantities of these [essential] commodities without actually lifting them. They therefore meant to sidetrack the Essential Commodities Act' (*Hindustan Times*, 7 January 1992: 9). Official circles were quoted as being 'baffled' by price rises and described them as 'totally inexplicable' (ibid.). Unchecked greed by a handful of wrongdoers was one explanatory narrative for the *de facto* exclusion of millions of families from accessing public food supplies.

The newspapers reported a parallel but slightly altered story about government restructuring and the PDS. The Indian government formally announced austerity measures on 25 December 1991. Four days later, government officials stated that the cost of wheat and rice would rise in order to reduce the costs of subsidizing essential food and commodities. Government economists estimated a savings of almost Rs 700 crore from the higher costs and narrower distribution of PDS food stocks.[3] In the same story, the Government of India explicitly denied that the rise in basic commodities was due to IMF pressure. The government enacted its policy quickly; by 2 January 1992, the government-set prices of wheat and rice rose in the PDS system. Its explanation for this rise was the necessity to 'pay farmers fairly'. In January, the Indian government also received an additional $1.8 billion loan from the IMF.

Economist Madhura Swaminathan described this policy shift regarding subsidized food and commodities in systemic terms:

[3] The government's economists figured the costs for PDS in 1990–91 to be Rs 2,450 crore, against the estimated costs of Rs 1,800 crore in 1991–92. *The Times of India*, 29 December 1991: 1.

The first change has been in the principles underlying policy and objectives of PDS. The second feature of policy change has been the steady increase in food prices. Thirdly, there has been a decline in the supply of food to the distribution system. Fourthly, the policy has attempted to cut back coverage and consumption by means of targeting and a denial of the principle of universalism. (Swaminathan 2000: 78)

Swaminathan illustrates how this cutback on the costs of PDS to the Indian government's budget was linked to the stabilization goal of decreasing the fiscal deficit. These policies fall under the name 'debt reduction' and are central mandates (or conditionalities) to the loans disbursed by supranational lending agencies like the World Bank and the IMF. A report in *The Indian Express* published one day before the government released its budget foretold the contraction of the PDS programme for subsidized food and linked it to the agreements signed with the IMF (Girimaji 1991: 1). Indian government officials downplayed their own role in the food shortage or simply lied about it, but as food costs rose and affordable supplies dwindled, residents in the capital city faced measurable hardships.

Protests in New Delhi were one public response to the price hikes and other changes in government policies. On 25 November 1991, the fair price

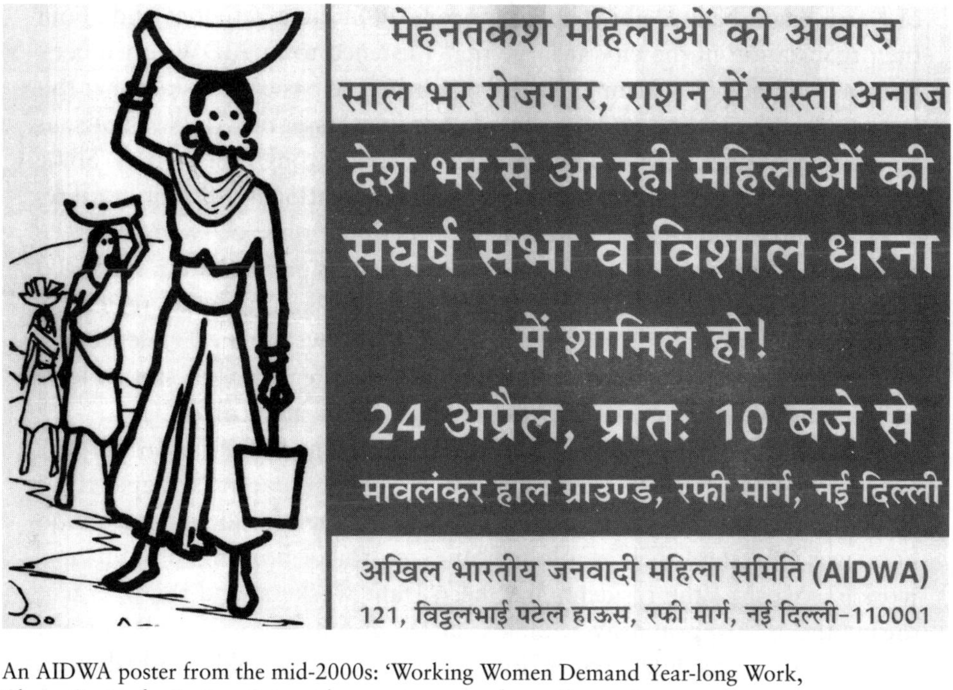

An AIDWA poster from the mid-2000s: 'Working Women Demand Year-long Work, Cheap Grains for Ration. Join with women coming from all over the country to hold a struggle convention and an important demonstration! 24th April, 10 am, Mavlankar Hall Ground, Rafi Marg, New Delhi.'

shop owners called a *dharna* (protest) demanding public attention to address the unavailability of subsidized food for one month in the 3,600 fair price outlets in the city. Planned four days after this protest, on 29 November, a united strike against the government's industrial policies was called by left trade unions and their allies. Participants shouted slogans like 'Down with the anti-people government!' and 'IMF *murdabad*!' (Death to the IMF!) as they marched towards the Boat Club in central Delhi. AIDWA's banners also flew at this march and rally in solidarity with unionized workers at banks and other government offices. Threats of downsizing and computerization galvanized the workers to save their jobs. Among AIDWA participants in the rally were women from a neighbourhood unit that had organized local women and men to end the violence faced by a woman who sought their help. They were part of the city's working poor and they were visibly angry. They were not waiting while the government crafted new excuses.

New Delhi, 1991–1992

Fallout from the supranational finance meetings had not yet trickled down to the streets in November of 1991 when I began to spend time with a neighbourhood branch of AIDWA in a working-class, largely Dalit residential area of Karol Bagh, New Delhi. The discussions about area activities and about the organization in the city at large that I listened to in AIDWA members' houses contained no warning of the deprivations in basic necessities that followed. Neighbourhood and city-based coordinators of the AIDWA units, as well as neighbours, friends and members passed through the houses. Some of the women I subsequently met in the AIDWA national office or at rallies in other parts of the city, though many I met only once or twice, between September 1991 and July 1992. AIDWA during this period had over 57,000 members in New Delhi. Its members across the city ran national, regionally coordinated campaigns for better laws around dowry-related violence and domestic violence, as well as neighbourhood-based campaigns, staffed legal aid centres, and published a new magazine in Hindi and English.

The first week I arrived in an AIDWA member's house in the Regharpura neighbourhood of Karol Bagh, I heard about their recent struggle for a woman who was not a member but lived down the block. The neighbourhood was one established in colonial times to provide housing for municipal workers. Most of the residents had been Dalit workers, and this was true during the 1990s, primarily Balmikis, Jatavs and Reghars, as well as some residents from Scheduled Tribes. Everyone in the households worked: men, women, young men and young women who had finished schooling, though not all for the municipality of Delhi. Some ran small shops, or worked as mechanics or domestic servants. As a working-class and working-poor neighbourhood, Regharpura was a relatively stable one that had the security of governmental housing and adequate work opportunities.

The local AIDWA unit worked to secure the woman's safety from domestic violence. Members described how they successfully negotiated an end to the abuse she suffered. The woman endured domestic abuse at the hands of her husband and her parents-in-law, finally leaving to stay in her own parents' house. Her parents-in-law threatened to take legal custody of her three children if she did not return. The local AIDWA unit, at the woman's request, stepped in to find a solution. Ashalata, then a full-time AIDWA organizer and area coordinator for New Delhi, helped to develop the Regharpura unit's strategy. As is common in AIDWA's handling of domestic violence cases across the country, the Karol Bagh chapter organized meetings with the household members involved in the violence. Usually, though not always, the woman who suffered the violence joined the negotiations. In this case, Ashalata aided their efforts through training members in legal aid and negotiation techniques, and did not conduct the meetings entirely herself. Members of the Regharpura unit began intensive discussions with the woman's mother-in-law, stressing a local ethics that made her violence against her daughter-in-law unacceptable for the entire neighbourhood.

The neighbourhood's political affiliations were primarily split between two parties: the Congress Party, the longest ruling party in India; and the Bharatiya Janata Party (BJP), that saw a marked increase in its popularity across the country during the early 1990s. None of the Communist Parties had a dominant presence in the area; however, in addition to the AIDWA unit, a few communist sympathizers and party members lived there, and the CPI(M)-affiliated union CITU (Centre of Indian Trade Unions) maintained a small membership in the area. Former textile mill workers kept their CITU affiliation active even after the textile factories had closed and union jobs had moved to other localities. On AIDWA organizers' request, men from the local chapter of CITU spoke to the woman's husband and father-in-law about the unacceptability of domestic violence in the neighbourhood. The CITU members were instructed by Ashalata and others of how to handle the discussions to gain their acquiescence to the conditions sought by the woman. Through a series of meetings, AIDWA members worked out an arrangement that was agreed upon by everyone involved. The woman returned to the house on the condition that the violence would cease. If the violence recurred, she would leave with monetary restitution and her children. The enforcement of this agreement rested upon the organizations involved in the discussions, AIDWA and CITU, as well as its public recognition and acceptance by neighbourhood residents. It did not involve the local police or national legal apparatus; though AIDWA's city-wide New Delhi office provided extensive legal expertise for the woman in the negotiations.

For the man and his parents, taking the case to court would have meant hiring a lawyer at considerable expense. For the woman, the counsel provided by the legal centre was free of charge, regardless of whether the two parties created a settlement in a formal court or not. Due to time, expense and outcome in different measures for both parties, finding a compromise outside of the courts benefited everyone.

Ashalata pointed out the differences between American solutions like shelters, placement centres, telephone hotlines and restraining orders to fight domestic violence. She stressed the differences within the Indian context where financial independence for many women with children is almost impossible. While women's financial independence is also in jeopardy for single women (with or without children) in the United States, AIDWA activists explained their model in contradistinction to the US.[4] Both models have their limitations, as Ashalata pointed out, since one works by a seemingly neutral negotiation with all parties to create a solution that often works to keep the woman in her in-laws' home with her husband. The other rests on the 'freedom' of the individual woman to make her own future without violence – a freedom often unsupported by the conditions that a woman (whether Indian or American) faces upon leaving the immediate site of violence.

The Regharpura unit in Karol Bagh worked through, even as it challenged, the social fabric of its locality to end the violence. Members built solidarity within the neighbourhood through their cross-gender alliance with the left-wing trade union that had a strong membership in that locality. They worked to shift tacit acceptance of, or looking the other way from, privatized familial violence against women through their encompassing negotiations to end the violence faced by one local woman. Through its organizational alliances, AIDWA's campaign fought to strengthen rather than break locality-based relationships between neighbours to stop the violence faced by a woman. Members built the campaign on several aspects of this locality. First, they approached the issue upon request by the woman facing the violence. They took direction from her, particularly who they included in negotiations and how to frame their negotiation goals. They drew on the resources of CITU to strengthen their campaign on the woman's behalf. Importantly, the unit mobilized its own members and other neighbourhood women effectively in the woman's support. They did not advocate a more individualist solution

[4] Critical feminist, anti-racist analyses of US liberal feminist solutions to domestic violence and alternate models for resistance are remarkably parallel to those developed by Indian women's groups like AIDWA. Likewise, the character of women's survival of violence and domestic abuse in India and the US shares structural forces of economics and political dependence allied against women who leave violent partners. See Bhattacharjee 1997; Davis 2000; Smith 2000.

where the woman leaves the site of violence, in this case her in-laws' home, as they stressed to me, because they could not ensure that a woman with three children and no education could survive alone. Neither could they expect her to gain custody of her children from her in-laws without a negotiated settlement including alimony. The physical and emotional violence may end, but an economic violence would take its place.

In late November 1991, AIDWA was a central organization sponsoring a city-wide march against the rise in costs of the basic commodities in the PDS and other neoliberal mandates. The crowds of women and men, as well as young people without children revealed the broader alliances of AIDWA's network. Trade unions, Communist Parties and student groups joined the chants of 'IMF *murdabad*!' against neoliberal policies, and the Indian government's active complicity with these punitive demands. A palpable anger against imperialism fuelled the chants of tens of thousands of protestors. In this context, I joined AIDWA members from Karol Bagh within a month of its neighbourhood chapter's negotiation to end a woman's domestic violence. AIDWA emphasized the connection between the loss of affordable food for women and children, and the erosion of the Indian government's accountability to its citizens. It fought to reassert the role of the Indian state as a site to support women's economic, social and political rights. Women and children, in its analysis, experienced the ebbing of state sovereignty and the transmutation of the state's role viscerally, through hunger.

Globalization intensifies women's economic insecurity, a fact powerfully illustrated by newspaper photos of the long lines of women and children futilely waiting for the government-run milk centres to open. As the New Delhi march in November 1991 showed, to fight structural adjustments meant to fight for affordable milk, race and *dal*. It meant a demand for the basic necessitics of women's economic independence. For women like the one in the Regharpura neighbourhood of Karol Bagh, the global forces of multinational capital closed opportunities to leave violent relationships. But these forces may have strengthened, at least in part, the imperatives behind AIDWA's more creative demands. AIDWA's campaign reinforced, as it renegotiated a Karol Bagh neighbourhood's community values against that violence. Women and men, at AIDWA's instigation, fought against the atomised view of domestic violence and eroded norms of privacy that shield the victimizers from sanction. The terms of the local feminist struggle at the onset of neoliberal social and economic policy shifts were not simply fixed or delimited by the terms of economic globalization. Domestic violence, in this instance at least, became a coalitional issue, one built upon AIDWA's analysis that cultural and social struggles for justice are interconnected with class-based struggles. Instead of the fight against domestic violence being added on to class-based demands, AIDWA brought CITU members into the issue on their terms. As such, this one example illustrates another political (and inter-personal) terrain to fight for goals of women's equality and liberation in a neoliberal context.

North Chennai, 2006

The buildings of the subsidized public housing complex in north Chennai seemed to look inwards as we parked on a wide but empty street on their outskirts. I travelled to the complex in the early evening with Lakshmi, the AIDWA area president for north Chennai, and Padma, who translated Tamil interviews into English for me, in the early evening in March 2006. The 4,000 residents of this housing estate in north Chennai lived in the concrete high-rise buildings or in smaller thatched houses along their perimeter; 500 of the women who lived here were AIDWA members. Before we entered the complex, we passed a row of palm-thatched stands, with a well-maintained but equally empty paved base beneath. Lakshmi informed me that the local fish market was held there in the mornings, and by late afternoon the women had returned home, most of whom lived nearby. Even though Lakshmi's work stretches across north Chennai, she lives roughly ten minutes away, and she knows the complex and its residents well. She lived here for several years before she was married. Her mother still resides here. I met Lakshmi the year before, only two weeks after the tsunami had devastated the lives of so many families who lived close to the shoreline, many of whom worked in the fishing industry for a living. In January of 2005, I joined north Chennai AIDWA members in a protest against the unfair distribution of aid to victims of the disaster. The protest had been ugly and the stakes clear. Callous local officials were first joined by the police, and then, as the conflict and abuse escalated, by area politicians. The women's anger, hurt and frustration gained no immediate audience, but AIDWA pursued the case and filed complaints against the police and officials involved. They won an apology almost immediately, but even a year later, continued to press for equal disaster relief compensation for all women from the area's fishing community. I wanted to return to the same neighbourhood after the floodwaters had receded, to interview women from the fishing community, when I returned to Chennai in early 2006.

This complex was too far inland to face the immediate devastation of the floodwaters, Lakshmi reported. But the women here still felt the aftereffects of the disaster since many of them earned their livelihood as fish sellers. The December 2004 tsunami hit the coastline of southeast India late in the morning on a Sunday, a very busy market day. Many women lost their fish, worth up to Rs 2,000, their bicycles and their cash as they fled from the waters. The fish were bought from loans, and their sale usually resulted in a day's profits of Rs 100–150. After the tsunami, daily-waged fish sellers, all of whom are women, received no compensation from the government. Men who fished for a living and who were members of the fishermen's cooperative received Rs 2,000, often without proof of their losses. But fish-selling women were not allowed to join the cooperative and therefore received nothing to help repay the loans they had taken to buy the fish that day. While the women were not members of the fishermen's cooperative society, they were active members of the CITU's fish workers' union. AIDWA was joined by the CITU union in its struggle to gain tsunami compensation for women in the fishing industry and for women's right to join the cooperative society. This struggle was two-pronged in its targets as well as its goals, since it both took on the government for fair compensation and pushed the insular fishing people's community to overturn rules that excluded women in the fishing industry from membership in the cooperative. Neither struggle had abated since the tsunami.

The CITU fish workers' union represented 2,000 people in this area of Chennai; in total, 8 per cent of the 50,000 people who comprised the entire fishing industry in Chennai. Women accounted for 50 per cent of CITU's membership in the fish workers' union, since their eligibility for membership was based on one's working status within the fishing industry alone and not on one's gender. This union was the only fish workers' organization that represented daily-waged fish workers, a category of workers that was largely women. Large and small boat owners, middle-level traders and international seafood corporations relied on a number of business consortiums to maintain a powerful role in the fishing industry (Karunanidhi interview, 9 March 2006). Several ward associations also represented members of the fishing community for non-work-related issues. AIDWA members I spoke to saw the CITU as leading the struggle to gain entry into the fishermen's cooperative, and AIDWA as taking the lead to gain governmental compensation for fish lost in the tsunami. One woman who was a member of CITU and AIDWA described her attempt to gain restitution for fish lost in the tsunami by presenting a petition signed by forty other fish-selling women to the Chief Minister:

> We brought our petition, but were not allowed to see anyone from the Chief Minister's cabinet. We were ignored. Outside her offices we were told we couldn't see anyone regarding our case. So we gave them our petition, but nothing happened. But when we returned we were advised to join AIDWA and take up the issue. To better fight for my rights, I joined AIDWA. (North Chennai AIDWA members interview, 18 March 2006[5])

[5] All names of AIDWA members in the north Chennai unit have been changed.

When describing these ongoing campaigns, AIDWA members from this area of Chennai did not bemoan the lack of success, but saw the campaigns as important and well fought against difficult odds.

We walked past many blocks of apartments, through the early evening labours of preparing food, watching children or relaxing with friends. We turned right into the passageway that measured roughly 25 feet across between the last two blocks of apartments. We arrived in the two-room apartment of Shanti, a woman with four children, all of whom were married. She welcomed us in, and we sat on the bed and on a woven run on the floor. Her eldest son and his wife lived with her. He left as soon as we entered, but his wife sat in the room and chatted with the women in our small delegation, including Lakshmi, Padma, two other AIDWA organizers from the complex and me. Her niece Pushpa arrived with her sister and spoke about her membership in AIDWA along with several other women who joined us soon after we arrived. I had not met Pushpa in early 2005, for although she was a member of AIDWA in 2004, before the tsunami, she only became an active member after May of 2005. She described the difference: 'Now I go to all of AIDWA's meetings. If they call me for a rally or an action, I come' (ibid.). She joined AIDWA in dues *and* participation after a particularly vicious public beating by her husband in the courtyard of the housing complex.

Pushpa described what happened. 'My husband beat me publicly with a cricket bat. Nobody asked why he was beating me and nobody intervened on my behalf. My aunt's [Shanti's] son rescued me from the beating and took me to the hospital' (ibid.). Pushpa's husband had significant power in the housing complex due to his sister who had ties with the political party that represented the area. After Shanti's son brought Pushpa to the hospital, her husband's sister filed a false complaint against him. The police arrested Shanti's son, locked him up and demanded that he submit to the charges of sexual harassment lodged against him. Pushpa's sister spoke up: 'We went to speak to Lakshmi to get AIDWA's help' (ibid.). An AIDWA delegation was formed to speak to Pushpa in the hospital to determine what happened. They contacted Shanti's son and heard his story. They spoke to residents in the housing complex. After consultation with the seven members on AIDWA's north Chennai area secretariat, local AIDWA leaders decided upon their plan of action. Lakshmi led an AIDWA delegation to file a complaint against Pushpa's husband on her behalf at the police station. They convinced the police to release Shanti's son since he had acted honorably by taking Pushpa to the hospital. AIDWA negotiated a settlement between Pushpa and her husband. He apologized to Pushpa for beating her and promised to never beat her again. Pushpa said: 'AIDWA produced this solution. Only they could intervene and solve these problems. Their actions gave us faith in AIDWA' (ibid.). Pushpa's sister described the galvanizing effect of this case on the entire area. 'We wrote a petition and walked door to door in the housing complex to raise funds for Pushpa's hospital bills and her legal case against her husband. Three hundred women joined because of AIDWA's actions in this case' (ibid.). By her estimation, AIDWA's membership in the housing complex more than doubled, from 200 members to 500, because of their involvement in this one case of domestic violence. Out of 2,000 adult residents in the housing estate, 500 women with very different levels of commitment were members of AIDWA in 2006. This case also unearthed another layer of neighbourhood control by the sister-in-law who had connections to the local representative political party, which heightened the impact of AIDWA's successful intervention. When AIDWA confronted the husband's violence against Pushpa, it also had to quash his sister's corrupt use of political influence over the housing complex residents. AIDWA's positive reputation, in this case, had to do with how its members handled the mediation between a wife and her violent husband. But it also stemmed from the strength they displayed to gain justice from the police, the courts, the locality's political machinery and the husband's well-connected family.

Information collected by AIDWA members in Tamil Nadu suggests that these numbers for new members after AIDWA unit members intervene in domestic violence against women are the rule rather than the exception. Recently, AIDWA activists in Tamil Nadu began to collect figures of how members joined the organization. In 2005, delegates to the Tamil Nadu state conference tabulated that over the past three years more than a tenth of the new units formed were directly related to ADIWA's domestic violence intervention work; 17,747 new members and 124 units were formed due to AIDWA's work on domestic violence cases across the state (Vasuki, 'Further Strengthen AIDWA in Tamilnadu', 2005: 3). When Pushpa finished telling her story, her aunt, Shanti, spoke up. 'After joining AIDWA we are not afraid. We are equal to anyone. After the incident and after joining AIDWA, troublemakers keep their distance' (north Chennai AIDWA members interview, 18 March 2006). During the interview one incident illustrated the weight of her words. When Pushpa told me her story, alongside at least ten other AIDWA members, she discovered that her husband was listening at the window. Even after this knowledge, she continued to discuss the details of her recovery from his beating. The next day when I returned to interview more AIDWA members from the complex, Pushpa was outside in the courtyard with her husband who was playing cards. She smiled at us, waved and went inside to her apartment.

The differences in AIDWA's strategies for these two cases of domestic violence are slight – due more to region, resources and activists at the fore of the struggle, than to the economic structures and political forces that support neoliberalism. In both cases AIDWA was already established and had strong allies in the neighbourhoods. In both its strongest open alliance was with the local CPM-affiliated union. AIDWA activists were alerted to the violence and asked to intervene by the abused women themselves, in both of these cases, with the support of their natal family members. Local activists in Delhi and Chennai reported to their district or city committees when they found out about the cases. They also developed their next actions in consultation with AIDWA leadership. They raised funds and awareness in the immediate locality of the violent incidents and built strength in their negotiations from that publicity. In New Delhi they explicitly did not involve the police; while in Chennai, activists used the police to release an intimidated witness and thereby establish their power to negotiate a solution. Women described their pride in AIDWA's power, and their own power as part of that collectivity, as well as the wisdom of the settlements negotiated by AIDWA between the women and their families. In both areas, AIDWA consolidated their membership by signing up new members and widening existing members' involvement in other issues, such as the rise in the prices of food and other essential commodities, the government's unfair distribution of aid after the tsunami, and the demand that the state actively support women's ability to thrive.

Violence and the Rupee

In 2000, AIDWA joined with five other national women's organizations, including the All India Women's Conference (AIWC), the Centre for Women's Development Studies (CWDS) and the YWCA of India, to organize 'Global March 2000', a conference about the effects of structural adjustment policies on women's lives. Representatives from over 80 women's groups attended the conference and endorsed the coalitional document that emerged from the discussions, entitled *Women Speak: United Voices Against Globalization, Poverty and Violence in India* (AIDWA *et al.* 2000). The document provides invaluable insight into how a broad range of women's groups across India understood the issue of violence and women in neoliberal times:

> To see domestic violence only in terms of a man–woman relationship or non-relationship would be to miss out the essence of the problem, which is the institutionalized nature of female second class citizenship as . . . a part of the system as it exists in India today, but also . . . a necessity for [India's] further development. (Ibid.: 58)

The forces of liberalization, in their analysis, demanded (rather than passively accepting) the relations of gender inequality. Among other benefits for the architects of neoliberal policy, women could continue to cushion their blows to the social fabric of daily reproduction, such as the rise in unemployment, the increasing scarcity of food, fuel and clean water supplies, the declining value of working-class wages, to name just a few assaults on women and men's standard of living (Elson 1994; Rakowski 2000; Sparr 1994). The family perpetuates and polices women's unequal gender roles – therefore, to fight domestic violence means for AIDWA and its allies in the women's movement, 'a complete restructuring and democratization . . . of *all familial relations*' (AIDWA *et al.* 2000: 57; their emphasis). AIDWA, like its allies, linked individuals' struggles against domestic violence to their fight against globalization in ways that made domestic violence campaigns a critical first step to dismantling systemic forces that support neoliberal social, economic and political policies. If globalization depends upon existing familial relations to maintain dominance, even as forces of globalization strengthen existing ideologies about gendered and unequal familial roles, then one fight can never be wholly disarticulated from the other.

The connections that AIDWA and the other signatories to this coalition document draw between one woman's fight against violence and the gendered impact of globalization are not the norm in Indian debates about gendered violence. A common frame to understand the differences in the Indian context has pitted a Marxist feminist economic analysis against a radical feminist cultural explanation. Using this culturalist model, Gail Omvedt's work suggests a third path of building from indigenous traditions against violence to mobilize a mass of rural poor women (Omvedt 1990b: 9–15). This explanatory narrative greatly oversimplifies not only India feminist analyses of violence against women, but also the campaigns, strategies and organizations that combat it. In painstaking detail, Veena Poonacha and Divya Pandey's overview of twenty anti-violence organizations in Karnataka and Gujarat shows how widely the praxis on domestic violence ranged during the 1990s (Poonacha and Pandey 2000). In their study, they list time- and cost-cutting strategies that garner community support for women survivors, sanction violent men and educate women about their rights. They note enduring weaknesses of money, resources and support infrastructure in the struggles against gendered violence. They describe how even systemic analyses in some organizations that connect the violence to women's unequal status in society do not change profoundly individualized responses of one-on-one service provision of counselling, legal aid, housing referrals or vocational training.

Importantly, Poonacha and Pandey locate several organizations, such as the Kasturba Stree Vikas Gruh (KSVG) in Jamnagar, Gujarat, that use community-based pressure to change ideologies about domestic violence and women's equality. But they worry about concomitant problems that such reliance on caste/community structures create. 'By utilizing these traditional structures,' they ask, 'are organizations inadvertently strengthening the hold of regressive caste organizations thereby preventing the development of a more egalitarian social system?' (ibid.: 572). Their grave distrust about using community/caste structures is particularly vital as Omvedt's indigenous solution continues to hold credibility among some social scientists as a viable alternative to their assumed alternative of external, homogenizing nongovernmental organizations that address domestic violence among disenfranchised people. Poonacha and Pandey disrupt the simplicity of Omvedt's insider/outsider approach to domestic violence by questioning the inequities ingrained in 'community', whether defined by indigeneity, oppressed-caste status or working-class background. For example, in another scholar's study of domestic violence politics, she (Leela Visaria) only lists the family and the community as sites to resolve high rates of domestic violence, irrespective of class or caste specificities (Visaria 2000). To reassert the links between domestic violence and globalization as AIDWA and its allies do, drastically shifts the focus from the family as a community-defined or even nation-based entity alone, to its importance in the architecture of neoliberalism. The family in neoliberal social policy must privately bear the costs of economic austerity. The family's privacy from public view, in AIDWA's analysis, must be scrutinized anew, since this privacy is won by sanctifying 'the family' as a normative ideal of the social order. AIDWA's publications propose an alternate argument: that the systemic inequality of women channels the hardships of neoliberalism to women and girls, whether those costs are smaller food supplies, decreased access to public education or lack of vaccinations. The privatized family, AIDWA's analysis shows, enforces these hardships in deeply gendered ways. An important facet in its struggles against domestic violence reasserts *and produces* public facets of the family in its present context.

AIDWA's analysis of globalization and domestic violence informs its approach in local struggles and national campaigns. The domestic violence campaigns in New Delhi in 1991 and north Chennai in 2005 began the conversation about women's equality and right to live without physical and sexual intimidation in their locality. They strengthened organizational allies that included men as members. They confronted ideological ties that bind women to their abusers, even while they could not always alleviate the material ties of a woman's economic stability, or her custody of her children in separation and divorce. AIDWA's campaigns also measurably built membership in these neighbourhoods. Neither its ideology nor its activism can be wholly separated from how the organization funds itself. The problem in struggles against domestic violence is not solely one of donor-directed palliatives that attempt to smooth over disruptions caused by disinvestments in social welfare. Nor is the problem just westernized and individualist solutions of care provision in domestic violence initiatives. Rather, it is how a women's organization understands 'women's equality' such that it creates the horizon of its strategies to strengthen women's empowerment.

AIDWA's ideological vision and organizational methods are embedded in its member-funded and member-run character. Vasuki, the general secretary for the state of Tamil Nadu, pointed to the slogan, 'Democracy, Equality, and Women's Emancipation', to clarify AIDWA's goals and ideological underpinnings. As she remarked, these are difficult goals to discuss in everyday terms. To imagine these goals, likewise, demands profound ideological shifts in the ways power operates. 'Democracy' as a goal, even in the pared-down neoliberal framework, can demand the state work for all the people it represents – a challenging, reformist goal. The police should file, investigate and prosecute each claimant's case with an impartiality guided by the law. 'Equality' also carries demands on the state, on social relations between oppressed groups, across cases, across castes, across religions, and among women and men, that all people are treated equally in the law. But equality also alludes to something within: an equal right to humanity, dignity and human value. 'Women's emancipation' as a goal exceeds the demands for a more just state, and reaches towards something more than democracy or even equality. Its claims have more utopian possibilities.

Vina Mazumdar makes a distinction between the contingency of empowerment to the goal of equality that illuminates AIDWA's understanding. Empowerment, she argues, cannot be the end result of any feminist campaign. Women's empowerment is a necessary precondition, the *means* for women to build the material conditions of their equality (Mazumdar 2000). Through member-sustaining fund-raising, AIDWA organizationally endorses women's empowerment not as an end, but as the necessary means to organizationally build women's equality (Vina Mazumdar interview, 5 January 2002). Likewise, its method of funding itself empowers women organizationally to produce women's equality as lived relations through their activism. The members who fight in their neighbourhood for each woman's right to live in a non-violent household are not being 'serviced' by their organization, since they are the organization and its organizers. Their strategy confronts the violence against women as a *public* practice, an understanding that enlarges the very terrain of 'women's equality'.

Organizers and the Rupee

AIDWA's activists discuss their work in different terms from the organization's programmatic publications about gendered violence. Lakshmi, the area leader in north Chennai, talks about the courage and respect she gains from organizing as part of AIDWA, in both personal and political terms. She described her lack of fear in daily negotiations with unjust social structures and relationships. Lakshmi recounted why she decided to become a more active member:

> I have two lakhs rupees of debt. Last year I was fed up with my huge debts, depressed about all the money I owe. I realized that if I go and fight for these issues then I can forget about all these problems. My work with AIDWA gives me courage that I will be able to repay my debts. I concentrate on educating my daughters so they can build a good life for themselves. If I stay at home, all I do is fret about my debts. AIDWA gives me courage that I can repay the money one day. (Lakshmi interview, 20 March 2006)

While Lakshmi sees her debt as an important reason for becoming the area president, she receives no monetary compensation for any of her AIDWA work. Yet, the connection she draws between debt and her activism is more than just symbolic, since she gains 'courage', in her words, rather than hope or faith that she can repay her loans. She directed her energy towards her daughters' futures and her activism, yet she also set her sights further toward a future free of debt. Her courage is built every day through her confrontation with people and systems of power.

Alongside courage, Lakshmi used the term 'respect' to describe her dealings with the police and local officials when she fights women's cases. She revealed her demands on the state through respect.

> At the police station women never get any respect. But if we go under the banner of AIDWA they give us respect. They don't ask us to buy them cigarettes and tea for the inspectors and ACP [Assistant Commissioner of Police]. We aren't afraid of them. They work for us, that is what we believe. So why should we be afraid? (Ibid.)

Lakshmi provided a lesson she learned about shedding fear after joining the organization: that police officers work for its members and for all women. The state works for *them*. That reformist knowledge of a representative state is not lightly won. That knowledge is also a power that must be repeatedly proved through AIDWA's political demands on that state apparatus. As a collective force, it has managed to counter dominant discourses of women's worthlessness. Even as an individual member, Lakshmi can go to the police station with that collective power writ large behind her. 'I will go alone, as the representative of AIDWA that is enough. They have to listen. If we come with twenty or thirty people, then they know something big has happened and they ask right away what the matter is' (ibid.).

Lakshmi used her skills in her own neighbourhood when women questioned her constant movements outside the home and their locality. 'They asked if I had boyfriends, and wondered what kind of man my husband was to let me go alone from the house', she described with a subtle light in her eyes. 'They kept talking and talking about my honour even when I tried to explain what I was doing. So I showed them in a way they understood.' Lakshmi pointed to fused streetlights that everyone complained about. Nothing was ever done to change the bulbs or restore the power. 'Come with me, and we will fix them', she told them (ibid.). She led her neighbours, none of whom were women active in AIDWA, to their local representative with a petition signed by everyone who lived along and near the street. The women saw that these officials knew Lakshmi and treated her gingerly, even with respect. They witnessed Lakshmi's confidence in their presence and even felt their own power. The streetlights were repaired soon thereafter, reported Lakshmi with a laughing sparkle in her eyes, and since then no one ever challenged her right to come and go as she pleased. A few of them even joined the local AIDWA unit.

In every locality, AIDWA makes choices informed by its political analysis that affect its activism – but the wider terrain of feminist NGO activism also marks these strategies. While AIDWA refuses funds from outside its organizational scope for its activism, the organization still must operate in relation to other NGOs and the changing field of civil society organizations (Brinda Karat interview, 19 December 2002). Unlike many NGOs, AIDWA cannot afford to pay the bulk of its lead organizers. In the country as a whole, in 2002, only 600 of its full-time activists drew a salary for their work. In effect, the organization must compete with other NGOs to retain its organizers. These non-governmental groups may raise similar concerns, use similar language and promote similar agendas in the same neighbourhoods as AIDWA does. The competitive logic of the free market operated among NGOs in their relationship to each other in what Sonia Alvarez called the professionalization or 'NGOization' of activism (Alvarez 1998). Alongside quantifiable results, or 'donor accountability' demanded by donor agencies, that enumerated the changes/actions/solutions effected by an NGO to justify money spent, came enumerations of other kinds (Markowitz and Tice 2002). Activism became a profession in new ways. An activist could count her rewards, quite literally, with each paycheck. Efficiency slid into efficacy when the politics of an NGO became measured in these more easily quantified ways.

Amy Lind emphasizes the silver lining of movements' competition with each other for funding. She argues that the more challenging terrain of social activism, with fewer groups receiving funding and greater donor control over what counts as legitimate activism, creates more militant strategies and more radical demands, particularly by the groups denied donor largesse (Lind 2000). But to equate competition and ensuing loss of funds to the rejection of outside funding glosses over the daily negotiations around money that all oppositional movements must make in their quest for structural social change (INCITE! Women of Color Against Violence, ed. 2007). The development and invigoration of AIDWA's leaders, members, campaigns, literature, analysis and organizational structure, all face additional pressure from the global shift in the 1980s and 90s from international donors primarily funding governments, to their new target of opportunity, NGOs.

A more important radicalization takes place when funding by outside agencies does not propel an organization as a negative or a positive force. Without a salary to measure her worth, to retain an AIDWA activist, the organization must produce palpable, though often qualitative changes (Indu Agnihotri interview, 8 January 2002). Likewise, its campaigns must gain for their localities material, even if incremental benefits from the ever-shrinking public sphere (Brinda Karat interview, 18 December 2002). The particularities of local groups' activism, marked by neighbourhood alliances or histories of struggle, have regional, national and potentially transnational effects. AIDWA's local units and campaigns expanded the political imaginary of women's equality as they challenged what constitutes 'private' values, and who can police those designations. In cases of domestic and neoliberal violence, the organization quite literally publicized, or forced into a renegotiated public space, previously private values and increasingly privatized solutions for gendered violence. Tactically, AIDWA mobilized 'community' not as a romantic hold-over against a rapacious modernity, but as a complex and unfolding set of social relationships that wield a public sphere to combat neoliberal privatization. Its struggle for ethical transformations in the everyday fabric of life became more than its hallmark, since the non-commodifiable character of these goals made its organizational survival possible.

Lakshmi described her own fearlessness in the face of daily injustices she witnessed. She gave daily examples to illustrate her freedom to contest those violations of the dignity of other women and herself.

> After joining AIDWA I gained awareness and experience. I can talk to others with spirit and courage. If I go to the police station I introduce myself as a member of AIDWA with a case to file. I can talk to them without inhibitions and without fear. And at home I talk freely without any fear I could be beaten up. (Lakshmi interview, 22 March 2006)

Her personal difficulties with large, seemingly insurmountable debt are not distinct from her reasons for becoming an active, unpaid member of AIDWA. Lakshmi explicitly connected her gains in her understanding of the state, of women's right to have the police work for them, to her own 'free' speech at home and in public. In these ways she suggested a much wider sphere of its influence. Her liberation as a woman exceeds equal protections promised by the state. Her freedom from fear and inhibition had much wider consequences as a precondition for further struggle.

Nine Million Rupees Strong

In many respects, the members I talked to in north Chennai and New Delhi used language that was more limited in scope than that of these cities' organizers. Many talked about 'protection' for themselves and their daughters. Others used the word 'safety' to explain their satisfaction with their membership. Others talked about the 'peace' that the organization brings them and their families. One member in north Chennai described the change in their housing estate. 'Our only issue in this area is that woman [the violent man's sister]. She's the one who creates the problems. Now we are not afraid of anything. And we have peace. After we've joined AIDWA she's not fighting as much and not lodging complaints with the police. So now we have our peace' (north Chennai group interview, 18 March 2006). These descriptions of AIDWA as a women's organization contain some aspects of a group that provides services to its members. Another member from north Chennai said, 'If someone makes trouble, or if there are any police cases, we don't know how to lodge a complaint. AIDWA helps us deal with the police procedures. So now we are in peace' (ibid.).

Likewise in New Delhi, women in AIDWA's legal centres were equally blunt about the legal knowledge and experience in dealing with court systems that the organization provided them. Their husbands' families faced a difficult choice: negotiate with AIDWA on the organization's terms, or enter the expensive legal system against a formidable force. In New Delhi, to solve disputes of familial violence, members drew upon and strengthened their coalitional ties with other movements active in the neighbourhood. The local unit's campaign success depended on an ideological interrogation of community-wide assumptions about violence against women. It did not end with the services provided in curbing one family's transgressive violence or ensuring one woman's safety.

In its literature, AIDWA draws explicit ideological connections between these struggles, since a woman's inability to leave a violent household is directly linked to her lack of economic independence, and her ability to gain custody of her children and to demand her rights under the law. Its analysis of gendered violence links the changing neoliberal state to women's relationship to domestic violence. An AIDWA pamphlet titled *Women and Violence* (1999) outlined the following argument: as the state's role in the distribution of resources and common wealth as well as its social welfare role retracted in the 1990s, a woman's chance to survive without violence shrank with it. Solutions began with the transformation of daily acceptance of violence against women, but made explicit demands of the state and the legal system alongside local struggles. But the organization's more mundane practicalities of membership and funding have an analogous logic that weaves its analysis of women and violence into its organizational structure. AIDWA does not solely provide services for and by women, but builds the capacity of women to fight for their own lived equality. Likewise, the women who pay dues to AIDWA also define their struggles, join coalitions, create campaigns and build their unit's membership.

In daily cases of domestic violence, AIDWA provided services to members and non-members that were much more valuable than its modest dues. Free legal aid, support in police cases, money to pay for hospital bills, and protection from powerful individuals and political parties were services that with some attention can be designated by their monetary value. But here, Vasuki's point about the two-sided coin of membership is important: membership has rights and it has duties. These duties have a less tangible quality. The same member in north Chennai satisfied by the peace wrought in her housing complex described her own stakes in AIDWA using a wider lens. 'Everyone should receive justice', she said. 'We fight for that justice' (north Chennai group interview, 18 March 2006).

Safety, protection, peace, equality and justice threaded their way through interviews I held with rank-and-file members on different days, and in different locations around north Chennai. These terms mirrored language I have heard from members in New Delhi. The women members did not explicitly connect these goals to AIDWA's slogan, 'Democracy, Equality, Women's Emancipation'. They did suggest, however, that a membership that cost one rupee per member per year allowed difficult conversations to begin about fighting for those larger goals. Both analytically and strategically, organizational praxis connected domestic violence to discriminatory hiring policies, the devaluation of girl children, restrictive rules about women's political participation and encroaching neoliberalism.

Each year the membership must be renewed, and if a member does not feel well represented by the organization, she will not pay her one-rupee dues. For that reason, any understanding of AIDWA's national campaigns, whether against structural adjustments or in favour of women's property rights, depends upon an analysis of its locally run campaigns, the leaders it developed, the conditions and practices it changed, and the people it benefited. In short, the continuity of AIDWA depends upon its accountability in its goals, results and ideology to its members, and the varied communities the organization produces and circulates amongst. Its members, in an increasingly competitive landscape of foreign-funded NGO activism, fuelled the constant demand for material changes in women's lives as they fought to win those gains. The tight web of membership initiative, organizational coordination and AIDWA's accountability to its members' daily struggles to survive give an urgency to even seemingly distanced 'global' or 'international' issues like structural adjustment policies. The inter-sectoral work of building solidarity gains its anti-imperialist potential with the ideological work of creating new cultures of anti-violence and peace during the daily, local and intra-communal, intra-familial struggles against violence. As those new ideologies pervade the difficult inter-sectoral work of building linkages across communal identities and formations, the potential for an anti-imperialist solidarity gains the solidity of praxis. Finding commonality across differences does not lie in the supposed universality of the issue, such as violence against women, but in the courage to build more inclusive, more just ideologies in the communities one inhabits. Global imperialism and national capitulation were also local issues for members like the women in Karol Bagh who joined the march against neoliberalism in late 1991 and the demonstrations that followed. The horizon of women's equality receded farther from view when equality in the marketplace seemed the only, in fact, the ideal end result of long-range struggles for justice. AIDWA's politics against the forms of violence that women face also sustained a social imaginary that envision a world where women's equality marks a catalytic beginning for women's possibilities, not its end.

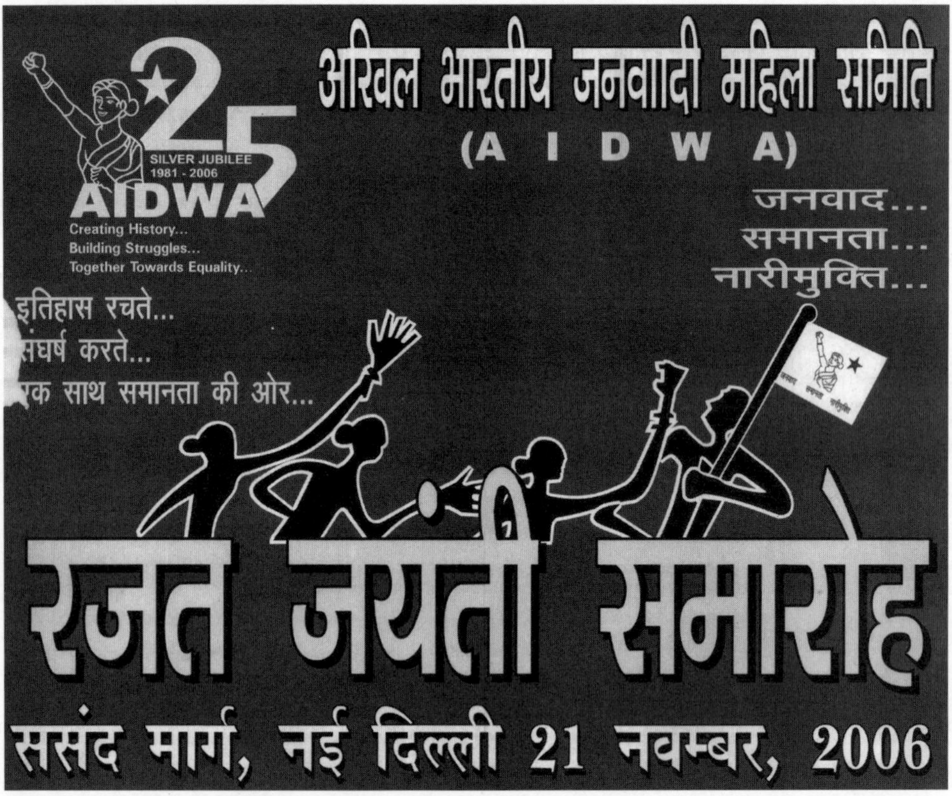

An AIDWA poster advertising its 'Silver Jubilee Celebration', New Delhi, 21 November 2006.

SEVEN

AIDWA in the World

Beginning 30th August 1995 and continuing through 15th September, the United Nations held two inter-related conferences on women hosted by the People's Republic of China. The opening conference gathered together upwards of 40,000 participants for the Non-Governmental Organization (NGO) Forum on women held in Huairou, a town situated roughly an hour outside Beijing. The second conference was the official United Nations Fourth World Conference on Women, and brought together 189 nations with their roughly 10,000 delegates, to assess the status of women in their countries and to move beyond the consensus built around the UN Forward-Looking Strategies for Action to support women's rights signed in Nairobi, Kenya ten years before. They sought to gain agreement by all member nations on the wider Beijing Declaration and Platform for Action, a document that reportedly had one-third of its language still under discussion when the conferences began. By the end of the UN Conference, the statement with its twelve areas of concern for women were finalized and signed by 180 UN member nations.

This chapter travels in two directions of scale that portray how AIDWA brings an internationalist analysis to women's lives, but also how the organization demands that women's lives shape internationalist policy. First, AIDWA organizers described their struggles to make imperialist wars relevant to their members. Through kerosene costs, through the shared lack of basic health and education necessities, this chapter traces how international and transnational solidarity depends upon the mundane yet meaningful objects and feelings that give the strength of collective will to social change. Second, this chapter traces the channels that AIDWA took to represent the hardships of their members' lives in order to shape national policies, international agreements and transnational debates. Neither process, of changing one person's consciousness about her links to other women across the globe, nor of demanding anti-imperialism in the face of G7 hegemony, can be easily modelled; yet for feminist transnationalism and women's internationalism, both are equally necessary.

During the 1995 UN Conference on Women held in Beijing, the feminist language of women's empowerment and equality finally gained a visible place in the discourse of the development circles that included international policy makers, large donors and governments. The 1990s marked a time of newly-won legitimacy for local and regional women's groups as well as transnational feminist networks. Public recognition, funds and governmental partnership welcomed many scrappy feminist groups with their hard-fought struggles into their fold. As representatives from feminist collectives around the world prepared to join the UN Conference on Women, major donors, like Ford Foundation and MacArthur Foundation, poured money into trainings, staff salaries, organizational infrastructure and transportation to ensure women's unprecedented participation in the NGO forum held in Huairou, China alongside the official UN proceedings.

For a number of reasons, many within the radical and left women's movement did not fully trust that the windfall of funds and international attention spurred by the UN Conference on Women heralded the beginning of a brighter feminist future. The focus on small feminist groups, the grassroots women's movement, in the lead-up to Beijing and its aftermath inspired a prophetic if bitter insight by women active in national, left-wing women's organizations. The grassroots, they joked, is where the trees can't grow. These activists contested the ways that their large and often politically and organizationally connected groups were deliberately sidelined in the heyday of transnational feminism in the 1990s. They upheld the importance of changes fought for through the mass mobilization of women, a mobilization that sometimes drew on leftist solidarity by gender-mixed groups. They asked how systemic change could be won solely through small or 'grassroots' feminist units of political vision and will.

In the case of the 1995 UN Conference, AIDWA members described being actively marginalized from well-funded official and unofficial planning meetings. Kept out of most regional planning meetings, they spearheaded a coalitional campaign to criticize structural adjustment policies for targeting women and children first for austerity measures. This was a national campaign within India first. They drafted a coalitional document, *Towards Beijing*, to describe their alternate vision for women's future. The coalitional partners sought to pressure the Indian delegation to critique structural adjustments in the UN Platform for Action, a document that historically had rendered structural adjustments invisible as a women's issue.

To build their coalition, AIDWA members drew on a national network of women's organizations that was over a decade older than the network of women's groups set up in 1993 and 1994 by the Ford Foundation and other funding organizations. Since its inception, AIDWA was part of a powerful coalition of seven, then eight and later nine national women's organizations. They first came together to advocate for a stronger commitment to women's issues in the government's Sixth Plan in the early 1980s. During 1994 and 1995, the national women's groups created a counter document to the UN Platform for Action that demanded 'structural transformation', not 'structural adjustment' (AIDWA *et al.* 1995). Over 800 small and large women's groups co-signed the document that was presented to the Indian government and distributed at the NGO Forum in Huairou. The coalitional protest against the detrimental effects of neoliberal economic restructuring in India was mirrored across the NGO Forum. Women from countries in Latin America, Africa, East Asia and Southeast Asia voiced similar experiences and parallel critiques. The issue of structural adjustments was added to the final UN document, but in coded language which suggested that a better future for women would emerge through their current austerity hardships.

Feminist language, though not always feminist goals, trickled into the very heart of international development discourse over the 1980s and 90s. Alongside this appropriation of feminist language in powerful places, autonomous feminist groups that were not linked to trade unions or left political parties faced their own set of challenges and changes, that have been particularly well documented in the Indian and the Latin American contexts. The autonomous women's movement in the 1990s witnessed a shift from a less capitalized politics of volunteer-run feminist groups to a more professionalized politics of service provision. Service provision, with its carefully measured outcomes and an organizational presentation with an eye to international donors, grants, conferences and networks, is the outcome of what Sonia Alvarez called the 'NGOization' of women's political activism (Alvarez 1999). The autonomous women's groups did not necessarily become NGOs, but felt their influence in their functions, goals, ideologies and even their politics.

Charities and government-supported women's aid groups often did transition into an NGO-ized protocol without much visible difficulty in India. But most autonomous women's groups were formed during the heady days of feminist activism after the Emergency ended in 1975, and these influences ran counter to many groups' mandate.[1] The rich outpouring of feminist energies of the 1970s and 80s created a wide range of autonomous women's groups, located mostly in cities and large towns, and run by middle-class and elite women. From their outset, they did not seek to simply ameliorate gendered inequities of resources. Nor did they want to confine their

[1] For a clear discussion about the theoretical and organizational definitions of 'autonomous' to describe an important wing of the Indian women's movement, see Purkayastha, Subramaniam, Desai and Bose 2003.

activities to the distribution of scarce resources and skills. They held deep commitments to social justice, and the eradication of patriarchal values and structures. Autonomous women's groups described their alienation from the depoliticized language of NGOs and their sense of isolation from this style of working within dominant systems of politics (CWDS 1995). Many of these groups, though certainly not all, did not survive the 1990s with their autonomy from the government and political parties intact.

Feminist scholars and activists in India have charted the effects of these changes with distress. They described a powerful sense of loss and also hope among feminist activists that they could harness the funds and linkages to powerful institutions to the benefit of women, and towards more equitable ideologies of gender relations (Roy 2009; Govinda 2009). Some scholars of the movement were more sanguine. One report about the Indian women's movement, first written for the World Bank, also noted the movement's increasing dissipation. However, the report's author saw little need for unity or 'a revitalized national women's movement', and suggested that the women's movement's vibrant history of networking and mobilizing women would be sufficient to carry it forward (Samita Sen 2000).

The NGO-ized turn located by so many scholars of women's movements around the world was not the only response to the sticks and carrots of neoliberal globalization forces. Activists in AIDWA continued to fund their campaigns and organization through member dues and individual donations. AIDWA built its service provisionary work, such as the legal aid centres, its social reform agenda, such as laws to mandate the reservation of seats in parliament for women, alongside its demands for systemic change in ideologies of girl children's worth, the dowry system and casteist practices of untouchability. It also held on to its central commitment to socialism and demands for people-centred governance that enabled fair distribution of monetary, land and other resources. AIDWA's most active women members continued to be volunteer, and the few full-time organizers were paid modest salaries. It continued to build its linkages to CPM-affiliated mass organizations through joint actions. It continued to seek wide coalitions within the women's movement on specific women's issues. This is not to say that AIDWA was not affected by the NGO-ization of the Indian women's movement at large; it was, in a number of ways. One facet mentioned by AIDWA's activists around the country was the rise in salaries offered to local women activists by NGOs, promises that their organization could not match. The loss of seasoned activists to better paying work for NGOs with a feminist politics is an example cited by many AIDWA activists.

The UN Fourth World Conference on Women in Beijing

The Platform for Action (PfA) forged in the UN Conference on Women in Beijing has guided the goals for signatory nations in their commitment to women's rights, and provided leverage for activists within these countries.[2] The 50,000 attendees at both conferences still represent a watershed participation level for UN Conferences on Women, held in 1975, 1980 and 1985. Due to a range of factors, including the threat by the Bush administration to dismantle key elements of the PfA signed in Beijing in 1995, the UN Conferences in 2000 (Beijing +5), 2005 (Beijing +10) and 2010 (Beijing +15) were effectively placeholders, since they did not include substantial renegotiation of the Beijing document, nor did they host an open non-governmental forum alongside the constrained UN meetings. The Beijing PfA, for almost two decades, has held material resonance for regional, national and local women's organizing around the world, even as memories of the actual conference events fade. In this context, the 1995 UN Conference and the NGO Forum provide a window on women's internationalism that includes nations, NGOs and less formally organized political actors during a critical decade for the consolidation (and some have argued undoing) of a capitalist global economy (Bello 2006).

Over ten years after the UN Conference on Women held in Beijing in 1995, the nine AIDWA members who had attended the conference remembered their participation in the international gathering. Their memories of the conference, their impressions that continued to resonate thirteen years later, and the impact these conferences had on AIDWA's organizing are the central subjects of this chapter.[3] The summer preceding the conference, many of these women were immersed in AIDWA's national campaign to shift the complacent language of the national *Status of Women* document that the official Indian delegation would submit to the United Nations. They built a wide coalition around an alternate document about women's lives in India called *Towards Beijing: A Perspective from the Indian Women's Movement* (AIDWA *et al.* 1995).

By the time the NGO Forum began in late August, over 90 Indian women's groups had signed on to *Towards Beijing*, a report that supported the Indian government-led research on women's lives but sharply contradicted the government's conclusions about that data. The alternate report excoriated the policies driven by structural adjustments, and demanded the Indian govern-

[2] Aili Tripp's work has followed women's organizing in the continent of Africa with a particular focus on Uganda, and the Beijing Platform for Action as a spur in these efforts. See Tripp 2006. For discussion of other regions in the world, see also, Rai, ed. 2003.

[3] Indus Chadha was a vital research assistant for this chapter. She conducted two richly informative interviews during 2008.

ment give critical voice to the intensified poverty of poor women due to these changes. *Towards Beijing* also forcefully imagined other necessary structural changes: what it called structural transformation of wealth redistribution for the Indian polity, a vision that hailed the international community. The coalition document begins with the language of the UN Conference:

> We as women, as workers, as cultivators, as producers, as consumers, as mothers, as citizens, as human beings: . . . Demand not structural adjustment but structural transformation. The former leads to feminization of poverty and redistribution of hunger between men and women. The latter is based on the redistribution of wealth with equal rights to women and an end to patriarchal structures and values. (Ibid.: 5)

I spent the summer as a witness to the coalitional campaign in New Delhi, but did not attend the conference in Beijing. Instead, I returned to the United States with vivid memories of their demand for international women's solidarity against neoliberal globalization, a globalization driven by the United States but invisible to most of its citizens, women and men alike. Once in the US, American activists who attended the NGO Forum led conversations, held presentations, and wrote articles for the feminist and general media that burned with anger at structural adjustments and our own complicity of silence around the dominant 'Washington Consensus'.[4] These discussions contradicted the tepid and even gloating language about neoliberal economic policies that was finally incorporated into the Beijing Platform for Action:

> Recent international economic developments have had in many cases a disproportionate impact on women and children. . . . For those States that have carried a large burden of foreign debt, structural adjustment programmes, and measures, though beneficial in the long term, have led to a reduction in social expenditures, thereby adversely affecting women. (UN 1995)

Structural adjustment policies became a visible women's issue in the United States after Beijing.[5] The inception of the American anti-globalization movement is usually dated by the wholesale disruption of the World

[4] The Washington Consensus emerged in direct opposition to the framing of the economic way forward by the Global South Commission for Third World countries. Peggy Antrobus locates the turning point in 1980 when the G7 (Group of Seven Industrialized Countries) meeting in Cancun, Mexico, led by Ronald Reagan and Margaret Thatcher of the US and the UK respectively, quashed the economic strategies for third world economic autonomy. See Antrobus 2004: 31. Devaki Jain names the International Monetary Fund (IMF) and World Bank as the two supranational lending organizations that defined what forces, besides the US and the UK, consolidated Washington's consensus on structural adjustment policies. See Jain 2005: 102.

[5] A number of articles provide an overview of responses to the Beijing Conference, but not all of them mention the economic issues under debate. Notably, most of the reports that make explicit mention of structural adjustments and US imperialism are by and/or about US women of colour. See Mallika Dutt 2000; Spivak 1996.

Trade Organization (WTO) meeting in Seattle in 1999. The groundwork for these protests began in many sites, from the labor movement, the environmental movement, the left, and from community organizers. The Non-Governmental Forum held in Huairou alongside the UN Conference on Women in Beijing in the summer of 1995 provided early, critical, distinctly feminist and too often unrecognized momentum to the anti-globalization movement in the United States.

Internationalism and Transnationalism

AIDWA's internationalism in the 1990s developed on a neoliberal political landscape that values quick-moving non-state actors, like non-profit, non-governmental organizations, that can turn on a dime to provide human services as the nation-state recedes from the business of resource redistribution and representation of the greatest numbers of its citizens. What does internationalism mean when transnational networks between outfits reign? What does it mean when the most influential women's organizations parley with international leaders over human rights declarations, or debate the terms of conflict resolution or the role of women in energizing the informal economy? Perhaps the most marked trait of these non-profits powered by feminism, women or both, is their inattention to organizing women, creating a membership base and becoming a vehicle for desires larger than their charter's ambit.

Transnational feminist theories of organization stress issue-based coalitions, regional alliances across continents, and, above all, a network of people and NGOs. Christa Wichterich exemplifies these celebrated organizational forms in her description of Huairou as 'a festival of networking' (Wichterich 2000: 147). She argues that this diffuse model of building connections mirrors globalization since women 'have spread to the farthest corner of this patriarchal planet and succeeded in forging closer links with one another, but at the same time they have remained diverse and fragmented' (ibid.). Wichterich's metaphor of globalization illustrates transnationalism more generally as a broad connection between women that extends beyond regional and national contexts, yet does not demand homogeneity of experience, analysis or goals. In less metaphorical terms, for Valerie Moghadam, globalization materially produces transnational feminist networks as 'one positive aspect' (Moghadam 2005: 19). The very terms of conversation among transnational feminist theories of organizing depart radically from those used by AIDWA members.

Interviews with AIDWA's representatives to the Beijing women's conference in 1995 reveal how imperialism and the opposition to imperialism continued to vex and inspire the internationalism of a socialist women's organization fuelled by its mass membership rather than its cultural or financial capital. Even ten years after their participation, these women, a fair number of whom have not left the country since that conference, still actively grappled with the problem of international solidarity for a capital-poor organization, one powered by the yearly one-rupees dues from its now 10 million-strong membership. What did internationalism mean when just entering a transnational feminist network requires substantial infrastructural support, of computers, technicians and full-time communicators with groups outside local, regional and national contexts? The AIDWA participants consistently framed their answers about AIDWA's internationalism through their commitment to anti-imperialism rather than anti-globalization. They also referenced the international connections AIDWA had built with other socialist women's organizations, and anti-imperialist women's movements in Iraq and Afghanistan, rather than with women aligned against current neoliberal policies of globalization, with the exception of the 2000 Global March of Women held in Montreal, Canada on International Women's Day.

Solidarity of a Pencil

Sonya Gill was AIDWA's secretary of Mumbai during the 1990s. During an interview with her in 2008 – when she was the Mumbai district president, the Maharashtra state vice president, and the Maharashtra member of AIDWA's Central Executive Committee – she reframed the general questions we asked about AIDWA's participation in the UN Conference: 'Could you define internationalism in AIDWA's politics?' and 'How is internationalism a part of different levels of the organization?' (Sonya Gill interview by Indus Chadha, 25 July 2008). Rather than answer functional questions about what their internationalist campaigns look like, she began with the lives and knowledges of AIDWA's members to ask what shaped their internationalist consciousness. Once international solidarity is a mass membership question rather than an organizational one, the problem shifts from campaign pathways to structural analysis. Sonya Gill laid out its contours clearly:

> Our mass membership and our mass activists come from a working-class background, in whose lives, for women as a whole, their exposures to begin with are very limited in that sense. So it is a question of how you involve them in campaigns and to what extent you are able to give them a sense of being part of a much, much wider struggle. Everyone knows this slogan, 'We are all one', and 'Women of the world unite'. But behind these slogans who are these 'all' and these other 'women', and what are they struggling for? (Ibid.)

To attend the conference in Beijing, even if AIDWA could have pulled together money for more than a handful of activists to go, could not solve the problem of answering these questions for all the members of AIDWA. Neither does a national campaign to critique the negative gendered affects of structural adjustments stretch members' daily experiences of those hardships to an internationalist critique of globalization. To ask, in internationalist terms, who is all and who are women in that solidarity, is to develop a systemic analysis of capitalism, of patriarchy and of imperialism which produces a category that integrates all, and substantiates women as a medium of commonality between oppressed and exploited people across regions and nations.

Our current framework of transnational feminism is the network, but to participate in a transnational feminist network, of conjoined strategizing between regions of women's organizing campaigns, does not begin to facilitate an answer to the question Sonia Gill articulates of what all women, in solidarity, are struggling for. The transnational feminist network can obscure precisely these questions of building internationalist consciousness among oppressed women. Nimble non-governmental organizations that traverse these networks are not equipped to aid the process of what women want to change and what alternatives women want to build across the globe. The shift to mass membership returns 'internationalism' to solidarity among and between women around the world; or, to that rephrasing of *The Communist Manifesto* echoed by Sonya Gill's slogan, 'women of the world unite'. Similarly, the emphasis of women's organizations and their members reasserts a socialist goal of building power for and by the mass of women, rather than exercise the means at hand to push existing power relations to accede to women's issues. Paradoxically, however, a focus on the outlook of the mass of AIDWA's members requires an internationalist consciousness to be developed by AIDWA as an organization, and by regional and state organizers to shape the understandings of local AIDWA members.

Sonya Gill's answer to her own question about international solidarity surprised me most: a pencil. AIDWA's campaign to build a wide coalition of Indian women's groups before the Beijing conference demanded a national level of coordination among women's groups across the country. But AIDWA had developed another kind of campaign to raise international solidarity against the crippling effects of structural adjustments on Indian women to the national level, with individual women, members and non-members in mind. Organizers used the symbolism of a pencil to create linkages across national polities, and build a critique of structural adjustments and war. Sonya's answer of 'how to take [international solidarity] into the mass of your membership' focused on an object of solidarity that, in her words, allowed AIDWA to 'be very conscious of how to make for our cadre a vivid, a real, a lived experience of how to show solidarity with women in other parts of the world and what is happening to their lives' (ibid.).

AIDWA's mass membership includes 10 million women; 75 per cent of them are from rural agricultural livelihoods, most work in the informal economy, a majority are from oppressed-caste, indigenous populations or religious minorities, a large proportion are landless women with no reliable means of survival except their own hands. Poverty, deeply riven by gendered inequities of experience, marks the lives of almost all of AIDWA's members in brutally direct and daily forms.

In this context, Sonya Gill defines international solidarity in prosaic terms. 'We're all the time talking and fighting and struggling about our issues, but there are others doing the same thing, and these same kinds of issues are much more global' (ibid.). Solidarity, in these terms, centred on a mundane and useful object of emancipation: the pencil. As a tool to write and a symbol of literacy, the pencil gave resonance to the campaign's message. Gill described organizing against the US occupation of Iraq after 2002:

> Iraqi children not having pencils, or Iraqi women having to go without anaesthesia for an operation, these are very vivid, and things that any person can relate to, although they may not be able to visualize what an Iraqi woman looks like, and where possibly Iraq is, because, you know, it's a very long time back they looked at a map. (Ibid.)

In a neoliberal world, where solidarity between neighbours, across community, caste and religious lines, is the defining imprint of AIDWA's work, the shared erasure of a pencil for children, the shared denial of anaesthesia for women around the world, best describe the lines that link women and create an all to unite.

AIDWA's public campaign in 2003 to collect pencils for Iraqi schoolchildren, and their petitions against US occupation and bombardment of Iraq, were both internationalist solidarity actions that sought to shape the consciousness of its members (and non-members), as they materially showed solidarity with unfamiliar women of different nationalities. They sought to link local deprivation of goods and services to international issues using transnational means; yet their visible symbols, whether books, anaesthesia or signatures, do not materially differ from a range of transnationalist women's campaigns waged on the internet and in person. The primary differences between AIDWA's internationalism and other transnational networks are ideological and organizational. AIDWA mobilized their campaigns to impart a socialist analysis of imperialism, capitalism and patriarchy that would build a more internationalist consciousness among its members. Through its internationalism, AIDWA sought to organizationally channel the central concerns of who are the women in joined (yet disparate) struggle and what goals should bring them together; that is, what should women of the world fight for.

Mass Membership

In early August of 1994, almost exactly one year before the UN Conference in Beijing, AIDWA held its Fourth National Conference in Coimbatore, Tamil Nadu. The draft report published beforehand and distributed at the conference opens with invocations of internationalist solidarity: in celebration of South Africa's hard-fought independence from the apartheid regime, in solidarity with the people of Cuba facing a crushing US-led blockade, and different greetings to 'people of the Third World', to women fighting exploitation, oppression and inequality in 'developed Capitalist countries' (AIDWA, *Draft Report*, 1994: 1–2). The greetings give special mention to women combating religious fundamentalism around the globe, and links women fighting for reproductive rights in Ireland, the US and Italy to women fighting for women's rights in Iran and Afghanistan. The opening also expresses AIDWA's solidarity with the people of the 'former Socialist countries who are learning the realities of capitalism' (ibid.: 2). On the back page of its conference draft report, AIDWA mentions its membership tallies from 1990 to 1993: over 3 million members in 1990, 2.8 million members in 1991, back to 3.1 million in 1992, and a jump to 3.7 million members in 1993.

AIDWA's internationalism in the 1994 document has an unadorned leftist character, with homage to struggles in the anti-imperialist third world, the previously socialist second world, and mention of the endemic travails of women in the first world. Internationalist solidarity is explicitly anti-capitalist, and anti-imperialist rather than anti-American, anti-British or anti-first world; that is, it is overtly ideological rather than geo-political. AIDWA's membership numbers tell that more complicated story of the early 1990s: the hegemony of globalization, the rise of Hindu fundamentalism in India, and a concomitant wavering of support for a working-poor, rural and urban women's organization with strong ties to the organized Communist Parties. The sharp dip in membership numbers from 1990 to 1991, years of the final dissolution of the Soviet Union, could signify an ideological defeat of Marxism, what some commentators from the time called the 'End of History'. Yet a more careful look at these numbers shows that the state of Kerala lost fully 200,000 members, Tripura lost 20,000 members, and Punjab and Orissa lost around 10,000 members between them. Other states either gained members or remained relatively steady. The changes, then, probably reveal more about local or regional organizational trends than a referendum on the feasibility of leftist women's politics after the dissolution of the Soviet Union.

The uneven connections between local realities, national shifts in policy direction and global politics are described in self-critical terms in the state reports delivered at this conference. The most common locus of internationalist work across the states over these years was the International Women's Day on 8th March. States like Kerala reported themes such as Peace, Anti-Gulf War and against New Economic Policies, while others briefly described rallies, speeches and programmes they held on the day. Tamil Nadu's state report is particularly sharp in its assessment of International Women's Day festivities. It notes their attempts to use the day for coalition work with other women's organizations, but due to competition with the state government's concurrent events, 'our show is restricted to a smaller circle and does not make any great impact' (AIDWA, 'Tamil Nadu: Work Report Submitted by the State Committee', 1994: 122). In addition, the Tamil Nadu state committee's report noted with dismay a rote quality to their actions on this day: 'March 8 is observed more as a convention, with the militancy it deserves generally lacking. In future, we have decided to take the initiative well in advance' (ibid.: 123).

Yet the same report describes another internationalist action against the US-led war in the Gulf that included a range of leftist mass organizations, and was joined by 500 members of AIDWA. The police charged the rally in Chennai and AIDWA members were among the injured; yet, as the report enthusiastically detailed, the second rally saw an even greater number of women participants. The report describes AIDWA's success in local–internationalist terms: 'In our campaign against the Gulf war, we found that linking up of price rise (especially petrol) with war made the issue alive for women' (ibid.). The coalition work with other women's organizations to condemn the Gulf War fell short of its goals however. In its petition against the war, the Tamil Nadu AIDWA could not convince its allies in the women's movement to name the primary role the US played in precipitating, escalating and prolonging the violence. The compromise document, states the report, was sent to the Secretary General of the United Nations as well as the presidents of the United States and Iraq.

Other states are less detailed in their internationalist campaign reports. In many states, the reports mention internationalism briefly through a resistance to the Dunkel Draft agreement released in December of 1990, which brought agriculture for the first time into the multilateral trade negotiations headed by the increasingly powerful body known as GATT, the General Agreement on Trade and Tariffs (De Rosa 1992). The agreement marked the shift from a commitment to technology transfer from the global North to the global South, to an enforcement role in handing over the monopoly rights of patentees (Dhar and Rao 1992). Other protests against the emerging global order included those against the IMF/World Bank New Economic Policies (NEP), as well as protests against the Gulf War. Over the three years from 1991–93, the state reports suggest they concentrated their internationalist actions on two particular days: International Women's Day and International Children's Day, alongside the less predictable actions with their allied leftist organizations. Apart from these two days, the Gulf War and the New Economic Policy protests, little other political work rose to the surface of the reports to suggest any deeper international alliances or campaigns.

Measures of internationalist consciousness are poorly served by state reports at a national conference – they can only suggest whether members around the country make connections between the high cost of rice and India's shift toward export-oriented economic policies during this period. Campaigns that make the pages of the state report are the barest surface of the fights won and lost across the regions. Perhaps what state reports reveal most clearly are the desires and priorities of the states. In what they report to the national organization, we can see what resonates in the state's leadership circles: from the units to the neighbourhoods, to the taluks, to the districts, to the cities, to the state, in ever-increasing rungs of accountability that the state reports reflect. Publications at national conferences have a simultaneously formal and rushed character; the state reports that were not submitted in time do not appear, the self-criticisms are phrased anecdotally rather than as lasting guides for change, and there are sweeping generalizations about the thousands of struggles, each with its own specific contours, waged by AIDWA members against violence and injustice. Neither can conference publications attempt to measure the consciousness of its members, or their newfound understandings about the systemic character of global changes in governance and economy.

These reports do carry vital glimmers of internationalism in AIDWA's mass membership, however. The members who better understood the Gulf War through the rise in petrol prices, for example, shed light on why AIDWA saw increasing numbers of women in the second anti-war demonstration, even in the face of concerted police aggression. Subhashini Ali, who held the all India joint secretary office during AIDWA's Fourth National Conference in 1994, adds a cautionary note about assessing internationalism in local and regional politics. 'We have not been good enough', Ali stated about AIDWA's efforts to strengthen internationalism at the local levels of its mass membership. She continued: 'for a poor woman in some village or some slum to conceive of imperialism and of Palestine, it's very difficult, it's very, very difficult, so sometimes it's like tokenism' (Subhashini Ali interview, 22 July 2008).The tokenism of assessing women's consciousness continues to vex this chapter: how does one shift from the reassuring language of transnational networks between women's NGOs to the immensely complex lives of the women in the world? These conference documents cannot be asked to illuminate the internationalist solidarity within all of AIDWA's members.

Socialism and Anti-Imperialism

Yet the contrast is startling between the solidarity invoked in the 1994 Fourth National Conference document and the 1998 Fifth National Conference document. The form of the draft report is identical in many respects: it is a small booklet measuring 5.5 by 9.5 inches, held together by staples along the spine, and printed by a movement printing press. Judging by its less markedly yellowed pages, it was printed on newsprint of slightly better quality in 1998 than in 1994. The Fifth National Conference was held in Bangalore, Karnataka, in the middle of June 1998, and its report considers the organization's work during the four years of 1994, 1995, 1996 and 1997. This draft report, as in 1994, also dedicates its opening to the international context of AIDWA's political work, but with marked differences. Instead of three pages of bulleted pledges of solidarity with women's struggles around the world, the 1998 report provides a thorough seven pages of cutting-edge analysis of the 'International Status of Women'. It begins with the Beijing Conference, lays out global trends, cites growing inequality, the rise of cultural imperialism and fundamentalism, provides an overview of socialist countries, and gives special attention to the issue of national sovereignty. AIDWA's especial solidarity with those who fight imperialist domination gains brief mention at the end of the report, and includes the people of Cuba, Iraq, Zaire and Palestinians. It concludes: 'We pledge to intensify our own struggles against imperialism and in solidarity with all those struggling for freedom' (AIDWA, *AIDWA 1994–1998, Women's Status*, 1998: 12). The invocation of solidarity has lost none of its leftist, more specifically socialist, character from the Fourth National Conference report. In 1998, the discussion of internationalism and solidarity devotes fully six pages to its analysis of global capitalism, and concludes with women's common struggle against imperialism. These intervening years between 1994 and 1998 also saw the consolidation of AIDWA's inter-sectoral organizing strategy and its more methodical use of research activism in states around the country. As AIDWA's lens on women's lives in India sharpened, the linkages with the global economic and political shifts that consolidated neoliberalism gained increasing clarity as well.

Over a decade after the conference, much of the opening section from the 1998 draft report regarding the rise of globalization in the 1990s enjoys the status of consensus in the women's movement – but this consensus had not yet solidified when the report was published. The report narrates how globalization gained steam after the dissolution of the Soviet Union and the collapse of socialist governments in Eastern Europe, in part through the promise to spread democracy as well as an improved standard of living to all. Globalization as an economic, political and cultural programme, AIDWA reports, proved starkly detrimental to poor women around the world. Instead of the promised alleviation of poverty, globalization policies further concentrated wealth in the hands of the moneyed and the powerful. Today, AIDWA's assessment in 1998 reads descriptively as much as polemically: 'The new world order is an order of growing inequalities, between developed capitalist countries and the third world, between the poor and the rich within these countries, and between men and women in the entire capitalist world' (ibid.: 6). It based its analysis on widely available research reports, like the *Human Development Report* on rural India, and reports by ILO (International Labour Organization) and UN agencies. Today, it could also cite the World Bank in support of its conclusions.

Similarly, AIDWA's analysis of globalization's cultural project and effects are not analytically far from a range of feminist theories about global culture. The conference report criticizes the values that cultural globalization pushes, rather than the homogeneity or westernization of the specific cultural products it sells. Under the sub-heading 'Cultural Imperialism' the draft states:

> The new order also extends to the cultural fields with the US leading the global attempt to impose its market-based values and blind consumerism on the rest of the world. At present the powerful electronic media and the entertainment industries are dominated by powerful Western conglomerates committed to these values, which are based on crass individualism at the expense of the common good. In a cynical manipulation of the concept of women's independence the new attempt is to portray women in the guise of the protagonist, the active agent who in the name of freedom of choice aggressively supports capitalist life styles. Women's sexuality is equated with the portrayal of women as sex objects. (Ibid.: 9)

After the pitched campaign against the Miss World pageant held in Bangalore in 1996, AIDWA developed a well-honed position on globalized culture in India. During this campaign, the media often collapsed AIDWA's opposition to the beauty pageant with the Hindu nationalist opposition to the pageant as symbolic proof of the encroaching loss of Indian women's traditional values of modesty and sexual control. AIDWA's argument about women's sexuality (debated most fiercely through the pageant's swimsuit competition) shows the clarity the organization gained as it distinguished its opposition to the pageant from that of the neo-traditionalist nationalists. AIDWA refuses to reassert an Indian patriarchal control over women's sexuality, it argued here, but seeks to delink women's sexual expression from their sexual objectification. An opposition to the profit motives of capitalism permeates the analysis of global cultural flows, an opposition not dissimilar to a range of feminist cultural analyses. AIDWA's general analysis of the effects of globalization on women's decreased quality of life, and even its resistance to the current circulation of global cultural flows, stay within active currents of the wider women's movement debates.

AIDWA's opening assessment includes two markedly socialist aspects that distinguish its analysis of globalization from the breadth of the women's movement, ideologically and in its goals. First, it draws on Lenin's analysis in *Imperialism: The Highest Stage of Capitalism* in its discussion of structural adjustments. 'Structural adjustment policies', begins an early paragraph, 'are a blueprint to the shift the burdens of the capitalist crisis on to the shoulders of the working people, in the interests of increased profits of big business' (ibid.: 7). The second phrase of this sentence is ubiquitous in critiques of global capital. Globalization is often cited as a profit-driven force. Multinationals utilize this assumption when they argue why they have to move their factories overseas: to compete with the laws of supply and demand, they must produce the cheapest goods possible. Since labour is the most fungible cost of production, they move where the workers accept the lowest wages. Yet this logical chain contains the assumption that globalization brooks no resistance, that maximizing profit must determine all actions. AIDWA looks at increased profits from a less fatalistic lens.

The beginning of the sentence – 'Structural adjustment policies are a blueprint to shift the burdens of the capitalist crisis on to the shoulders of the working people' – draws directly from Lenin's theory of imperialism and capitalist overproduction. In Lenin's analysis, the engine of profits drives capitalism to imperialism to seek out additional markets to buy excess commodities. 'The necessity of exporting capital', Lenin writes, 'also gives an impetus to the conquest of colonies, for in the colonial market it is easier to eliminate competition' (Lenin 1939: 84). The distinctly capitalist crisis of overproduction, he argues, lies behind the quest for new territories to conquer economically and politically. AIDWA's understanding of the impetus behind globalization builds directly on Lenin's central insight. As analysts of globalization largely agree, structural adjustment policies (SAPs) written into IMF/World Bank loans and various 'free trade' agreements like the North American Free Trade Agreement (NAFTA) open up national economies to penetration by multinational corporations, to global speculation on currencies and commodities, as they simultaneously seek to dismantle national trade barriers and shrink widely utilized social safety nets for more delimited (and therefore cheaper) public health, education and anti-poverty schemes. In these ways, SAPs attempt to create new markets for capitalism, in what capitalism buys (labour power and resources) and what capitalism sells (commodities), in order to move the capitalist crisis of overproduction to 'the shoulders of the working people'. Goods may be less costly in this regime, but as wages shrink and jobs disappear, even the most cheaply made goods, and, more starkly, essential commodities like food, water and shelter, are out of reach for the working people. Imperialism, in AIDWA's draft report, is not a catch-phrase to signify a political relationship alone; that is, third world or developing countries' national sovereignty in the face of colonial and neo-colonial forces. Imperialism describes a capitalist logic powered by countries like the US, and supported by allied supranational agencies like the World Bank and the IMF. AIDWA's understanding of what drives globalization is not along the grain of the majority of feminist analyses of globalization, but builds a gendered Marxist analysis which resists the very tenets of capitalism that anchor neoliberal globalization.

The second specifically socialist distinction in AIDWA's internationalism lies in how it seeks to build solidarity and what it seeks to create as an alternative to imperialist globalization. AIDWA's draft report draws from Beijing a lesson of solidarity: 'the need for a much wider solidarity between likeminded organizations across the world to counter global trends inimical to women's interests' (AIDWA, *AIDWA 1994–1998, Women's Status*, 1998: 5). This solidarity is not a simple one between socialist (or 'likeminded') women's organizations, but is one that requires strengthening an active support for socialist governments and policies. Under globalization, worsening women's conditions provide the ground for increased solidarity between women across polities. AIDWA's conference report argues that its ideological struggle in the international and transnational realm lies in defining the shared goals supported by these ties of solidarity among (likeminded) women of the world. As AIDWA argues, 'a much bigger ideological struggle is required worldwide to meet the continuing offensive against socialist thought and practice' (ibid.: 11). AIDWA does not aspire to anti-globalization solidarity actions alone, but imagines a solidarity where women unite in support of a common goal of socialism.

By 1998, AIDWA clearly articulated the solidarity it envisions between women on a transnational scale. The differences between its Fourth and Fifth Conference documents reveal a movement from vague invocations of women's solidarity against capitalism in favour of socialism, to a sharply delineated argument about the state of the world for women and AIDWA's goals to build pro-socialist solidarity movements among women around the world. The years of political activism the Fifth Conference assessed, from 1994 to 1998, were defining ones: as AIDWA clarified its commitments against communalism and neoliberal capitalism, it developed a strategy that gave precedence to the most marginalized women in India – Dalit women, women from minority religious communities, particularly Muslim women, rural women, and women working in informal industries. The organization sought to focus its daily organizing efforts on the very women least valued by the neoliberal economic order. These priorities sought to build leadership within the organization to reflect its mass-based political work within these communities of women. While AIDWA's report in 1998 gleans analytic support from internationally recognized agencies like the UNDP and the ILO, it had begun to pursue research methods that developed its own members and researchers and objects of study to understand what structural adjustment living meant for its constituency. Due to the grassroots methods of analysis that AIDWA's state and local units began to develop in the late 1990s, the shift in clarity between these two AIDWA conference documents may mirror the consciousness of AIDWA's members to women's shared struggle against imperialism and their shared goal of socialism.

To read these conference documents as symptomatic of a change from the ground up hearkens back to Sonya Gill's observations at the beginning of this chapter about how to understand the relationship between the internationalism of the leadership of AIDWA and the transnational sense of solidarity among its membership. Sonya talked about internationalism as travelling from the leadership of the organization to its cadre:

> We continuously stay in touch, you know, very conscious of how to make for our cadre a vivid, a real, a lived experience, as to what is happening, and how to show solidarity with women in other parts of the world and what is happening to their lives. We're all the time talking and fighting and struggling about our issues, but that there are others doing the same thing and that issues are much more global, you have to constantly bring it in. (Sonya Gill interview by Indus Chadha, 25 July 2008)

Sonya Gill in Maharashtra and Subhashini Ali in Uttar Pradesh both displayed a sharp unease about the direction in which solidarity training travels, from AIDWA's state leadership to its mass membership. They were keenly aware that our current historical epoch has intensified this troubling character of building internationalist solidarity among women. Sonya described the ebbing of a strong class consciousness as a factor: 'Previously, when there was a very strong working-class movement here [in the state of Maharashtra], I feel, that gives, that would sort of help also to give a more broad perspective' (ibid.). Subhashini Ali defined the shift in more generational terms, of the clarity of past anti-imperial struggles and the complexity of current ones. She said: 'Our state leadership has a big movement, you know, we who come from the sixties, we can't help but be international because that's where we're coming from, the ones who've come from the Vietnam War . . . most of us have been pushed into the movement by American imperialism' (Subhashini Ali interview, 22 July 2008). In these two AIDWA leaders' discussions of internationalism, one emphasized the regional politics of strong working-class movements and the other stressed the international politics of anti-war movements in Asia. Yet the national context that shapes internationalist consciousness has its own contours, as revealed by AIDWA's national conferences. Internationalism, and a vision of the struggles women shared around the world, provided AIDWA the scaffolding to combat the two most central national fields of struggle throughout the 1990s to the present: the simultaneous dominance of neoliberalism and the hegemony of communalism.

AIDWA's increased clarity between 1994 and 1998 could be explained, in part, by the 1995 UN Conference and NGO Forum in Beijing, and what AIDWA members learned from that interaction with activist women around the world. If so, what happened during the UN Conference on Women to sharpen AIDWA's official position on women's internationalism? AIDWA's specific organizational history, its strategies in the face of neoliberalism and the demise of the socialist bloc, are part of a larger story about socialist women's organizing during this period of neoliberal capitalism's consolidation of global economics. The Fourth UN Conference on Women held in Beijing and the NGO Forum held in Huairou outside Beijing, more than ever before at a UN-sponsored conference on women, reverberated with the concerns of poor women, rural women and disenfranchised women from countries outside the Euro-American ambit. Structural adjustment policies were forced on to the table and included (however tepidly) into the Platform for Action. One quarter of the 40,000 participants in the NGO Forum came from Asia (*Beijing!*, 1998: 166). Many others came from Latin America and the African continent. Even with 50 per cent of the NGO Forum being from the United States and Canada, a trenchant and systemic critique of structural adjustment policies and the Washington Consensus as a whole entered the gathering (Agnihotri 1996: 122).

United Nations, Imperialism and Women: A History

Brinda Karat, AIDWA's general secretary during this period, viewed the UN world conferences as contradictory and even hostile sites, not as platforms to sustain a socialist internationalism. Months before the meeting, she publicly announced her low expectations for the meeting in Beijing: 'No one expects anything earth-shaking to emerge from the Beijing conference' (Brinda Karat interview by Asha Krishnakumar, 'Papering It Over', 1995: 110). In another interview just a month later, Karat outlined her analysis of the Beijing Conference for the third world women's movement as one of multiple locations for struggle:

> So there are two processes for Beijing. One is, because we don't expect very much from Beijing, we're very clear about that: because given the global hierarchies, and given the correlation of forces at the international level, and given the complete dominance of the Group of 7, led by the United States of America. We're very clear that all international conferences now have very strong US hegemonic roles. . . . So Third World movements have two levels: one, within their own countries, against their own governments. And at the international level, primarily against the

entire imperialist content of policies which are being put forward as blueprints for the rest of the world. . . . So it's a dual role, a dual challenge, which Third World movements have to play. (Brinda Karat interview, 6 June 1995)

Karat described her distrust of international fora, particularly those organized by the United Nations, through the context of the hegemony of the Group of Seven Industrialized Nations, or G7, and the overwhelming dominance of neoliberalism. Importantly, she did not entirely dismiss either venue for struggle: against the Indian government's acquiescence to neoliberal economics, or against the supportive role to neoliberalism played by the United Nations and its affiliated agencies like the World Bank (Winslow 1995). By the time of the Beijing Conference in 1995, even UN agencies considered most attuned to the lives of third world women, like the *Human Development Reports* published by the United Nations Development Programme (UNDP), were pledging their allegiance to the free market doctrine as the best way to support development (Pietila and Vickers 1996: 153). Yet Karat's well-modulated enthusiasm, one bordering on dismissal, has an older history that marked the potential role for the United Nations to mediate imperialism, and its impact on women, after its formation in 1945.

By most accounts, the United Nations provided very limited venues for women and women's issues before 1972: what Devaki Jain has called a *nethi nethi* (neither this nor that) 'evolution of the spaces the United Nations has offered women activists' (Jain 2005: 7). She invokes a phrase about the quest for truth from the *Upanishads*, a quest marked by a process of uncovering 'not this, not this'. Two early victories usually begin these narratives of women's participation. The first regards the wording of the UN Charter and the Universal Declaration of Human Rights. Amalia Caballero de Castillo Leon from Mexico, Bertha Lutz from Brazil and Minerva Bernardino from Dominican Republic were all members of the Inter-American Commission on Women, and all were present in San Francisco at the founding conference of the United Nations. They, and Jessie Street from Australia, are credited with the added language in the UN Charter that affirms 'the equal rights of men and women' alongside its commitment to human rights (Pietila 2002: 9–10; Rupp 1997: 223; Stienstra 1994: 76–80). Yet, even in the wake of this victory, Bertha Lutz expressed doubts about the United Nations as 'an oligarchy of five nations' (cited in Rupp 1997: 223).

The second early struggle won by women in the UN was the full commission status (rather than a sub-commission) of the Commission on the Status of Women (CSW) within the Economic and Social Council (ECOSOC) in 1946 (Stienstra 1994: 83–84). A year later, in 1947, the CSW held its first meeting with fifteen countries in attendance and twelve international women's groups presenting reports. However, after these two early gains, most histories of the UN agree that much of the following two decades provided more internal and hidden opportunities within the UN for the supporters of women's rights and equality (Antrobus 2004; Stienstra 2000). Until the early 1970s, when activists managed to declare 1975 as International Women's Year, and organize the first UN Conference on Women in Mexico City, the work of CSW was not able to secure a platform to organize women. Instead, during these years, the CSW worked within UN agencies, primarily ECOSOC, but also the ILO, to push for women's suffrage rights, and, in the 1960s during the UN's Decade for Development, women's individual rights and working women's rights in the informal economy (Jain 2005: 25–29; Nijehlt, Swiebel and Vergas 1998: 26). Margaret Galey describes the CSW between 1947 and 1974: 'In the critical formative period, Western and pro-Western members from Latin America, Asia, and the Middle East dominated the CSW as well as the UN generally' (Galey 1995: 15). The early years of the United Nations, whether viewed as an 'oligarchy of five nations', or as a body representing western and pro-western views, did allow newly independent nations from Asia, Africa and the Caribbean to join. Yet the opening was for those nations who had achieved formal post-colonial status rather than those with active anti-colonial movements, and therefore was not realized to a large extent until the mid to late 1960s when representatives from around the decolonized world began to join UN committees, subcommittees and initiatives.

Even in the heady days of the 1960s, when the UN declared its first Decade of Development, Peggy Antrobus characterizes the UN's perspective as entirely reliant on neoclassical economics. She writes: 'These theories held that the wealth generated from economic growth would trickle down to the poor and thus reduce poverty' (Antrobus 2004: 29). Underdevelopment of colonized territories was the central challenge for newly autonomous nations, and trickle-down theories of wealth distribution did little to create an industrial base or economic self-sufficiency in these countries. At the level of its guiding theories for world governance and development, the UN did not buck the doctrine of the capitalized west. The distrust for the UN that Brinda Karat articulated in 1995 is not simply about the UN's role in sustaining the movements for women's rights and equality, but also about the economic and political role the UN played more generally throughout the 1960s, 70s and beyond. The UN did not act as an entirely reactionary force for independence movements or newly independent nations, but neither has the inter-governmental body played a wholly supportive role. In this sense, the UN has always been a site for struggle over imperialism, capitalism and what constitutes human and women's rights.

The CSW burrowed into the agencies of the United Nations with its mandate for women's equality, but as historians of the international women's movement have documented, even without the United Nations, women from around the world continued to meet during the 1940s, 50s and 60s.[6] One important international women's federation during this period, that had consultative status with the United Nations, was the Women's International Democratic Federation (WIDF), which emerged the same year as the United Nations in 1945. WIDF was based in Paris, but as a socialist women's organization, it coordinated women's groups in socialist countries like the USSR and Eastern Europe, and had members from socialist women's groups from forty countries. In 1949, WIDF organized the Conference of the Women of Asia, held in Beijing, with women from Vietnam, Burma, Malaya, Iran, Indonesia, China and Iran attending. Betty Millard, an American member of the Communist Party, described a speaker from a contingent of anti-imperialist movements of women in Africa who 'arose and greeted the Chinese victory "in the name of the millions of black women who, back in my country, are dreaming of liberty"' (Millard 1952: 24). The solidarity among participants at this conference was reflected in the reports submitted by national representatives. Iranian women at the conference described national liberation movements through the lens of International Women's Day. 'Iranian women, in spite of jailing and torture, were fighting the rule of the British oil company which was the chief factor in the impoverishment of their country', reported Millard. 'Huge numbers of women have come out in the streets to demonstrate for the nationalization of oil. On International Women's Day 15,000 women assembled before the headquarters of the Iranian Peace Committee in Teheran and paraded through the streets' (ibid.: 20). This meeting actively sought to make the connections between women around Asia and Africa who fought colonialism and imperialism, a solidarity marked not just by the similarities of economic and political exploitation, but also through the specific struggles fought in each region and country. WIDF's multinational conferences of women, both regional, like the conference held for Women of Asia in 1949, but also their larger membership meetings, were not the only conferences held in the 1940s. WIDF was, however, the only organization providing a specifically anti-imperialist platform for women's movements. It was also the only women's organization that organized women from colonized countries as members autonomous from their colonizers' patronage.

[6] Deborah Stienstra has cited the International Planned Parenthood Federation and WIDF as the two most active international organizations on women's issues during this period. See Stienstra 1994: 86–88. She argues that the International YWCA, the International Council of Social Democratic Women, the International Alliance of Women (IAW) and other older women's international organizations also continued to meet and build their membership in these decades, though many did not build their membership among women from newly independent nations.

Like other international women's organizations, WIDF held international member meetings periodically; its first and second meetings were held in 1947 and 1948 respectively. At its Second Congress held in Budapest, Hungary, it adopted a radically anti-imperialist resolution: 'A Resolution on the Development of the Democratic Women's Movement in the Countries of Asia and Africa'. The resolution listed a series of four demands framed explicitly for the United Nations on the basis of its own commitment of 'respect for the principle of equality of rights of nations and their right of self-government'. These demands sought to widen the role the UN played to support anti-colonial movements around the world. The first demand sought general support: 'Protect the countries of Africa and Asia against the cruel domination of the imperialists and colonial extortioners.' And the last demand sought relief for freedom fighters and colonized people alike: 'Organize moral and material aid to the women and children of the native populations fighting for liberty and pace, by collecting money, food, clothing and medical supplies' (WIDF 1948: 535). The demands crafted for the United Nations were both limited and general: as a helpmate and moral arbiter in the military struggles around the world. They stand in stark contrast to the rest of the document that incites wider participation, through solidarity actions, for anti-colonial struggles, and cheers anti-imperialist women as well as their anti-colonial struggles as the bastion of 'democratic liberties'. The demands for the UN imagine a supportive forum to level the playing field between colonial nations like Britain and France, and not-yet-decolonized regions like Algeria, Indonesia and Madagascar.

Not until 1953, when WIDF held its Third International Women's Congress in Copenhagen, with 1,990 delegates from 70 countries, did it attract the active concern of the United States government.[7] Worried that women's organizations would be used as vehicles for communist propaganda, the US government utilized its contacts with the United Nations to set up a counter-organization to WIDF called Women United for the United Nations (Laville 2002: 172). This organization became known as the Committees of Correspondence (CoC) until it dissolved in 1967, when it was revealed to be a CIA (Central Intelligence Agency, US) front organization (ibid.: 171). During the mid-1950s through the early 60s, the CoC developed contacts with sympathetic women's groups around the world, primarily through letters, newsletters and informal gatherings around UN meetings held in New York. It also organized tours of the United States to develop 'female leadership in the Anti-Communist World' ('Twelve Asian Women Study Life in

[7] Kate Weigand shows in vibrant detail how early the American government became concerned about the American-affiliated organization, Congress of American Women (CAW). CAW formally began in 1947, was forced to disaffiliate with WIDF in 1949, and shut down by 1950. Weigand 2001: 46–55.

the US', *New York Times*, 29 April 1956). CoC did not attempt to organize international women's forums, however, until the 1960s.

Yet WIDF was not the only organization developing international platforms for discussion among women in the 40s and 50s. The Non-Aligned Movement (NAM) of third world nations that coalesced after the Bandung Conference in 1955 generated two international conferences for women. The 1958 Asian–African Conference of Women, held in Colombo, Sri Lanka, was organized by a range of nationalist women's groups in the third world 'to meet and discuss on a common platform some of the basic problems affecting women and children . . . in the spirit of the resolutions of the Conference of Asian–African Nations held at Bandung in April 1955' (Invitation letter to the first Asian–African Conference of Women, from Avabai B. Wadia). Women from independent nations could be delegates or observers, while women from still colonized nations could participate only as observers. Avabai Wadia, a member of the All India Women's Conference (AIWC) and the International Alliance of Women, was the organizing secretary of the conference. The sponsors were women's organizations in Asia, including Burma (Myanmar), Ceylon (Sri Lanka), India, Indonesia and Pakistan. The topics for discussion focused primarily on social and civic issues like health, education, citizenship and franchise, enslavement and traffic in women and children, and bonded and child labour (ibid.). The conference framed women's rights issues and its structure of member-nation participation along the grain of the United Nations' standards at the time.

Wadia began her preparations for a second conference in 1960 when she toured East Africa for a suitable place to hold it. She described her meetings with women's organization and government leaders in Uganda and Tanzania (then Tanganyika) in careful detail (Letter by Avabai B. Wadia, 'Tour in East Africa', 20 January 1961). She repeated her descriptions of the conference in terms that suggest an early NGO rubric: 'The women feel that it [Asian–African Conference] would help to rouse interest and enthusiasm for social work among the local women and be very educative. They are beginning earnest work on non-political and non-racial lines and this sort of Conference would give a real fillip to such trends' (ibid.). 'Non-political', she stressed, supported women's full civic participation, but did not include pushing for the structural transformation of gender norms. 'Non-racial', for East Africa in the 1960s, meant reformulating (or at least combining) women's organizations with exclusive Asian, white or African memberships that were the norm. Conference plans circulated in 1960 described the debates that it hoped to resolve in order to institute the constitution and structure of a formal Asian–African Organization of Women. Two issues that Wadia outlined were: first, the limits of participation due to colonial governance, since only formally independent nations could have fully participatory members; second, she questioned whether the organization's definition of 'Asia' would include the 'Soviet-Asian Republics'. Both of these issues suggest the complex cold war debates around colonialism and communism that had direct implications for 'Bandung' or third world countries that may or may not have yet gained independence in the 1950s and 60s. The preparatory document for the Second Asian–African Women's Conference outlined modest aims: (1) to support 'cooperation among women in Asia and Africa'; (2) to support women's 'equal status, rights and responsibilities'; and (3) foster women's welfare 'in the social, economic and cultural spheres' ('Asian–African Conference of Women'). The organizations represented on the first conference letterhead were ones with multiple strands of analysis and activity within them, as the discussion in Chapter One of this book about Avabai Wadia's own organization, the All India Women's Conference (AIWC), illustrates. These goals were modest because they hailed women participants as individual members of their nations, with unspoken assumptions about their relative privilege and the ability to take a leading role in social welfare and uplift of the less fortunate. The refusal to allow non-independent countries active membership in the Asian–African Women's Conference, as well as the financial means the women needed to participate in the conference, created a relatively elite rather than mass-based horizon for the conference. While the conference held no mention of anti-communist aims, nor allow membership by representatives from non-Asian or African countries, its strictly non-political purview provided a more conservative means to organize for 'women's rights' through international women's civic participation.[8] This Second Asian–African Conference as a kind of proto-NGO women's movement for third world women was never held however.

Instead, the same year Wadia scouted for suitable East Africa host nations, the Bandung countries held their own explicitly political and openly anti-imperialist 'First Afro–Asian Women's Conference' in Cairo, Egypt, early in 1961 (Armstrong and Prashad 2006: 36–37). Another AIWC member, Hajrah Begum, attended this international conference. She also attended WIDF meetings and was a member of the Communist Party of India. She held the post of secretary of the National Coordinating Committee for WIDF. The cleavages of the cold war can easily be traced along the grain of regional and international women's meetings during these decades, and in the ways that 'women's issues' were framed either broadly or narrowly.

The Asian–African Women's Conference sought to develop social welfare activities among women across newly independent African and Asian countries. The Afro–Asian Women's Conference developed regionally spe-

[8] Wadia also wrote to the CoC thanking them for contributions made by its office-holding members towards the Second Asian–African Women's Conference. See Letter from Avabai B. Wadia, 1960.

cific as well as universal recommendations for women, and 'for the Struggle of National Independence and Peace'. The aims of the Conference articulated the wider definition of women's and human rights that was also being debated in the United Nations. They sought: '(1) The role of women in the struggle for national independence and the maintenance of peace. (2) Political and legal rights of women. (3) Equality between men and women in the economic field. (4) Social rights of women. (5) Cultural rights of women' (*The First Afro-Asian Women's Conference, Cairo, January, 1961*: 3). Many of these recommendations directly countered conservative forces within independence struggles that sought to limit women's roles after independence. The second conference recommendation targeted the United Nations and revealed its stakes in the struggle: 'The Conference decides to demand firmly of Afro–Asian member states of the United Nations, that women should participate in the delegations that are sent to attend the annual sessions of the United Nations, and allow qualified women to take up diplomatic posts' (ibid.: 19). The invocation of the UN in many of these regional women's conference documents is important. Their attention to what the UN could be as an international body reveals a series of hopes and struggles, some realized and some still fought.

Regional women's conferences and international women's organization meetings during the 1940s, 50s and 60s fuelled the demand for a UN-sponsored international women's conference. WIDF first circulated the demand for the 1975 International Women's Year and Conference in the CSW, but could not raise it because of its observer status to the UN. WIDF drafted the proposal, the Romanian representative to CSW raised the proposal, and the Finnish representative seconded it (Pietila and Vickers 1996: 76). CSW then brought the proposal to the UN General Assembly, which adopted it in December 1972. When the proposal passed, WIDF members were exultant. Fanny Edelman, the WIDF general secretary, addressed the 'Third World Trade Union Conference on the Problems of Working Women' held in Prague in April 1972. She spoke in anticipatory terms of the International Women's Year events: 'our joint initiatives, our cooperation, and the contribution of other organizations interested as we are in the advancement of women will be of major importance in giving International Women's Year great international portent' ('Documents and Information: International meetings attended by the WIDF', 1972: 5).

The international conferences that included women from colonial and newly independent nations were deeply invested in the definition of women's rights in the context of human rights more generally. They foreshadowed how UN conferences on women could foster wider conversations and provide a forum to air disagreements about women's, and thereby human rights. In the conferences sponsored by WIDF and third world countries, human rights did not just include political and civic rights, but also economic, cultural and social rights – a definition that did not find favour in the US government, or in Anglo-European countries so recently divested of their colonial territories. Economic rights, such as the right to food and the right to living-wage work, rights these conferences emphasized, were also women's rights. The Soviet Union's Universal Declaration of Human Rights, that specified these additional rights beyond the UN-accepted purview, gave the disagreement a cold war cast (Manisha Desai 2002: 26). The faultline of disagreement on the definition of human rights did not fall entirely along cold war borders, as the two overlapping Asian–African and Afro–Asian women's conferences sponsored in the name of Bandung and the third world illustrate. The demands for a broadly conceived definition for women's rights also represented cleavages within third world nations over how to instantiate women's rights in liberated nation-states.

Challenging India's Country Document, Challenging the United Nations

AIDWA's campaign before the UN Conference on Women had two tracks that dated from the early months of 1995. One set its sights on India's country document and the official UN Conference held in Beijing. As Brinda Karat, the general secretary of AIDWA stated in June of 1995:

> So we are totally and utterly opposed to the Government of India's position paper, to its policies. There is no meeting ground. In fact, there is a confrontation, a widening confrontation between the women's movement and the Government of India despite all of its claims. We do not trust the Government of India in international fora because of its vacillating policies vis-a-vis imperialism and the interests of multinational corporations. (Brinda Karat interview, 6 June 1995)

The other challenged the structure of preparations for the NGO Forum by targeting how operatives built the national network of Indian NGOs to attend the NGO Forum in Beijing. Subhashini Ali recalled this movement in the following terms: 'We had a huge campaign in India at the cooptation of the non-governmental delegations to Beijing' (Subhashini Ali interview, 22 July 2008). The first campaign built a wide coalition of national, regional and grassroots women's groups to condemn India's weak position on the worsening poverty of Indian women, and its refusal to criticize or even take into account the structural adjustment policies implemented by the Indian government. The second campaign sought to challenge a new structure set up by the UN and international funding agencies to mobilize Indian women's NGOs to participate in the NGO Forum.

Brinda Karat described the UN preparatory process as particularly troubling in the Indian context. Rather than utilizing existing networks of women's organizations and groups, as in other countries, the UN created the means to build a new network for the Conference on Women. They built the new network rather simply:

> They put together five or six women, brought together well-known women activists to form what is known as the Coordination Unit. These five or six women were then given the responsibility of contacting a whole lot of groups all over the country. Micro-level groups. So in the name of networking with grassroots-level organizations, what they actually wanted to do is to divorce the entire process from the politics and the national vision which a big organization will have. (Brinda Karat interview, 6 June 1995)

This Coordination Unit invited women's groups across India to meetings to learn skills such as how to lobby for changes in the UN draft documents. The Coordination Unit also disbursed the international donor funds that allowed women's groups to attend the NGO Forum in Huairou. As Subhashini Ali described it, AIDWA refused to go along with the process.

> We went into battle mode, and we got people to sign against this, to say that this was actually going to curtail the autonomy of women's groups and this was setting the agenda for them, because this was just when globalization and neoliberal policies started being talked about, and there was this whole talk at the time that this was very good for women, women are getting much more employment, and the structures are breaking down so there's more space for women. (Subhashini Ali interview, 22 July 2008)

Indu Agnihotri participated in the NGO Forum in Huairou as an AIDWA delegate. She also worked for the Centre for Women's Development Studies (CWDS) in New Delhi; and in her capacity at CWDS, attended the preparatory meetings arranged by the Coordinating Unit (CU) head, Asha Ramesh. Agnihotri did not represent AIDWA, she remembered clearly: 'I was not there from AIDWA, because AIDWA was not invited and was not part of those discussions' (Indu Agnihotri interview, 29 July 2008). She also remembered the CU's haphazard functioning, particularly regarding the government office-holders who attended meetings to report on the government's progress on the *Status of Women* country report: What struck me as odd was that the convention is being organized by a unit which has been set up by donors' (ibid.). Agnihotri reiterated this concern in her report after the Beijing conference when she argued that this funding and organizational structure reflects the wider, pro-western role that the UN played. She wrote:

> This is not to understate the domination of the advanced West in the international political configuration which was apparent right from the preparatory stage of the

> Conference and in the selective nature of accreditation given to non-governmental organizations (NGOs). Here the influence of the donor agencies was clear. The First World dominated in terms of the presence of their governments and in the sense that the First World-based donor agencies had in deciding who went to Beijing. (Agnihotri 1996: 112)

The AIDWA campaign against the preparations for the NGO Forum, its determination to expose the process, the international aid agencies and the actors behind this new national network created for the UN Conference, had some success among the women's organizations it contacted. AIDWA formally refused any sponsorship from the Coordination Unit, in part because it had the membership to do so. As Subhashini Ali recounted pragmatically: 'The problem is one of money, how do you get to Beijing? The ticket is expensive. Where do you stay? So a lot of people who even agreed with us, and agreed with our objections, they couldn't really say no to a free ticket' (Subhashini Ali interview, 22 July 2008).

The AIDWA delegation included nine members from across the country who attended the NGO Forum; one AIDWA member also attended the UN Conference as part of an Indian government delegation of women Members of Parliament. The AIDWA delegation raised their funds for the airplane tickets, their registration, food and lodging through donations mostly from AIDWA's membership. Many members remember the difficulty of pulling together all the money and documents, but reflect with appreciation on the support they received from a wide range of women, AIDWA members and non-members. Vimala Kalagar movingly recalled how some of her funds to attend the conference were raised by the Karnataka-based coalition she joined as an AIDWA member to fight the upsurge of visual and physical violence against women, called the Forum Against Atrocities. She said: 'At that time of the Beijing Conference, those organizations [in the Forum Against Atrocities] felt they must send me as a delegate of Karnataka, representing all of them. . . . And I really feel so grateful to them, even this financial thing, they started collecting for me' (Vimala Kalagar interview by Indus Chadha, 9 July 2008).

AIDWA directly linked its campaign against creating an NGO-based network as a proxy for the national Indian women's movement to its campaign against the Indian government's document. Brinda Karat excoriated India's country document even as it was still being finalized:

> As far as the government of India's document is concerned, it's just full of platitudes. . . . It's just the same platitudes about poverty, about discrimination. But for god's sake, it is your policies that are responsible for this. Structural adjustment programmes which you are pushing with all the power and vigour at your command. (Brinda Karat interview, 6 June 1995)

Karat connected the empty concern in India's country document about women's impoverishment to the Coordination Unit's strategy for NGO mobilization.

> What they're really trying to do is claim that they have a consensus with the women's movement. Unfortunately, the reason they've been able to make that claim is because for the first time, international funding agencies have succeeded in setting up a national network in the name of grassroots organizations, a network that has manipulated the entire agenda of these organizations. Many of them sincerely believed they were going to have a voice. (Ibid.)

By all accounts, including by Karat and other members of AIDWA, the CU meetings were highly critical of India's structural adjustment programmes. S.K Guha, secretary of the Government of India, was another organizing member of the Coordination Unit. He described two years of debate, from late 1993, by CU members about India's liberalization and structural adjustment policies (Guha 1998: 165). The Indian NGO Coordination Unit criticized the Beijing Draft Platform for Action because it merely sought funds for social welfare programmes that provide basic services to women, and refused to target the reasons for women's impoverishment. An Indian report on the draft document described the Indian CU's strong disagreements with the Draft Platform for Action: 'the document does not take a position on the structural causes of poverty; not does it make any attempt to situate it in a political and economic perspective. Such analysis presumably lies outside the purview of women's issues' (Pratap 1995: 109). The report also listed issues held off the agenda for Beijing by the west: any questioning of the geo-political power structures that limit what 'women's empowerment' can mean; debt cancellation for Sub-Saharan countries; the demand that multinational corporations abide by the ILO's labour conventions in export processing zones; and the recognition of 'the right to development as a human right' (ibid.: 108–10).

Early in 1995, over a year after the Coordination Unit began its meetings in India, the so-called 'seven sister' organizations – a group of seven national women's organizations – met in New Delhi to draft a alternative declaration to the Beijing Platform of Action, that became the coalition's centrepiece.[9] Each organization took responsibility for drafting different sections. They met in New Delhi in early 1995 to compile the sections and write the document as a whole. Called *Towards Beijing: A Perspective from the Indian Women's Movement*, the coalition published many copies of this alternative

[9] The 'seven sisters', as they were known at that time, included the following organizations: AIDWA, the All India Women's Conference (AIWC), Centre for Women's Development Studies (CWDS), Joint Women's Programme (JWP), Mahila Dakshata Samiti (MDS), National Federation of Indian Women (NFIW) and the YWCA.

document to distribute at the NGO Forum. They listed the convening all-India organizations' names on the inside cover and 98 signatory organizations after their introduction. By the time of the Beijing Conference, many other women's organizations had signed on to the document. The report focused on neoliberal economic policies primarily, and religious fundamentalism, to reframe the standard UN women's issues of human rights, violence and development. The alternative document begins with structural adjustment policies in general, then breaks down their impact into four central areas: food security, women's paid employment, rural women, and the cuts in social-welfare spending like health and education. It includes a passage on violence against women exacerbated by SAPs. The recommendations are primarily national in scope, for example, that the Indian government should implement land reforms for women and enforce women's right to own land. It includes international recommendations, that the Indian government should renegotiate its membership of the WTO. They begin with the recommendation that the World Bank and the IMF should 'fundamentally change their present blueprint for developing countries which has led to increasing poverty, distress and marginalization for women' (AIDWA *et al.* 1995: 22).

Almost all the AIDWA members I talked to were chary that their alternative document had substantially changed India's final country document on the *Status of Women* submitted to the United Nations. The changes allowed to both the country document or the Draft Platform, many argued, were in any case too subtle to matter. Both Indu Agnihotri, who attended many of the CU meetings in New Delhi, and Brinda Karat, AIDWA's general secretary at the time, made this point through 'the lobby' to change the official draft documents. Karat astutely framed AIDWA's critique as one of political process.

> If we're having a very big struggle in which we want certain demands we will go and meet members of Parliament and ask them, lobby with them to support our struggle. . . . But you know there's no given framework in which we're saying, 'add this, and subtract that'. We're putting our own agenda. So when lobbying forms part of a basic struggle, then it is an instrument of strength to the movement. But when lobbying forms the basis of it, then the agenda is already determined. You get coopted into the agenda which is determined and then you lobby for whatever little compromises you can get. (Brinda Karat interview, 6 June 1995)

Neither were AIDWA members certain that their pressure on the Coordination Unit yielded any tangible results in how the process of building a national network for India worked. But, in their estimation, their campaigns held other successes. Indu Agnihotri noted with satisfaction AIDWA's learning curve since the UN's Third World Conference on Women, held in Nairobi, Kenya, in 1985. Only one AIDWA member attended that conference. AIDWA's national-level protests around India's country document did not have as strong a coalitional character. Agnihotri described the protests leading up to the 1985 UN Conference:

> . . . we had drafted a memorandum which we gave to Rajiv Gandhi in April, 1985. We also held a week-long campaign which focused on the International Women's Decade. . . . And I remember we published a small pamphlet which was called *A Decade in Decline*. It was a public campaign, we went to resettlement colonies [for Sikhs displaced by the anti-Sikh riots in 1984], it was like a *jatha* [procession) where we focused on women's issues. . . . And one of the activities was a poster workshop, on Parliament Street, where almost all of the top artists of this country who were in Delhi came and painted a poster for us. (Indu Agnihotri interview, 29 July 2008)

Agnihotri described an impressive array of protests organized by AIDWA in 1985, but she lauded two aspects that changed in 1995. First, AIDWA organized a delegation of nine activists to attend the conference, where they led two workshops about SAPs generally, and one in relation to health and reproductive justice issues (ibid.). Second, she valued the process of building an alternate national network of women's organizations through their alternative document: 'we were part of a joint effort to make a statement about women, and do a kind of stocktaking' of women's status in India (ibid.). Agnihotri saw the success of AIDWA's campaign in another light, of the organization's increasing ability to join international debates.

One other member of AIDWA travelled to China for the conference. Malini Bhattacharya was a woman Member of Parliament (MP) in the Rajya Sabha, representing the CPI(M) in West Bengal. All Indian women MPs joined the UN Conference on Women held in Beijing, roughly 60 women or 9 per cent of all MPs in India, ferried by a special plane at the government's expense. Bhattacharya attended a session for parliamentarians that she described as formal and brief. In contrast, she remembered the NGO Forum in Huairou as 'a very very active place, which was the hub of a great deal of interchange and a great deal of interaction was going on' (Malini Bhattacharya interview, 4 August 2008). Like Bhattacharya, all the AIDWA delegates carried their booklets and papers to distribute among the Forum attendees. They tended to discount the effect these publications had on the tenor of the Forum or the closed-door negotiations on the Platform for Action in Beijing. From her perspective travelling between the two conferences, Bhattacharya suggested a more porous character between the two, with debates among Beijing delegates being led by the NGO Forum. 'So what struck me was that while at another formal and institutional level certain discussions were going on, the NGO Forum was able to put a certain pressure on the proceedings of the conference. Which I thought was a very good thing' (ibid.). Yet even

Malini Bhattacharya, who recognized the importance of the coalition document she distributed, hesitated to give that one document credit for changing the tenor of UN conversations. She widened the field of actors considerably: 'It would be too much to say that it was because of ADIWA's document, but in that conference I think this aspect of the effect of liberalization in the third world countries, that did become an issue' (ibid.). Most tangibly, then, AIDWA's campaign before the Fourth World Conference of Women wrought its own alternate or parallel country platform for action, and its own alternate national network of women's organizations. Most importantly to AIDWA members well after the events, the coalition document and the national network cohered around an ideological commonality, rather than monetary incentives, or simply in the service of the international event they targeted.

Over two months before the conference in the People's Republic of China began, AIDWA's general secretary, Brinda Karat, presciently assessed the anti-imperialist critique of the American role in UN conferences, particularly around women's rights. She spoke about the 1994 UN International Conference on Population and Development held in Cairo, Egypt, just a year before. She described the betrayal many women from Latin America, Africa, Asia and elsewhere felt when a delimited reproductive rights agenda pushed by American and European feminist delegations superseded health infrastructure concerns, and the rise of Malthusian population control masked by some international birth control programmes. Karat delineated a global South/North split that extended beyond issues of reproductive health and justice:

> Sisterhood for whom? And against whom? We're going to have a situation where the global women's movement is going to be very sharply divided into two different sections. What happened in Cairo and what happened in Copenhagen is really the prelude to what is going to happen in Beijing, we feel. Because there again, certain groups, representing 'women's movements or organizations' belonging to the G7 [Group of Seven Industrialized Countries] basically hijacked the entire conference with the acquiescence of vested interests.

She presaged a critique of American imperialism that emerged again in Beijing. Karat stated the lessons AIDWA learned in 1994 after Cairo, ones that included a direct message to women in the United States:

> Third World women have to come out very certainly, very strongly against this whole imposition. We have to say, 'We do not agree with you on this. And there's a gap here.' What we're saying is, 'You are in your own countries and your movements have to make your governments accountable.' Who's going to make the US government accountable unless the women's movement in the United States

> is going to get up and say, 'Look! You're talking about women's rights, and what are you doing globally to these rights?

Brinda Karat was not part of the AIDWA contingent in China that summer, but her analysis prophesied a spontaneous protest in Huairou, a protest that received no attention or was blatantly misrecognized by the international press corps who attended the event.[10]

AIDWA Goes to Beijing

Hillary Clinton gave two speeches in the China: one on 5th September at a Plenary Session of the UN Conference on Women in Beijing, the other on 6th September at the NGO Forum in Huairou. Even before she spoke, her presence in Beijing was controversial. Protests in the US, and US senators and representatives called for Clinton to boycott the conference due to its location in a socialist country. She narrowly avoided being forced by American conservatives to cancel her appearance. The imprisonment of Harry Wu, an outspoken critic of the Chinese government, became the symbol of Chinese human rights violations, specifically their suppression of free speech. Harry Wu's sudden release before the conference began gave Clinton an opening to join the conference.

Her speech at the official UN Conference was delivered to the official delegates from among the 181 member nations in Beijing from 4–15 September. Largely through innuendo, it attacked the Chinese government for its suppression of political independence. As recently as her 2008 presidential primary race, Clinton described this speech as 'standing up against . . . the Chinese government over women's rights' (Hillary Clinton, CNN interview on 'American Morning', 5 March 2008). Clinton's speech in Beijing relied on a repetition of the conference theme, 'Women's Rights are Human Rights', to lambast the Chinese government by deed rather than name. Rhetorically, she hewed to the Christian conservative issue of forced abortion as a critique of the Chinese governmental policy of one-child families.[11] She said, 'It is a violation of human rights when women are denied the right to plan their own families, and that includes being forced to have abortions or being sterilized

[10] Articles by participants noted the backlash of international media attention across the board. The press refused to ask or answer basic questions about what was at stake in either the UN Conference or the NGO Forum. Radhika Mongia details the many questions *The New York Times* did not answer in its coverage: 'What, for instance, did women of NGOs have to say about the "starkest forms of the kinds of violence and discrimination" that were to be "topics at the Fourth World Conference on Women"? What is their relationship to State policy and politics? What are their organizational strategies?' Mongia 1995: 24–26. See also Danner and Walsh 1999.

[11] *The Christian Science Monitor* reported on Clinton as an 'odd bedfellow' with the Vatican in its celebratory report on her speech. Tefft 1995: 7.

against their will' (Clinton, 'Remarks to the UN 4th World Conference on Women', 1995). She based her demands for women's rights in their reproductive roles in the family, as mothers and care givers, and as productive members of society. She never figured women's rights in economic terms, for example, as the right to a living wage.

In explicit, and culturally specific detail, she also listed the cacophony of violence women faced around the world, including honour killings, dowry murders, militarized rape and domestic violence. Her invocation of American women's rights was reassuringly vague: 'I want to speak for those women in my own country, women who are raising children on minimum wage, women who can't afford health care or child care, women whose lives are threatened by violence, including violence in their own homes' (ibid.). The contrast could not have been more stark: where American women fought for the vote and good schools in Clinton's speech, women around the third world fought dehumanization of the most vicious kind. Human rights, in Clinton's speech, reiterated the greater humanity of western countries, and the difficult but autonomous lives led by western women. Clinton used her speech to assert American superiority over the rest of the world in ways that reverberated far beyond her coded chastisement of the Chinese government. The US provided the model for women's development, for women's human rights, in ways that could not be easily ignored. The Chinese authorities were not the only people incensed by her speech in Beijing, although no record of that anger remains in international news reports of the event.[12] Clinton was scheduled to speak in Huairou to the Forum for Non-Governmental Organizations the following day.

Intermittent yet heavy rain showers and constant mud marked the 1995 Non-Governmental Forum of the UN Conference on Women in Huairou, China. From 30 August to 8 September, many outdoor events, meetings, speeches and marches contended with the downpours, but most festivities continued as planned. Hillary Clinton's plenary, 'Strategies for the Future', held on 6 September, was no different; her planned open-air location in a former soccer stadium was relocated to the biggest indoor venue on the Huairou conference grounds, a theatre with seating for roughly 2,000 people. Forum officials relocated her speech from a large outdoor soccer stadium to a much smaller indoor theatre because of the promise of rain, a promise kept throughout that morning. An AIDWA delegate to the NGO Forum from Bangalore, Vimala Kalagar, remembered the day vividly even thirteen years later, both for the storm and another kind of protest of Clinton's speech:

[12] Even one short article that noted the roughly 2,000 women outside Clinton's forum building inaccurately reported that all of the women wanted to enter the building, but were kept out by the Chinese police force. 'Women kept out as Mrs. Clinton speaks to forum in Huairou', Deutsche Press-Agentur, 6 September 1995.

> And I still remember, one day, Hillary Clinton was there. In the whole NGO Forum, that was the biggest hall. . . . On that day there were very heavy rains in Beijing, very heavy downpours in the morning only. And Hilary Clinton was speaking inside the auditorium about human rights violations, specifically in China. . . . Inside there were 2,000 people. Outside I don't know how many thousands were there in that heavy rain shouting slogans against America: 'Hillary Clinton, go back and see what sort of human rights violations are being perpetuated by America's dictated policies elsewhere in the world.' (Vimala Kalagar interview by Indus Chadha, 9 July 2008)

Kalagar emphasized the importance of this protest as bringing together women to redefine human rights violations as also economic violence. This protest brought up a long-standing controversy in the history of the United Nations around human rights to include the economic rights to food, shelter and land, in addition to civil and political rights. The protest against Clinton's speech in Huairou demanded recognition of economic human rights violations wrought by IMF / World Bank structural adjustment policies; in Kalagar's words, violations by 'America's dictated policies'. AIDWA's nine delegates joined the protest with hundreds of other leftist women in pouring rain to demand that Hillary Clinton be held accountable for the economic imperialism of globalization. Inside the Forum, Clinton lauded the US government for funding educational programmes, 'to enhance educational opportunities for girls so that they could attend school in Africa, Asia, and Latin America. Today that effort, funded with United States' dollars, is being organized in countries throughout those continents by NGOs' (Clinton 2002: 362). The contrast between the protests outside of Clinton's speech and her own blindness to the effects of the Washington Consensus around the world was stark. Whereas protestors demanded a systemic condemnation of neoliberalism, Clinton applauded palliatives to patch slashed education budgets in African, Asian and Latin American countries due to structural adjustment policies. Like the Beijing consensus document, Clinton never mentioned any underlying causes for her cure to girls' inability to attend primary schools in the global South.

Unlike Clinton's speech, the protest was not carefully planned but percolated through word of mouth, by informal billboard notices and impromptu planning meetings, like so many of the activities at the NGO Forum. Subhashini Ali, another AIDWA participant at the NGO Forum, described the process: 'somebody talks to somebody, and then nobody knows who initiated that demonstration' (Subhashini Ali interview, 22 July 2008). As Kalagar recalled, the protest gave voice to a leftist definition of human rights to include the economic realm of political rights:

> And finally after the conference Hillary could not go away from the main door,

> she had to run away from the back door. I just can't forget that moment because America is lecturing as if it is the champion of so many things, [with a] big brother attitude. We are experiencing it so visibly, whether it is in Iraq, or its attitude about Palestine. . . . Even in that demonstration, many American women were there. They were saying [to Hillary Clinton], 'No, your policies are the main reason for the violation of human rights.' (Vimala Kalagar interview by Indus Chadha, 9 July 2008)

For Subhashini Ali, the protest revealed 'a huge feeling of solidarity', since 'you come to know about how many communists there are also, because they're there in all the NGOs, they're there everywhere, at many places where the communist party is banned, whatever is leftist . . . but they all come out when something like this happens' (Subhashini Ali interview, 22 July 2008). Indu Agnihotri attended the tail end of the protest, and expressed astonishment at the *Time* magazine's coverage of the event that suggested the protesters were trying to stampede their way into the hall, completely obscuring their choice to stand in the rain and challenge Clinton's limited stand for human rights (Walsh 1995: 14). Agnihotri saw a wilful blindness in *Time*'s portrayal since 'the protest expressed the anti-imperialist sentiment of the women's movement across the world. Not just anti-imperialism, but more specifically structural adjustment programmes' (Indu Agnihotri interview, 29 July 2008). She extended this sense beyond the one protest: 'third world women protesting was very much my understanding, but the sharp statements being made by some first world women was more interesting for me, and more reassuring in a sense' (ibid.). Many members of AIDWA's delegation talked about how the protest against Hillary Clinton signified something larger: the possibility of anti-imperialist solidarity among women who fought for gender equity and justice, an internationalism that emerged from the cover of the official transnational feminism fostered by the United Nation's NGO Forum.

Yet *Time*'s was not the only English-language report that either misread the significance of the protest or missed the protest altogether. Many of the feminists reporting back on what they saw in Huairou and Beijing mentioned Hillary Clinton's speech without reference to the protesters. High-profile second wave feminists from the United States like Jo Freeman and Robin Morgan lauded Clinton for her bravery against American conservatives and Chinese officials (Morgan 1996). These same commentators often underplayed and ignored critiques of structural adjustment policies and economic globalization. Jo Freeman wrote enthusiastically on the conference issues and demands, and only deep into her report comes the following characterization: 'Women from the Third World complained that investment in women is being undermined by structural adjustment programs demanded by the

World Bank so countries can repay their foreign debts' (Freeman 1996). While Freeman accurately represented the criticism of structural adjustment policies, her report quickly added the World Bank's interpretation, that it was 'government policy and not international monetary policy that caused women to bear the brunt of economic hardships' (ibid.).[13] Freeman's choice of the word 'complained' and her refusal to assess the relative merits of the two positions on SAPs, as well as the brevity of her discussion, suggests the issue of globalization and economic human rights carried little weight in her assessment of the conference.

Yet US feminists like Freeman and Morgan could not entirely set the tone for what mattered about the Beijing and Huairou meetings. Many feminists returned to the United States with a new understanding of globalization. 'The global economy was the lightbulb that went on in everybody's head in Beijing', described Linda Burnham, the executive director of the Women of Color Resource Committee based in Oakland, California (Burnham 1996: 9). And as delegates from AIDWA experienced, some American women joined the conference with an analysis of the complicity of the United States already in their grasp. They were part of a women's movement that Kalagar and Agnihotri found particularly interesting.[14] Burnham organized a delegation of about 100 participants, mostly American women activists of colour from the Bay Area, to travel to Huairou. She remembered the Forum as a critical juncture in bringing globalization, as a doctrine and set of policies, home to the United States:

> I think it forced us to engage with issues having to do with the impact of globalization on women around the world and also to start to understand how global economic policies, or the parallels to the kinds of global economic policies that were impacting women in other places, how they were impacting women here in the US. And I think one of the things that was most important about that gathering was to really understand that for many women in other parts of the world, their thinking and understanding and work around women's issues was framed by how they understood the impact of transnational capital on their communities. (Linda Burnham, interviewed by Loretta Ross, 18 March 2005, Oakland, CA)

Marcy Rein, in her article 'Beijing Bound: Local Women Make Global Links', anticipated the connections between structural adjustment policies within the US and those outside. She described Cherri Gomez, a member of Women's Economic Agenda Project in Northern California as joining Burnham's delegation for precisely these reasons:

[13] She cited the World Bank report, *Toward Gender Equality: The Role of Public Policy* (Washington, D.C.: The World Bank, 1995): 54, 67 and back cover.

[14] For reports describing the importance of globalization to the international women's movement, see Streeter 1996: 200.

> Touched off by socialism's demise and the free market's triumph, the global changes come into individual women's lives in ways that become clear as they talk about Beijing.
>
> Cherri Gomez felt the brunt of one of those changes, the structural adjustment policies that shredded safety net programs around the world. Gomez had her first child at 16, was a single mom, sometimes on welfare, sometimes making a sparse living picking fruit. (Rein 1995: 3; see also Kirshenbaum 1995: 92.)

Some activists from the United States came to the conference looking for precisely the global connections around American imperialism that AIDWA's campaign in India portended. They may or may not have joined the spontaneous protest of Hillary Clinton's speech at the Huairou Forum on 6 September 1995. They may have found other sites of commonality, like the workshop audience members who shouted down Ishrat Husain, the World Bank's director of poverty and social policy, and his protestations of looking out for women's interests in their structural adjustment programmes.[15] They may have built ties through informal conversations with activists, and through pamphlets against neoliberal globalization like the ones distributed by AIDWA. In preparation for Beijing, Gayle Kirshenbaum, an editor at *Ms. Magazine*, lamented the lack of organization by US women's groups towards the Beijing conference. She linked American women's apathetic international activism to anti-poor government policies. She wrote: 'For US activists reeling from the current scorched-earth approach to domestic social programs the notion of demanding accountability from Washington for a global vision of social reform is hard to contemplate' (Kirshenbaum 1995: 92). Women from the US may have gained insights about their own means to demand national accountability from the US government through participation in the 'Women's Eyes on the World Bank' campaign run by a network of NGOs from around the world, or the many workshops held by women from the global North and the global South against economic liberalization.

The Next UN Conference on Women

The protest of Hillary Clinton's speech in Huairou was, in effect, a protest of her speech that she gave the day before in Beijing. That protest was also the high point in AIDWA delegates' memories over ten years after the festivities ended. In the context of a longer anti-imperialist third world women's movement, this spontaneous international response was also a protest for women's rights: a definition of women's rights that included women's right to sovereignty, to survive with dignity, and to control their own future. Subhashini

[15] For footage of this confrontation, see Shirini Heerah's documentary, *Beyond Beijing*, Women Make Movies, 1996.

Ali stressed the numbers of women who held citizenship in G7 countries who also protested as proof of internationalist solidarity, of an ongoing possibility for a future without imperialism. Vimala Kalagar stressed the strength of their anger as the women outlasted the rain coming down in sheets around them. Sonya Gill remembered the numbers of people who shouted slogans, openly distinguishing themselves from those outside who still wanted to enter the filled hall. This more far-reaching definition of women's rights, one that includes national independence and the struggles within the nation-state that entails, as well as economic rights, is a third-worldist women's demand that continues in a post-third world context. The window for a mass movement of marginalized, working-poor and agricultural women depends upon women's rights that go beyond Hillary Clinton's limited vision of women's individual rights to autonomy.

Shyamali Gupta was another AIDWA delegate who in 1995 was the president of West Bengal's AIDWA, by far its largest state committee. She foretold another lesson from Huairou when I asked her about any future UN Conference on Women and Forum for NGOs:

> There is no hope for that! The NGO conference is going on, usually, every ten years. . . . But after Beijing there has been no NGO conference due to America's significance. America stopped it, they gave direction to the UN. Because there was so much talk against American imperialism, against their politicians, against liberalization, against globalization, against structural adjustment policy. That's why they're not letting them continue. (Shyamali Gupta interview, 16 July 2008)

AIDWA's scepticism about the UN did not prevent them from organizing carefully before the Beijing Conference. Their frustration with India's country document spurred them to write an alternative analysis as a basis to build a national network of women's organizations and an outreach document to distribute among conference goers in China. Their refusal to tap funds from international aid agencies may have given a stronger mandate to their nine-member delegation, since these women actively represented their regional coalitions to join the conference. In Huairou, AIDWA participants witnessed the ongoing possibility for a socialist women's solidarity through their global commitment to confront imperialism. Yet, as Gupta's speculation suggests, the UN continues to be a contested site for negotiation, one that allows for difficult international conversations to develop, and one that could see those possibilities denied by hegemonic forces. Yet, in Gupta's reading, the Beijing Conference's success for anti-imperialist internationalism in 1995 spelled its own demise.

Gupta also mourned the lack of a forum for socialist women alongside (but not wholly dependent upon) the future loss of meaningful UN conferences on women. She celebrated AIDWA's active efforts to build regional ties of solidarity by hosting women from Bangladesh, Afghanistan, Iraq and China at its national conferences. She mentioned other AIDWA delegations: to the Asia Social Forum held in Hyderabad in 2003, the World Social Forum (WSF) held in Mumbai in 2004, to the regional WSF held in Karachi in 2006, to the Cuba Solidarity meetings held in Chennai in 2006, and to the Montreal March against Hunger, Poverty and Violence held on International Women's Day in 2000. She saw these efforts to build an international community, however, in the larger neoliberal backdrop: 'there is no platform' (ibid.). By platform, Gupta did not mean a set of common demands, or a political platform upon which to build an internationalist women's movement, but a literal platform or organizational site to host those events, to fund the delegates, and to build a mass-based women's movement for socialism. Thus far, analysts of Beijing +5 and Beijing +10 have similar assessments to Gupta's (McFeatters 2000: 1). Progress reports were presented in 2005 and the Beijing PoA was re-affirmed, but 'there was little excitement; the outcome was predictable, and the atmosphere was subdued' (Molyneux and Razavi 2005: 984). Perhaps most significantly, these conferences did not include the same breadth of participants, nor did they inspire tangible solidarities of pencils or medicine. If in Beijing globalization was 'the lightbulb that went off in everybody's head', the links between women's activism, their differential experiences in the face of globalization's benefits, and their potential for shared politics were noticeably absent in 2000 and 2005. The largely symbolic, yet potentially real benefits encoded into the PoA depend upon our consciousness of international and transnational solidarity: that is, what issues, goals and horizons link women in struggle, and who takes the lead in defining this movement.

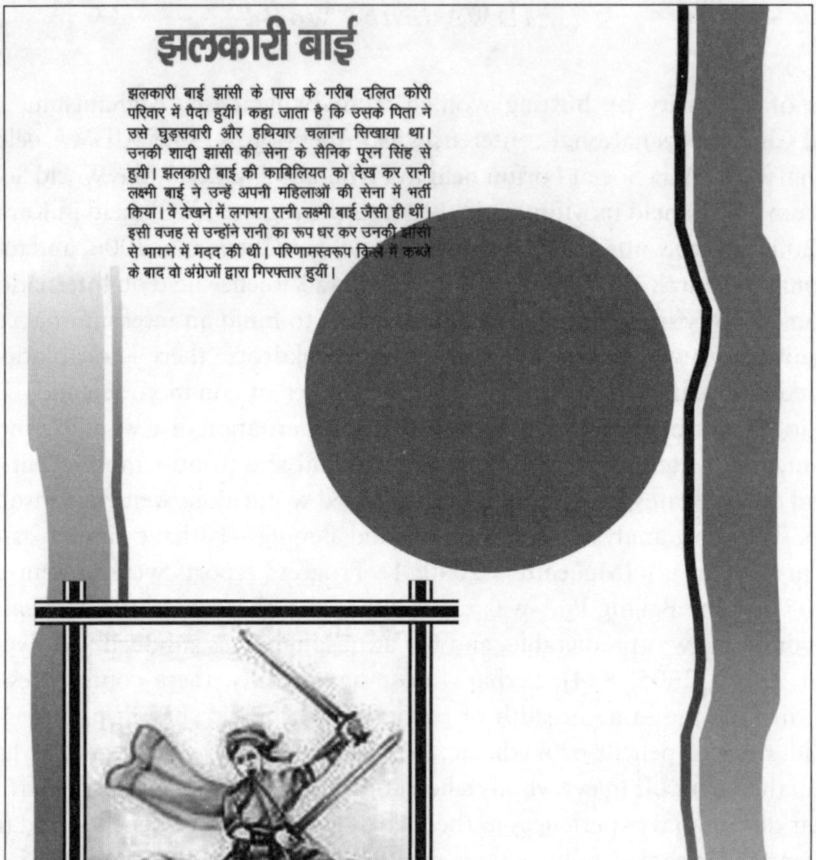

A leaf from AIDWA's 2010 calendar. The text describing Jhalkaribai's image reads: 'Jhalkaribai was born in a poor Kori (Dalit) family near Jhansi. . . . her father trained her in horse-riding and the use of weapons. She married Puran Singh who was a soldier in the Jhansi forces. There are reports that Laxmibai recruited Jhalkaribai into a women's force that she created, and also that she resembled the queen very closely. This led to her masquerading as the queen and helping her to escape from Jhansi. . . . she was arrested by the British after they overran the fort.'

Conclusion

Over the 1990s and 2000s, AIDWA developed methods to successfully organize where the greatest numbers of Indian women lived: both in rural and urban areas. They accomplished their substantial increase in numbers while the Indian state and economy moved towards the neoliberal 'free market' policies. In the first ten years, the organization grew from 590,000 women at their founding convention in 1981, to 2,876,000 members in 1991. Ten years later, in 2001, this number had more than doubled to 5,950,000 members. By the end of this study, in 2006, there were 10 million women who composed AIDWA from every state in the country. The numbers tell of careful work on the ground, building from successful local campaigns for affordable food, fair working conditions and basic equality through demanding laws for women's right to live without violence. The lives of the women who joined AIDWA are set within a context that creates their own expendability, an economy of 'disposable people'.

The Indian government midwifed the economic shift during this period from a planned economy to a market economy with considerable pressure from the 'Washington Consensus' forces: the International Monetary Fund (IMF), the World Bank, the World Trade Organization (WTO) and the United States government, to name a few of the best known players. In the process, Indian governance underwent its own transformation from one that gave some weight to representing the interests of its population to the neoliberal stance that explicitly emphasized its pro-business, pro-military priorities. These are well-documented transformations. The economic features of the neoliberal model have also been given ample study across the globe: from the financialization of the economy where the engines for growth lie in the financial instruments over productive capacity, to the shift from production of goods to the service sector and the move away from production-based jobs towards increasing service jobs. The 'jobless growth economy' emerged from these larger trajectories. Even the most basic rights for workers have been further eroded, as wages fell and the reserves of unemployed people grew. The devastation of labour politics across the globe is not just about shifting processes of production or the disarticulation of workers' consciousness, but about the disappearance of work and the insecurity of the work that remains. In India's rural areas, 79 per cent of the women are agricultural workers. But women's days of paid work in the fields have decreased dramatically in the 2000s and the National Rural Employment Guarantee Act (NREGA) has not increased the number of work-days to provide women with living wages. In urban areas, the greatest increase in work for women is not in the higher-waged work of information technology (IT) or tourism, but in the low-waged work of domestic service and construction. The role of women as workers in the neoliberal era has meant positive changes for a few women, but for the vast numbers of women their wages and work have decreased over the last twenty years.

Concurrent to these economic trends, the global women's movement during the 1990s and 2000s witnessed a move away from organizing, and sometimes even mobilizing women, in favour of networking women. Networks, connectivity and transnational linkages, supporters argued, heralded the future. Mass protests, neighbourhood-based groups and reaching out to the greatest number of women were methods to leave behind. Advocates of networking in the women's movement did not explicitly say that organizing women was a waste of time. However, their analysis of what could change social policy most effectively made it difficult to prioritize the work of building a mass movement of women. These feminist networks began to slide into functioning like transnational lobbies. AIDWA read the challenges of the neoliberal order quite differently. As the needs and opinions of the mass of people, and of working-class and agricultural women in particular, became less important, AIDWA more vociferously asserted the worth of their voices and lives. It reasserted its historical emphasis on the mass organizing and mass mobilizing of women. AIDWA members stressed the importance of creating local units in the least powerful communities of people to build their membership and develop their leadership. The women first left behind in the juggernaut of liberalization policies were the women AIDWA sought to reach. Long-term campaigns and inter-sectoral organizing methods allowed them to build a critical base among a wide swathe of women assumed to be voiceless in the neoliberal project.

AIDWA made a critical pivot in its theories of organizing women. It did not abandon the organization's historic methods of organizing around women's common concerns, whether food security, equal wages or dowry violence. Issues like these that crossed class divisions continued to energize their members across the country. What they developed in addition was recognition of the reassertion of community boundaries – of caste and religion in particular. The sharpened boundaries of caste, religion and other community affiliations developed alongside increasing economic exploitation of women workers. The rise of unstable casual labour for women in the 2000s has far outpaced women's self-employment in the informal sector. Women's economic insecurity and joblessness is a constitutive feature of the Indian neoliberal economy. In her study of Gujarat, Nikita Sud powerfully argues that the retreat into the fortress of exclusionary and bigoted community networks is linked to neoliberal shifts in Indian governance and the economy (Sud 2012).

AIDWA's identification of particularly vulnerable sectors of women led to the second even more deeply transformative shift. It built an inter-sectoral praxis that formulated women's common issues, against caste violence for example, as a cross-caste and cross-religion issue. Inter-sectoral praxis fuelled powerful campaigns even from within its membership, so that women from majoritarian identity positions fought for the issue from their social location. As public campaigns, all AIDWA members were organized to join the struggle as their own issue, not just the issue of the sector who felt the worst of the repression.

AIDWA's current work continues to press these issues. *Khap panchayat*s are finally an ongoing part of the national conversation, not just a regionalized one for north India. Rural and Dalit women's issues continue to galvanize powerful campaigns for land rights, water rights, dignity and bodily autonomy. Rape laws, divorce and maintenance laws, sexual harassment laws, and domestic violence laws are not left on the books with flaws intact. Instead, partial gains in laws are continually challenged. When a topical crisis of women's inequality flares into public view, activists are ready with research reports, analysis, bills and demands to take full advantage of the opportunity. Government officials are not allowed to gloss their commitment to women's rights with shoddily constructed bills without a fight. Since 1996, neither have they been allowed to forget the Women's Reservation Bill to reserve for women 33 per cent of seats in parliament and state assemblies. The imbalanced sex ratio, female foeticide and infanticide are ongoing campaigns. The explicit inclusion of women workers in the NREGA came out of a coalitional effort, led in no small part by AIDWA. The organization's deep research about the wages and conditions of work for women in rural areas gave vital strength to their demands for a better employment Act for women.

The challenges AIDWA faces in the current period have been well articulated by the organization's general secretary since 2004, Sudha Sundararaman. She emphasized the importance and the difficulties in reaching out to young women (Sudha Sundararaman interview, 12 July 2012). She talked about the media campaign run by AIDWA that gave a critical eye to women's sexual objectification and the overemphasis on women's beauty, including light skin tone and flawless looks. These efforts reached some young women attuned to these inequities. Yet the largely spontaneous upsurge of young women's activism in the Delhi rape case beginning in December 2012 revealed a widespread and largely untapped potential to bring more young women into the organized women's movement. One critical challenge for AIDWA and other women's groups is to understand the aspirations held by young women in urban and rural areas. The promises of empowerment and freedom held out in the media (alongside women's objectification), government rhetoric and the global emphasis on women's rights are embedded in the dreams of young women. Finding the language and the methods to hear these unfulfilled aspirations and give them a sustained voice through organized politics is the work that lies ahead.

Bibliography

Published Work

Agarwal, Bina, 1985, 'Work Participation of Rural Women in the Third World: Some Data and Conceptual Biases', *Economic and Political Weekly*, 20, nos. 51–52: A155–A164.

Agarwal, Bina, 1994, *A Field of One's Own: Gender and Land Rights in South Asia*, Cambridge: Cambridge University Press.

Agnes, Flavia, 1995, 'Redefining the Agenda of the Women's Movement within a Secular Framework', in Tanika Sarkar and Urvashi Butalia, eds., *Women and the Hindu Right*, New Delhi: Kali for Women: 136–57.

Agnihotri, Indu, 1996, 'The Fourth World Conference on Women: A Report from Beijing', *Indian Journal of Gender Studies*, 3, no. 1: 121–24.

Agnihotri, Indu, 2009, 'Women in the Struggle for Food Security in India', Global Food Security Initiative, available at http://www.globalfoodsec.net/modules/gfs/knowledge_resource/gender_and_food?debut=46, accessed 12 March 2011.

Agnihotri, Indu and Vina Mazumdar, 1995, 'Changing Terms of Political Discourse: Women's Movement in India, 1970s–1990s', *Economic and Political Weekly*, 30, no. 29, 22 July: 1869–78.

Ahlawat, Neerja, 1995, *Women's Organizations and Social Networks*, Jaipur and New Delhi: Rawat Publications.

Ahlawat, S.R., 1988, *Green Revolution and Agricultural Labour*, New Delhi: Deep and Deep Publications.

AIDWA (All India Democratic Women's Association), 1981, *Aims and Objects Programme Constitution of All India Democratic Women's Association, Adopted at the First Conference of the All India Democratic Women's Association, held in Madras on 10–12 March 1981*, New Delhi: AIDWA.

'AIDWA Memorandum to the President of India on Sati Bill', 1988, *Equality*, 2, no. 1, January–March: 21.

AIDWA, 1993, 'Communalism: "Not Just Another Issue"', *Women's Equality*, 5, no. 1, January–June: 2.

AIDWA, 1994, *Draft Report: Issues, Struggles, Organization, AIDWA Fourth National Conference, August 11–14, 1994, Coimbatore, Tamil Nadu*, New Delhi: AIDWA.

AIDWA, 1998, *RSS: The Ideological Onslaught on Women*, New Delhi: AIDWA.

AIDWA, 1999, *AIDWA 1994–1998, Women's Status: Issues and Struggles, Draft Report, 5th National Conference, Bangalore, 11–14 June 1998*, New Delhi: AIDWA.

AIDWA, 1999, *Not a Uniform Civil Code but Equal Rights, Equal Laws*, New Delhi: AIDWA.

AIDWA, 1999, *Women and Violence*, New Delhi: AIDWA.

AIDWA, 2003, *For a New Food Policy: Low-priced Food Grains and Work for All, Sangharsh Sabha*, New Delhi: AIDWA.

AIDWA, 2010, *In the Name of Honour: Let Us Love and Live*, New Delhi: AIDWA.

AIDWA *et al.*, 1995, *Towards Beijing, A Perspective from the Indian Women's Movement*, New Delhi.

AIDWA *et al.*, 2000, *Women Speak: United Voices Against Globalization, Poverty and Violence in India*, New Delhi.

'AIDWA's Growing Path', 1987, *Magalir Sinthanai*, 27, May: 14.

'AIWC Meets: Demands Immediate Indian Freedom', 1946, *People's War*, 4, no. 32, 27 January.

Alexander, K.C., 1975, *Agrarian Tension in Thanjavur*, Hyderabad: National Institute of Community Development.

Alvarez, Sonia, 1998, 'Latin American Feminisms "Go Global": Trends of the 1990s and Challenges for the New Millennium', in Sonia Alvarez, Evelina Dagnino and Arturo Escobar, eds., *Cultures of Politics, Politics of Culture: Revisioning Latin American Social Movements,* Boulder, CO: Westview Press: 293–324.

Alvarez, Sonia, 1999, 'Advocating Feminism: The Latin American Feminist NGO "Boom"', *International Feminist Journal of Politics*, 1, no. 2: 181–209.

'Among Kisan (Peasant) Women', 1945, *People's War*, 3, no. 46, 13 May: 2.

Anonymous Labour Organizer, 1946, 'Sadistic Police Brutality: Firing on S.I.R. Strikers at Golden Rock, An Eyewitness Account', *People's Age*, 5, no. 12, 22 September: 4.

'Anti-Sati Bill and the Women's Movement', 1988, *Equality*, 2, no. 1, January–March: 18.

Antrobus, Peggy, 2004, *The Global Women's Movement: Origins, Issues and Strategies*, London and New York: Zed Books.

Armstrong, Elisabeth and Vijay Prashad, 2006, 'Bandung Women: Vietnam, Afghanistan, Iraq and the Necessary Risks of Solidarity', in Robin Riley and Naeem Inayatullah, eds., *Interrogating Imperialism*, New York: Palgrave Macmillan: 15–50.

Athreya, Venkatesh and R. Chandra, 2000, 'Dalits and Land Issues', *Frontline*, 17, no. 12, 10–23 June: 54.

Bacchetta, Paola, 1996, 'Hindu Nationalist Women as Ideologues', in Kumari Jayawardena and Malathi de Alwis, eds., *Embodied Violence: Communalizing Women's Sexuality in South Asia,* New Delhi: Kali for Women.

Bacchetta, Paola, 2004, *Gender in the Hindu Nation: RSS Women as Ideologues*, New Delhi: Women Unlimited.

Basu, Amrita, 1992, *Two Faces of Protest: Contrasting Modes of Women's Activism in India*, Berkeley: University of California Press.

Basu, Aparna, 1996, *Mridula Sarabhai: Rebel with a Cause*, New Delhi: Oxford University Press.

Basu, Aparna and Bharati Ray, 2003, *Women's Struggle: A History of the All India Women's Conference, 1927–2002*, New Delhi: Manohar.

Basu, T., Pradip Datta, Sumit Sarkar, Tanika Sarkar, Sambuddha Sen, *Khakhi Shorts and Saffron Flags: A Critique of the Hindu Right*, New Delhi: Orient Longman.

Baxi, Upendra *et al.*, 1979, 'Open Letter to the Chief Justice of India', 4 SCC (J) 17.

Bayliss, Kate, Ben Fine and Elisa Van Waeyenberge, 2011, *The Political Economy of Development: The World Bank, Neoliberalism and Development Research*, London: Pluto Press.

Beijing! U.N. Fourth World Conference on Women, 1998, New Delhi: Women's Feature Service: 166.

Bello, Walden, 2006, 'Globalization in Retreat', *Focus on the Global South*, 27 December.

Beneria, Lourdes, 2003, *Gender, Development and Globalization: Economics as if All People Mattered*, New York: Routledge.

Bhagwati, Jagdish, 1993, *India in Transition: Freeing the Economy*, New York: Oxford University Press.

Bhalla, Sheila, 1989, 'Technological Change and Women Workers: Evidence from the Expansionary Phase in Haryana Agriculture', *Economic and Political Weekly*, 24, no. 43, 28 October: WS67–WS73, WS75–WS78.

Bhattacharjee, Anannya, 1997, 'The Public/Private Mirage: Mapping Homes and Undomesticating Violence Work in the South Asian Immigrant Community', in M. Jacqui Alexander and Chandra Mohanty, eds., *Feminist Genealogies, Colonial Legacies, Democratic Futures*, New York: Routledge: 308–29.

Bidwai, Praful, 1995, 'Making India Work – For the Rich', *Multinational Monitor*, 16, nos. 7–8: 3–10.

Bose, Mandakranta, ed., *Faces of the Feminine in Ancient, Medieval and Modern India*, New Delhi: Oxford University Press, 2000.

Byres, Terence, 1997, 'Introduction: Development Planning and the Interventionist State Versus Liberalization and the Neo-Liberal State: India, 1989–1996', in Terence Byres, ed., *The State, Development Planning and Liberalization in India*: 1–25.

Byres, Terence, ed., 1997, *The State, Development Planning and Liberalization in India*, New Delhi: Oxford University Press.

Byres, Terence, ed., 1998, *The Indian Economy: Major Debates Since Indian Independence*, New Delhi: Oxford University Press.

Centre for Women's Development Studies (CWDS), 1995, *Confronting Myriad Oppressions, Voices from the Women's Movement in India, The Western Regional Experience*, No. 1, New Delhi: CWDS.

Chandra, R., 1986, 'It is Our Great Fortune to be Born Women...?' *Magalir Sinthanai*, 19, July: 3.

Chandra, R., 2002, 'AIDWA Takes Initiative: Women's Inspiring Conference Against Untouchability', *People's Democracy*, 25 August.

Chandra, R., 2004, 'Tamil Nadu: AIDWA Holds Inspiring Conference Against Untouchability', *People's Democracy*, January.

Chattopadhyay, Suhas, 1973, 'On the Class Nature of Land Reforms in India since Independence', *Social Scientist*, 2, no. 4, November: 3–24.

Chakravarti, Uma, 2003, *Gendering Caste through a Feminist Lens*, Calcutta: Stree.

Chakravarti, Uma, 2005, 'From fathers to husbands: of love, death and marriage in North India', in Lynn Welchman and Sara Hossain, eds., *'Honour': Crimes, Paradigms, and Violence Against Women*, Karachi, Pakistan: Oxford University Press: 308–31.

Chakravartty, Renu, 1980, *Communists in Indian Women's Movement*, New Delhi: People's Publishing House.

Chandrasekhar, C.P. and Jayati Ghosh, 2000, *The Market that Failed: A Decade of Neoliberal Economic Reforms in India*, New Delhi: Leftword Books.

Chandrasekhar, C.P. and Jayati Ghosh, 2003, 'Why is Farm Employment Generation Falling?' *Business Line*, 4 April; available at http://www.thehindubusinessline.in/2003/04/22/stories/2003042200851100.htm, accessed 27 June 2011.

Chaudhuri, Kalyan, 1977, 'Women Prisoners in Presidency Jail', *Economic and Political Weekly*, 12, no. 19, 7 May: 755–57.

Chaudhuri, Maitrayee, ed., 2003, *Feminism in India*, New Delhi: Women Unlimited.

Chaudhuri, Maitrayee, ed., 2004, *Issues in Contemporary Indian Feminism: Feminism in India*, New Delhi: Kali for Women.

Chaudhuri, Tripti, 2000, 'Women in Radical Movements in Bengal in the 1940s: The Story of the Mahila Atmaraksha Samiti (Women's Self-Defence League)', in Mandakranta Bose, ed., *Faces of the Feminine in Ancient, Medieval and Modern India*: 304–21.

Chowdhry, Prem, 'Redeeming "Honour" through Violence: Unravelling the Concept and its Application', available at http://cequinindia.org/pdf/Special_Reports/Honour%20killings%20by%20Prem%20Choudhury.pdf, accessed 29 June 2011.

Chowdhry, Prem, 1993, 'High Participation, Low Evaluation: Women and Work in Rural Haryana', *Economic and Political Weekly*, 28, no. 52, 25 December: A135–A137, A140–A148.

Chowdhry, Prem, 1994, *The Veiled Women: Shifting Gender Equations in Rural Haryana, 1880–1990*, New Delhi: Oxford University Press.

Chowdhry, Prem, 2007, *Contentious Marriages, Eloping Couples: Gender, Caste and Patriarchy in Northern India*, New Delhi: Oxford University Press.

Chowdhry, Prem, 2011, *Political Economy and Production and Reproduction: Caste, Custom and Community in North India*, New Delhi: Oxford University Press.

Clinton, Hillary Rodham, 1995, 'Remarks to the U.N. 4th World Conference on Women', Beijing, 5 September, available at http://5wcw.org/docs/Clinton_Speech.html, accessed January 16, 2010.

Clinton, Hillary Rodham, 2002, 'Remarks to the NGO Forum on Women (1995)', in Dawn Keetley, ed., *Public Women, Public Words: A Documentary History of American Feminism*, vol. 3, Lanham, Maryland: Rowman and Littlefield: 359–62.

CPI(M) (Communist Party of India [Marxist]), 1981, *On Mass Organizations: CPI(M) Central Committee Resolution*, New Delhi: CPI(M).

CPI(M), 1992, *Central Committee Document: On Mass Organizations*, second edition, New Delhi: CPI(M).

CPI(M)–AIDWA, 2003, *State-Sponsored Carnage in Gujarat, March 2002*, New Delhi.

Danner, Lauren and Susan Walsh, 1999, '"Radical" Feminists and "Bickering" Women: Backlash in U.S. Media Coverage of the United Nations Fourth World Conference on Women', *Critical Studies in Mass Communication*, 16: 63–84.

Das, S.K., 1998, *Civil Service Reform and Structural Adjustment*, New Delhi: Oxford University Press.

Datar, Chhaya, 1995, 'The Women's Movement in Maharashtra: An Overview', in Chhaya Datar, ed., *The Struggle Against Violence*, Calcutta: Stree.

Dave, Naisargi N., 2011, 'Activism as Ethical Practice: Queer Politics in Contemporary India', *Cultural Dynamics*, 23, no. 3: 3–20.

Davis, Angela, 2000, 'The Color of Violence Against Women', *Colorlines*, 3, no. 3: 4–8.

DeRosa, Dean, 1992, 'Concluding the Uruguay Round: The Dunkel Draft Agreement on Agriculture', *The World Economy*, 15, no. 6, November: 755–60.

Desai, Manisha, 2002, 'Transnational Solidarity: Women's Agency, Structural Adjustment, and Globalization', in Nancy Naples and Manisha Desai, eds., *Women's Activism and Globalization: Linking Local Struggles and Transnational Politics*, New York: Routledge: 15–39.

Deshpande, R.S. and Nagesh Prabhu, 2005, 'Farmers' Distress: Proof beyond Question', *Economic and Political Weekly*, 11, nos. 44–45, 29 October: 4663–65.

Dhar, Biswajit and C. Niranjan Rao, 1992, 'Dunkel Draft on TRIPS: Complete Denial of Developing Countries' Interests', *Economic and Political Weekly*, 27, no. 6, 8 February: 275–78.

Dutt, Kalpana, 1945, 'Where Civilization Ends and Hell Begins ... Down the Arakan Road', *People's War*, 3, no. 50, 10 June: 6–7.

Dutt, Mallika, 2000, 'Some Reflections on United States Women of Color and the United Nations Fourth World Conference on Women and NGO Forum in Beijing, China', in Bonnie Smith, ed., *Global Feminism since 1945*, New York: Routledge: 305–13.

'Editorial', 1987, *Equality*, 1, no. 1, October–December: 2.

Elson, Diane, 1994, 'Micro, Meso, Macro: Gender and Economic Analysis in the Context of Policy Reform', in Isabella Bakker, ed., *The Strategic Silence: Gender and Economic Policy*, London: Zed Press: 33–45.

Engineer, Asghar Ali, 1987, *The Shah Bano Controversy*, Bombay: Orient Longman.

Fernandez-Kelly, Patricia, 1983, *For We Are Sold, I and My People: Women and Industry in Mexico's Frontier*, Albany: State University of New York Press.

Fernandez-Kelly, Patricia, 2007, 'The Global Assembly Line in the New Millennium: A Review Essay', *Signs*, 32, no. 2: 509–21.

Forbes, Geraldine, 1996, *Women in Modern India*, Cambridge: Cambridge University Press.

Frankel, Francine, 1971, *India's Green Revolution: Economic Gains and Political Costs*, Princeton, NJ: Princeton University Press.

Frankel, Francine and M.S.A. Rao, eds., 1989, *Dominance and State Power in Modern India, Decline of a Social Order, Vol. 1*, New Delhi: Oxford University Press.

Freeman, Jo, 1996, 'The Real Story of Beijing', *off our backs*, 26, no. 3, March: 1, 8–11, 22–27.

Galey, Margaret E., 1995, 'Women Find a Place', in Anne Winslow, ed., *Women, Politics and the United Nations*, Westport, CT: Greenwood Press: 11–38.

Gandhi, Nandita and Nandita Shah, 1991, *The Issues at Stake: Theory and Practice in the Contemporary Women's Movement in India*, New Delhi: Kali for Women.

Ghosh, Jayati, 1998, 'Liberalization Debates', in Terence Byres, ed., *The Indian Economy: Major Debates since Independence*: 295–334.

Ghosh, Jayati, 1999, 'Perceptions of Difference: The Economic Underpinnings', in K.N. Panikkar, ed., *The Concerned Indian's Guide to Communalism*, New Delhi: Viking: 107–30.

Ghosh, Jayati, 2001, 'Skewed Reforms and the Slowdown', *Frontline*, 18, no. 3, 3–16 February: 101.

Ghosh, Jayati, 2004, 'Informalization and Women's Workforce Participation: A Consideration of Recent Trends in Asia', *Labour and Development*, 10, no. 2, December: 4–44.

Gill, Sonya, 1993, 'Bombay: Communal Carnage', *Women's Equality*, 5, no. 1, January–June: 25.

Gill, S.S., 2011, 2003, 'Diluting Mandal', *The Hindu*, 24 June, available at http://www.hinduonnet.com/2003/06/24/stories/2003062400731000.htm, accessed 18 July 2011.

Girimaji, Pushpa, 1991, 'Government May Restrict PDS to the Poor', *The Indian Express*,23 July.

Glaeser, Bernhard, ed., 1987, *The Green Revolution Revisited: Critique and Alternatives*, London: Allen and Unwin.

'Global Framework', 1995, *Beijing Declaration and the Platform for Action*, United Nations.

Gopalan, Susheela, 1987, 'The Challenge Before Us', *Equality*, 1, no. 1, October–December: 5.

Gorringe, Hugo, 2005, *Untouchable Citizens: Dalit Movements and Democratization in Tamil Nadu*, New Delhi: Sage Publications.

Gothoskar, Sujata, Vithubai Patel, Vibuti Patel and Carol Wolkowitz, 1982, 'Documents from the Indian Women's Movement', *Feminist Review*, 12: 92–103.

Gough, Kathleen, 1973, 'Harijans in Thanjavur', in Kathleen Gough and Hari P. Sharma, eds., *Imperialism and Revolution in South Asia*: 222–45.

Gough, Kathleen and Hari P. Sharma, eds., 1973, *Imperialism and Revolution in South Asia*, New York: Monthly Review Press.

Govinda, Radhika, 2009, 'In the Name of "Poor and Marginalized"? Politics of NGO Activism with Dalit Women in Rural North India', *Journal of South Asian Development*, 4, no. 1: 45–64.

Guha, Ramachandra, 2007, *India After Gandhi: The History of the World's Largest Democracy*, New York: Harper Collins.

Guha, S.K., 1998, 'India: It's a Long Haul, But We'll Make It', in *Beijing! U.N.Fourth World Conference on Women*, New Delhi: Women's Feature Service: 164–66.

Gulati, Ashok and Sudha Narayanan, 2003, *The Subsidy Syndrome in Indian Agriculture*, New Delhi: Oxford University Press.

Gulati, Leela, 1981, *Profiles in Female Poverty: A Study of Five Poor Working Women in Kerala*, Delhi: Hindustan Publishing Corporation.

Gupta, Amit Kumar, 2001, 'Forest-fire in the Sundarbans: The Communists and the Kakdwip Rising, 1946–1950', in Maya Gupta and Amit Kumar Gupta, eds., *Defying Death: Struggles against Imperialism and Feudalism*, New Delhi: Tulika Books: 39–52.

de Haan, Francisca, 2010, 'Continuing Cold War Paradigms in the Western Historiography of Transnational Women's Organizations: The Case of the Women's International Democratic Federation (WIDF)', *Women's History Review*, 19, no. 4, September: 547–73.

Hajrah Begum, 1945, 'UP Women's Conference Welcomes Draft Code: Reactionaries Boycott Attempts Defeated', *People's War*, 3, no. 40, April: 7.

Hajrah Begum, 1962, *Why Women Should Vote Communist*, New Delhi: People's Publishing House.

Hanumanthan, K.R., 1979, *Untouchability: A Historical Study up to 1500 A.D. with Special Reference to Tamil Nadu*, Madurai: Koodal Publishers.

Harvey, David, 2008, *A Brief History of Neoliberalism*, Oxford: Oxford University Press.

Hasan, Zoya, 1988, 'A Perspective of the BKU Agitation', *Equality*, 1, no. 3, March: 3–4.

Hasan, Zoya, 1989a, 'Minority Identity, Muslim Women's Bill Campaign and the Political Process', *Economic and Political Weekly*, 24, 7 January: 44–50.

Hasan, Zoya, 1989b, 'Power and Mobilization: Patterns of Resilience and Change in Uttar Pradesh Politics', in Francine Frankel and M.S.A. Rao, eds., *Dominance and State Power in Modern India*: 133–203.

Hasan, Zoya, 1990, 'Changing Orientation of the State and the Emergence of Majoritarianism in the 1980s', *Social Scientist*, 18, nos. 8–9, August–September: 28–32.

Hindustan Times, 14 February 1991: 1.

Hindustan Times, 7 January 1992: 9.

'Housewives Express Shock, Anger', *Times of India*, 23 December 1991: 3.

Human Rights Watch, 1999, *Broken People: Caste Violence Against India's "Untouchables"*, New York: Human Rights Watch.

INCITE! Women of Color Against Violence, ed., 2007, *The Revolution Will Not Be Funded: Beyond the Non-Profit Industrial Complex*, Boston: South End Press.

'Introductions', 1987, *Magalir Sinthanai*, 26, February: 3.

Jaffrelot, Christophe, 2003, *India's Silent Revolution: The Rise of the Lower Castes in North India*, New York: Columbia University Press.

Jain, Devaki, 2005, *Women, Development and the U.N.*, Bloomington and Indianapolis: Indiana University Press.

James, K.S. and S. Irudaya Rajan, 2004, 'Respondents and Quality of Survey Data', *Economic and Political Weekly*, 39, no. 7, 14 February: 659–63.

Jayawardena, Kumari and Govind Kelkar, 1989, 'The Left and Feminism', *Economic and Political Weekly*, 24, no. 38, 23 September: 2123–26.

Jha, Satish, 1996, 'Economic Reforms: Impact on Rural Poverty', in *Economic Liberalization and Rural Poverty*, Population, Rural and Urban Development Division, United Nations: 64-70.

John, Mary E., 1999, 'Gender, Development and the Women's Movement: Problems for a History of the Present', in Rajeswari Sunder Rajan, ed., *Signposts: Gender Issues in Post-Independence India*: 100–24.

Joshi, Vijay and I.M.D. Little, 1996, *India's Economic Reforms, 1991–2001*, Oxford: Oxford University Press.

Kak, Shakti, 1994a, 'Rural Women and Labour Force Participation', *Social Scientist*, 22, nos. 3–4, March–April: 35–50.

Kak, Shakti, 1994b, 'Subsistence Economies and Women's Work: A Case Study of India', Occasional Papers on Perspectives in Indian Development, Number 47, Nehru Memorial Museum and Library, New Delhi.

Kannabiran, Vasanth and Kalpana Kannabiran, 1995, 'The Frying Pan or the Fire?

Endangered Identities, Gendered Institutions and Women's Survival', in Tanika Sarkar and Urvashi Butalia, eds., *Women and the Hindu Right*: 121–35.

Karat, Brinda, 1988, '"There is no work, yet the grind of work is killing me...": A Comment on *Shramshakti* (Report of the National Commission on Self-Employed Women)', *Equality*, 2, no. 2, April–July: 22.

Karat, Brinda, 1993, 'Equal Rights, Equal Laws', *Women's Equality*, 5, no. 1, January–June: 5.

Karat, Brinda, 1995, 'Papering It Over', interview by Asha Krishnakumar, *Frontline*, 19 May: 110.

Karat, Brinda, 1997, 'Crying out for Social Justice', *Indian Express*, 1 August.

Karat, Brinda, 2003, 'Fighting for a Basic Human Right: A Life Free from Hunger', *Women's Equality*, 17, no. 1, January–March: 25–32.

Katzenstein, Mary Fainsod, 1989, 'Organizing Against Violence: Strategies of the Indian Women's Movement', *Pacific Affairs*, 62, no. 1, Spring: 53–71.

Kelkar, Govind, 1992, 'Stopping the Violence Against Women: Fifteen Years of Activism in India', in M. Schuler, ed., *Freedom from Violence: Women's Strategies from Around the World*, Washington D.C.: OEF International: 75–99.

Khullar, Mala, 1997, 'Emergence of the Women's Movement in India', *Asian Journal of Women's Studies*, 3, no. 2: 94–129.

Kirshenbaum, Gayle., 1995, 'Getting U.S. Feminists Psyched About Beijing', *Ms. Magazine*, March: 92.

Kishwar, Madhu, 1990, 'Why I Do Not Call Myself a Feminist', *Manushi*, 61, November/December: 2–8.

Krishna, C.S., 1980, 'The Madras and Southern Mahratta Railway Strike: 1932–1933', *Social Scientist*, 8, no. 9, April: 12–24.

Krishnaraj, Maithreyi, 1990, 'Women's Work in the Indian Census: Beginnings of Change', *Economic and Political Weekly*, 25, nos. 48/49, 1–8 December: 2663–72.

Krishnaraj, Maithreyi, ed., 1990, *Feminism: Indian Debates, Readings of Women's Studies Series 1*, Mumbai: Research Centre for Women's Studies, SNDT Women's University.

Krylova, Anna, 2010, *Soviet Women in Combat: A History of Violence on the Eastern Front*, Cambridge: Cambridge University Press.

Kumar, Avinash, 2011, 'The Battle for Land', *Economic and Political Weekly*, 44, no. 25, 18 June: 20–23.

Kumar, Radha, 1993, *A History of Doing: An Illustrated Account of Movements for Women's Rights and Feminism in India, 1880–1990*, New Delhi: Kali for Women.

Laville, Helen, 2002, *Cold War Women: The International Activities of American Women's Organizations*, Manchester and New York: Manchester University Press.

Lenin, V.I., 1939, *Imperialism, The Highest Stage of Capitalism*, New York: International Publishers.

Leydesdorff, Selma, Luisa Passerini and Paul Thompson, 1996, 'Introduction', in Selma Leydesdorff, Luisa Passerini and Paul Thompson, eds., *Gender and Memory: International Yearbook of Oral History and Life Stories, Vol. IV*, Oxford: Oxford University Press: 1–16.

Lind, Amy, 'Negotiating Boundaries: Women's Organizations and the Politics of

Restructuring in Ecuador', in Marianne Marchand and Anne Runyan, eds., *Gender and Global Restructuring: Sightings, Sites and Resistances*, New York: Routledge, 2000: 161–75.

Liddle, Joanna and Rama Joshi, 1986, *Daughters of Independence: Gender, Caste and Class in India*, New Brunswick, NJ: Rutgers University Press.

Loomba, Ania and Ritty A. Lukose, eds., 2012, *South Asian Feminisms*, Durham, NC: Duke University Press.

Lycklama a Nijeholt, Geertje, Joke Swiebel and Virginia Vergas, 1998, 'The Global Institutional Framework: The Long March to Beijing', in Geertje Lycklama a Nijeholt, Virginia Vargas and Saskia Wieringa, eds., *Women's Movements and Public Policy in Europe, Latin America, and the Caribbean*, New York: Garland Publishing: 1–30.

'Magalir Sinthanai', 1987, *Magalir Sinthanai*, 25, January: 3.

Mahbub ul Haq Human Development Centre, 2002, *Human Development in South Asia 2002: Agriculture and Rural Development*, New Delhi: Oxford University Press.

Majumdar, Asok, 2011, *The Tebhaga Movement: Politics of Peasant Protest in Bengal, 1946–1950*, New Delhi: Aakar Books.

Malik, Bela, 2005, 'Untouchability and Dalit Women's Oppression', in Anupama Rao, ed., *Gender and Caste*, London and New York: Zed Books: 102–05.

Markowitz, Lisa and Karen Tice, 2002, 'Paradoxes of Professionalization: Parallel Dilemmas in the Americas', *Gender and Society*, 16, no. 6, December: 941–58.

Mathew, Molly, 1981, 'Constant Underemployment: Women in Kerala's Coir Industry', *Manushi*, 9: 27–29.

Mathew, P.M. and M.S. Nair, 1986, *Women's Organizations and Women's Interests*, New Delhi: Ashish Publishing House.

Mathur, Kanchan, 2004, *Countering Gender Violence: Initiatives towards Collective Action in Rajasthan*, New Delhi: Sage Publications.

Mathur, Kanchan, 2007, 'Body as Site, Body as Space: Bodily Integrity and Women's Empowerment in India', Working Paper 148, Institute of Development Studies Jaipur (IDSJ), June.

Mathur, Shubh, 2008, *The Everyday Life of Hindu Nationalism: An Ethnographic Account*, Gurgaon: Three Essays Collective.

Mazumdar, Vina, 2000, 'Political Ideology of the Women's Movement's Engagement with Law', Occasional Paper No. 34, New Delhi: Centre for Women's Development Studies.

McFeatters, Ann, 2000, 'Women's Conference Breaks No New Ground', *Post-Gazette*, 10 June: 1.

Mendelsohn, Oliver and Marika Vicziany, eds., 1998, *The Untouchables: Subordination, Poverty and the State in the Modern India*, Cambridge: Cambridge University Press.

Menon, Nivedita, ed., 1999, *Gender and Politics in India*, New Delhi: Oxford University Press.

Menon, Parvathi, 2004, *Breaking Barriers*, New Delhi: Leftword Books.

Menon, Ritu, ed., 2011, *Making a Difference: Memoirs from the Women's Movement in India*, New Delhi: Women Unlimited.

Menon-Sen, Kalyani, 2001, 'The Problem', *Seminar*, 505, http://www.india-seminar.com/2001/505/505 the problem.htm#top, accessed 31 July 2012.

Moghadam, Valerie, 2005, *Globalizing Women: Transnational Feminist Networks*, Baltimore, MD: John Hopkins Press.

Moghe, Kiran, 1999, 'AIDWA Convention Against Untouchability and Oppression of Dalits', *People's Democracy*, 3 January: 8.

Mohapatra, Satyen, 1991, 'Price hikes hit the poor most', *Hindustan Times*, 29 December: 5.

Molyneux, Maxine and Shahra Razavi, 2005, 'Beijing Plus Ten: An Ambivalent Record on Gender Justice', *Development and Change*, 36, no. 6: 984.

Mongia, Radhika, 1995, 'Reflections on the NGO Forum or What I Didn't Learn from *The New York Times*', *Bad Subjects*, 21, October: 24–26.

Morgan, Robin, 1996, 'Dispatch from Beijing', *Ms.*, 6, no. 4, January: 12–21.

Mosse, David, 1994, 'Idioms of Subordination and Styles of Protest among Christian and Hindu Harijan Castes in Tamil Nadu', *Contributions to Indian Sociology*, 28, no. 1: 67–106.

Mukherjee, Kanak, 1944, 'Our Famine-Homeless Sisters' Plight: Bengal Government's Work Houses Closing Down', *People's War*, 2, no. 62, 24 September: 9.

Mukherjee, Kanak, 1989, *Women's Emancipation Movement in India*, New Delhi: National Book Centre.

Nair, Kusum, 1979, *In Defence of the Irrational Peasant: Indian Agriculture after the Green Revolution*, Chicago: University of Chicago Press.

Namboodiripad, E.M.S., 1975, 'Perspective of the Women's Movement', *Social Scientist*, 4, nos. 40–41, November–December: 1–8.

National Council of Applied Economic Research (NCAER), 2003, *North India Human Development Report*, New Delhi: Oxford University Press.

Noorani, A.G., 1989, 'Babri Masjid – Ram Janma Bhoomi Dispute', *Economic and Political Weekly*, 24, nos. 44–45, 4–11 November: 2461–66.

O'Hanlon, Rosalind, 1985, *Caste, Conflict and Ideology: Mahatma Jotirao Phule and Low Caste Protest in Nineteenth-Century Western India*, Cambridge: Cambridge University Press.

Omvedt, Gail, 1975, 'Rural Origins of Women's Liberation in India', *Social Scientist*, 4, nos. 40–41, November–December: 40–45.

Omvedt, Gail, 1980, *We Will Smash This Prison!* London: Zed Press.

Omvedt, Gail, 1990a, '"Twice-Born" Riot against Democracy', *Economic and Political Weekly*, 25, no. 39, September: 2193–96.

Omvedt, Gail, 1990b, *Violence Against Women: New Movements and New Theories in India*, New Delhi: Kali for Women.

Palriwala, Rajni and Indu Agnihotri, 1996, 'Tradition, the Family, and the State: Politics of the Contemporary Women's Movement', in T.V. Sathyamurthy, ed., *Region, Religion, Caste, Gender and Culture in Contemporary India, Volume 3*, New Delhi: Oxford University Press: 501–23.

Panini, M.N., 1996, 'The Political Economy of Caste', in M.N. Srinivas, ed., *Caste: Its Twentieth Century Avatar*, New Delhi: Viking: 28–68.

Paschim Banga Ganatantrik Mahila Samiti, *Paschim Banga Ganatantrik Mahila Samiti Golden Jubilee (1943–1993)*, Calcutta, 1993.

Passerini, Luisa, 1989, 'Women's Personal Narratives: Myths, Experiences and Emotions', in Personal Narratives Group, ed., *Interpreting Women's Lives: Feminist Theory and Personal Narratives*, Bloomington and Indianapolis: University of Indiana Press: 189–97.

Pasha, Mustapha, 2000, 'Liberalization, State Patronage, and the "New Inequality" in South Asia', *Journal of Developing Societies*, 16, no. 1: 70–90.

Patel, Vibhuti, 1994, 'Women and Structural Adjustment in India', *Social Scientist*, 22, nos. 3–4: 18–32.

Patel, Vibhuti, 1985, 'Women's Liberation in India', *New Left Review*, 1, no. 153, September–October: 75–86.

Patnaik, Prabhat, 2011, 'Economic Growth and Employment', *Economic and Political Weekly*, 44, nos. 26–27, 25 June: 172–76.

Patnaik, Prabhat and C.P. Chandrasekhar, 1996, 'Investment, Exports and Growth: A Cross-Country Analysis', *Economic and Political Weekly*, 31, no. 1, 6 January: 31–36.

Patnaik, Utsa, 1991, 'Devaluation, IMF Conditionalities and Their Implications', *Women's Equality*, 4, no. 3, July–September: 1–5.

Patnaik, Utsa, 1999, *The Long Transition: Essays on Political Economy*, New Delhi: Tulika Books.

Patnaik, Utsa and Manjari Dingwaney, eds., 1985, *Chains of Servitude: Bondage and Slavery in India*, Madras: Sangam Books.

Patnaik, Utsa and Prabhat Patnaik, 2001, 'The State, Poverty and Development in India', in N.G. Jayal and S. Pai, eds., *Democratic Governance in India*, New Delhi: Sage: 32–65.

Pietila, Hilkka, 2002, *Engendering the Global Agenda: The Story of Women and the United Nations*, United Nations Non-Government Liaison Service (UN-NGLS) Development Dossier.

Pietila, Hilkka and Jeanne Vickers, 1996, *Making Women Matter: The Role of the United Nations*, London: Zed Books.

Poonacha, Veena and Divya Pandey, 2000, 'Responses to Domestic Violence: Government and Non-Government Action in Karnataka and Gujarat', *Economic and Political Weekly*, 35, no. 6: 566-574.

Pratap, Sangeet, 1995, 'The Beijing Meet: Critical Concerns over Women in Society', *Frontline*, 19 May: 109.

Purkayastha, Bandana, Mangala Subramaniam, Manisha Desai and Sunita Bose, 2003, 'The Study of Gender in India: A Partial Review', *Gender and Society*, 17, no. 4, August: 511–13.

Rai, Shirin M., ed., 2003, *Mainstreaming Gender, Democratizing the State? Institutional Mechanisms for the Advancement of Women*, Manchester and New York: Manchester University Press.

Rajalakshmi, T.K., 2001, 'Slavery amidst Prosperity', *Frontline*, 18, no. 15, 21 July – 3 August: 42–44.

Rajalakshmi, T.K., 2004a, 'Caste Terror', *Frontline*, 21, no. 25, 4–17 December: 75–77.

Rajalakshmi, T.K., 2004b, 'Murder for "Honour"', *Frontline*, 21, no. 3, 31 January – 13 February: 47–48.

Rajalakshmi, T.K., 2008, 'AIDWA National Convention against Fraudulent BPL Targeting', *Women's Equality*, 22, no. 2, April–June: 2–6.

Rakowski, Cathy, 2000, 'Obstacles and Opportunities to Women's Empowerment under Neoliberal Reform', *Journal of Developing Societies*, 16, no. 1: 115–38.

Ramachandran, V.K., 1990, *Wage Labour and Unfreedom in Agriculture: An Indian Case Study*, Oxford: Clarendon Press.

Ramachandran, V.K. and M. Swaminathan, eds., 2005, *Financial Liberalization and Rural Credit in India*, New Delhi: Tulika Books.

Ramachandran, V.K., Madhura Swaminathan and Vikas Rawal, 2002, 'Agricultural Workers in Rural Tamil Nadu: A Field Report', in V.K. Ramachandran and Madhura Swaminathan, eds., *Agrarian Studies*, New Delhi: Tulika Books: 445–72.

Ranadive, Vimal, 1986, *Feminists and Women's Movement*, New Delhi.

Rani, R. Swarupa, 2003, *Women's Associations in Telengana*, Hyderabad: Booklinks Corporation.

Rao, Anupama, 2005, 'Introduction', in Anupama Rao, ed., *Gender and Caste*: 1–47.

Rao, Anupama, ed., 2005, *Gender and Caste*, New York: Zed Books.

Rao, C.H. Hanumantha, 2005, *Agriculture, Food Security, Poverty and Environment: Essays on Post-Reform India*, New Delhi: Oxford University Press.

Rao, J. Mohan and Servaas Storm, 1998, 'Distribution and Growth in Indian Agriculture', in Terence Byres, ed., *The Indian Economy: Major Debates Since Indian Independence*: 193–238.

Rawal, Vikas, 2004, 'Agricultural Labour and Unfreedom: *Siri* Workers in a Village in Western Haryana', *The Marxist*, 20, no. 2, April–June: 35–52.

Rawal, Vikas and Keya Mukherjee, 2006, 'Debt and Unfreedom among Landless Manual Workers in Rural Haryana', in V.K. Ramachandran and Madhura Swaminathan, eds., *Financial Liberalization and Rural Credit*: 178–203.

Ray, Bharati, 1995, 'The Freedom Movement and Feminist Consciousness', in Bharati Ray, ed., *From the Seams of History: Essays on Indian Women*, New Delhi: Oxford University Press: 174–218.

Ray, Raka, 1999, *Fields of Protest: Women's Movements in India*, Minneapolis: Minnesota University Press.

Ray, Raka and Mary Katzenstein, eds., 2005, *Social Movements in India*, New York: Rowman and Littlefield.

Reddy, D. Narasimha and Srijit Mishra, 2009, 'Agriculture in the Reforms Regime', in D. Narasimha Reddy and Srijit Mishra, eds., *Agrarian Crisis in India*, New Delhi: Oxford University Press: 3–43.

Rege, Sharmila, 1998, 'Dalit Women Talk Differently: A Critique of "Difference" and Towards a Dalit Feminist Standpoint Position', *Economic and Political Weekly*, 33, no. 44, 31 October – 6 November: WS43.

Rein, Marcy, 1995, 'Beijing Bound: Local Women Make Global Links', *News for a People's World*, 3, no. 2, March: 3.

'Report of the Women's Delegation to Bhopal, Ahmedabad and Surat', *Women's Equality*, 5, no. 1, January–June: 10–22.

Rupp, Leila, 1996, 'Challenging Imperialism in International Women's Organizations, 1888–1945', *NWSA Journal*, 8, no. 1, Spring: 8–16.

Rupp, Leila, 1997, *Worlds of Women*, Princeton, NJ: Princeton University Press.

Sainath, P., 1999, 'Caste, Glass and Other Struggles', *International Gallerie*, 2, no. 1: 71–74.

Sangari, Kumkum, 2002, 'A Narrative of Restoration: Gandhi's Last Years and Nehruvian Secularism', *Social Scientist*, 30, nos. 3–4, March–April: 3–33.

Sangari, Kumkum and Sudesh Vaid, 1999, 'Institutions, Beliefs, Ideologies: Widow Immolation in Contemporary Rajasthan', in Nivedita Menon, ed., *Gender and Politics in India*, New Delhi: Oxford University Press: 383–440.

Sangwan, Jagmati, 2010, 'Making Honour Crimes Visible: 25 Years of Struggle by AIDWA, Haryana', interview by Indu Agnihotri and Manjeet Rathee, in AIDWA, *In the Name of Honour*: 69–81.

Sarkar, Sumit, 1987, *Modern India*, New York: St. Martin's Press.

Sarkar, Sumit and Tanika Sarkar, 2007, 'Introduction', in Sumit Sarkar and Tanika Sarkar, eds., *Women and Social Reform in Modern India*, vol. 1: 1–9.

Sarkar, Sumit and Tanika Sarkar, eds., *Women and Social Reform in Modern India*, vol. 1, Ranikhet: Permanent Black, 2007.

Sarkar, Tanika, 1991, 'The Woman as Communal Subject: Rashtrasevika Samiti and Ram Janmabhoomi Movement', *Economic and Political Weekly*, 26, no. 35, 31 August: 2057–62.

Sarkar, Tanika, 2001, *Hindu Wife, Hindu Nation: Community, Religion and Cultural Nationalism*, New Delhi: Permanent Black.

Sarkar, Tanika, 2002, 'Semiotics of Terror: Muslim Children and Women in Hindu Rashtra', *Economic and Political Weekly*, 37, no. 28, 13 July: 2872–76.

Seabrook, Jeremy, 1992, 'The reconquest of India: the victory of International Monetary Fundamentalism', *Race & Class*, 34, no. 1: 1–16.

Sen, Atreyee, 2007, *Shiv Sena Women: Violence and Communalism in a Bombay Slum*, Indianapolis: Indiana University Press.

Sen, Bhowani, 1945, 'Slave Trade in Chittagong: Gruesome Pictures of Traffic in Women Destitutes', *People's War*, 3, no. 27, 11 February: 3.

Sen, Gita and Chiranjib Sen, 1994, 'Women's Domestic Work and Economic Activity: Results from the National Sample Survey', *Economic and Political Weekly*, 20, no. 17: WS49–WS56.

Sen, Ilina, 1989, 'Feminists, Women's Movement, and the Working Class', *Economic and Political Weekly*, 24, no. 29, 22 July: 1639–41.

Sen, Samita, 2000, 'Toward a Feminist Politics? The Indian women's Movement in Historical Perspective', Development Research Group/Poverty Reduction and Economic Management Network, The World Bank, April, available at http://www.worldbank.org/gender/prr, accessed 25 July 2008.

Sen, Sunil, 1985, *The Working Women and Popular Movements in Bengal*, Calcutta: K.P. Bagchi and Company.

Sharma, Kumud, 2003, 'Institutionalizing Feminist Agenda(s)', *Economic and Political Weekly*, 38, no. 43, 25–31 October: 4565.

Shiva, Vandana, 1998, *Globalization of Agriculture, Food Security and Sustainability*, New Delhi: Research Foundation for Science, Technology and Ecology.

Shiva, Vandana, 1999, 'Monocultures, Monopolies, Myths and the Masculinization of Agriculture', *Development*, 42, no. 2: 35–38.

Singh, Kirti, 1987, 'The Dowry Prohibition Act', *Equality*, 1, no. 1, October–December: 19–20.

Singh, Kirti, 1994, 'Obstacles to Women's Rights in India', in Rebecca Cook, ed., *Human Rights of Women: National and International Perspectives*, edited by Rebecca Cook, Philadelphia, PA: University of Pennsylvania Press: 375–96.

Singh, Ujjwal Kumar, 1998, *Political Prisoners in India*, New Delhi: Oxford University Press.

Sivaraman, Mythily, 1973, 'Gentlemen Killers of Kilvenmani', *Economic and Political Weekly*, 8, no. 21, 26 May: 927.

Sivaraman, Mythily, 1975, 'Towards Emancipation', *Social Scientist*, 4, nos. 40–41, November–December: 76–103.

Sivaraman, Mythily, 1992, 'Tribute: Remarkable Political Activist', *The Hindu*, 29 March.

Sivaraman, Mythily, 1999, 'In Defence of Dignity', *The Hindu*, 23 May.

Sivaraman, Mythily, 2006, *Fragments of a Life*, New Delhi: Zubaan.

Smith, Andrea, 2000, 'Colors of Violence', *Colorlines*, 3, no. 4: 4–7.

Sparr, Patricia, 1994, *Mortgaging Women's Lives: Feminist Critiques of Structural Adjustment*, London: Zed Books.

Spodek, Howard, 1990, 'Review: "Shramshakti: Report of the National Commission on Self Employed Women and Women in the Informal Sector"', *Economic Development and Cultural Change*, 38, no. 4, July: 896–901.

Sunder Rajan, Rajeswari, 2003, *The Scandal of the State*, Durham, NC: Duke University Press.

Sunder Rajan, Rajeswari, ed., 1999, *Signposts: Gender Issues in Post-Independence India*, New Delhi: Kali for Women.

Roy, Srila, 2009, 'Melancholic Politics and the Politics of Melancholia: The Indian Women's Movement', *Feminist Theory*, 10, no. 3: 341–57.

Spivak, Gayatri, 1996, '"Woman" as Theatre: United Nations Conference on Women, Beijing, 1995', *Radical Philosophy*, 75, Jan/Feb: 2–4.

Srinivas, M.S., ed., 1996, *Caste: Its Twentieth Century Avatar*, New Delhi: Viking.

Srinivas, M.N., 1991, 'On Living in a Revolution', *Economic and Political Weekly* 26, no. 13, 30 March: 834.

Staff Reporter, 2006, 'Economic Reforms No Panacea: CPI(M), 60th Anniversary of "Ponmalai Martyrs" in Tiruchi', *The Hindu*, 9 June, available at http://www.thehindu.com/2006/09/06/stories/2006090622290300.htm, accessed 12 May 2010.

Status of Women in India: A Synopsis Report of the National Committee (1971–1974), 1975, New Delhi: Indian Council of Social Science Research.

Stein, Burton, 1995, 'Situating Precolonial Tamil Politics and Society', in *Plenary Session Papers, VIII World Tamil Conference*, Chennai: International Association of Tamil Research.

Stienstra, Deborah, 1994, *Women's Movements and International Organizations*, New York: St. Martin's Press.

Stienstra, Deborah, 2000, 'Making Global Connections among Women, 1970–99', in Robin Cohen and Shirin M. Rai, eds, *Global Social Movements*, New Brunswick, NJ: The Athlone Press: 62–82.

Stree Shakti Sanghatana, 1989, *'We Were Making History': Women and the Telangana Struggle*, London: Zed Press.

Streeter, Nicole, 1996, 'Beijing and Beyond', *Berkeley Women's Law Journal*, 11, 31 January: 200.

Sud, Nikita, 2012, *Liberalization, Hindu Nationalism and the State: A Biography of Gujarat*, New Delhi: Oxford University Press.

Surya, Vasantha, 2003, 'Voicing Their Protests', *The Hindu*, 16 November, available at http://www.hindu.com/mag/2003/11/16/stories/2003111600110400.htm, accessed 13 July 2010.

Swaminathan, Madhura, 2000, *Weakening Welfare: The Public Distribution of Food in India*, New Delhi: Leftword Books.

Tamil Nadu Democratic Women's Association, 1981, *Third State Conference Report for Tamil Nadu*, translated by B. Padma.

'Tamil Nadu State Conference, "Extracts from the Political-Organizational Report"', 2008, *The Marxist*, 24, no. 1, January–March: 6–12.

Tefft, Sheila, 1995, 'Clinton Chides China, Wows Women', *The Christian Science Monitor*, 6 September: 7.

Teltumbde, Anand, 2010, 'Counting Castes: Advantage the Ruling Castes', *Economic and Political Weekly*, 45, no. 28, 10 July: 11.

Teltumbde, Anand, 2011, 'Some Fundamental Issues in Anti-Caste Struggle', inaugural speech, Kula Nirmulan Porata Samiti conference, Guntur, Andhra Pradesh, 11 June, available at http://www.countercurrents.org/teltumbde130611.htm, accessed 19 July 2011.

Thapar-Bjorkert, Suruchi, 2006, *Women in the Indian National Movement: Unseen Faces and Unheard Voices, 1930–42*, New Delhi: Sage Publications.

Tharu, Susie and K. Lalita, eds., 1994, *Women Writing in India*, vol. 2, New Delhi: Oxford University Press.

'The Deorala Tragedy', 1987, *Equality*, 1, no. 1, October–December: 8.

'Third AIDWA Conference: A Report (9–12 November 1990), Jadavpur, West Bengal', 1990, *Women's Equality*, 3, no. 4, October–December: 3–4.

Thorat, S.K., 2001, 'Dalit Women Have Been Left Behind By the Dalit Movement and the Women's Movement', *Communalism Combat*, 69, May: 12.

Thorner, Alice, ed., 2001, *Land, Labour and Rights*, New Delhi: Tulika Books.

Towards Equality: Report of the Committee on the Status of Women in India, 1975, Ministry of Education and Social Welfare, Government of India.

Tripp, Aili Mari, 2006, 'The Evolution of Transnational Feminisms: Consensus, Conflict, and New Dynamics', in Myra Marx Ferree and Aili Mari Tripp, eds., *Global Feminism*, New York: New York University Press: 51–75.

Tukaram v. State of Maharashtra, 1979, SCC [Cr] 381.

'Turning Words in Action, Women Take the World Stage', 1996, *Issues Quarterly*, 2, no. 1, Fall/Winter: 9.

United Nations Development Program (UNDP), 1992, *Human Development Report*, New York: UNDP.

Vashishtha, Prem and Anindita Mukherjee, 1996, 'The Effects of Agricultural Price Liberalization and Market Reforms on Rural Poverty', in *Economic Liberalization and Rural Poverty*, Population, Rural and Urban Development Division, United Nations, 1996: 33–36.

Vasuki, U., 2004, 'Violation of Human Rights of Dalit Women in Tamil Nadu', *Women's Equality*, 18, nos. 1–2: 45.

Velayudhan, Meera, 1985, 'The Crisis and Women's Struggles in India (1970–1977)', *Social Scientist*, 13, no. 6, June: 57–68.

Vepa, Swarna Sadasivam, 2007, 'The Feminization of Agriculture and the Marginalization of Women's Economic Stake', in Maithreyi Krishnaraj, ed., *Gender, Food Security and Rural Livelihoods*, Kolkata: Stree: 1–23.

Visaria, Leela, 2000, 'Violence Against Women: A Field Study', *Economic and Political Weekly*, 35, no. 18: 1742–51.

Viswanathan, S., 2005, *Dalits in Dravidian Land*, Chennai: Navayana.

Visweswaran, Kamala, 1994, *Fictions of Feminist Ethnography*, Minneapolis: University of Minnesota Press.

Walsh, James, 1995, 'Spirit of Sisterhood', *Time*, 18 September.

Weber, Charlotte, 2001, 'Unveiling Scheheraazade: Feminist Orientalism in the

International Alliance of Women, 1911–1950', *Feminist Studies*, 27, no. 1, Spring: 125–57.

Weigand, Kate, 2001, *Red Feminism: American Feminism and the Making of Women's Liberation*, Baltimore, MD: John Hopkins Press.

West Bengal Government, 1955, *India's Villages*, Calcutta.

Wichterich, Christa, 2000, *The Globalized Woman: Reports from a Future of Inequality*, New York: Zed Press.

Winslow, Anne, 1995, 'Specialized Agencies and the World Bank', in Anne Winslow, ed., *Women, Politics, and the United Nations*, Westport, CT: Greenwood Press: 155–74.

'Women kept out as Mrs. Clinton speaks to forum in Huairou', 1995, *Deutsche Press-Agentur*, 6 September.

World Bank, 1991, *Gender and Poverty in India*, Washington D.C.: World Bank.

World Bank, 1995, *Toward Gender Equality: The Role of Public Policy*, Washington, D.C.: World Bank.

Writers, Sangtin and Richa Nagar, 2006, *Playing with Fire: Feminist Thought and Activism Through Seven Lives in India*, Minneapolis: University of Minnesota Press.

Yadav, Nomita, 2002, 'Other Backward Classes: Then and Now', *Economic and Political Weekly*, 37, nos. 44–45, 2–15 November: 4495.

Zelliot, Eleanor, 1996, *From Untouchable to Dalit*, New Delhi: Manohar.

'5000 Golden Rock Workers on Strike: Bosses Launch Offenses on S.I.R.', 1946, *People's Age*, 5, no. 6, 11 August: 7.

'11th State Conference Resolve: Further Strengthen AIDWA in Tamilnadu', 2005, *People's Democracy*, 29, no. 36, 4 September: 4.

Unpublished Documents

AIDWA, 'Memorandum to the Parliamentary Standing Committee of the Ministry of Rural Development on the National Rural Employment Guarantee Bill, 2004', 15 February 2005, personal copy.

Ali, Subhashini, 'Survival in a Time of Violence', Opening Plenary Session, Annual Conference of International Association for Feminist Economics (IAFFE), Hangzhou, China, 24–26 June 2011.

'Asian-African Conference of Women', Box 20, Folder 203, International CoC Collection, Sophia Smith Collection, Smith College, USA.

Burnham, Linda, interviewed by Loretta Ross, 18 March 2005, Oakland, CA, tape 3 of 4, page 32, Voices of Feminism Oral History Project, Sophia Smith Collection, Smith College, USA.

Chakravartty, Renu, National Federation of Indian Women, 'Documents and Information: Leaders of National Women's Organizations Exchange Experiences', Budapest, Hungary, 10 October 1970, pages 24–25, Box 4, Folder 37, Communism Collection, Sophia Smith Collection, Smith College, USA.

Chandra, R., Joint Secretary, AIDWA, Tamil Nadu State Committee, 'Fourth Conference on Eradication of Untouchability: Research Paper', translated by B. Padma, personal copy.

Clinton, Hillary Rodham, CNN interview on 'American Morning', 5 March 2008.

'Documents and Information: International meetings attended by the WIDF', Issue 7, 1972, p. 5, Box 4, Folder 37, Communism Collection, Sophia Smith Collection, Smith College, USA.

Hajrah Begum, Secretary of the National Coordinating Committee, India, 'XIV Session Executive Committee', World International Federation of Democratic Women, 1954: 18–20, Box 2, Folder 16, Sophia Smith Archives, Smith College, USA.

Hajrah Begum Ahmad, Oral History Project, 19 September 1994, Nehru Memorial Museum and Library Archives, New Delhi, India.

Indian School of Women's Studies and Development (ISWSD), 'Women Workers in Rural Haryana: A Field-Based Study', Ministry of Labour, Government of India, New Delhi, 2003.

Indian School of Women's Studies and Development (ISWSD), 'Monitoring and Evaluation of National Rural Employment Guarantee Scheme with Special Focus on Gender Issues', October 2006.

Indian School of Women's Studies and Development (ISWSD) and Janaki Amma Trust for Welfare of Women and Children, 'Impact of Fish/Prawn Culture on Women in Rural Orissa and Andhra Pradesh', Department of Women and Child Welfare, Government of India, New Delhi, 1998.

Invitation letter to the first Asian-African Conference of Women, from Avabai B. Wadia, Box 20, Folder 203, International Committee of Correspondence Collection, Sophia Smith Collection, Smith College, USA.

Karat, Brinda, 'On the Occasion of AIDWA's Fourth National Conference', n.d., personal copy.

Karat, Brinda, 'Agricultural Workers Bill: And What About the Women?', n.d., personal copy.

Letter by Avabai B. Wadia, 'Tour in East Africa', 20 January 1961, Box 20, Folder 203, International Committee of Correspondence Collection, Sophia Smith Collection, Smith College, USA.

Letter to Chairperson, National Commission for Women, New Delhi, signed by U. Vasuki, dated 22 May 2004, personal copy.

Letter to Poornima Advani, Chairperson of the National Commission for Women, signed by U. Vasuki, dated 27 October 2003, personal copy.

Mazumdar, Vina 'Inaugural Address by Dr. Vina Mazumdar, First National Conference of All India Democratic Women's Association, Madras, 10th March 1981', photocopy.

Millard, Betty, 'Women on Guard', 1952, pp. 19–20, Box 1, Folder 13, Communism Collection, U.S. Pamphlets, Sophia Smith Collection, Smith College, USA.

'Twelve Asian Women Study Life in the U.S.', *New York Times*, 29 April 1956, clipping, Box 20, Folder 217, International Committee of Correspondence Collection, Sophia Smith Collection, Smith College, USA.

Vasuki, U., 'Further Strengthen AIDWA in Tamilnadu', 11th State Conference Resolve, 4 September 2005, personal copy.

WIDF, 'Second International Conference Proceedings', 1948, p. 535, Box 3, Folder 22, Communism Collection, Sophia Smith Collection, Smith College, USA.

Archives

International Archives for the Women's Movement, Aletta Institute for Women's History, Amsterdam, Netherlands.

International Institute of Social History Archives, International Institute of Social History, Amsterdam, Netherlands.

Nehru Memorial Museum and Library Archives, Nehru Memorial Museum and Library (NMML), New Delhi, India.

P.C. Joshi Archives on Contemporary History, Jawaharlal Nehru University, New Delhi, India.

Sophia Smith Collection, Smith College, Northampton, Massachusetts, USA.

Interviews

Indu Agnihotri, interview by author, New Delhi, 29 July 2008

Subhashini Ali, interview by author, Kanpur, Uttar Pradesh, 22 July 2008.

Ashalata, interview by author, New Delhi, 2 July 2005.

Malini Bhattacharya, interview by author, Kolkata, West Bengal, 4 August 2008.

R. Chandra, interview by author, Chennai, Tamil Nadu, 17 March 2006.

Fatehabad district AIDWA group, interview by author, Fatehabad, Haryana, 13 June 2003.

Sonya Gill, interview by Indus Chadha, Mumbai, Maharashtra, 25 July 2008.

Indian School of Women's Studies in Development (ISWSD) research group, interview by author, Bhirdana, Haryana, 13 June 2003.

Indu, interview by author, Bandh, Haryana, 24 June 1999.

Jatinder Kaur, Fatehabad AIDWA group interview, interview by author, Fatehabad, Haryana, 13 June 2003.

Shakti Kak, interview by author, New Delhi, 18 June 2003.

Vimala Kalagar, interview by Indus Chadha, Bangalore, Karnataka, 9 July 2008.

Brinda Karat, interview by author, Kolkata, West Bengal, 6 June 1995.

Brinda Karat, interview by author, New Delhi, 19 December 2002.

Brinda Karat, interview by author, Kolkata, West Bengal, 24 December 2004.

Brinda Karat, interview by author, Kolkata, West Bengal, 26 December 2004.

Brinda Karat, interview by author, Kolkata, West Bengal, 28 December 2004.

Brinda Karat, interview by author, Kolkata, West Bengal, 29 December 2004.

Karunanidhi, general secretary of CITU fish workers' union, interview by author, translated by B. Padma, Chennai, Tamil Nadu, 9 March 2006.

Lakshmi, interview by author, translated by B. Padma, Chennai, Tamil Nadu, 20 March 2006.

Vina Mazumdar, interview by author, New Delhi, 5 January 2002.

Vina Mazumdar, interview by author, New Delhi, 10 January 2002.

Vina Mazumdar, interview by the author, New Delhi, 19 June 2003.

Keya Mukherjee, interview by author, Bhirdana, Haryana, 13 June 2003.

North Chennai AIDWA unit, interview by author, translated by B. Padma, Chennai, Tamil Nadu, 18 March 2006.

Risik Kaur, interview by Keya Mukherjee and Vikas Rawal, Bhirdana, Haryana, 13 June 2003.

Veena Rani, Fatehabad AIDWA group, interview by author, Fatehabad, Haryana, 13 June 2003.

Vikas Rawal, interview by author, Bhirdana, Haryana, 13 June 2003.
Vikas Rawal, interview by author, Bhirdana, Haryana, 14 June 2003.
Jagmati Sangwan, interview by author, Rohtak, Haryana, 12 July 2005.
Sennelkulam hamlet group, interview by author, Sennelkulam, Tamil Nadu, 13 February 2006.
Sugonthi, interview by author, Virudhunagar, Tamil Nadu, 13 February 2006.
Mythily Sivaraman, interview by author, Chennai, Tamil Nadu, 16 February 2006.
Sudha Sundararaman, interview by author, New Delhi, 12 July 2012.
Pappa Umanath, interview by author, translated from Tamil by B. Padma, Chennai, Tamil Nadu, 26 March 2006.
U. Vasuki, interview by author, Chennai, Tamil Nadu, 15 January 2005.
U. Vasuki, interview by author, Chennai, India, 14 March 2006.
U. Vasuki, interview by author, Chennai, Tamil Nadu, 26 March 2006.

Index